History of the Tow

New Hampshire

With genealogical record, 1763-1910

(Volume I) Narrative

William H. Child

Alpha Editions

This edition published in 2020

ISBN : 9789354013126

Design and Setting By
Alpha Editions
email - alphaedis@gmail.com

HISTORY

OF THE

TOWN OF CORNISH

NEW HAMPSHIRE

WITH GENEALOGICAL RECORD

1763-1910

By WM. H. CHILD

IN TWO VOLUMES

Vol. I.

NARRATIVE

Recording all events we can,
Is rendering good service to fellow-man

THE RUMFORD PRESS
CONCORD, N. H.

MOTTOES AND QUOTATIONS.

"How carefully should we secure the memorials, while we may, of the long procession of true-hearted men and women that have borne with many tears, toils and prayers the precious Ark of God's Covenant, and of our liberties down to the present hour. We will not, we cannot forget those who toiled and dared and endured so much for God and for us."—*B. W. Dwight.*

"A town exists in its history. Take away the memory of the past, and what remains? Only a name. Take away the example of the recorded wisdom of the past, and what ray of light would be left for our guidance? What could we do but wander in the maze of perpetual childhood? If we are bound to respect the claims of posterity we likewise owe a debt to our ancestors."
—*Chipman.*

"He that is not proud of his ancestors, either has no ancestors to be proud of, or else he is a degenerate son."—*From Walpole History.*

"A people who do not look back to their ancestors, will not look forward to their posterity."—*Burke.*

In no way can the Divine Command, "Honor thy father and thy mother," be so completely obeyed as in tenderly recording their deeds and words.

PREFACE.

THE writer of this history, although somewhat advanced in life, is yet comparatively a novice in the work. Being called to it in the midst of the onerous cares and labors of a farm, which already absorbed most of his time and energy, it may lack somewhat in literary merit from what it otherwise would, while under any circumstances the writer could lay no claim to literary qualification or essential merit. It has, however, been his aim to give a fair, truthful and impartial record, and at the same time, making it as exhaustive as possible. He has also been deeply impressed with the magnitude and importance of the work in hand, and has carefully and prayerfully sought to do it, so that all interested in it shall be satisfied.

A powerful source of inspiration is found in the history of those ancestors whose achievements have been for the betterment of the world. There is an intellectual and moral power in such an ancestry which elevates the character and improves the heart.

The history of a town is scarcely more than the collective history of the families composing the town. The writer has felt it his duty to collect as much as possible, realizing that it is a duty we owe both to the living and the dead, to the future as well as the present, that these memorials of the past and present be preserved. It does not seem right that the memory of the dead should perish, that they who have done and suffered so much for their posterity should be forgotten on the earth.

It is true that many do not highly appreciate researches of this nature. This lack of interest arises generally from too intense a contact of the mind with the *present*, excluding almost wholly the influences of the *past* and even of the *future*. It is no credit to us to be reckless of that *past* from whose womb the *present* has sprung, and without which the *present* cannot be interpreted.

In New England there is a type of religious and moral character coupled with strong intellectual power such as the world has never

elsewhere seen. Does any one inquire the cause? The answer
is found in the *personal character* of the men and women who first
settled here, who, under God, laid the foundation of all we so
highly prize. They had an elevation of aim, a purity of purpose,
a steadiness of resolve, a fortitude under trial, and above all, a
deep sense of responsibility to God never elsewhere seen in the
world's history. Their characters were formed in the school of
adversity and thus they were prepared for the noblest of all
human achievements, the *founding of a Christian Republic*. To
such an ancestry we owe, under God, all that is valuable in the
character and institutions of the American people.

The town of Cornish has enjoyed her full share of these
influences from the first. Her early settlers were men and
women who were ready to stake their all upon the principles
of political and religious liberty. Their venture proved a mag-
nificient success. The lustre of their teachings and examples
has been reflected upon their sons and daughters, as their record
will show on the pages of this work.

TABLE OF CONTENTS

VOL. I

LIST OF ILLUSTRATIONS.

VOL. I.

HISTORY OF CORNISH.

CHAPTER I.

GENERAL DESCRIPTION.

CORNISH, Sullivan County, New Hampshire, is situated on the east bank of the Connecticut River, which separates the states of New Hampshire and Vermont. It is situated about 43½ degrees north latitude and 72 degrees west longitude from Greenwich and 5 degrees east from Washington.

It is bounded on the north by Plainfield; on the south by Claremont; on the east by Croydon and part of Grantham, and on the west by the western bank of the Connecticut River, at low-water mark. According to the terms of the grant it was at first the equivalent of six miles square and contained 23,040 acres by measurement.

On June 24, 1809, a portion of Croydon, by legislative act, was annexed to Cornish, and on December 25, 1844, a portion of Grantham also was annexed. This latter addition soon after received the name of, and has since been known as "Texas," as its annexation occurred a year previous to the admission of Texas into the Union. These additions to Cornish considerably increased her territory, but since then, no changes have taken place in the boundaries of the town. These changes were a great convenience to all of the families settled on farms west of the mountain ridge. Heretofore, the owners of these farms were practically isolated from the main portions of their respective towns by reason of this abrupt ridge between them, while by their annexation to Cornish they could readily join with her in all town affairs. The new line on the east was made to conform as nearly as practicable with the greater height of land.

The approaches to Cornish, both by roads and railway are chiefly from the north and south, as the Connecticut River and Valley generally trends in that direction. A single bridge, on its western boundary, crossing the river at Windsor, Vt., furnishes the

2

only approach from the west, and the mountain ridge on its eastern boundary seems to forbid extensive intercourse in that direction.

Cornish received its name from some of the grantees of the town whose families came from the famous mining town of Cornish, England, but it did not receive the name until it was granted in 1763. A camp, however, had previously been established in the town near the river, which has ever since been known as "Mast Camp." Here the officers of the Crown with their workmen were sent to select and cut choice timber for the Royal Navy. This was cut in the winter and hauled to the river, and in the following spring when the water was high, it was floated down stream to some point where it was to be used for ship-building. There is no known record of how much timber had been thus used, or when the first white man came here in quest of it, but the forests were subsequently found to contain much timber suitable for such use.

A point in the Connecticut River, at low-water mark, opposite the center of the town, is said to be 212 feet above sea-level. On leaving the river and going east, this altitude is rapidly increased by the successive elevations of land. The surface is diversified with meadows and hills, thus gradually rising to the summit of Croydon and Grantham mountains on the east. The soil is equally diversified, and in places rocky, but taken as a whole, judging by its appearance, or the record of its production, Cornish compares favorably with the best towns of the state. These elevations in the surface are favorable to good drainage. But little stagnant water is to be found. Miasma is unknown. The brooks, two of which are of considerable size, find their source in the mountain sides on the east, flow westward and empty into the Connecticut River. Of this beautiful river which fringes our entire western border, a poet has well said:

"Nor drinks the sea a lovelier wave than thine."

This river renders no small contribution to the pleasure of the tourist while journeying along its beautiful banks. Its valley is celebrated for its beautiful and variegated scenery. On either side of the river are wooded heights sometimes projecting and almost overhanging its banks and sometimes receding, leaving the beautiful meadows and fertile farms spread out in full view of the tourist. In the near distance on the west stands in silent majesty the stately Ascutney ever in view, and the beautiful and historic village of Windsor lying between.

The town has no lakes to add their charms to the beauty of the landscape, neither are there deep ravines or gorges and water-falls to thrill the beholder; but otherwise, Nature in her lovely garb is here in manifold combinations. Cultured taste seems to admire the scenery of Cornish, as the variety of its scenery seems inexhaustible. Verdant hills, rich pastures, and smiling meadows and pure streams of water, all combine to render it the seat of ideal homes. The hillsides and valleys, too, abound in springs of purest water, while beautiful forests crown the summit of most of the hills, and pure air breezes over all.

> "I love thy rocks and rills,
> Thy vales and templed hills."

CHAPTER II.

CHARTER—GRANTS, ETC.

THE charter for Cornish was granted June 21, 1763, to Rev. Samuel McClintock of Greenland, N. H., and sixty-nine others. The charter was renewed December 21, 1768.

The following is a copy of the charter of the township of Cornish as granted by King George the Third to the original proprietors of the town:

Province of New Hampshire.

[L. S.] George the Third, by the Grace of God, of Great Britain, France and Ireland, King, Defender of the Faith &c. To all Persons to whom these Presents shall come, Greeting:

Know ye that We of our special Grace, certain Knowledge and meer motion, for the due Encouragement of settling a New Plantation within our said Province, by and with the advice of our Trusty & Well Beloved Benning Wentworth Esqr. Our Governor and Commander in Chief of our said Province of New Hampshire in New England, and of our Council of said Province, Have, upon the Conditions and Reservations here-inafter made, given and granted, and by these Presents, for us, our Heirs and Successors, do give, and grant in equal Shares unto our loving Subjects, Inhabitants of our said Province of New Hampshire and our other Governments and to their Heirs and Assigns forever whose names are entered on this Grant to be divided to, and amongst them into Seventy Six Equal Shares all that Tract or Parcel of Land Situate, lying and being within our said Provience of New Hampshire containing by Admeasurement, 23040 acres, which Tract is to Contain Six miles square and no more: out of which an allowance is to be made for High-Ways and unimprovable Lands by Rocks, Ponds, Mountains and Rivers. One Thousand and Forty Acres free according to a Plan and Survey thereof made by our said Governors orders, and returned into the Secretary's Office and

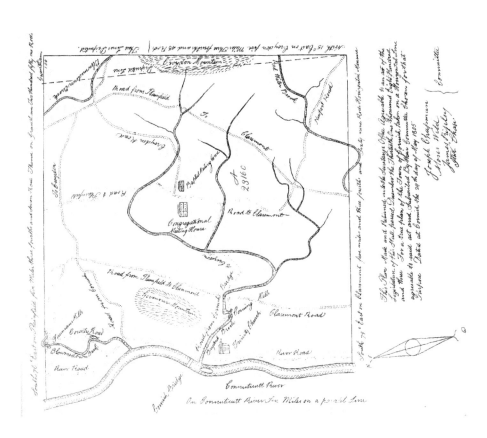

On Connecticut River Six Miles on a paral Line

hereunto annexed, butted and bounded as follows: Viz: Beginning at A Tree marked with the Figures 2 & 3. Standing on the Bank of the easterly side of the Connecticut River,which is the South Westerly Corner Bounds of the Town of Plainfield, from thence running South, Seventy Six degrees East by Plainfield to a stake and Stones which is the South Westerly Corner of Gran tham and North Westerly Corner of Croydon, thence South fif͞ teen Degrees West by Croydon Aforesaid, Six Miles to the North Westerly Corner of Newport, thence turning off and running North 77 deg. West. Six Miles to a Tree Standing on the Easterly Bank of Connecticut River, marked with the Figures 1 & 2, then up the river as that Trends, to the Bounds begun at, and that the same be and hereby is Incorporated into a Township by the name of Cornish, and the Inhabitants that do, or shall hereafter inhabit the said Township are hereby declared to be Enfranchised with, and Entitled to all and every the Privileges and Immunities that other Towns within our Province by Law Exercise and enjoy:—and further, that the Said Town, as soon as there shall be Fifty Families resident and Settled thereon, shall have the Liberty of holding two Fairs, one of which shall be held on the   and the other on the   annually, which Fairs are not to continue longer than the respective   following the said   and that as soon as the said Town shall consist of Fifty Families, a market may be opened and Kept one or more Days in each Week, as may be thought most advantageous to the Inhabitants.

Also that the first Meeting for the choice of Town Officers agreeable to the Laws of our Said Province, Shall be held on the Second Monday of July next which said meeting shall be notified by Clement March Esqr. who is hereby also appointed the moderator of the said first Meeting, which he is to notify and Govern agreeable to the Laws and Customs of our Said Province; and that the Annual Meeting forever hereafter, for the Choice of such Officers for the said Town, shall be on the Second Tuesday of March annually.—To Have and to Hold the said Tract of Land as above expressed, together with all Privileges and Appurtenances to them and their respective Heirs and Assigns forever upon the following Conditions: (Viz.)

I. That every Grantee, his Heirs or Assigns shall plant and cultivate five Acres of Land within the Term of five years for every fifty acres contained in his or their Share or Proportion

of Land in said Township, and continue to improve and settle
the same by Additional Cultivations, on Penalty of the Forfeiture of his Grant or Share in the said Township, and of its
reverting to Us, our Heirs and Successors, to be by us or them
Re-granted to such of our Subjects as shall effectually settle and
cultivate the same.

II. That all White and other Pine Trees within the said Township fit for Masting our Royal Navy, be carefully preserved for
that use, and none to be cut or felled without our Special License
for so doing, first had and obtained, upon the Penalty of the Forfeiture of the Right of such Grantee, his Heirs and Assigns, to us,
our Heirs and Successors, as well as being subject to the Penalty
of any Act or Acts of Parliament that now are, or hereafter shall
be Enacted.

III. That before any Division of the Land be made to and
among the Grantees, a Tract of Land, as near the Center of the
said Township as the Land will admit of, Shall be reserved and
marked out for Town Lots, one of which shall be allotted to each
Grantee of the Contents of one Acre.

IV. Yielding and paying therefor to us, our Heirs and Successors
for the space of ten years, to be computed from the date hereof,
the Rent of one Ear of Indian Corn only, on the twenty fifth
day of December annually, if Lawfully demanded, the first Payment to be made on the twenty fifth day of December 1763.

V. Every Proprietor, Settler or Inhabitant, shall yield and pay
unto Us, our Heirs and Successors yearly, and every year forever
from and after the Expiration of ten Years from the above said
twenty fifth Day of December, namely, on the twenty fifth day
of December which will be in the year of our Lord 1773, one
Shilling Proclamation money for every Hundred Acres he so owns,
Settles or Possesses, and so in Proportion for a greater or lesser
Tract of the Said Land; which money shall be paid by the respective Persons abovesaid, their Heirs or Assigns in our Council
Chamber in Portsmouth, or to such Officer or Officers as shall be
appointed to receive the same; and this is to be in Lieu of all other
Rents and Service whatever.

In testimony whereof we have caused the Seal of our Said
Province to be hereunto Affixed.

Witness Benning Wentworth Esqr; our Governor and Commander in Chief of Our Said Province; the Twenty first Day of

June, in the Year of Our Lord Christ, One Thousand Seven
Hundred and Sixty three, and in the Third Year of our Reign.

B. WENTWORTH
  By His Excellency's Command
  with Advice of Council.
THEODR ATKINSON *Junr Sec^ry*

Prov° of New Hamp^r October 1.
1763. Recorded according to
the original Charter, under
the Prov. Seal.
T. ATKINSON *Junr Sec^ry*.

Names of the Grantees of Cornish:

Rev. Sam^ll McClintock
Ensign John Whidden
Samuel Ayers
Capt Philip Johnson
Josiah Clark
Willm Wallis Junr.
Thomas Berry
Capt. George Frost
Noah Emery
John Hill
Jon^a Barker
Hunking Wentworth Esq.
Nathan Goss
John Grow
Wyseman Claggett Esq.
Nath^ll March
Thomas March
Capt George March
Lieut Paul March
William Blazo
Willm MC. Clane
The Honble John Temple
Theod^r Atkinson
Wm Temple
Mark Hun^g Wentworth
Joshua Haines
Eleaz^r Cate
Thomas Sherburne
Enoch Clark
Willm Jenkins Junr.

} Esq^rs

Josiah Foss
Willm Berry
Benj^a Philbrook
Nath^ll Huggins Junr.
Capt John Dudley
Thomas Johnson
John Weeks
Dea^n Ebenezer Cate
Philip Babb Junr
Lieut Ebenezer Clark
Daniel Pierce Esq
Mr Jon^a Greely
George Bracket
Stephen March
Clem^t March Esq
Doct^r John Hall
John Fisher
Wm Cate Junr
Samuel Whidden
Walter Bryant Esq.
Greenleaf Clark
Simeon Dearborn
Capt James Neal
Nathan Marston
Sam^ll Haines
John Huggins
Bracket Johnson
Lieut. Nathan Johnson
Capt William Weeks
Willm Pottle Junr

Samuel Dearborn	Joseph Jackson Esq. Boston
Daniel Cate	Joseph Stores Esq.
Maj^r Jon^a Moulton	Leveret Hubbard
Capt. Nath^ll Bracket	Nath^ll Dowse
Doctor Hall Jackson	Sam^ll Fabion

Reservations and Conditions of the Grant:

Executed and recorded in due form.

(It is not known why this part of the document was deferred so long after the main part was executed—over three months.)

His Excellency Benning Wentworth Esqr. A Tract to Contain five Hundred acres as Marked B. W. in the Plan which is to be Accounted two of the within Shares,—one whole Share for the Incorporated Society for the Propagation of the Gospel in Foreign Parts—One Share for A Glebe for the Church of England as by Law Established—One Share for the first Settled Minister of the Gospel & one Share for the Benefit of a School in S^d Town.

Province of New Hampshire—Octo—1—1763. Recorded according to the Original on the Back of the Original Charter of Cornish.

T. ATKINSON Junr Sec^ry

Provc. New Hampshire. Oct. 1st 1763.

Recorded from the Back of the Original Charter of Cornish, Under the Prov^e Seal.

T. ATKINSON Junr Sec^ry

Comparatively, but few of the Grantees ever settled in town, as their names have never appeared on the town records as landholders after the settlement of the town. They, however, employed every available method to promote the early and rapid settlement of the town by offering flattering inducements to influence emigration thither. Several of the grantees deeded their shares to others who were more hopeful in the venture and desired to settle in town.

The proprietors held meetings and continued to legislate upon the affairs of the grant until the town had a population sufficient to manage them itself. The first proprietors' meeting was held in Greenland, N. H., August 15, 1763, nearly two months after the grant was made, and, in the absence of recorded authority, we have reason to believe meetings were held at such times and places as became necessary to meet the requirements of the landowners; but records of these have not been obtained.

The British workmen at "Mast Camp" were not settlers, and made no attempt at settlement. It is claimed, however, that Daniel Putnam who soon afterwards became one of the first settlers of Cornish, spent the winter of 1764–65 at the camp, also a Mr. Dike and family were staying there to assist, perhaps, in boarding the mast-cutters.

It cannot be expected the historian of today will antedate the times already named, or even to record all events that occurred during the time of the settlement of the town. Much, indeed, lies buried in the centuries preceding and during the time these known events took place that would be of great interest to record; but the revolving ages have forever hidden them from the present generation, and no power can recover them. Fanciful tradition might be employed to some extent to gratify the curious reader, but it is thought better to record only authentic facts, even though the record be fragmentary and less entertaining.

The first provincial governor of New Hampshire, Benning Wentworth, was appointed by the Crown and served from 1741 to 1767, a period of nearly twenty-six years. It was during his administration that the township grants of Cornish and adjoining towns were made. He was succeeded by his nephew, Sir John Wentworth, who served until 1775, at which time all British rule ceased among her New England colonies. These were the only governors New Hampshire ever had that received their appointment from Great Britain. It may not be amiss to mention for the benefit of the general reader, that our ancestors were, previous to 1775, all supposed to be loyal and loving subjects of England, our mother country; but, for reasons hereafter given, this relationship ceased to exist about that time.

It was the custom of Gov. Benning Wentworth to make reservations of five hundred acres of land in a single body in each of the townships granted by him. These were usually selected with reference to their situation and value. On all the early township maps these reservations were designated by his initials, *B. W.* The motives prompting him to make these reservations are matters of conjecture. It is evident that he believed their proprie-

torship would be entailed upon his successor in office. In this
he was mistaken, for it was found that his successor, Sir John
Wentworth, possessed *no* right in said reservations, and therefore
they were still ungranted lands, and subject to the same modes
of disposal as the rest of the towns had been at the first. In Cornish such reservation was a very desirable tract situated near the
northwest part of the town, and bordering on the Connecticut
River. In order to make this land available for settlement, putting it on a par with the rest of the town, it must needs be granted
to the town or to some individual. A petition was issued by
Moses Chase, then a prominent citizen of the town, to Sir John
Wentworth, and the following grant was made by him to Moses
Chase, Esq.

Grant to Moses Chase, 1772.

Province of New Hampshire   George the Third, by the Grace

[L. S.]   of God, of Great Britain, France

MOSES CHASE'S   and Ireland, King, Defender of the
                       Faith &c. To all to whom these
Grant   Presents shall come, Greeting:

Know Ye that we of our special grace, certain Knowledge and
mere Motion for the due encouragement of settling and cultivating our Lands within our Province aforesaid, by and with
the advice of our Trusty and well beloved John Wentworth Esqr.
our Governor and Commander in Chief of our own said Province
of New Hampshire & of our Council of the same, Have (upon the
Conditions and Reservations herein particularly recited and
expressed.) given and granted & by these Presents for us our
Heirs and Successors do give & grant unto our leige and loving
Subject Moses Chase of Cornish in the County of Cheshire and
Province aforesaid Esqr. and to his Heirs & Assigns forever, a
certain Tract or parcel of Land containing by Admeasurement
Five Hundred Acres, situate lying and being in our Said Province
as by a plan or Survey thereof (exhibited by our Surveyor General
of Lands for our Said Province by our said Governor's order and
returned into the Secretary's office of our Said Province; a Copy
whereof is hereunto annexed) may more fully and at large
appear; Butted & Bounded as follows Viz.

Beginning at a Stake and Stones standing on the bank of Connecticut River on the north side of Blow-me-down Brook (so

called) from thence running south 76 degrees East 288 Rods to
a Stake and Stones, from thence running South 15 Degrees West
283 Rods to a Stake and Stones, from thence running North 76
Degrees West 286 Rods to a Stake and Stones standing on the
bank of Connecticut River aforesaid, from thence up said River
to the Bounds first mentioned.   To Have and to Hold the said
Tract of Land as above expressed to him the said Moses Chase
and to his Heirs and Assigns for Ever upon the following Terms
Conditions and Reservations Viz:

First that the said Grantee shall cut, clear and make passable
for Carriages &c. a Road of three Rods wide thro' the said Tract
as shall at any Time hereafter be directed or Ordered by the Governor & Council aforesaid, which Road Shall be Completed in
Two years from the date of Such order or direction of the Govnr.
& Council aforesaid on penalty of the forfeiture of this Grant &
of its reverting to us, our Heirs and Successors.

Second. That the said Grantee shall settle or Cause to be settled Two Families in Three Years from the date of this Grant, in
failure whereoff the Premises to revert to us our Heirs and
Successors to be by us or them entered upon & regranted to
such of our Subjects as shall effectually settle and cultivate the
same.

Third. That all white and other Pine Trees fit for Masting our
Royal Navy be carefully preserved for that use; & none be cut
or felled without our special License for so doing first had and
obtained on penalty of the forfeiture of the Right of the Grantee
in the Premises his Heirs and Assigns to Us our Heirs and Successors as well as being subject to the penalties prescribed by
any present as well as future Act or Acts of Parliament.

Fourth, Yielding and paying therefore to us our Heirs and Successors on or before the 24th day of January 1774, the Rent of
one Ear of Indian Corn only if lawfully demanded.

Fifth That the said Grantee his Heirs & Assigns shall yield
& pay unto us our Heirs and Successors yearly and every year for
ever from and after the expiration of Two Years from the date of
this Grant; one Shilling Proclamation Money, for every Hundred Acres he so owns settles or possesses, and so in proportion
for a greater or lesser Tract of the Land aforesaid, which money
shall be paid by the respective Proprietor Owner or Settler in our
Council Chamber in Portsmouth, or to Officer or Officers as shall

be appointed to receive the same: And these to be in lieu of all
other Rents and Services whatsoever.

In Testimony whereof we have Caused the Seal of our said
Province to be hereunto affixed. Witness: John Wentworth
Esqr. our aforesaid Governor & Commander-in-Chief, the 24th
day of January in the 12th year of our Reign Annoque Domini
1772.

J. WENTWORTH.

By His Excellency's Command }
With advice of Council   }

The words "money for every Hundred acres" being interlined
previous to signing & Sealing.

THEODORE ATKINSON, Secretary.

Province of New Hampshire 25th. Jan[ry] 1772.

Recorded according to the Original Patent under the Province
Seal.

The Surveyor's Certificate of this grant to Moses Chase was
as follows:

Province of New Hampshire, Portsmouth 22[d]. January 1772.
These may Certify that this Plan Beginning at a Stake & Stones
standing on the bank of Connecticut River, &c. (according to
terms of the aforesaid grant) Contains 500 acres of land, and is
a true copy of an Original Plan or Survey of said Tract as taken
and returned to me by Capt[n]. Jonath[n]. Chase Dept. Surveyor.

ATTEST. Is[l]. RINGE,

Surv[r]. Gen[l].

The French and Indian war (1754–1763), had just closed and
many of the troops who had served in it were from Massachusetts
and Connecticut. These on going to, and returning from, Canada passed through the Connecticut River Valley. They saw
it was indeed a "goodly land," and brought flattering accounts
of it home. These reports had a marvelous effect upon many,
especially upon those who were anxious to try their fortunes in
a new country. Applications to the proper authorities were
soon made, and two tiers of towns on each side of the river were
surveyed and severally granted and many of them were incorporated as early as 1761.

Nearly two years elapsed after the town was granted before any active measures were adopted regarding the settlement of the town. But in the spring and summer of 1765, the first actual settlement began. Previous to this time the only item of Cornish history known was the establishing of a station called "Mast Camp" not far south of the present site of Windsor Bridge. This was established by order of British authority for the purpose of selecting trees suitable for the British navy. How long this had existed there is no record to show.

In 1765, two years after the grant was made, Judge Samuel Chase of Sutton, Mass., and others of his family and relatives who had become enamored by the descriptions of the beautiful scenery, the tall forests and rich lands of the Connecticut River Valley resolved to make the venture. It was a long and tedious journey of 140 miles, first reaching the river by going in a westerly direction, and then ascending the river into the then unknown wilderness.

They ascended the river until they reached Walpole, N. H., the extreme uppermost known settlement at that time on the river, unless we except that of Charlestown where a fort had been established several years before. At Walpole a part of the family tarried nearly two years. Judge Chase had meanwhile made extensive purchases of land of the proprietors of Cornish. At this time he was nearly sixty years of age and decided to stay at Walpole until the following year. His son, Dudley Chase, and son-in-law, Daniel Putnam, and Dyer Spalding, with their workmen, were the first men who came up the river in a canoe for the purpose of making a settlement in the virgin forests of Cornish.

They landed on the river meadow near the mouth of Blow-me-down Brook in the northwest part of the town, on land now (1906) belonging to the estate of C. C. Beaman, Esq. Here they began to make a clearing, the first made in town.

There is an absence of recorded authority; tradition says it was in the early days of June, when Nature was at her loveliest and the "leaves were green," that the woodman's axe first resounded through those forests. At this season they scarcely thought of a shelter except of the rudest kind, so intent were they upon clearing and preparing ground for the season's crops. During the season now before them, until the season's crops could be grown,

they were wholly dependent for their supplies of provision upon
Fort No. 4 at Charlestown, sixteen miles away, down the river.

It was at this fort that the family of Dea. Dudley Chase had
been left for safety while on their journey up the river, as the husband and father with his associates went on to prepare for them
their future home in the "township of land" just across the river
from what is now Windsor, Vt., in full sight of the dome of Ascutney. This family consisted of his wife and seven small children.
It appears to have been a sore trial to her to be thus compelled
to remain within the prison-like walls of the fort with no con-
genial associate except her little children.

These circumstances, and those that followed, with their
interesting outcome, are best described by herself as quoted by
her youngest son, Bishop Philander Chase:

"Days seemed weeks and weeks seemed months, and scarcely
did a sun rise without witnessing my wandering on the bank of
the flowing stream where I had parted with your father and his
company of Cornish workmen. It was in one of these walks
with my children by my side, that I saw at sunset a canoe coming
round a point of the river bank, towards me. At first I thought
of the approach of savages, but I soon recognized the well-known
canoe of your father, and in it our trusty neighbor Dyer Spalding.
My heart leaped with joy, and no sooner did the canoe reach
the shore than the children were in it, and on his knees; nor did
they allow him to stir till they told him that I was resolved that
we should all return with him to their father in the woods. 'Do
you know, dear Madam,' said he, 'that our anxiety to put in a
crop and plant the ground for the coming summer has been such
that we have had no time to build even the semblance of a house?
I am come to tell you that your husband is well and to learn of
your safety and health and to carry back a supply of provisions.
We have all slept upon the uncovered ground, and as yet have no
shelter for ourselves—much less for you, and your little ones.—
Will you venture with them into the woods before you are sure
of a refuge?'

"To this I replied: 'I will go, and with all my children endure
any storm if you will give me but a safe and steady conveyance
to my husband. If there be no shelter, nor fence, nor fort, his
faithful arm will guard me, and his trusty men will aid him, and
their God, who is above all, will provide.'"

CORNISH

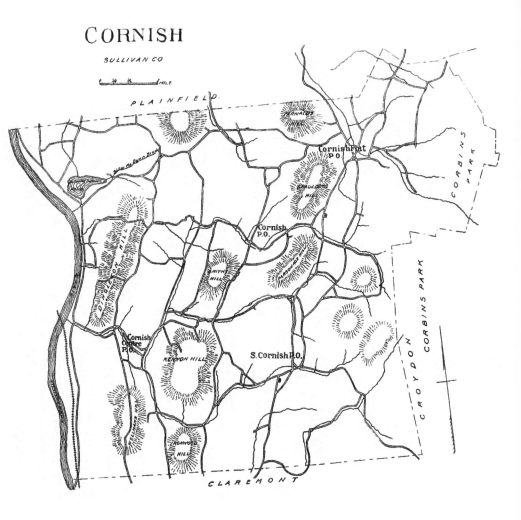

SULLIVAN CO

PLAINFIELD

CLAREMONT

A much smaller degree of sagacity than Dyer Spalding possessed would have convinced him that Mistress Alice was mistress of the situation.

The question decided, all the resources of his mind were called into action to make things ready for the journey up the river. "Such goods as we needed least were secured in the fort; and such as the boat would carry and were needed most, with ample provisions, were put on board and the morning sun was scarcely risen, ere by Spalding's help and that of the older boys, all things were ready for the voyage.

"Spalding was a good canoe-man, and with the boys to lend a hand we made good progress, slow but unceasing. It was in time of Indian warfare, in a frail Indian canoe, and going up a rapid stream, yet we reached the little opening among the towering trees before nightfall. 'There they are' cried the children. 'There are father and his men; I hear his voice and the sound of their axes.' For a moment all was hidden from our view by the tall forest trees; this gave me time to utter a prayer of faith and benediction; 'May the God of our fathers bless your father and me, your helpless mother, and you, my dear children, now, even now, as we shall take possession of this, our dwelling-place in the wild woods; and though like Jacob of old, we have but a stone for a pillow and the canopy of Heaven for a covering, we may find God in this place, and may it be to us as the House of God and the Gate of Heaven.''

How the prayer of this faithful woman was answered, time has told. "Pilot Spalding made fast the canoe to the willows and asked us to await his return. Your father could get no direct answer to his inquiries: 'Is all well? and have you brought us a supply of food?' &c. 'Come and see,' replied Spalding and as they stood upon the bank, he saw the frail bark in which were his wife and children. The emotion of the moment was almost too much. I sprang forward, the little ones following. He received us with joy mixed with agony. 'Are you come here to die,' he exclaimed, 'before your time? We have no house to shelter you, and you will perish before we can build one.'

" 'Cheer up, my faithful,' I replied. 'Let the smiles and the rosy cheeks of your children, and the health and cheerfulness of your wife make you joyful! If you have no house, you have strength and hands to make one. The God we worship will bless us and help us to obtain a shelter. Cheer up! Cheer up! my faithful!'

"The sunshine of joy and hope began to beam from his countenance, and the news was soon told to the company of workmen, and the woods rang with their shouts in honor of the first white woman and her children, on the banks of the Connecticut River above the Fort No. 4.

"All hands assembled to welcome the strangers. Trees were felled and peeled, and the bark in large sheets was spread for a floor. Other sheets were fastened by thongs of twisted twigs to stakes driven into the ground and were raised for walls or laid on cross-pieces for a roof, and a cheerful fire soon made glad our little dwelling. The space of three hours was not consumed in doing all this, and never were men more happy than those men who contributed so speedily to our wants. Beds were brought from the canoe to the rustic pavilion, and on them we rested sweetly fearless of danger, though the thick foliage was wet with the dew, and the wild creatures of the woods howled around us. The next day all hands were called to build a cabin which served us for the following winter, and in which, cheered by the rising prospects of the family, and the mutual affection of all around us, my enjoyments were more exquisite than at any other period of my life."

One cannot but admire the spirit of this pure and high-minded woman; far from all the comforts of ordinary life; so full of courage and possessing such a perfect trust in God. She was, indeed, a woman fitted by nature and grace to become the mother of such men and women as Cornish can gladly boast.

On the 17th of October following, she gave birth to the first child born in Cornish,—a daughter who received her mother's name.

It may be of interest to mention that this first family in town, soon after this, settled three miles further south on "Cornish Plain," on the farm now (1907) owned and occupied by William E. Chadbourne. Here they spent the remainder of their lives, each living to be more than fourscore years of age. (See Dudley Chase.) Other settlements soon followed by other families coming to town. In 1766 Judge Samuel Chase came with others of his family, who mostly settled in town. Prominent among these besides Dudley were Samuel, Jr., Solomon Chase, the first physician in the town; Jonathan who afterwards attained military distinction during the Revolutionary War. Moses Chase, a younger brother of Judge Samuel, with his family also came and settled in town within a year from the date of the first settlement. His name appears as one of the selectmen at the first meeting of the town in 1767. Many of his descendants remained in town for two or three generations following. Caleb Chase, another brother of Moses and Samuel, with a portion of his family came soon after. The children of these families of Chases were generally quite numerous; so those named *Chase* in town, for years, exceeded in number that of any other, or all other names combined.

The name *Bellows* was as strong numerically in Walpole, N. H., as the name *Chase* was in Cornish. The families intermarrying brought them into very friendly relations. A member of the Cornish family was one day boasting to one of the Walpole families that "there were Chases enough in Cornish to chase all others from out the town into Walpole." The other replied, that "there were Bellows enough in Walpole to blow them all back again." Besides the Chase families, there were at the first Dyer Spalding and Daniel Putnam. These were soon followed by the Cadys, Wellmans, Richardsons, Bartletts and many others.

All these very naturally selected desirable situations, chiefly at first along the banks of the Connecticut River. These estates have all "passed out" of their family names except that of Daniel Putnam whose estate is still retained by his descendants of the same name. Possibly there are remote descendants of those early families still living who retain interesting traditions of the settlement by their ancestors, including many facts of interest, but unhappily these are mainly beyond our reach and knowledge.

The number of settlers were few during the years 1765–66, but all worked for the general good of the whole. Of course, there were diverse opinions regarding religious and political matters, but the time had not yet arrived for any organization to materialize. Probably they did not feel the need of any during this time. Hard work and happiness joined hand in hand and as a result harmony prevailed. A general spirit of helpfulness and interest in each other's welfare existed on every hand.

The two years of which we have no authentic record may be

termed "assembling years" for the colony. Their numbers the first year were too few to coöperate in a formal way, but in the autumn of 1766, the people had so increased in numbers that they became anxious to try the experiment of self-government on the following year. Accordingly they presented a petition to Judge Samuel Chase (he having become authorized to receive such petition), for a meeting of the town to be holden on the 10th of March following. Their petition was granted; therefore he, on the 28th day of February, 1767, issued a call for the first meeting to be holden as above.

The following is a copy of the original call which is presented in its original form, etc.:

Province of   )
New Hampshear   )
    Pursuant to a Request of yᵉ Inhabitance & Free holders of yᵉ Town of Cornish To me directed one of his majestys Justices of yᵉ Peace for yᵉ Province of New Hampshere for calling a Town meeting In sd Town of Cornish.
    These are to notify and warn the free holders and other Inhabitance of yᵉ Town of Cornish, To meet at yᵉ Dwelling House of Mʳ. Jonathan Chase In sᵈ Cornish on Tuesday yᵉ tenth day of March Next at Ten of yᵉ Clock In Yᵉ forenoon. Then & There To act upon the following artichels (Viz.):
    1ˡʸ To chuse a moderator To regulate sᵈ meeting.
    2ˡʸ To chuse a Town Clark.
    3ˡʸ To chuse Selectmen
    4ˡʸ To chuse a Constable or Constables.
    5ˡʸ To chuse any other Town officer as yᵉ Law Directs.
    Dated at Cornish Feb. 28ᵗʰ A. D. 1767.
                            SAMUEL CHASE Justice of yᵉ Peace
Recorded by Daniel Putnam—Town Clark.

    The following is the response to the above call,—the first recorded meeting of the free-holders of the town:

Province of   )
New Hampshear   )
    At a meeting of yᵉ free-holders & Inhabitance of yᵉ Town of Cornish & Province aforesᵈ Held (Pursuant to a Notification) at the Dwelling House of Mr. Jonathan Chase In sᵈ. Cornish on

Tuesday yᵉ tenth day of March anno Domini 1767 at ten o'clock in yᵉ forenoon, The following votes were passed (Viz.):

1ˡʸ Voted and Chose Samˡˡ Chase Esq. Moderator for sᵈ meeting.

2ˡʸ Voted and Chose Daniel Putnam Town Clark.

3ˡʸ Voted and Chose five Selectmen Viz: Samˡˡ Chase Esq. Mr. Elijah Cady, Mr. Jonathan Chase, Mr. Dudley Chase, & Mr. Moses Chase.

4ˡʸ Voted and Chose Mr. Tisdale Dean Constable.

5ˡʸ Voted and Chose Samˡˡ Chase Esq. Town Treasurer.

6ˡʸ Voted that swine should Run at Large this Present year Being Yoaked & Ringed according to law.

7ˡʸ Voted and Chose Mr. Joseph Tinsur 1ˢᵗ. Haward.

8ˡʸ Voted and Chose Phinehas Powers 2ᵈ. Haward.

9ˡʸ Voted and Chose Mr. Elijah Cady Leather-Sealer.

SAMˡˡ CHASE ESQᴿ. Moderator.

Recorded by Danˡˡ Putnam, Town Clark.

In the charter, already mentioned, the date of the town meetings had been fixed for the second Tuesday of March of each year. Every year since the above-mentioned meeting, the annual meetings have been called for this date.

CHAPTER III.

PIONEER LIFE—EARLY CUSTOMS, ETC.

THE early customs, manner and means of living in all the towns of New England were so similar that a record of them in any one town would not be unlike that of other towns in the same section. Recognizing this, the writer takes the liberty of quoting somewhat from contemporaneous writers on the subject, being careful to mention only such things as have often been verified by tradition and observation. The histories of Charlestown, Keene, Richmond, Washington, Bristol, Plymouth, Warren and others have contributed their aid to this department; for which the writer hereby renders his grateful acknowledgment.

When the pioneer settlers first started for their new home in the unbroken wilderness, they generally left their families behind them in comfortable homes in the older settlement. They usually went in small parties of two, three or more. This they did for protection and mutual aid, as wild beasts and Indians might be encountered at any time. Each man took his trusty gun with a supply of ammunition, an axe, knife and tinder-box, and such other articles as might be most needed, together with a liberal supply of provision.

This was the outfit of the first party who came up the Connecticut River from Walpole in the spring of 1765 and landed on the meadows now owned by the heirs of the late C. C. Beaman, Esq. (See Settlement.) It is said by historians of other towns that a liberal supply of rum and tobacco was counted among the necessaries or essentials brought into the new settlements or towns; but no such tradition is known to exist regarding the first settlers of this town, although those articles were subsequently used quite extensively.

After the arrival of the settlers upon their lot, one of the first things was to provide a shelter for themselves and their effects. The spring was the most favorable time of year for them to make a beginning. At this time hemlock would readily peel. After felling and peeling a tree or two, the bark was placed on opposite sides of a pole which was supported at each end by crotched stakes six or eight feet long. In this way a very good temporary shelter was quickly prepared. From this same pole their kettle was suspended for cooking purposes. Excepting a few dishes and utensils brought with them, the dishes at the first were of the rudest kind,—all wooden; plates, bowls, platters, etc., being split from small logs, and then hollowed and curved as best they could with the axe and knife. At first they slept upon the ground or on beds of leaves in their rude shanties, using such scant covering as they had.

These extreme conditions generally lasted only while land was being cleared, prepared and seeded for the season's crop. This being done, their next thought was the building of a log-house. Abundance of timber of the right kind was ever near at hand. The houses were built of straight, smooth logs, hewed on upper and lower sides and locked together at the corners so as to bring the logs into close contact. The unavoidable cracks between the logs were filled with mud or clay. Sometimes, when they could afford it, the logs were hewn smooth inside, but generally they were left round. One opening was left for a door and one for a window. Each of these were to be closed by shutters made of slabs split from logs, as there were no boards or sawmills at first. The roofs were covered with bark supported by poles. After the first season many of the roofs were thatched with rye straw. The earth still formed the floor, which was rendered hard and smooth by use. Generally there was but one room, sometimes two, partitioned by logs like the walls.

The chimney was the hardest problem to solve; sometimes, none at all, with simply a hole in the roof for the escape of smoke; sometimes, with stone, topped out with short logs, built like the walls and plastered inside with clay, and generally built outside the cabin at one end of it. At other times, when the weather would permit, the open fire was used wholly outside the house. In this case a pole was supported on crotched posts from which the kettles were suspended by wooden hooks with the fire beneath.

Poles were laid across overhead, in the cabin, for storing articles. Sometimes the loft was made a sleeping apartment for children or hired man. This was reached by a ladder.

For a cellar, an excavation was generally made outside of

sufficient depth and covered with logs and dirt, so that articles stored should not freeze.

The first farming tools of the early settlers were few and rude, but their stock of these gradually increased in quantity and improved in quality. At first they were chiefly hand-tools, as hoes, spades, mattocks, forks, etc. The ground at this time could not be plowed, neither were there teams at first to do it.

One of the first crops grown by the settler was rye, the seed having been obtained from some older settlement. This was "scratched in" the first autumn, using a pronged hoe for the purpose. Corn would also be planted the following spring, by opening the soil with a hoe or spade and putting in a "hill" wherever there was room for it among the rocks and stumps. Pumpkins, peas, beans and vegetables were planted in like manner. Crops of all these were generally satisfactory. The soil was new and fertile, yielding abundantly. The cultivation of the crops was but trifling, as there were no weed-pests at first to prevent full development of the crops. Potatoes were scarcely known and but little used at the time the town was settled. In two or three years the farmer would have grass on his place and there was always browsing and some native grass on the lowlands, so he could keep a cow, which added quite a little to the support of the family. He could soon have young cattle and a yoke of steers and a few sheep. Hogs and poultry he could have from near the first, but the horse was a luxury that usually came later. Seeds would be brought at the first, and one of his first acts was to plant a nursery of fruit trees, and a few years would bring him an abundance of apples, plums, and other fruits; and the women never forgot to bring a few seeds of their favorite flowers, also bulbs and roots for the garden. Every mother knew the medicinal qualities of many herbs and plants and was thus qualified to become her own family physician.

The "sweetning" of the pioneers was wholly made from the sap of the sugar maple, caught in troughs made from small logs, split in halves and hollowed out. At the close of the sap season these troughs were inverted under the trees, and so were ready for use the following year. Such troughs were still used for that purpose within the memory of some people still living. The sap was boiled down in kettles suspended from poles, over an open fire, and when reduced to a syrup, was carried to the kitchen to be further boiled and clarified by the good wife. This furnished the only kind of sugar used by the families during all the earliest years.

Later in the spring came soap-making. The waste grease was tried out and boiled with lye, and a sufficient amount of soft soap was made to last the family a year.

Mechanics of all kinds were very important members of the community; for all tools and implements had to be made by hand. Scarcely any ready-made article could be bought. Coopers were much relied upon for making all sorts of wooden vessels. They not only made casks, tubs, barrels, buckets, but also the keeler, piggin, noggin, and all other wooden vessels in common use.

Farming tools of all kinds were made by hand, and were generally of a clumsy make, and hard to obtain at first as no manufactories were convenient. Nearly everything had to be made at home from necessity. Even the entire clothing of the family was made within its own home. The cloth was made of wool and flax, spun and woven at home and made up by some good tailoress who came and spent several days in the family, doing up the family sewing for a year. The shoemaker, too, with his kit of tools and bench made his annual visits to each family, usually in the fall of the year and made up the necessary foot-wear for the entire family. The good housewife, aided perhaps by one or more of her daughters, was expected to do all the knitting for the family. Each woman, too, was always expected to be her own milliner and dressmaker. Few were the ornaments worn in those early days, except the beautiful ornaments of self-reliance and independence, coupled with contentment.

When the settler first built his house he took care that it should be located near a fine spring, or by a running brook of pure water. The supply of water was brought from the spring or brook in buckets or pails. To furnish a more constant supply, and more even temperature, a well was dug, and the water drawn by a bucket fastened to the end of a long, slender pole with a spring. Later the "well-sweep" was erected, and the "oaken bucket" attached.

As time progressed, the carpenter and brick-maker appeared in the settlement, so that framed or brick houses could be built when desired; but the log-cabin remained for many years. The entrance to these cabins was secured by a heavy latch on the inside, to be raised from the outside by a raw-hide string running through the door. To fasten against intruders the string was pulled in, but this was seldom done, even at night, except in time of hostile Indians. The phrase, "The latch string *out*," is still used as an expression of hospitality.

During the first season of the settlement, while the men were "roughing it," their wives and children usually remained at home in the old settlement where they could enjoy better privileges and remain in safety. Very seldom did the wife and children accompany the husband and father during his "shanty life"; but after the log house appeared and provision secured for their support, they rejoined him in the wild, and their real life as a pioneer family began.

All the food at this time was the product of the farm, forests and waters of the vicinity. No fancy dishes of food adorned their rude table at the first, but only plain, substantial food such as the farm produced. Pork was the usual meat, varied occasionally by poultry or mutton or wild game. Wheat and corn bread, hot rye cakes with maple syrup, bean porridge— made of the broth of meat and vegetables, thickened with beans —"good hot or cold, but best when nine days old," were the first staple articles of food. After the advent of the cow, their diet was more varied and bread with milk, butter and cheese and pumpkin pie were then the daily articles of food the year around.

Rude as were the habitations of our forefathers and apparently devoid of what we term luxuries, and even necessaries, they were, nevertheless, the abodes of contentment and happiness to a degree as great as is enjoyed in the more luxurious homes of the present.

These homes all had huge fireplaces, in which, during the long winter evenings there was kept up a blazing fire that threw a ruddy glow over the healthful countenances of the happy group seated around. There were *fire-sides then*, and influences going out from them that are *lost* since the gloomy stove has taken their place. There may be centers of attraction in our homes now, but there are none equal to the "fire upon the hearth." "The fire upon the hearth is the center and symbol of the family

life. When the fire in the house goes out, it is because the *life*
has gone out. Somewhere in every house it burns in constant
service, and every chimney that sends its incense heavenward
speaks of an altar inscribed to *Love* and *Home*."

The social gatherings during winter evenings in these rude
homes, in which the young men and maidens met, clad in
their homespun attire and engaged in their innocent sports, were
seasons of enjoyment and mutual interest in each other not
less true and pure than similar gatherings now, in which there
is more display and more tyranny of fashion.

Simplicity of dress, manners and equipage continued to be
a characteristic of our forefathers until after the Revolutionary
War. As wealth increased, the home-made garments, vehicles,
etc., gave place to those of a more modern type.

There were but few ornaments that adorned those cabin walls
or shelves. The day of bric-a-brac had not arrived. The trusty
gun and powder horn seemed to occupy the post of honor above
the fire-place, while around the walls of the cabin hung crook-
necked squashes, festoons of red peppers and medicinal herbs,
and apples on strings, "quartered and cored," while on poles
overhead were rings cut from the yellow pumpkin, all drying
for winter use. Practical articles like these constituted the chief
ornaments of these homes.

The fireplaces were at first the only sources of heat for the
entire household. If the house had other apartments than the
kitchen, the sleeping rooms in the winter would be like the frigid
zone, and the children sleeping in such rooms would often feel
the snow sifting in their faces during violent storms, and find
their beds covered with it in the morning, and have to wade
through small drifts with bare feet to get to the kitchen; and
as the family gathered around the rousing fire, their faces would
be nearly scorched while they shivered with the cold from the
rear. But as wood was plenty, the householder took care that
the fires were liberally supplied, and an air of comfort soon
pervaded the kitchen, or "living room." Warming pans were
sometimes used to warm beds situated in rooms remote from the
fire. These consisted of a covered brass pan with a long handle
attached. Coals of fire were put in and then it was inserted
and slid about in the bed by the good housewife until the bed

became warm and comfortable,when it was ready for its occupant. But this was a luxury too expensive to be afforded by all.

The fireplace was also the principal source of light for the family at night. This was generally ample for the "living room," so that the family could see to read and sew, and perform nearly all of their household labors. Pine knots were much used to obtain an increased light by throwing one or more of them upon the fire in the fire-place. But if a member of the family had occasion to go to some other room or to the cellar, some other light was needed. The tallow-dip or candle was the light generally used for this purpose. These were made by suspending wicks at proper distances apart on slender rods which were dipped in melted tallow in cold weather when the tallow would adhere and quickly cool. These were suspended between two poles. After repeated immersions the tallow dips would grow to a proper size and be ready for use. These candles were the main light aside from the fire-place. Oil and lamps did not come into general use for several years.

The wearing apparel of our ancestors was likewise all home-made, and the materials were home-grown. Every farmer kept, at least, a few sheep and raised his own wool for family use. The sheep were sheared at the proper time and the wool stored. When the women were ready for the work, the wool was sorted, scoured and carded into rolls and spun into yarn, all by hand. Wool was spun on a large wheel turned by hand, the spinner walking back and forth to draw and renew her thread. The yarn thus made was knitted into stockings and mittens, and woven into cloth for the clothing and bed clothing of the family. Some of the woolen yarn was dyed, and the indigo blue dye pot stood in the chimney corner always ready for use, potent with its vile odors whenever it was stirred. Other dyes were used for other colors, as the butternut, sumac and golden rod. These with other combinations furnished all the varieties of color the artistic housewife needed for the family. Cotton goods were almost an unknown article. Many years elapsed after the settlement of the town before cotton fabrics were generally used in it. Flax was raised for the family linen. This is a plant grown like wheat or oats. When matured it was pulled up by the roots and, after threshing, was laid in gavels to "rot," so that the woody part of the stalk would separate from the fiber.

Then it was gathered and stored. The winter's work of the farmer
was to break his flax with a break, swingling it on a swingling
board so as to remove the woody part. This latter work must
be done on a clear, cold day. It was then hatchelled and ready
for spinning. This was done on a foot-wheel, the spinner sitting,
furnishing the power by the foot. The flax was wound on a
distaff and carefully fed to a spindle. From the spindle, the
yarn was reeled off into knots and skeins and was then ready for
weaving. All farmers' daughters learned to spin and weave
and they usually made their own marriage outfit. The following
lines by Ebenezer Morse, in the history of Walpole, N. H.,
have a significance here:

> "The boys dressed the flax, the girls spun the tow
> And the music of mother's foot-wheel was not slow.
> The flax on the bended pine distaff was spread
> With the squash shell of water to moisten the thread.
> Such were the pianos our mothers would keep
> Which they played on while spinning their children to sleep.
> My mother, I'm sure, must have borne off the medal,
> For she always was placing her foot on the pedal.
> The warp and the filling were piled in the room,
> Till the web was completed and fit for the loom.
> Then labor was pleasure and industry smiled
> While the wheel and the loom every trouble beguiled.
> And here at the distaff the good wives were made,
> Where Solomon's precepts were fully obeyed."

Leather breeches of deer or sheep-skin were much worn by
men for heavy work, also leather aprons. The women also used
the strong, coarse cloth made of tow, or the combings of flax.
The Scotch-Irish brought with them the art of making striped
frocking, and it became an article of universal wear for farmers
and laboring men, and was made in nearly every family.

In the early days the woman's work was not only spinning,
weaving, making butter and cheese and doing general housework,
but they milked the cows and fed the hogs and poultry and
gathered the vegetables for the table. During the Revolutionary
War the women took almost the whole care of the farm and stock
and performed the labor of the field during the absence of their
husbands and brothers. It must not be inferred that the men

were idle. Far from it. The farm needed and received the
incessant and vigorous labor of the men to cut, clear, fence and
prepare land for the future crops, and then to care for the same.

The farmer had but little food-stuff to buy. Nearly every
thing needed in the family was raised on the farm. He soon
began to raise a surplus from his fresh and unworn soil, and this
sold for good prices. Every thrifty farmer was supposed to
make at least one trip annually to Boston to dispose of the surplus
products of his farm. In winter there might be seen, almost
any week-day one-horse pungs and two-horse box sleighs winding
their course to Boston. The body of the load consisted of dressed
poultry, butter, cheese, beans, peas, grain, dried apple on strings,
woolen mittens and stockings, woolen yarn and sometimes
woolen and linen cloth made by the thrifty women. Sometimes
there were pelts, furs and skins of various animals. Frequently
such loads were "topped out" with one or more dressed frozen
hogs. Frequently a number of neighbors started at the same
time and kept company on the road. They carried their food
with them—bread, cheese, cooked sausage, and frozen bean-
porridge. Sometimes they trudged along on foot and sometimes
on the circular step in the rear of their pung. When night came
they paid ten cents or so for the privilege of warming their
porridge by the tavern fire and sleeping on the bar-room floor.

The return freight would be salt, molasses, a few gallons of
the indispensable rum, a little salt fish, tobacco, a few spices, a
little tea and a few yards of dress goods and ribbons for the wife
and daughters. The arrival home of the thrifty farmer at these
times brought joy to the whole household. In this way the
goods and luxuries of the city came to be known and appreciated
by those living in the wilderness.

Cooking was mostly done by the open fire and the brick oven.
Cakes were often baked on the hot stones of the hearth, and
potatoes roasted in the ashes. Meat was roasted by being hung
before the fire and kept constantly turning. In every good
fire-place a large iron crane was hung which supported all kettles
hung upon it. It was constructed on hinges, so that pots and
kettles suspended from it could be swung backwards over the
fire, or forward whenever desired. By this means all boiling
of food, clothes washing, etc., was readily done.

Stoves did not come into general use until near the middle of the nineteenth century. The brick oven was also a great aid to the housewife, which turned out its great loaves of brown bread, its pots of beans and pork, its roasts of beef, fowl and mutton, its delicious mince and pumpkin pies—all put in at night, and taken out steaming hot in the morning, the materials of which were all produced on the farm except the salt and spices. The modern butcher and baker were yet unknown. A little later they began to raise wheat, but that was a luxury, and the economical housekeeper would make the upper crust of her pies of wheat flour and the under crust of rye. From that custom came the term "upper crust" as applied to aristocratic society.

As before stated the fire on the hearth was seldom allowed to go out. To prevent this, a large brand was buried in the embers each night for a bed of coals the next morning. If by any chance the fire was lost, coals had to be brought from a neighbor's, perhaps over long distances; or by flashing powder with a flint-lock gun. Friction matches were then unknown, and were not used until about 1830. Clocks and watches were not generally owned, but the hour-glass, sun-dial or noon-mark were used, and when an evening meeting was announced, it was called at "early candle-lighting."

The kitchen was the sleeping apartment of the farmer and his wife, the bed standing in one corner, with the wheel or loom in the opposite corner. The children slept in the loft above, or in a trundle-bed drawn from beneath their parents' bed. The only brooms the good housewife had, were made of hemlock brush tied in a bundle around a handle, or one of "birch-peel." These were made by cutting a yellow birch about three inches in diameter, and four or five feet long, taking off the bark of about a foot of the upper end, then peeling that end into thin narrow strips for the brush, and using the other end, shaved down, for a handle.

The Bible and an almanac constituted about all the literature found in their homes.—No libraries, no newspapers.

The sports of today were unknown a hundred, or more, years ago. *Then* it was working bees, raisings, wrestling matches, corn-huskings, etc. Women visited, but worked, taking their work with them. Quilting and carding bees were much their employment during the daytime. In the evening, both sexes came in for a jolly good time, the occasion often ending up with a dance in the big kitchen. The huskings were delightful festivities, closing with a supper of pumpkin pie, "nut-cakes," cheese, apples and cider. A red ear of corn husked by a young man entitled him to go the rounds with kisses, and one husked by a girl gave her the right to kiss the lad of her choice, or, if her courage failed, to be kissed by every lad present. The only light furnished for these occasions was a tallow dip in a perforated tin lantern, which gave only a feeble light. Later in the season came the paring bees, where the apples were pared, quartered and strung to dry. After the feast came the social hour, usually devoted to playing of games; all games having fines and all fines being paid with a kiss. After these jolly frolics each young man was expected to "beau" his "best girl" home.

Postal facilities were very limited in those days, even to the close of the eighteenth century. Mail was at first carried on horseback, once in two weeks or so; and this only along the principal routes. These routes were very few, and but few post offices were established at first. Farmers living away from these routes often had to travel many miles to obtain their mail. The condition of the roads, too, was very unfavorable. In the earliest days oftentimes a bridle-road afforded the only means of communication between neighbors. After highways were laid out the roads were made in better condition, so that carriages became more common, and travel more rapid.

In those times, church and state were united. The church was sustained by the whole community under the management of the political machinery of the state and town; a tax for its support being laid on every propertyholder. This action was required by Great Britain in all her colonies, and therefore one of the conditions of the township grants was that a certain part of said grant should be set apart for the propagation of the gospel, etc. This practice continued even after British rule had ceased in our colonies. The emancipation of the church from political authority was largely due to the Baptists, whose tenets forbid magisterial authority or interference in religious affairs. (See Baptist Church.) All other churches soon after followed in their wake.

The first meeting houses in town were plain buildings, but little better than barns, without much finish. The men sat on one side, and the women on the other. There were no means of warming them in winter; and yet everyone was required to go to meeting, even though thinly clad and poorly shod, and remain through two long services, each sermon being at least an hour long, besides two prayers and psalm-singing to each service. Between the two services there was an hour's intermission.

It was a common custom on Sunday morning in winter to yoke the oxen to a sled, put on a few boards, put on a chair for "mother" or "grandpa," take blankets in which the children cuddled down, and drive, in some cases, miles to meeting, stay through both services and intermission with no fire in the meeting house, and then drive home through the snow to a cold house. Women sometimes carried heated stones for their hands and feet; and later foot-stoves were used. These were filled with live coals at the start, and sometimes replenished for the return ride home, at the house of a friend near the meeting house. It was thought essential that a child should be baptized soon after birth, and it is said that babies were sometimes taken to those cold houses for baptism before they were a week old. In summer most of the people walked to meeting. If a horse was owned, the man would take his wife on the horse with her youngest child on a pillion behind him, and the children walked barefooted, the older girls carrying their shoes and stockings and putting them on just before they arrived at church. The mother of the writer has often avouched the truth of this custom, as she was one of the many big girls who practiced it.

The minister was regarded as a superior and sanctified being and entitled to great reverence and respect. At the close of the services the congregation would rise and stand while he passed out through the central isle. The early ministers preached morality as an essential element of true religion, and practiced it in their lives. Children were taught to show them great respect. If they met the minister on the highway, the boys would remove their hats and bow their heads, and the girls would make a low courtesy. Their visits in the family were not always relished by the children. The restraint on these occasions was irksome, and the fear of being catechised so great that they were glad to see him take his departure.

Deacons' seats were built at the base of the high pulpit, facing the congregation. Here those officials sat each Sabbath adding much to the apparent sanctity of the services.

Tithingmen, chosen by the town and sworn to the faithful performance of their duties, armed with a long staff, took position overlooking the congregation, or walked the aisle, to preserve order and keep all the drowsy ones awake.

The singing was performed by the reading of a line of a hymn by the minister or leader, who gave the key-note with his pitch-pipe or tuning fork, the choir singing it after him, and then taking the next line in the same way.

The observance of the Sabbath was very strict; its hours begun at sunset on Saturday, and ended at sunset on Sunday night. All customary labors were suspended. All things savoring of levity or even mirthfulness were to be repressed, and *all* must go to meeting whatever the distance or the weather. Almost the only public and secular intercourse the people had on Sunday was during the hour intervening between the two solemn services of the sanctuary, when they caught a few moments for gossip. The less devout men of the congregation had their weekly chat in the horse-sheds at the rear of the church.

Puritan morals frowned upon amusements generally. Card-playing, theater-going and dancing were considered abominations by all good church-goers.

The free use of ardent spirits was not tabooed as at present. Ordinations and dedications, and even funerals were made occasions of feasting, and great freedom in those indulgences, and excess did not then seem to incur any disgrace.

The first schools were primitive affairs. Owing to the lack of text-books and competent teachers, but little could be learned beside the "three R's:" (Reading, "Riting" and "Rithmetic.") Schoolhouses were rude and uncomfortable. In winter the teachers were men, and the schools were effective and practical so far as they went. (See Educational Department.)

"As a rule, the pioneers heretofore described, and their wives and the large families of girls and boys reared in those primitive homes, were among the purest and noblest of men and women. Though parents were austere and apparently unsympathetic, their hearts were warm under a stern exterior. Their Puritan principles were of the highest, and their industry, frugality and integrity made them the best of citizens; and most of those homes were pure fountains whence flowed the streams that formed the mighty rivers of the states and the nation. From such homes came the men, always nobly seconded by the women, who beat back the savages, subdued the forests; carried on the affairs of each little independent government, the town; organized the states; won their separation from Great Britain, and laid the foundation of this grand republic."

The early settlers of these towns were a hardy and vigorous people, inured to hardship and danger. They were generally the young, energetic and enterprising members of the older communities. Respect for the authority of the church and state were striking features in the character of our forefathers.

While not highly educated in the schools, they became liberally educated in the arts and methods of pioneer life. The rugged life they were compelled to lead developed new energies and made them the heroes of their own success.

With all their devotion to law and authority they possessed a love for freedom from restraints of society which is fascinating to many men and women. Their own lives as pioneers were divested of all such restraints and so they were at liberty to devote all their energies to the founding and growth of their homes in the wild. Their lives were a repetition of that of their ancestors nearer the coast who had fought and driven the Indians back and established homes the century before; the account of which stimulated these, their descendants, to a similar work and experience.

The rugged experiences of the first settlers served to develop them in every way and fit them for still greater achievements. It made them a class of men and women of a type apparently superior to those who were never called to such experiences.

The following incident is a specimen of multitudes of similar experiences by early settlers: It is related by Levi N. Barnard, Esq., of Springfield, Vt.:

"Nathaniel Gowing, who was born in Sutton, Mass., in 1734, came to Chester, Vt., soon after the settlement of that town in 1763. The summer of 1765 was a barren one and the following winter was very cold with deep snows. Provisions were scarce, and Mr. Gowing, who lived in the north part of that town on a high hill, was forced to travel on snowshoes to Cornish, N. H., where the only grist-mill within many miles was located. He tramped across Weathersfield and reached the river (there were no highways then), went up the river on ice to Cornish and

secured sixty pounds of Indian meal, he then retraced his steps.
The load proved heavy and he became nearly exhausted. In this
condition he was tempted to lie down in despair, but the thought
of his wife and children famishing at home kept him going, and
after a long and weary tramp he reached home with his meal on
his back, and on that they managed to worry out the balance
of the winter."

Mr. Barnard, now (1908) in his 99th year, has often heard
Mr. Gowing relate this incident among other experiences of his
early life. Many a like incident has been told where our ancestors, when driven to straits, have performed heroic deeds and
conquered difficulties that would seem well-nigh impossible in
our day. To the masterful deeds of our forefathers, we owe the
comfortable conditions of the present. Their heroic achievements
paved the way for the generations that have since followed them.

In all the early settlements of New England a vigilant system
of self-defense was the only safeguard for the settlers. The
dangers of the forests from Indians and wild beasts developed
this spirit and made the hardy pioneers brave and warlike.
Thrilling feats of bravery and valor were often displayed by
individuals and by organized forces. The necessity of organized
force was realized by all. The French and Indian War had
been precipitated. French and English were rival claimants
for vast tracts of the territory of North America. The French,
joined by Indian allies, sought to drive the English settlers from
their just claims. The English very naturally resented all these
attempts, and a war lasting nine years ensued, resulting in a victory for the English colonists. This was called the "French and
Indian War."   It ended in 1763,—two years before the settlement
of the town. Cornish, therefore, as a town, played no part in
this strife. Hostile forces may have marched through the
solitude of her forests, but they left no record there.

The principal, if not the only hero of that memorable strife,
who afterwards made Cornish his home, was Capt. Joseph Taylor,
whose interesting experiences are recorded in the genealogy of
the Taylor family. (Which see.)

Wild Beasts, Etc.

The forests of Cornish, like those of other towns in this section,
at first abounded with wild game of all kinds common to the

latitude and climate. The most dangerous and most dreaded
animals were the black bear, wolf and catamount. The wolves
often made the night hideous by their howling, two or three
making sounds as if there were a dozen or more of them.
But these seldom attacked men unless pinched by extreme hunger.
Children, however, were in much greater danger from them.
Bears and wolves especially were counted a terror and a scourge,
as they were ever ready when opportunity presented, to prey upon
such domestic animals as might come within their reach. The
raising of sheep was next to an impossibility by reason of their
depredations. The state therefore offered and paid bounties for
their destruction. We can realize that it was a pressing necessity
that prompted the offering of *liberal* bounties for their extermina-
tion. For several years it was necessary that all domestic animals
be secured by corralling them at night to render them as secure
as possible. It was no uncommon thing for the weary owner to
be aroused from his slumbers at midnight by the dismal wail of
his affrighted animals, caused by the stealthy approach of vora-
cious beasts. Incessant war, therefore, was waged against them.

Trapping the bear was a common method resorted to. Shooting was considered less safe than trapping them, as a wounded
bear becomes a terrible foe unless the hunter has made a fortunate
shot, which he is not always sure to accomplish.

The traps were made of iron and steel with long sharp teeth inside the jaws which closed with a savage and relentless grip upon
its victim which could in no way extricate itself. When caught
in this way the bear or other animal could easily and safely be
dispatched.

Doubtless many a thrilling adventure with these animals
occurred during the earlier years, which, had they been recorded
would furnish an interesting chapter; but unfortunately not many
of these are left on record, or even handed down by tradition.

Col. Jonathan Chase was the owner of a bear-trap. He
oftentimes loaned it among his neighbors on condition that he
should have the hide of all animals caught in it, while the trappers
could have the carcass, and all the fun and satisfaction of the
capture.

The story has often been told of his loaning his trap to Benjamin Dorr and other parties in the east part of the town. The
trap was set on the hill of the farm of Stephen Child near the line

of the adjoining farm of Mr. Dorr. The land was but partially cleared, being covered with underbrush, fallen trees, etc. They set the trap by the side of a huge log or fallen tree. The following day Mr. Dorr and his companion sought the place to ascertain if they had caught any game. Evidently they had mistaken its locality. Mr. Dorr mounted a log and pointed to another log a little way off, saying to his companion, "There is the place where we set the trap," and suiting the action to the word he stepped off the log, intending to go to the other log, and stepped directly into the trap which closed upon him, piercing his ankle and holding him fast. His companion seeing his condition, at first endeavored to liberate him, but soon found that it required, at least, another man to aid in mastering the sturdy jaws of the trap.

The next thought was to go to the nearest neighbor for help. Meanwhile Mr. Dorr was suffering severely from the lacerations of the cruel spikes of the trap, which held him firmly in their grip. His companion ran to the house of Mr. Child for help, and hurriedly told him the circumstances, urging him to come at once to the aid of Mr. Dorr. They went to the place where the unfortunate man was pinioned, and with considerable effort they extricated him from his unenviable predicament. His leg had received severe injuries, from which he never fully recovered, and, though he afterwards lived to a good age, was always lame in consequence of this event.

But the joke came in on the settlement for the loan of the trap according to the terms then specified. Tradition does not say how the matter was adjusted, but it is hardly supposable that Colonel Chase claimed the "hide," for in this case the "game" lived until nearly 79 years of age. The writer well remembers, when a little boy, of seeing Mr. Dorr, as an aged and lame man.

The event of the "capture" of Mr. Dorr gave occasion for many jocular remarks, doubtless enjoyed by all better than by himself. The locality where this event took place was said to be a favorite resort for bears. A clearing was made on the hill and a field of corn planted as a decoy for them. The rows or ridges made at that time are plainly visible at this day.

One morning Mr. Child saw a bear leisurely sauntering about the barn evidently in search of a breakfast. Seeing the bear was disposed to leave, he seized a lever near at hand, and followed the bear towards the woods on the east, until the bear was crossing a shallow pond on a log, when Mr. Child sprang forward and struck the bear a vigorous blow, breaking his back, after which he was easily dispatched. This little incident has often been told the writer, also the place designated where it took place.

Ezra Stowell, who lived on the mountain in the edge of Grantham (now Cornish), during the early part of the last century had one year an unusually fine piece of corn. He not only took great pride in it, but it was to be the chief dependence of the family for food during the coming winter. So it was with great concern that he discovered that the bears had also got their eyes on it, and were helping themselves to it freely. His wife sympathized with him in the loss, but when he declared his intention of going out that night to shoot the bear, she brought all her powers of persuasion to bear to dissuade him. She argued that if he failed to kill the bear, the bear might kill or injure him, and such a loss would be greater than any amount of corn. She finally wrung from him a reluctant promise to let the bear alone, and she retired to rest with a mind free from anxiety.

But there appears to have been a mental reservation in the promise made by Ezra for he loaded his gun that night with a large charge of shot, adding two good bullets. He stood the gun in the hall near the door of the sleeping room, covering it with his coat; and when the regular breathing of his wife convinced him that there was no likelihood of argument being renewed that night, he softly arose, and taking the gun started for the cornfield.

It was bright moonlight. As he crept along he heard the bear at work, and soon could see him as plainly as by day, going along between the rows, and every now and then reaching for a particularly juicy ear, which he would twist from the stalk, munch with great relish, and then pass on for another morsel. As the bear approached he presented a fine target, and taking good aim, Mr. Stowell fired. The bear went down in a heap, and in a moment lay still. He seemed to be dead, but Mr. Stowell, with the caution of a frontiersman, would not risk a nearer approach without better evidence of death. He prepared to put another charge in the gun, but after the powder was down the muzzle he found that in his haste he had forgotten to bring the shot-pouch. He would not risk a return to the house, where his wife might already be awake; he dare not leave the bear without a complete settlement. He finally slid the long iron ramrod down the barrel, and fired that into the bear. There was no responsive movement, and he was fully satisfied that his first shot had killed the bear. He returned to the house, where he found his wife peacefully sleeping. She knew nothing of the adventure until he confessed to her.

The morning came, a complete examination was made. It was found that one of the bullets had passed through the bear's heart and must have caused instant death. The other bullet had severed a corn-stalk as neatly as a knife could have done it.

The ox team was brought into play and the bear's carcass drawn down to the house. He was a big fellow. His meat was a welcome addition to the homely fare of the day, and the thick, warm bearskin did duty for many years.

These dangerous animals have long since disappeared except an occasional straggler, lured by the "Blue Mountain Game Preserve," may have been seen within a few years.

Beside the dangerous animals was the beaver, once numerous, judging by the remains of their dams on meadows through which flow large streams of water. These are now entirely extinct, but the fox, mink, muskrat and raccoon still exist, despite the wary hunter's skill, also the woodchuck, rabbit, hedgehog and skunk.

Of the feathered tribe the hawk, owl and crow are still plentiful, causing more or less trouble to those who raise poultry. The sparrow, robin, bobolink, swallow, oriole, blackbird, bluejay and many other kinds still exist, charming us with their beauty and filling our forests and meadows with their cheerful songs. Occasionally the whip-poor-wills' plaintive note may be heard on a summer evening.

Forests.

When the first settlers came to Cornish they found the country an almost unbroken wilderness. The land was covered with a heavy growth of wood and timber, all in its original stateliness and grandeur. The settlers were attracted by these conditions of the forests, as they furnished abundant evidence of the fertility of the soil. Many of the trees were of immense size, especially the white pine. At first these were reserved for "His Majesty's masts," according to the terms in the original grants. This reservation continued only during the continuance of British rule in the grants. After this all timber remaining belonged to the owners of their tracts.

Other varieties of trees common to the latitude abounded in all their primeval grandeur. The evergreens, hemlock and spruce, the former occupying a conspicuous share in the general forest, while the latter crowned the mountain's top and sides.

Of the deciduous trees, the different varieties of beech, birch and maple, seem to have formed a large percentage of the bulk of the forest in many places. To these were added the oak, poplar and basswood, while the stately elm and ash were to be found on the meadowlands, or beside the streams of water.

The above-named varieties have constituted the chief bulk of all the forests of the town, while many other varieties of less importance were found interspersed among them.

The forests, at the first, were comparatively continuous and uniform; covering *all* the land except swale bogs and craggy heights, or where a tornado may have partially denuded it.

With such a growth of wood and timber covering the land one may easily imagine what a task our forefathers had to prepare for the raising of the first crop of provisions. Yet they faltered not, and the forests rang with the sound of the merry woodman's axe mingled with his cheerful song.

Legislation to protect the forests was not needed in those days. The significance of the modern title "forester" was then unknown. But on the other hand, the most effective means were employed whereby large tracts of land could be cleared as speedily as possible of its immense growth of trees. Oftentimes the best wooded and timbered tracts were the fields chosen for crop-growing, especially if near the building, and so the fine growth of wood and timber had to be sacrificed.

A very common way of beginning a clearing was to cut several adjacent trees two thirds or more off at the stump and then to fall one large tree against the one nearest it, causing it to fall in turn against others, and so the whole would be carried to the ground. This was called "driving a piece." The trees were allowed to lie one season to dry, after which they were cut, piled and burned.

Another way was to girdle all the large trees and then remove all the smaller growth by grubbing and burning. The large

trees dying, their shade was not sufficient to materially affect
any growing crop. These might stand for years before they fell.
Millions of feet of the finest timber, and wood beyond all estimate,
were destroyed by these methods. There seemed to be no other
alternative as they had no market value at that time, and so the
chief aim of the settler was to *destroy*, which was chiefly done
by burning. The clearing involved much hard labor. A portion
of the logs were used to build a fence around the tract, and
some of the finest were used for building the house, which
was generally constructed of logs; and the remainder, the main
portion, were cut, piled and burned.

These methods were the common experiences of all pioneers
who attempted settlement in the primeval forests.

Sometimes the settlers would exchange work with each other,
and at other times join in "bees" to hasten the work.

It is said that some secret tact in planning and preparing log-
piles for burning, gave rise to the satirical term of log-rolling.

So hardy and physically powerful were many of these settlers
and so skilled in the use of the axe, it is said that many a man
"felled" his acre of timber in a day, and that some of them would
drink a quart of rum, and chew a "hand" of tobacco while
doing it.

To the present generation, the destruction of those beautiful
and valuable forests, seem little short of vandalism; but the
exigencies of the times required it, as man must subsist on the
products of the soil, and these could not be obtained until after
the removal of the trees.

Sawmills, however, soon began to be erected, and in this way
some of the best timber came to be of great use to the settlers,
enabling them to build better houses and materially adding to
the comforts of life.

Flora.

Not unlike the record of other towns of central New England,
is Cornish, in regard to the wild flowers of the forest and the
field. The history of man cannot antedate their existence in
great profusion and variety. Our Savior evidently alludes to
the wild flowers when he speaks of the lilies of the field whose
beauty and glory outrivaled that of King Solomon.

In all the centuries following until our forefathers opened up their settlements, have the forests and fields been decked with wild flowers.

"God might have made the earth bring forth enough for great
    and small,
The oak-tree and the cedar-tree without a flower at all,

"We might have had enough, enough for every want of ours,
For luxury, medicine and toil and yet have had no flowers.

"The clouds might give abundant rain, the nightly dews might
    fall,
And the herb that keepeth life in man, might yet have drunk
    them all.

"Then wherefore, wherefore were they made, all dyed with crim-
    son light—
All fashioned with supremest grace, upspringing day and night—

"Springing in valleys green and low, and on the mountain high,
And in the silent wilderness, where no man passes by?

"Our outward life requires them not, then wherefore had they
    birth?
To minister delight to man, to beautify the earth."
                                            —*Mary Howitt.*

An observant mind, instructed in the love of the beautiful discovers that Nature has bestowed with unstinted measure the wild flower upon our hills and through our valleys. "Every-where about us they are glowing." In great variety, each in its own season, from early spring until the severe frosts of autumn these lovely messengers are sent for the pleasure and inspiration of man. Their varieties are almost numberless, and even un-named. They would teach us wisdom and incite to praise.

"Were I in churchless solitude remaining,
    Far from all voice of teachers or divines,
My soul would find in flowers of God's ordaining,
    Priests, sermons, shrines."
                                            —*Horace Smith.*

The wild flowers of our primeval forests possessed charms hardly excelled by those of the present day. Ages before man

saw them, they annually sprung up, flourished in their beauty,
performed their mission, and then lay down awaiting the resurrection of the following year.

After the removal of the forests, the flora of the field underwent a change. The soil of the cultivated fields was now open to
the reception of any foreign seeds which might be brought to it,
and in place of the wild flower were the cultivated grasses with
their flowers. So in the open field have the clovers and daisies,
with their sweet flowers, in part supplanted the many varieties
of the wild flower; while in their wild retreats, the latter still
maintain their pristine excellence and beauty.

A corresponding change of the flora has taken place in the
gardens of cultivated flowers. Our grandmothers were content
with a few lilacs, hollyhocks, poppies and moss pinks, and a few
medicinal and fragrant herbs, but the modern housewife now
revels among a great profusion of cultivated flowers of almost
endless variety.

CHAPTER IV.

THE NEW HAMPSHIRE GRANTS.

THE tract of country situated west of the Connecticut River, and now known by the name of Vermont was originally claimed by both New Hampshire and New York. In 1741, Benning Wentworth became governor of New Hampshire, receiving his commission from the king. He continued in office until 1767. In 1749, he received a commission giving him power to issue grants of the unimproved lands, including those lying west of the Connecticut River. He and his successor continued doing so until the year 1764, when the king and council, revoking their former action, decided in favor of New York by declaring the eastern limits of their state to be the western bank of the Connecticut River, and that said line should be the western boundary of New Hampshire.

The grants which Governor Wentworth had made during this period of fifteen years, of lands west of the river, was 138 towns. At this point begins the celebrated conflict of jurisdiction, which lasted twenty-six years, over the "New Hampshire Grants," now known as the State of Vermont.

Cornish, owing to its location in such close proximity to the territory in dispute, became a party in the bitter political strife of those years. Its inhabitants became such active participants in the controversy, that it is deemed proper to here record the leading features of that eventful period. Cornish, too, at that time, had her share of men of mental stature and influence that could not be defeated by any trifling opposition. Their intentions were doubtless in favor of the public good, even if in the heat of the controversy they have been charged with ambitious designs.

The grants issued by Governor Wentworth of lands west of the Connecticut River, the government of New York now declared to be void and called upon the settlers to surrender their charters and purchase new titles to their lands of the government of New York at exorbitant prices. Some of the towns complied with

this unjust requisition, but the larger portion of them refused
to do so.

These lands, or towns, which the settlers refused to repurchase
were granted to others by the governor of New York, and actions
of ejectment brought and judgment obtained against the settlers
in the courts at Albany. The settlers, seeing no hope through
the law, determined on resistance to the arbitrary and cruel
decisions of the court. Having fairly purchased their lands of
one royal governor, they were determined not to submit and
repurchase them of another. The attempts of the New York
executive officers to enforce their governor's decrees were met
with avowed opposition and they were not suffered to proceed
in the execution of offices. The settlers who so resisted were
indicted as rioters, but the court at Albany found it impracticable
to carry their decisions against the settlers into execution. This
opposition soon became organized under the lead of Ethan Allen,
Seth Warner and others, who stirred up the minds of the people,
who met in their several towns and appointed "committees of
safety," and concerted measures for the common welfare. Their
principal object, at first, was resistance to the high claims of
New York. In 1774, the government of New York passed an
act declaring that unless the offenders surrendered themselves
to their authority within seventy days they should, if indicted, be
convicted and suffer death without the benefit of clergy. At the
same time a reward of fifty pounds was offered for the apprehension of eight of the principal leaders who had become distinguished in the opposition. This threatening state of affairs
continued without abatement until the war commenced between
Great Britain and her colonies, which event was close at hand.
This probably prevented the parties from proceeding to open
hostilities.

During these years of strife and conflict of claims, another
sentiment found birth in the minds of the settlers of these grants.
They owed no allegiance to the State of New York, neither
regarded any of her claims, save that of contempt. They began
to regard it as no violation of compact, or of good feeling with
New Hampshire, their mother state, should they become a separate and independent people. The sentiment rapidly developed
in intensity and force that they, the inhabitants of the New
Hampshire Grants ought, for certain reasons which they set forth,

to be an independent state by themselves. Accordingly, conventions were held at Dorset, Vt., in July, 1776, and also September 25th of the same year, and at Westminster, Vt., January 15, 1777. At this last convention it was resolved that the New Hampshire Grants be a new and separate state. This convention adjourned to meet at Windsor, Vt., July 2, 1777, when a constitution was adopted. It adjourned again to meet on December 24 following at Windsor, when the constitution was revised, and the day set for election of officers March 1, 1778, and the Legislature of the new state to be held at Windsor on the second Thursday of the same month.

For months, previous to this the Province of New Hampshire had been taking steps to formally sever its connection with Great Britain and set up an independent state government. A series of provincial congresses had been holden at Exeter, N. H. The fifth and last of these was held December 28, 1775, when a committee was appointed to draft a new constitution for the government of the colony. This committee completed their work and reported the draft of the new constitution January 15, 1776. The convention adopted and voted to be governed by it. These acts virtually changed the *Province* of New Hampshire, politically, into the *State* of New Hampshire. This seems to have been a *transition* period, more so than was realized at the time, for the government of the province and of the towns passed almost imperceptibly from the government of a king to a government of the people, and yet the records of those years hardly showed the change which had actually occurred.

The severing of the relations between Great Britain and the Province of New Hampshire gave rise to this peculiar idea: that as the Crown had given towns charters, they were, by virtue of said charters, independent corporations of themselves, and that after their allegiance to the Crown was dissolved, they had a right to form confederations of their own, or to ally themselves with other federations as they saw fit or deemed best. This idea of independence became developed, especially in that portion of New Hampshire lying west of "Mason's Line" (so called). The Province of New Hampshire was originally granted to John Mason on November 7, 1629. The limits of his grant extended "sixty miles west of the sea." The region between this line and the Connecticut River had subsequently been annexed to the Province of New Hampshire by royal authority. This authority now being annulled, the people believed they were under no obligation to continue under the government of New Hampshire, but had the privilege of choosing for themselves the jurisdiction to which they should belong.

Vermont having just organized as a state, was holding a session of its assembly at Windsor, in March, 1778. This seemed a favorable time for those towns east of Connecticut River in New Hampshire to take some concerted action to be admitted into the State of Vermont. By reason of kinship and similarity of habits they preferred to unite with Vermont, rather than remain with the people of eastern New Hampshire.

A committee from sixteen towns east of the river presented this petition to the Vermont Legislature in their first session at Windsor on the second Thursday of March, 1778. They represented that they were not under the jurisdiction of any state, and asked that they might be admitted to, and constitute a part of, the new State of Vermont.

The towns east of the river represented at Windsor at this time were: Cornish, Lebanon, Hanover (then Dresden), Lyme, Orford, Piermont, Haverhill, Bath, Lyman, Littleton (then Apthorp), Dalton, Enfield, Canaan, Orange (then Cardigan), Landaff, Lisbon (then Granthwaite), Franconia (then Morristown). The town of Cornish was especially active in this movement. February 9, 1778, they chose a committee consisting of William Ripley and Moses Chase to meet a general committee assembled at Lebanon on May, 1778, which committee voted to join the State of Vermont. So the town, at a meeting on June 2, 1778, likewise passed the same vote. Another town meeting was holden on August 11, 1778, to choose a justice of the peace, agreeable to an act of the Vermont Assembly and William Ripley was chosen.

The Legislature of Vermont was undecided at first as to what to do with the petition. Members of the assembly from towns of Vermont on and near the river were inclined to favor the petition and even threatened to withdraw from the state, unless the petition of their friends across the river was granted. This induced the Vermont Assembly to accede to the union, provided the assent of the several towns of Vermont could be obtained, and the matter be acted upon at the next meeting of the assembly. This convened in June, 1778, and it was found that thirty-seven out of forty-nine towns represented were in favor of a union with the New Hampshire towns. An act was passed at this time enabling the sixteen towns to elect and send representatives to their Legislature, and also that other towns east of the river might by a majority vote be admitted to the union. But the controversy did not end here. It was found that many of the inhabitants of those towns were strongly opposed to their union with Vermont. New Hampshire, too, also put in a vigorous protest. Mesheck Weare, the governor of New Hampshire, wrote the governor of Vermont, protesting against the course she had taken in admitting those towns to a union with herself. This evidently unsettled the minds of many of the leaders of public opinion in Vermont, who had been looking forward to a union with the thirteen original states. Therefore the governor and council of Vermont sent a messenger to Congress to see how the new state was viewed by them, and the course they had pursued in receiving the sixteen towns across the river.

The messenger soon learned that Congress was unanimously opposed to the union of the sixteen towns with Vermont, but had no objection to the independence of the new state—the representatives from New York alone dissenting. This information produced a radical change of sentiment throughout Vermont.

At the next session of the Vermont Assembly at Windsor, in October, 1778, the members from the sixteen towns east of the river, having taken their seats, demanded that they be attached to some county or counties in the state. But this request was denied them. This plainly indicated a change from their former opinions, and that they would doubtless seek to undo what they had already done. The members from the sixteen towns in New Hampshire indignantly protested against the action of the assembly and promptly withdrew. They were followed by many members in sympathy with them, from the towns in Vermont west of the Connecticut River. These seceding members from both sides of the river immediately (October, 1778) resolved themselves into a convention, and after conference decided to call a convention of delegates from towns both sides of the river to take measures to form a new state independent of either Vermont or New Hampshire. This convention was called to meet at the "Cornish meeting-house on December 9, 1778." The convention met at the time and place designated and twenty-two towns from both sides of the river were represented by their delegates. They agreed to act together and disregard the limits established by the king in 1764. Anticipating the action of the Vermont Assembly, they now decided to make proposals to New Hampshire in substance as follows: "Since Vermont has taken us and then discourteously rejected us we will now unite with *you* (New Hampshire) and give you our aid and influence in laying claim to all the New Hampshire Grants lying west of the Connecticut River, thus making one entire state subject to the approval of Congress." Until this be consummated they proposed to trust in God and defend themselves.

While these schemes concerning New Hampshire and Vermont were under consideration, the State of New York was pressing her claims of jurisdiction over the territory of Vermont and taking active measures to enforce her authority. Massachusetts, too, at this time was claiming a portion of the southern part of Vermont.

These circumstances, together with the vigorous policy of New Hampshire and New York, induced Vermont to gracefully recede from her former position, so that at her next assembly in February 1779, a majority of the members were in favor of annulling their union with the sixteen towns east of the river. An act was then passed dissolving their union with those towns.

This action of Vermont ought to have ended the whole controversy, but instead it afforded a fresh cause for dissatisfaction especially with the inhabitants of the sixteen towns that had recently been in union with Vermont.

The convention in Cornish of December 9, 1778 (already alluded to) consisted of determined men, not easily deterred from carrying out any policy in which they engaged. Most of the prominent men of Cornish were strong advocates of the action of this convention. They voted in Cornish town meeting the following April (1779) that they were desirous the New Hampshire Assembly "should extend their jurisdiction over all the New Hampshire grants."

The petition of the Cornish Convention of December 9, 1778, was presented to the New Hampshire Legislature April 2, 1779, by Jacob Bailey and Davenport Phelps. A committee was appointed on the petition, who reported to the Legislature June 24,

1779. The House of Representatives took it into consideration and adopted it in substance, thus laying claim to all of Vermont, with this provision: "Unless Congress should choose to allow the grants west of the river to be a separate state by the name of Vermont," in which case they (New Hampshire) would relinquish its claim to said territory. Congress, at this time, was appealed to by delegates from both Vermont and New Hampshire, each state representing its own case. Congress sent a committee to inquire into the merits of the controversy. Upon the report of this committee, Congress recommended that New Hampshire, New York and Massachusetts each pass acts giving Congress power to settle all boundaries and adjust all conflicting claims between these three states, thus ignoring Vermont, the most interested party of them all. Congress had postponed any decided action, trusting the excitement would subside, and that they might adjust the difficulties among themselves. But this could hardly be possible owing to the diversity of schemes and opinions regarding the grants. These may be summarized in part as follows: New York claimed all of Vermont. Massachusetts also claimed a part of the southern portion of it. New Hampshire also desired to extend her claim west to the eastern boundary of New York, while, on the other hand, Vermont desired her independence as a state with her eastern boundary still unsettled; and the grants of New Hampshire between "Mason's Line," and the Connecticut River clamoring either for independence as a state with many of its inhabitants desiring union with Vermont on the west or with New Hampshire on the east. Each of these schemes had its able advocates possessing but little spirit of concession, which fact rendered the solution of the difficulties hard to reach.

A convention met at Walpole, N. H., November 16, 1780. Col. Jonathan Chase had been chosen delegate from Cornish. They appointed a committee of representative men to formulate some plan of action in regard to boundaries and jurisdiction. They called another convention on January 16, 1781, at Charlestown, N. H., and caused one or more delegates to be appointed from each town in the grants to unite if possible on measures needful for the times. The convention met. Hon. Samuel Chase of Cornish was chosen chairman. Delegates from forty-three towns from both sides of the river were present. The convention adopted a set of resolutions claiming a right to join Vermont or submit to

5

the jurisdiction of New Hampshire.   An able and numerous committee was chosen to confer with the assembly of Vermont on the subject of union with that state.

The convention adjourned to meet at Cornish meeting house on February 10, 1781.   They met agreeable to call, chose Hon. Samuel Chase chairman.   Col. Ira Allen from Sunderland, Vt., told the members of the convention that the governor and council and leading men of Vermont were in favor of extending their claim in New Hampshire to "Mason's Line," sixty miles west of the sea.   The effect of this communication was very marked. The convention therefore reported that all the territory of New Hampshire west of "Mason's Line" to the Connecticut River be united to the State of Vermont.   This report was adopted by a great majority of the convention.

The assembly of Vermont, now in session at Windsor, gave a hearing to the action of the Cornish convention, and a mutual agreement followed, subject to a certain provision, namely: that the question of union should be referred to towns exceeding twenty miles from the river, and if two thirds of such towns were in favor it should be considered settled.   On the 22d of February, 1781, the terms of union were confirmed between the Vermont Assembly and the convention at Cornish.   The two bodies adjourned to meet in their respective places on April 15, 1781.

They met according to adjournment, the Vermont Assembly at Windsor and the convention at Cornish.   The committee of the convention reported thirty-four towns east of the river favored the union and none opposed it.   The Vermont Assembly from the west side reported thirty-six towns favoring and seven opposed to the union.   The assembly informed the Cornish Convention that the union was agreed upon by a major part of the towns of the state, and that they would receive members returned, to sit in the assembly.   This was accordingly done, each taking the necessary oaths of office.   The member from Cornish was William Ripley, Esq.   Thus the sixteen towns which united with Vermont a few years before, so soon to be dropped, were again brought in union with Vermont and as many more towns with them.

The necessary political machinery of government was put in motion in the towns now united, agreeably to the constitution and laws of the State of Vermont.   The government of New

Hampshire energetically opposed this action of the towns east of the river, as well as the aggressive movement of Vermont. Through its delegates to the Continental Congress, New Hampshire made a strong appeal for Congress, in some way, to settle the controversy.

New troubles now arose to add to the already serious complication, a large minority of the inhabitants of the towns now united to Vermont still rejected the union with much opposition, consequently the laws and the civil officers frequently came into collision. Disputes and contention prevailed and party spirit run high. Both Vermont and New Hampshire found it very difficult to extend their complete jurisdiction over those towns. Finally Congress appointed a committee to investigate the merits of the case, and hear both sides of the controversy through delegates from both parties.

The State of Vermont at this time was seeking admission to the Federal union of the thirteen states, but on account of the claims of New Hampshire and New York to her territory, her request was denied. Finally Congress moved in the matter and sent an ultimatum to Vermont by a commissioner appointed for the purpose, viz.: that Vermont, before being admitted to the union, must confine her limits on the east to the west bank of the Connecticut River and give up to New York all the towns for a breadth of twenty miles east of the Hudson River, adopting a line from the northwest corner of Massachusetts to the south end of Lake Champlain. Accompanying this recommendation was a threat, in substance as follows: that in case of the refusal of Vermont to comply with those terms, all lands west of the Green Mountain range, running through the state, should be placed under the jurisdiction of New York, and all lands east of this line should be under the jurisdiction of New Hampshire; and that if Vermont neglects or refuses compliance with these terms, it would be deemed a hostile act, and that the forces of the state should be employed against them, unless these orders are carried into execution.

The assembly of Vermont considered these resolves of Congress and firmly declined to accede to them, and resolved that they would not submit the question of their independence to any power.

A period of excitement bordering on anarchy or civil war now reigned among the people. The majorities undertook to control the minorities, and the latter were not willing to submit to them. Both states appointed civil officers throughout all the towns that had united with Vermont. As a consequence, sheriffs, justices and courts came into collision in attempting to perform their duties as officers of their respective states. Many cases of injustice are left on record as occurring during this "reign of terror," orders were issued by the New Hampshire Legislature for three regiments of militia to be mustered, armed and provisioned and gotten in readiness to march into western New Hampshire to establish and maintain its authority to the Connecticut River. The governor and council of Vermont issued counter orders, and instructions were sent to General Payne to call out any or all of the militia east of the Green Mountains to assist the civil officers in the execution of the laws of Vermont, and, in case that New Hampshire makes an attack by force, to repel by force. Three regiments of Vermont troops were notified to be in readiness to act under the authority of Vermont. One of these regiments was Col. Jonathan Chase's Regiment containing the Cornish men. But they were never called to this service.

Events at this time seemed approaching a fearful and bloody crisis. Men of cooler and more considerate minds now came to the front, anxious to avoid, if possible, the bloodshed that seemed inevitable. Governor Chittenden of Vermont wrote to General Washington, defending the right of his state to independence, but disdaining the right of New York or New Hampshire over any of her territory, and humbly asked his interposition in behalf of Vermont.

General Washington replied (January 1, 1782) so wisely and pacifically as to put a better and brighter aspect upon the affairs in dispute. General Washington plainly told Governor Chittenden that Congress would admit Vermont into the Federal union upon the condition that she must relinquish all claims to lands east of the Connecticut River and that said river be her eastern boundary, and that she must also relinquish to New York all lands lying twenty or more miles east from the Hudson River, and their eastern limit be the western boundary of Vermont. Upon the acceptance of these terms, Congress would doubtless receive Vermont into the union as an independent state, and thus guarantee her limits.

The Vermont Assembly met at Bennington February 11, 1782. The letter of General Washington was laid before it. Its effect was immediate, and favorable to a settlement of the difficulty upon the terms it suggested, and a disposition to settle the matters in dispute pervaded the entire assembly. A resolution was soon passed, in substance, that Congress had determined and guaranteed the boundaries of New York and New Hampshire, and by so doing had determined the boundaries of Vermont. Accordingly on February 23, 1782, an act was passed establishing the west bank of the Connecticut River as the east line of the state, and that the State of Vermont relinquish all claim or jurisdiction over all territory east of said line. This act dissolved the union and excluded the members of the assembly from all towns east of the river. It is said that they withdrew from the assembly with some spirit of bitterness and chagrin. The inhabitants of these towns also shared in the disappointment, and it took several years for the animosity engendered by this long and bitter controversy to subside.

Probably no town east of the Connecticut River carried greater influence, or was more deeply interested in the strife than was Cornish. For these, and other reasons, the "New Hampshire Grants" have received the generous mention here bestowed.

It was a matter of regret that, following the political transactions just recorded, a small yet influential minority of Cornish, under the leadership of Judge Samuel Chase and others, would not yield to the will of the majority. Possessing a strong aversion to the government of New Hampshire, he, with others, seemed to possess the forlorn hope of independence, or of a union with any other government than New Hampshire. They called town meetings and elected their full boards of officers and undertook the management of town affairs. These doings, however, were met by the firm yet peaceful spirit of protest from the majority and after a few years this spirit of opposition slowly and reluctantly died away, and gave place to a better order of things.

CHAPTER V.

REVOLUTIONARY WAR.

"The land is holy where they fought,
   And holy where they fell,
For by their blood that land was bought,
   The land they loved so well.
Then glory to that valiant band,
   The honored saviors of the land."
                     —*MacLellan.*

NEW HAMPSHIRE was first organized into a separate province in January, 1680. The first General Assembly met on the 16th of March following, and at once enacted laws organizing the militia of the state, for the exigencies of the times seemed to demand the safeguard of an effective militia.

The conflicting claims of France and England were liable at any time to devastate New England. So the colonists were not only interested witnesses of the strife, but they vigorously participated to sustain the claims of England whose colonies they were.

The Indians, too, were a constant menace to the settlers, being liable to make murderous raids upon them at any time. They joined hands with the French, and the French and Indian War was precipitated, 1754–63. During this latter year, after the war had closed and all the clouds of war had disappeared, the militia of the state was found to consist of but nine regiments of infantry and one of cavalry. The colonists now enjoyed a few years of immunity from military strife and had the privilege of returning to their homes, cultivating their farms and enjoying the comforts of domestic life. During this period, however, the colonists continued to increase and strengthen their military forces. In 1773 there were twelve regiments in the state. Little did they dream that their mother country, the home of their birth, and of the graves of their ancestors, would be the power against which their military force would be employed!

At first the most amicable feelings existed between the colonies and their mother country. These friendly relations, however, were soon disturbed by various causes: Tyrannical governors were sometimes appointed over the colonies, from whose decision there was no appeal. Criminals from England were transported to America. "Navigation Laws" compelled the colonists to do their trading with England. The arbitrary collection of duties by custom house officers appointed by Parliament—these were some of the first causes that finally led to the separation of the colonies from England.

In 1764, the famous, or infamous, Stamp Act was introduced into Parliament. This was regarded by the colonists as an assumption of power on the part of England to oppress her subjects in America. Petitions, remonstrances, and protests from the people were presented to the king and his Parliament to prevent if possible the proposed enactment. But, in the words of Patrick Henry a little later: "Our petitions have been slighted; our remonstrances have produced additional violence and insult; our supplications have been disregarded, and we have been spurned with contempt from the foot of the throne."

The Stamp Act passed both houses of Parliament on March 22, 1765, by a majority of five to one in the House of Commons, while every member of the House of Lords voted in favor of it, and the royal assent was likewise given.

This action seemed to destroy all love and confidence heretofore existing between England and her American colonies and a storm of opposition arose on every hand. This was widespread and apparently universal. In many places it assumed very demonstrative forms, so much as to interfere with the royal authority, which, until now, had existed. British troops were therefore sent to Boston and other points to assist the royalists in maintaining the authority due the officers of the Crown. This, instead of quieting the opposition, inflamed the colonists all the more. Parliament seeing they had made a mistake in the passage of the Stamp Act, formally repealed it March 18, 1766, but while doing this they would not relinquish their right to tax the colonies. Repealing of the act, therefore, had but little effect in quelling the opposition which had been so thoroughly aroused.

While the popular clamor of the people was apparently unani-

mous in opposition to the policy pursued by England, there were
those who still remained loyal to the Crown and to their kindred
and ancestors in England, and regretted to see the breach widen-
ing that separated them from their kindred. They were not in
sympathy with the prevailing spirit of the times, but rather with
their mother country. These were by some called "Royalists,"
and by others "Tories." As a matter of course as well as a matter of history, these tories were an offense to all those aggrieved
at the course pursued by Parliament, and were considered enemies to the common cause. This element, though not large, had
its representatives all over the country, and even in many of the
towns of New Hampshire; but neither record nor tradition shows
that any of the citizens of Cornish entertained those sentiments.
The spirit and attitude that England manifested towards the
colonists was anything but conciliatory but, rather, was well
calculated to beget increased bitterness, and the people in all
parts of the country were becoming seriously in earnest. Civil
officers found it very difficult to maintain their authority, and
many of them threw up their commissions under the king.

The courts of justice were suspended, and the laws relating to
civil affairs were but partially executed.

By the militia law then in force, the execution of which was
in the hands of the "Committee of Safety" and the Provincial
Congress, every male citizen from sixteen to sixty years of age
was required to provide himself with a musket and bayonet,
knapsack, cartridge box, one pound of powder, twenty bullets
and twelve flints. Every town was required to keep constantly
on hand one barrel of powder, two hundred pounds of lead and
three hundred flints for every sixty men enrolled. Even the old
men, and those unable to do full military duty, were required to
keep on hand the same supply of arms and ammunition as the
active militia-men.

During the few years of peace prior to 1765, no thought of
another war had entered the minds of the colonists until now the
people were rudely awakened to the fact that there was less
than half the required amount of military stores in the country,
and also that the veterans of the Indian wars were fast passing
away, and their young men were learning nothing of military arts.

Attention was called to these facts by the committees of
safety and other prominent men. Accordingly, existing military

organizations were strengthened, and voluntary associations were formed for the purpose of learning military tactics. Drills and trainings became frequent. Companies of minute men were organized and instructed to move at a minute's warning, and the manufacture of arms, equipments and ammunition was stimulated. Subsequent events proved the wisdom of these precautionary measures. "Committees of Safety" were appointed in all the towns. They had the oversight and management of all affairs relating to movements of any militia; and exercised a general watch care against any threatened danger. The committee of each town were to apprize the committee of their neighboring towns, should necessity require, and thus they would be enabled to act together when any crisis should come. Expresses were kept in readiness to speed the intelligence to the country around and, in some cases, preparations were made to flash the news by signal lights.

The culmination of such a series of events seemed imminent at any time, but the "dogs of war" were not let loose until 1775. On June 29, 1767, Parliament imposed a tax on lead, glass, paper, tea and several other commodities. This added fresh fuel to the flames. Newspapers became more outspoken than before in their denunciation of Parliament and the king.

It soon became evident that the Crown was fast losing all patience with her colonies, and that it was about time she should show some intimations of chastisement. With a view of frightening the colonies into submission, General Gage, commander of the British forces in America, was ordered to take a regiment of soldiers from Halifax to Boston and quarter them on the citizens. This order being known, its effect was to intensify the bitterness already existing. It was sternly denounced by Samuel Adams and many others, and the press reëchoed the sentiment. Nevertheless, on September 28, 1767, the troops came fully equipped, with colors flying and paraded on Boston Common.

Collisions between the troops and citizens were liable to occur at any time, and on March 5, 1770, occurred the so-called "Boston Massacre," in which five citizens were killed and six wounded, by British soldiers. This event caused such an uprising of the people that the troops were sent away.

During nearly three years following this event, historians record but few striking events that were calculated to precipitate the

Revolution. It seems a little marvelous that at such high tide in
the passions of men as was exhibited in 1770, that so few historic
developments occurred during this time. There can be no doubt,
however, that affairs were ripening for the great events to follow.
Were they not years of gestation? *Liberty* had been *conceived*,
but was not yet *born*. Perhaps this comparative quietude was
needed for the full growth and development of the *new principle*
of *Liberty* which has since actually revolutionized the world.

On December 16, 1773, occurred the famous "Boston Tea
Party" when 340 chests of tea were broken open and their contents thrown overboard into Boston Harbor.

The news of this transaction was received in England on January 27, 1774. This threw her into a flame of wrath. Thereupon
the charter of Massachusetts was declared annulled, and the
people, *rebels*. She also passed the famous "Boston Port Bill,"
closing the port to all trade, said act to take effect June 18, 1774.

On September 5, 1774, the Continental Congress met at Philadelphia. All the states were represented except Georgia. It was
at this session that Patrick Henry in a burst of oratory uttered
those immortal words that fired every heart by their patriotic eloquence, saying in part that there was "no peace, but the war has
actually begun."

The British troops stationed in or near Boston were becoming
more bold and began acting on the offensive. This being reported,
continued to further arouse the people to a determination to
resist the further assumption of power by England. This spirit
extended to towns far remote, and men from those towns hurriedly left their homes for the threatened theater of strife. It
was now evident the "clash of resounding arms" was near at
hand.

The battle of Lexington soon followed, April 19, 1775. News
of the battle spread like wild-fire throughout all the colonies.
"It was the shot that was heard around the world."

After this, there was no need of conscripting or even urging
men to the opening conflict. No bounties were needed to induce
men to enlist, but they voluntarily rushed forward to the "ranks
of war" induced only by a love for *liberty and home*.

Nearly every town in the Province of New Hampshire sent
volunteers, so that by the 23d of April, 1775, 2,000 New Hampshire
men were on the ground at Cambridge and Medford, Mass.,

while the whole force of men from Massachusetts, Connecticut and Rhode Island numbered nearly 20,000. They were entirely ununiformed, and many of them without equipments.

Boston, with the British army, was now entirely enclosed on the land side. The patriots began throwing up entrenchments all along the lines, and the city was in a state of siege.

At this time there was no staff organization from New Hampshire on the ground, and no rations, ammunitions or supplies of any kind provided by the authority of New Hampshire. The New Hampshire men were advised to enlist for the time being in the service of Massachusetts in order to draw rations and quarters. An arrangement to that effect was made by a committee of the New Hampshire Provincial Congress with one from that of Massachusetts—the men to be accounted on New Hampshire's quota, and supplies were issued to some New Hampshire troops by the commissaries of Massachusetts. Even the commissions of colonel to Stark and Reed were issued April 26, by the Massachusetts Committee of Safety. These were accepted, to continue until New Hampshire acted. (McClintock's "History of New Hampshire," p. 332.)

Most of the men who had gathered in such haste were farmers, impatient to strike a blow for their country, or to be at home to plant their crops and attend to their affairs. Seeing no prospect of immediate action at the front, large numbers of them returned to their homes, many with the consent of their officers, others without asking consent. There was no power to hold them because they had not yet signed enlisting papers in any regular service; and in some cases they were advised by their commanders to go home and prepare for a war of indefinite length. (Keene History, p. 177.) These facts account for the limited number of names of soldiers on the Revolutionary rolls of the year 1775. That a considerable number of men from upper Cheshire County (now Sullivan County) went to Massachusetts at that time to render military assistance has been accounted a matter of fact, but only a portion of their names appear on the rolls. Perhaps, however, family tradition in some instances has preserved the names of some of them.

On the pay-roll of Capt. John Marcy's Company, Col. James Reed's Regiment, August 1, 1775, is the name of William Richardson and other Cornish men.

Joseph Taylor (then of Cornish) is found enrolled in Capt. Henry Elkins' Company, Col. Enoch Poor's Regiment, on July 7, 1775, August 1, 1775, and also on October 10, 1775.

On the 17th of June, 1775, the battle of Bunker Hill was fought. The whole number of Americans in that memorable battle did not exceed 1,700 men. Of these 1,230 men were from New Hampshire, and were largely from Cheshire County. The troops were under the command of Colonels Stark and Reed, both New Hampshire men.

Of this battle it is said that "it was the bloodiest fight that could be called a battle, in proportion to the numbers engaged, that has ever been fought on American soil." The loss to the British army was not less than eleven hundred, killed and wounded, or more than one third of the English army engaged. The loss on the American side was about four hundred and fifty men, or about thirty per cent. of those engaged.

The roar of cannon at the battle of Bunker Hill is said to have been heard by inhabitants of several towns along the Connecticut River. Citizens of Cornish declared they heard it, and, whether true or not, it has generally been so believed.

Among the events of 1775, it is of interest to record that John Wentworth, the last governor appointed by the Crown for New Hampshire, after several ineffectual attempts to convene the Legislature during the summer of 1775, finally in September, abdicated and went away in a British frigate for Nova Scotia. To the last he urged upon the Legislature, but without avail, a restoration of harmony with Great Britain. This ended the last vestige of British rule in New Hampshire. The early hesitating measures of resistance and defence on the part of the colonies, now assume the gravity and dignity of war. The British government no longer oppressed a dependent, but engaged in grim war with a nation.

On May 17, 1775, the Provincial Congress or Assembly met at Exeter, New Hampshire. Samuel Chase, Esq., attended it from Cornish. It was there recommended that "the selectmen of the several towns, parishes, and other places in the Colony, take an exact number of the Inhabitants of their respective Districts in classes, with the number of fire-arms and pounds of powder on hand, and the number of fire-arms needed, and that an account of the whole made under oath, be returned to the Committee of Safety for this Colony."

Agreeable to the foregoing recommendation the census of Cornish for the year 1775 was taken, which was as follows:

Males under 16 years of age	83
Males from 16 to 50 not in the army	77
Males above 50 years of age	9
Females (all)	136
Negroes & slaves for life	0
Persons in army	4
All	309

Fire-arms in Cornish fit for use	53
Number of fire-arms wanted to complete one for every person capable of using them	33

No powder in town but private property and that is 20 lbs.

Cornish Oct. ye 30th 1775.

Personally appeared Samuel Chase Esqr. and made solemn oath that he had acted faithfully and impartially in taking the above numbers according to the best of his discretion before me.

DANIEL PUTNAM—Town Clerk.

The records of Cornish, before 1776, are silent about everything that relates to the Revolutionary War. While a record of a deep interest in the war would afford gratification to later generations, yet the fact of such omission reflects nothing upon the loyalty of the entire town. It seems that, at this time, the good people of Cornish were all engaged in the erection of a house of worship that enlisted their interests, means, and energies to their utmost. To them, religious rights and privileges were second to no other, as manifestly shown in this.

After the British rule in New Hampshire was ended, the towns became aware of the fact that there was no general government. No courts were held in Cheshire County from 1774 to 1778, but each town instituted governments of its own and enacted laws for the management of its own affairs. Warrants for town-meetings were headed, simply "Cheshire

S. S." and were called by the town clerk upon the order of the selectmen. A similar state of affairs existed among all the colonies. It is not to be wondered if strange local laws were sometimes enacted.

The Provincial Congress on the 5th of January, 1776, adopted a temporary constitution. By the terms of this instrument a distinct and coördinate branch of the Legislature was created which was then called the Council. In later times this body has been styled the senate. During the Revolutionary War, and the period of this temporary constitution, there was no governor. The council and the house performed these functions during sessions, and the committee of safety during the recesses of the Legislature. For the year 1776, the councillors were elected by the house of representatives, and in subsequent years by the people.

Early in March, 1776, General Washington seized Dorchester Heights and thus compelled the British to evacuate Boston, and on the 18th he started for New York with five of his best regiments, including General Stark with all his New Hampshire men as one, and on the 27th General Sullivan followed with the remainder of his brigade, but the latter was soon afterwards sent with his New Hampshire regiments from New York to reinforce the army of the North which was now slowly retreating from Quebec under General Gates. The smallpox had broken out in the Northern army and General Thomas had fallen a victim to it, so General Sullivan succeeded to the command. The Northern army slowly retreating before a powerful British army under Burgoyne, from the north, naturally caused great alarm throughout New England, particularly as bands of Indians at this time were hovering on our frontiers, threatening to repeat their former atrocities.

Because of this, the government raised two additional regiments to reinforce the Northern army. These were commanded by Colonels Wyman and Wingate.

In the enrollment of Colonel Wyman's Regiment, August 20, 1776, are found the names of Peter Labere, J. Nathaniel Holden and Joel Rice, all of Cornish. (P. 324, Vol. 1, Rev. Rolls.)

On the 12th of April, 1776, the committee of safety for the state, sent to the selectmen of each town the "Association Test," which in form was as follows:

"To the Selectmen of———

"Colony of New Hampshire

"In Committee of Safety,

"April 12, 1776.

"In order to carry the underwritten *Resolve* of the Hon'ble Congress into Execution, You are requested to desire all males above Twenty-One Years of Age, (Lunatics, Idiots, and Negroes excepted) to sign to the *Declaration* on this paper; and when so done to make return hereof, together with the Name or Names of all who shall refuse to sign the same, to the *General Assembly*, or Committee of Safety of this Colony.

"M. WEARE, Chairman.

"In *Congress* March 14th 1776.

"Resolved, that it be recommended to the several assemblies, Conventions and Councils or Committees of Safety of the United Colonies, immediately to cause all persons to be disarmed, within their respective Colonies, who are notoriously disaffected to the cause of *America*, or who have not associated, and refuse to associate to defend by *Arms* the United Colonies against the Hostile attempts of the British Fleets and Armies.

"Extract from the Minutes.

"CHARLES THOMPSON, Secretary.

"In consequence of the above Resolution of the Hon. Continental *Congress*, and to show our Determination in joining our American Brethren in defending the Lives, Liberties, and Properties of the Inhabitants of the *United Colonies:*

"We the Subscribers, do hereby solemnly engage, and promise, that we will, to the utmost of our Power, at the Risque of our Lives and Fortunes, with *Arms* oppose the Hostile Proceeding of the British Fleets and Armies against the United American Colonies."

Copies of the above Association Test were sent to all of the colonies including the towns of New Hampshire. Returns from nearly a hundred of these towns have been preserved. No return from Cornish has been preserved, and if the paper was circulated and signed by the men of Cornish, it has been lost. The province of New Hampshire then numbered about 80,000 inhabit-

ants. Only 773 persons in the state refused to sign. In most
cases these were the wealthy and influential men.

The application of the foregoing test revealed the true attitude
of the American people, and furnished assurance of success in
the bold venture of July 4th when their independence was declared.
The new nation now felt her increased responsibility and she resolved to bend her every energy that the venture should prove
a triumphant success. The Declaration of Independence was
published by beat of drums in all the shire towns of New Hampshire. (Belknap's "History of New Hampshire," Vol. 2, p. 405.)
"It was received by the army, the legislatures and the people with
great rejoicing. That declaration brought great encouragement
to the patriots, gave them a more definite object for carrying on
the war, and united them in a common cause. That object had
now come to be the establishment of a nation of their own under
democratic rule; the dreaded alternative was the fate of conquered
rebels. There could be no more powerful incentive to fight; no
sharper spur to endure hardship and privation."

Because of the continued threatening attitude of the enemy
and the exposed condition of Ticonderoga, the assembly this year
voted that 2,000 additional men be raised to recruit the forces
already in service. At this time there were seventeen territorial
regiments in the state. Col. Jonathan Chase's regiment was the
seventeenth in number. The quota of men to be raised from his
regiment was sixty-one. The full enrollment of his regiment was
492 men, from which to enlist the quota. These enlisted September 24, 1776, and were mustered in October 14, following.
Colonel Chase marched with two companies, and Colonels Ashley,
Bellows and Hale with several companies each, all for Ticonderoga and vicinity. The record of their movements has not been
found, but they received hearty commendation for prompt
service, etc., from General Gates and were dismissed by him with
honor November 9, 1776.

Enrolled among the two companies under command of Colonel
Chase were the following Cornish men: Capt. Josiah Russell's
Company—Lieut. Daniel Chase, Ensign Josiah Stone, William
Paine, Benj. Comings, Zebadiah Fitch, James Cate, Samuel
Fitch, David Huggins, Thomas Hall, Jr., John Chase, Abijah Hall,
Robert Dunlap, James Hall, Joseph Vinsen, Elias Gates, Stephen
Cady, John Weld, James Wellman, Jr., beside several others

Gen. Jonathan Chase house as it appeared in 1870

who may have been of Cornish but whose identification is uncertain. In Capt. John House's Company, Colonel Baldwin's Regiment, in September, 1776, were enrolled the names of Briant Brown, Curtis Cady and Ebenezer Brewer, all Cornish men. (Rev. Rolls, pp. 422-23, Vol. 1.)

On December 12, 1776, Capt. Joshua Haywood's Company was paid off by Col. Jonathan Chase. John Weld, Eleazer Jackson and possibly other Cornish men were of the company. (Rev. Rolls, pp. 444-45, Vol. 1.)

As the year 1776 was drawing near its close the outlook of public affairs was so gloomy that Congress recommended all the states to appoint "a Day of Solemn Fasting and Humiliation."

The New Hampshire Legislature adopted the recommendation, and, on the 13th of December it dissolved with the invocation: "God save the United States of America."

The three New Hampshire regiments, Stark's, Poor's and Scammell's, had left the Northern army on the 16th of November and had marched down the Hudson River and joined General Washington on the 20th of December in time to take a leading part in the battles of Trenton and Princeton. Though worn by fatigue, and almost destitute of clothing at that inclement season, these New Hampshire regiments were counted by General Washington among the best troops of his army, and their arrival gave him great satisfaction. At Trenton, the main column of attack was led by Colonel Stark with his New Hampshire men, and the battle was saved; the same troops, with Gilman's added, saved the day at Princeton. The battle of Trenton was fought December 26, 1776, and that of Princeton on the 3d of January following.

These victories gave the colonists fresh courage, yet the winter of 1776-77 was, to the inhabitants of New England, a season of gloom and fearful apprehension, the regiments of New Hampshire troops having been withdrawn. This left their frontier exposed to the mercy of the British army, and the incursions of Indians. But a kind Providence seemed to intervene and the rest of the winter of 1776-77 passed without serious events happening to them.

The following Cornish incident found among the "Chase Papers" illustrates the spirit that animated our fathers during those days: "The house of Col. Jonathan Chase was for a time used as a station for collecting supplies for the government, and there was a guard left or stationed there in charge—a sergeant and a few men, as sentinels. These were detailed from a company of minute men that were enrolled in the town. On one occasion the guard was on duty when he saw something passing along near the river, which he hailed, but not being answered, he fired his gun at the object. This brought out the sergeant and guard. They decided to give the signal to call the minute men together: this signal was the firing of three minute guns. Before morning, without any other notice, fifty men rallied to headquarters, armed and equipped for service."

Early in the spring of 1777, the colonists felt the necessity of vigorous action. Pressing appeals from Generals Schuyler and Wayne came to the Committee of Safety of New Hampshire. On the 3d of May the state committee sent orders to the three colonels of militia in Cheshire County, "entreating you by all that is sacred, to raise as many of your Militia as possible and march them to Ticonderoga." In response to this call, Colonel Ashley raised, and marched from Keene with 109 men, Colonel Bellows from Walpole with 112 men, and Colonel Chase of Cornish with 159 men. These men were all enlisted in four days. This ready response revealed the active and determined spirit of the times. In Revolutionary Rolls, volume 2, pages 14–19 is the full list of Colonel Chase's men. Nearly thirty of these men were soldiers of Cornish. The other men from outside, came to town and together they marched on May 7, 1777, for Ticonderoga, ninety miles distant. On reaching their destination they found the alarm had subsided, and the men were discharged on June 18, after serving one month and twelve days. It is not clear why the alarm should subside so easily, while General Burgoyne with his forces were still hovering so dangerously near; yet such is the record.

The three New Hampshire regiments, Colonels (now Brigadier-Generals) Stark, Poor and Scammell who had rendered such valuable service at Trenton and Princeton were called north, and joined the Northern army in early summer.

General Burgoyne now commanded the British army of the North, 10,000 strong. Seven thousand of these were choice troops sent from England, with the finest train of brass artillery (forty-two pieces) that had ever been seen in America; besides thousands of Indians employed as allies "to use as instrument of terror" (Bancroft's History, Vol. 5, pp. 579, 587). Exaggerated reports of the strength of his army and the rapidity of his advance reached the states again causing great alarm throughout New England. Again the militia was ordered to the front, and turned out in greater numbers than before. Colonel Ashley having about 400 men and Colonel Chase 186. These latter left Cornish June, 27, 1777. Revolutionary Rolls, volume 2, pages 38–45, contains the full list of Colonel Chase's men. Thirty-three of these are recognized as Cornish men. While on their march they met troops returning home who informed them that Ticonderoga had capitulated with 3,000 men, on July 1st, to General Burgoyne.

The men with their officers returned home disheartened and were soon discharged, after having rendered a brief service of from four to fifteen days. Hardly had these men returned, when another alarm rang through the state. The evacuation of Ticonderoga and advance of General Burgoyne were threatening the subjugation of New England.

This was perhaps the darkest hour in the history of the war for the New England States. The situation was so alarming that the Committee of Safety of New Hampshire issued a call July 14, 1777, for the Legislature to convene on the 17th. A most depressing state of affairs existed. The treasury was empty. The state had no money, and no means of obtaining any. Heretofore there had been such a draught on the state for men and money, that it seemed nothing more could be done. And yet Burgoyne must be stopped, or his army would overrun their territory, and their homes and property be sacrificed. When the gloom of the situation had been portrayed, Col. John Langdon, speaker of the House, arose and made one of the most telling speeches of the Revolution, when he said: "I have one thousand dollars in hard money. I will pledge my plate for three thousand more; I have seventy hogsheads of Tobago rum which I will sell for the most it will bring. They are at the service of the state. If we succeed in defending our firesides and our homes, I may be remunerated; if we do not, then the property will be of no value to me. Our friend Stark, who so nobly defended the honor of our state at Bunker Hill, may safely be entrusted with the honor of the enterprise, and we will check the advance of Burgoyne." * * *

The effect of such patriotism and eloquence was magical. The offer was accepted with enthusiasm. The next day the Legislature promptly voted ways and means for the immediate increase of the army. The patriotism of Colonel Langdon was contagious. No draft was necessary. Swift couriers carried the news to the remotest towns in the state and 1,500 men sprung to arms.

The troops rendezvoused at Charlestown and General Stark took command.

About the first of August General Burgoyne detached Colonel Baum with about 700 men, veteran soldiers, two pieces of artillery and 150 Indians for a raid through the New Hampshire Grants. He was also joined by several hundred tories. He had received orders to collect cattle and horses, and to destroy all such stores as they were obliged to leave behind. Information was received by General Stark that the enemy designed to capture the stores at Bennington, Vt. Pressing forward with his troops he arrived at Bennington on the 9th of August. Baum's advance reached Cambridge, twelve miles northwest of Bennington on the 13th. On the 14th the two armies came in sight of each other, and General Stark invited attack, but Baum was cautious and entrenched. It being near night, Stark drew back about a mile, where his men lay on their arms that night. On the 15th it rained hard all day, and both parties remained in position. General Stark now had about 1,600 men.

On the morning of the 16th of August, General Stark, having decided to attack the enemy, sent Colonel Nichols with 300 men to his left, and Colonel Hendricks with 300 men to the right. Taking command of the main body in front of the enemy's breastworks, when all was ready, he, pointing to the enemy, made the short but immortal speech: "There are the Redcoats, they are ours, or Mollie Stark sleeps a widow tonight." Prompted by the same determined spirit his men entered the action, and the result was a complete defeat of Colonel Baum, who was mortally wounded, and a decisive victory on the part of General Stark. The result of this victory was far-reaching. It wonderfully cheered the spirits of the colonists, and was largely instrumental in the surrender of General Burgoyne at Saratoga two months later.

On the 23d of September, having received another requisition from General Gates, Colonel Chase again mustered the men of his regiment, then numbering 142 men, and marched from Cornish to Saratoga, September 26, 1777, a distance of 110 miles, to reinforce the army of General Gates, which was purposing to check the movements of General Burgoyne, and, if possible, to effect his overthrow. Two or three additional companies of men were subsequently placed under the command of Colonel Chase, so that when ready for action, his regiment numbered 235 men. After he had left Cornish, Colonel Morey with a company of thirty men marched to Cornish, reaching it October 1. He intended to turn over his men to Colonel Chase but, finding him gone, he sent the men forward under Captain Chandler, with orders to place themselves under Colonel Chase, and then he returned to enlist more men.

The first battle of Saratoga had been fought September 19. It being a drawn battle, the forces lay confronting each other for eighteen days following. Meanwhile Colonel Chase, with his men had joined the army of General Gates. On the 7th of October another battle was fought and a decisive victory over Burgoyne was the result. The regiment of Colonel Chase was engaged in this battle, though not seriously, and ten days later they witnessed the surrender of Burgoyne. After the battle of October 7 the situation of General Burgoyne become desperate. He was almost surrounded by the American troops; his supply of provisions were becoming exhausted; his men deserting; reinforcements for the patriots were constantly arriving. Burgoyne called a council of war, and it was unanimously agreed "to enter into a Convention with General Gates."

On the forenoon of October 17, 1777, General Burgoyne surrendered his entire army to General Gates. Nearly 6,000 officers and men thus became prisoners of war, among whom were six members of the British Parliament. The trophies consisted of a splendid train of brass artillery consisting of forty-two pieces, 5,000 stand of arms and an enormous quantity of ammunition and stores. The terms of capitulation were very favorable for the British: The troops to be conducted to Boston, and from thence returned to England; and the officers to retain all their horses, carriages and equipments.

The surrender of General Burgoyne was the most complete triumph thus far gained by the patriots in their struggle for independence. The joy it brought to all their homes was unbounded. It inspired the army with confidence, so that it became invincible and final victory was assured. The cause of the tantalizing alarm that had so long harrassed the patriots of New England was now removed, and the seat of war was transferred further south. Many of the troops who had been called into service for this special emergency were discharged. The men who formed the regiment of Colonel Chase in this campaign were chiefly farmers, who had hurriedly left their farms, leaving their crops unharvested. These were now anxious to return home and secure their crops, and make preparation for the coming winter.

On the day following the surrender, the following certificate of service and order was issued:

"H. Q. SARATOGA. October. 18, 1777.

These may certify that Col⁰ Chase with a regiment of volunteers have faithfully served until this date in the Northern Army and are now Discharged with Honor.

"By order of General Gates.

"JACOB BAGLEY, Brigʳ Gen¹"

On pages 373–376, volume 2, Revolutionary Rolls, is a list of 140 men of Colonel Chase's regiment who were discharged by the above order. The following named Cornish men were discharged the date named:

Lieut. Abel Spaulding	Caleb Plaistridge
Sergt. Samuel Chase	James Cate
" Joseph Spaulding	John Chase
Corp. Stephen Child	Solmⁿ Chase
Jos. Vinsen	John Morse
Jabez Spicer	Simeon Chase
Solmⁿ Wellman	Dyer Spaulding
Jonthⁿ Huggins	Ebʳ Brewer
James Wellman	Daniel Waldron

and possibly others who cannot be identified.

In the campaign to repel the invasion of Burgoyne, the little State of New Hampshire, then almost a wilderness, furnished more than 6,000 men, and contributed very largely to the grand results attained. (Keene History, p. 230.)

It has never been the purpose of the writer to attempt to prepare a history of the Revolutionary War only so far as to record some of the principal events in which the soldiery of Cornish played an important part.

As long as the principal theater of the war was in, and on the borders of New England, the New Hampshire troops were always available and cheerfully responded to every urgent call. While the greater number of these, since the surrender of Burgoyne, had returned to their homes, it is pleasant to record that there were quite a number of Cornish men left remaining in the service in other New Hampshire regiments which had now gone further south. Some of these men followed the fortunes of war to its close in 1783. During the terrible winter of 1777–78, at Valley Forge; at the battle of Monmouth, June 28, 1778; at the unfortunate battle of Camden, S. C., August 16, 1780; and in several other memorable engagements of the war, including the surrender of Cornwallis, October 17, 1786, the New Hampshire regiments were in active service.

In several companies of each of these regiments are found the names of Cornish men. It would indeed be very gratifying to know the exact number and names of men that Cornish furnished to aid in establishing our national independence; but from lack of certainty of identification, it is impossible to determine accurately in every case, as their names appear on the rolls.

The names of soldiers on these whose identity is comparatively certain are given below. Some of their names appear twice, or more, but occurring at different dates; presumably, having served out their former term of enlistment, they enlisted again, sometimes in the same regiment and sometimes in another.

In Capt. Wm. Scott's company, Col. John Stark's regiment, are the names of Jonathan Currier, William Richardson, Moses Chase, Loring Thompson, John Bartlett, Peter Spicer, Moses Brown and Nathaniel Bartlett. (Rev. Rolls, p. 614, Vol. 1, May 6, 1777.)

In Captain Wait's company, Col. John Stark's regiment, is the name of Nathaniel Curtis. (Rev. Rolls, p. 596, Vol. 1, May, 1778.)

On the muster roll of Capt. John House's company, Col. Baldwin's regiment, is the name of Daniel Putnam, aged thirty-seven. (No date.) (Rev. Rolls, p. 608, Vol. 1.)

In Capt. Joshua Hendee's company, Col. David Hobart's regiment, is the name of Lieut. Daniel Chase of Cornish. (No date.) (Rev. Rolls, p. 157, Vol. 2.)

Daniel Putnam's name is also found in Capt. Moody Dustin's

company, 1st regiment, February 13, 1781.   (Rev. Rolls, p. 223, Vol. 3.)

In the "Record of Town Returns" are the names of David Haskell, Joseph Spaulding and Daniel Putnam, soldiers, under date of May 10, 1782.   (Rev. Rolls, p. 502, Vol. 3.)

A pay-roll of men of Colonel Chase's regiment, raised October 28, 1776, and discharged November 18, 1776, contains the following names: Col. J. Chase, Solomon Chase, Reuben Jirould, Samuel Chase, Nathaniel Goodspeed, Elias Cady, William Richardson, Isaac Wellman, Simeon Chase and Moses Hall. (Rev. Rolls, pp. 108–9, Vol. 4.)

In Capt. Davenport Phelps' company, Colonel Bedell's regiment, whose services ended March 31, 1778, were the following names: Luther Hilliard, Briant Brown and Judah Benjamin, all credited to Cornish.   (Rev. Rolls, p. 120, Vol. 4.)

"We the Subscribers Being a Draft from the Militia of the Regt. of Col. Jono. Chase, Do Acnolege we have Rec'd of him, four pounds & ten shillings each, as one months Advanced pay agreeable to a Vote of the Council & Assembly of the State of New Hampshire:—Willm. Ripley, Samuel Hilliard, Samuel Fitch, Lieut. Daniel Chase, Nicholas Cady, Ebenezer Brewer, Benjn. Comings, John Whitten."   (Rev. Rolls, p. 143, Vol. 4.)

In Col. Joseph Cilley's regiment at Valley Forge, January 10, 1778, continued the names of Peter Spicer, Daniel Putnam, Curtis Cady.   (Rev. Rolls, p. 434, Vol. 2.)

Revolutionary Rolls, pages 602–4, volume 2, contains a list of men raised in Colonel Chase's regiment February 17, 1779, all from Cornish: Curtis Cady, Nathaniel Curtis, Daniel Putnam, Moses Brown, Peter Spicer, Nathaniel Bartlett, John Bartlett, Moses Chase, Jr., Jonathan Currier, Loring Thompson, William Richardson, David Currier, Gale Cole.

Kidder's history of the first New Hampshire regiment also makes mention of the continued service of several Cornish men as follows:

Curtis Cady entered Feb. 1777, disch. Apr. 4, 1778.

Daniel Putnam entered Feb. 12, 1777, disch. Dec.—1781.

Peter Spicer entered May 1, 1777, disch. Mar. 20, 1778.

Loring Thompson entered May 1, 1777, disch. May 1, 1780.

David Haskell entered Jan. 1, 1782, disch. Dec. 31, 1783.

Daniel Putnam entered Jan. 1, 1782, disch. ——— 1783.

The following list of Cornish men marched May 7, 1777, from Cornish in Col. Jonathan Chase's Regiment for Ticonderoga. Time of service, one month, twelve days:

Jonathan Chase, Col.
Solomon Chase, Capt.
Dyer Spaulding, Q. M.
Stephen Cady, Sergt.
Samuel Chase, 3d Sergt.
William Payn, Private
Briant Brown, Private
Solomon Chase, Private
William Richardson, Private
Moses Currier, Private
Isaac Wellman, Private
John Chase, Private

Nathaniel Hall, Sergt.
Stephen Child, Corp.
Benj. Cummins, Corp.
Gideon Smith, Corp.
Benj. Chapman, Drum.
John Whitten, Private
Joseph Vinsen, Private
James Wellman, Private
Moses Hall, Private
Andrew Spaulding, Private
Eben'r Brewer, Private
John Weld, Private

The following is the list of Cornish men who marched June 27, 1777, in Colonel Chase's Regiment for Ticonderoga. Time of service, from four to fifteen days:

Jonathan Chase, Col.
Moses Chase, Capt.
William Ripley, Adj.
Moses Chase, Jr., Private
Abel Stevens, Private
William Ripley, Private
Elijah Cady, Private
Eliphalet Kimball, Private
Gideon Smith, Private
Jabez Spicer, Private
Josiah Stone, Private
Jedediah Hibbard, Private
Joseph Vincent, Private
Moses Currier, Private
Thomas Hall, Jr., Private
Zebadiah Fitch, Private
William Richardson, Private
Nathan'l Dustin, Private
Abel Spaulding, Jr., Private

Abel Spaulding, Lieut.
Reuben Jerald, Lieut.
Elias Cady, Lieut.
Nicholas Cady, Private
Simeon Chase, Private
Isaac Wellman, Private
Moody Hall, Private
Samuel Fitch, Private
Ebenezer Brewer, Private
Salmon Chase, Private
David Huggins, Private
James Cate, Private
Samuel Chase, Jr., Private
Dudley Chase, Private
Caleb Plastridge, Private
Hezekiah French, Private
Benj. Swinnerton, Private
James Wellman, Private

The following is the list of Cornish men, not included in the foregoing organizations, who served more or less during the war. Great efforts have been made to make this list as complete and accurate as possible.

Lieut. Eleazer Jackson
Samuel Comings
Ebenezer Dresser
Frank Cobb
James Ripley
Samuel Paine
Joshua Page
Ezra Spaulding
Peter Chase
Nahum Chase
Caleb Chase
William Chase
Thomas Chase
Nath'l Huggins
Robert Wilson
Amos Chase
Daniel Roberts

Thomas Chamberlain
David Davis
Timothy Spaulding
Moses Vinson
Francis Dana
Hezekiah Fitch
James Wellman, Jr.
Andrew Spaulding, Jr.
Joseph Bartlett
Richard Hawley
Elijah Carpenter
William Darling
Peter Labere, Jr.
Joel Rice, Jr.
Nathaniel Holden
Deliverance Woodward

On June 24, 1779, the state voted that General Folsom shall forthwith issue orders to the several Colonels of regiments of this state for raising men to fill up the Continental Battalion belonging to the state and the regiment for Rhode Island, according to the order of the General Court recently passed, and the proportion of officers and privates to be raised in each regiment. The number of men thus called for was 280. Colonel Chase's regiment was to receive eight. (Rev. Rolls, p. 655, Vol. 2.)

Dr. Solomon Chase of Cornish was a very efficient and useful man in the entire Revolutionary service. At one time he commanded a company in Colonel Chase's Regiment; but chiefly his duties were confined to the hospital as a physician and surgeon. The following order is on record (Rev. Rolls, p. 144, Vol. 4):

Gen. Stark to Doctor Chase.

H Quar' C: Town, Aug. 3, 1777.

Doc' Solomon Chase—Sir—You are ordered and Required to take under your Care all the sick that is, or may be sent hereafter from my Brigade of Militia to this place—And you are to Receive medicines out of the State Chest for the purpose aforesaid. What medicines you use of your own private property, you'r to keep an exact account of—You'r also from time to time desired to send me an account of the State & Condition of the Sick under your Care, & this shall be your sufficient order—

JOHN STARK, B. D. G.

To Dr. Solomon Chase—Chirurgeon to Colo. Hobarts Regiment.

On the 16th of June, 1780, the Legislature passed an act ordering 600 men to be raised to recruit the three regiments in the Continental army in the state. The Committee of Safety gave orders to the regimental commanders to raise their several quotas, and 23 men was the quota of Colonel Chase. The men were to furnish their own Clothing, Knapsack & Blankets and serve till the last day of December next, or be liable to a fine of 500 dollars. "They were to be paid forty shillings per month in Money, equal to Indian Corn at Four Shillings a Bushel, Grass-fed Beef at Three Pence per Pound, or Sole-Leather at Eighteen Pence a Pound." They were also to have five pounds each for clothing money, two dollars in paper currency per mile for travel and money for rations till they could draw Continental rations. (Rev. Rolls, p. 58, Vol. 3.) N. H. troops did service this year (1780) at West Point and in New Jersey.

In the latter part of June (1780) the Legislature voted to raise 945 men for a term of three months to reinforce the army at West Point. These were to form two regiments. The men were apportioned to be drawn from the other regiments. Colonel Chase was to raise thirty-six privates and two officers. The men were enlisted early in July, and marched via Springfield, Mass., to West Point, where the vanguard arrived August 4. These were discharged the latter part of October, 1780. (Rev. Rolls, p. 104, Vol. 3.)

The burning of Royalton, Vt., October 16, 1780, was a lamentable affair. It was not done by an organized military body, but by Indian marauders accompanied by one lieutenant, one Frenchman and one Tory. They burned over twenty houses, and nearly as many barns, and slaughtered cattle, sheep and swine. They murdered two men and carried away about twenty-five captives. The attack was sudden and unexpected. The news of this event was quickly carried from town to town arousing the entire region and several companies of militia were soon marching to the relief of their brethren in Vermont. The companies were so hastily formed that the rolls, if there were any, have not been preserved. The records of several towns, including Cornish, testify to a remarkable and spontaneous muster of men about that time. But the enemy had escaped, and the soldiers soon returned to their homes. (Plymouth History, p. 130.)

A law was passed by the Legislature, November 8, 1780, that the state reimburse all military expenses incurred by officers of the army during any emergency campaign. The following bill was presented. (No date given):

To Sergeant & 8 men 6 months in Vermont.......	152–18
To 4 men 1 month Scouting & ammunition.......	25–14
To Capt. Solomon Chase, Roll to Royalton, Vt...	60–15–9
To Capt. Solomon Chase, Roll to Newbury, Vt. in 1781	16– 0–5
To Dudley Chase for supplies.................	3
To Moses Chase for supplies.................	17–2

From the third item above, one might infer a good number of Cornish men went to Royalton at the time of the alarm, under command of Capt. Solomon Chase. (Rev. Rolls, p. 537, Vol. 3.)

April 5, 1781, the Legislature voted to raise two companies of sixty-five men each, by June 1st to rendezvous at Haverhill. They were to be raised from the military regiments of Colonels Ellis of Keene, Chase of Cornish, Morey of Orford, Webster of Plymouth, and the regiment of the late Colonel Bellows of Walpole, and were to serve six months. (Rev. Rolls, p. 249, Vol. 3.)

On February 1, 1786, Daniel Putnam of Cornish petitioned the Honorable General Court of New Hampshire, then convened at Portsmouth, as follows: The petition showeth that he (Putnam) was engaged as a soldier, in the year 1776, in Capt. Esterbrooks company in Col. Bedell's regiment; that he marched with the troops to Quebec, when he was taken sick, and had the misfortune to lose all his clothes to the amount of 14 pounds & two shillings, and being left by the troops with no care, incurred the expense of 16 pounds for doctoring, which sum your petitioner was obliged to pay. Wherefore he prays your Honors to take his case and grant him the said sum, with interest, if you in your wisdom shall think proper. (Rev. Rolls, pp. 431–32, Vol. 3.)

DANIEL PUTNAM.

During the Revolutionary War the people suffered much inconvenience from the depreciation of the currency. It continued to depreciate, and the price of the necessaries of life continued to advance until the people became greatly alarmed. Legislation was sought to check the evil, but, whatever it may have done, proved of no avail. In 1780 it seemed to reach its climax. During this year Cornish voted to raise 800 pounds for schooling in town, also 2,000 pounds for mending highways, and the price of labor on highways in some towns was fifteen dollars per day; and wages and articles of commerce were correspondingly high.

Without special active cause, this state of things slowly subsided and normal conditions and prices again prevailed.

The cause of this inflation (as ever) was primarily due to the scarcity of gold and silver. Money must be had to equip soldiers for the service, and to pay them for their services. This led to the issuance of an undue amount of paper money whose value was uncertain. By resorting largely to a barter trade, or an exchange of commodities, using them as mediums of circulation at prices agreed upon by the authorities, the trouble gradually disappeared.

The condition of our troops on January 1, 1781, is thus described by Frederic Kidder in his History of the First Regiment:

"The new year opened with a deep gloom. The whole army, North as well as South, was suffering severely, both for clothing and provisions. The winter was unusually severe. The soldiers were often on the point of starvation, and for days without meat and nearly all the time on short allowance, while most of them had received no pay for almost a year. As for clothing, they were often so destitute that many of them could not do guard duty without borrowing from their comrades, while for shoes they were still more deficient, and parties who were on fatigue duty for

firewood and forage, could often be tracked by the blood from
their bruised feet. It was at this period that General Washington
addressed a pressing letter to President Weare of New Hampshire,
earnestly urging the state to make some further exertion to relieve the distresses of the army. He said: 'I give it decidedly
as my opinion, that it is vain to think that an army can be kept
together much longer under such a variety of sufferings as ours
has experienced, and that, unless some immediate and spirited
measures are adopted to furnish, at least three months pay to the
troops in money that will be of some value to them, and at the
same time provide means to clothe and feed them better than they
have been, the worst that can befall us may be expected.'

"The Legislature of the state nobly responded, and voted a gra-
tuity of twenty-four dollars in hard money to each of the non-com-
missioned officers and soldiers belonging to the state who were
engaged to serve for the war."

With the surrender of Lord Cornwallis and his army at Yorktown, October 19, 1781, the war was practically ended. The remaining part of the story of Cornish in the Revolution relates
mainly to the defence of the frontiers, and in coping with the
various financial problems touching the soldiers and their families.

The treaty of peace was concluded between the United States
and Great Britain, September 3, 1783.

In reviewing the immense sacrifices of our forefathers, it is
becoming us, their descendants, to render them the meed of praise
that is rightfully theirs, and that to these we are indebted for the
blessings of civil liberty we enjoy today.

CHAPTER VI.

MILITARY HISTORY, 1783-1861.

AFTER the war of the Revolution was ended and peace again restored, it was thought best that the military force of the country be maintained and that existing military laws be so amended and enforced that an effective army might be in constant readiness to meet any emergency that might arise. In 1792, the general government passed an act establishing a system of uniform militia laws throughout the United States. This required the enrollment of all free, able-bodied, white, male citizens between the ages of eighteen and forty-five.

New Hampshire being then a state, yielded a willing obedience to the law and took active measures to carry out all its provisions. The military officers who had served during the war, retained their rank and honors, and resumed their official functions, enrolling and drilling their men in their own towns or districts.

In June, 1808, the State of New Hampshire was divided into thirty-eight military districts. Each district was required to enroll and equip all its eligible men, and these constituted a regiment. Each of these regiments was composed of one company of artillery and about ten other companies— chiefly of infantry. The fifteenth district embraced Cornish, Claremont, Plainfield and "the west company in Grantham." The troops of this district were called "the 15th Regiment of New Hampshire Militia."

This regiment with six others, namely the 6th, 12th, 16th, 20th, 28th and 31st constituted the 5th brigade and 3d division of New Hampshire troops.

Various acts relating to the militia were passed from time to time by the Legislature, while parades and drills were kept up throughout the state. On December 22, 1820, a full and satisfactory code of laws was adopted, that, in the main remained in force until the militia laws of New Hampshire were repealed in June, 1850.

Cornish furnished three companies of troops for the 15th

Regiment; one of artillery and two of infantry. One of the latter bore the name of "Stubtoe" or "Floodwood," by way of derision. All of these companies with their officers were required, on parade day, to be "uniformed and armed as the law directs." The general features of their dress were:

The artillery were attired in red frocks trimmed with white, with dark caps and pants. The infantry were attired with dark blue or black coats, white pants. One of these companies wore high, bell-crowned caps with tall red plumes, tipped with white.

The state furnished all the arms needed for these two companies of infantry, and also the field-piece or cannon for the artillery.

The days of parade and drill during the year were usually three:

1st. The second Tuesday in May, called the "May training."

2d. A certain day usually in September. This was a day for a special drill preparatory to a general muster and parade of the whole regiment which occurred a day or two later.

3d. The general muster day. This was not only for parade but for the review and inspection of the entire regiment by military and civic officers of higher rank.

Muster day furnished the acme of interest to all. Early in the day each orderly sergeant marshalled his company, which soon after received its commissioned officers in martial form. About eight o'clock, the companies about ten in number, each headed by fife and drums, united in line upon the field, thus forming the regiment. After a period of united drill and march, the troops were placed in form to receive their superior officers.

The colonel, major, inspecting brigade general and other officers of note, with fiery, mettlesome steeds now rode upon the field with great pomp and the whole regiment was soon in obedience to the orders of the colonel for the day's parade.

The pen poorly depicts the grandeur of those scenes as they appeared to the eyes of the ordinary country boy seventy years ago; the immense gathering of the people of both sexes and all ages, with peddlers and fakirs in abundance at every street corner; the air filled with martial music; the uniformed companies of marching soldiery, were all matters of acute interest, especially to the young. Sometimes, too, the interest was intensified by occasional discharges of cannon by the artillery and later in the day by a sham fight.

All these scenes and experiences passed away upon the repeal of the law in 1850. The writer well remembers several occasions of this character, and the enthusiasm attending them.

Several fields in Cornish have been used for these muster parades. Three different fields at the Flat, two on "Cornish Plain," south of Trinity Church, have been used for this purpose, and perhaps several others. A level tract of dry ground of suitable area is all the condition needful for such a field. Some years the 15th regiment mustered in other towns of the district. The time and place for each annual muster was appointed by the colonel of the regiment with the advice of his subalterns.

The period of our national history following the Revolution was a constructive period and generally a peaceful one. The first note of war heard within our national realm was the war with Tripoli, 1803-05; when the American fleet under Commodore Decatur administered a chastisement upon that barbarous nation thereby conquering a peace instead of purchasing one.

It sent a thrill of satisfaction throughout our nation to know that a stop was put to their preying upon our commerce as heretofore. This over, the country generally enjoyed a few years of peace and prosperity until the war with England occurred, 1812-15. A brief account of the causes, progress, and outcome of this war is here given:

In the treaty of peace between the United States and Great Britain at the close of the Revolutionary War, were several provisions. Some of these, Great Britain had failed to fulfill, notably that of the evacuation of posts along the northern frontiers. This was a perpetual annoyance to the inhabitants of those sections, who continued to be fearfully apprehensive of further trouble.

The unfriendly attitude of England towards France, too, was also unfortunate for the United States; for by an order in Council the British government had declared that all vessels trading with France were liable to seizure, and that all vessels clearing from hostile ports must touch at a British port and pay custom duties. Because of this order, British naval officers claimed and exercised in the most arrogant and offensive manner, the right to search American vessels, and oftentimes to impress their seaman into the British navy, despite all the strong protestation of American officers and men.

7

President Madison urgently requested the withdrawal of this order in Council, and the discontinuance of this oppressive and unjust practice, but his requests were insultingly denied.

In November, 1811, the President called an extra session of Congress and laid these grievances before it, and recommended preparation for war.

On April 10, 1812, Congress authorized the president to detach 100,000 militia to be organized and held in readiness to serve six months after entering service. Congress was becoming convinced there was no hope of a change of policy on the part of Great Britain, and that a resort to arms was the only alternative to protect the persons and property of American subjects and maintain the honor of the nation, and so war was declared June 18, 1812. A month previous, in May, 1812, New Hampshire was called upon for 3,500 men.

At the first, the declaration of war was not a popular measure in New Hampshire, or in New England. For this reason enlistments were a little tardy, and a draft was enforced. The records of the town show that on November 2, 1812, an attempt was made in Cornish to raise the wages of men drafted for the army, but the project was voted down.

During the continuance of this war which lasted nearly three years it is stated that finally every requisition of the government was met with promptness on the part of New Hampshire, and that Cornish did her full duty and furnished her just proportion of men for the army.

It is a matter of regret that no rolls of enlistments or of drafted men have been preserved. Search has been made in the archives of the state, and none has been found.

On recent application to the War Department at Washington for the needful information, the following reply was received:

"ADJUTANT GENERAL'S OFFICE,
            "Washington, D. C., May 11, 1908.

"The War Department has no list of the soldiers from the town of Cornish who served in the War of 1812, and has no records from which such a list can be compiled.

                    "F. C. AINSWORTH,
                            "The Adjutant General."

During the summer of 1814, British war vessels lay off the coast of New Hampshire, and captured and burned several of our coasting vessels. A considerable force of New Hampshire men were therefore stationed at Portsmouth to be in readiness to repel any attack from the British. But fortunately no engagement took place. It is stated on good authority that several men from Cornish were among those stationed in Portsmouth. In August of this same year a British squadron sailed up the Chesapeake Bay and landed a force of 5,000 troops, which advanced on Washington, burned the public buildings, including many of the government archives, and without meeting any resistance they retired as they came. This dastardly act roused the people, stimulated enlistments and unified public sentiment.

It is possible and even probable that the paucity of war rolls may in part be due to the destruction of the public buildings with their contents at the time the British invaded Washington.

On the 24th of December, 1814, a treaty of peace was concluded at Ghent, and the War of 1812–14, was supposed to be at an end.

It is a remarkable fact, however, that the greatest engagement of the war took place at New Orleans after the treaty of peace was concluded. The British had evidently planned the capture of New Orleans and were so intent on accomplishing it, that the news of the treaty, if received at all, did not deter them from their purpose. The matter came to a final crisis on January 8, 1815, when General Jackson gained a decisive victory over the British army, which ended all strife of arms between the two nations.

The names and numbers of men who served in this war from Cornish cannot all be given. This is a matter of deep regret but all other towns have suffered a like experience. A few names can be gleaned from the traditional records of their families. These we append:

Benjamin Edminster, Clark Kendrick, Capt. Andrew Dodge, Capt. Eben Comings, Daniel Jackson, Walter Weld (died in service), Eben Weld (killed at Williamsburg, Can.), Samuel Bernum, Ebenezer Deming, Jr., Everett Robinson, Andrew Comings (son of Benj.), Capt. Eben Comings, Edward Kimball, Daniel F. Spaulding, and Jacob Newell.

After the war with England was over, thirty years of

peace and prosperity followed. The state made her appropriations and active military drill was maintained throughout the country. The Southern States increased in population and power. The slavery system also increased and sought fresh avenues for increasing and strengthening its power.

In 1846, the war with Mexico was ushered in. This lasted from April, 1846, until September, 1847. It was plainly a war of unjust aggression on a weaker power with the object of acquiring more territory for new slave states. As a matter of course the citizens of Cornish, with divided opinions, watched with great interest the opening, progress and termination of this war; but it is not known that they furnished any men for the service.

After the war with Mexico was ended, all appearances of war with any foreign power, entirely disappeared,

Another season of apparent peace and prosperity now followed. The warlike propensities, especially of the North seemed fading away. A generation had arisen which tried to believe that war was a relic of barbarism and that it never would again be employed for the settlement of disputes between enlightened parties or nations; that our people were too highly civilized to engage ever again in the destruction of their fellowmen on the battlefield. Military drill, especially in the North, had become unpopular. The glamour of military display presented fewer attractions than formerly. As a result of these causes, the existing militia laws of New Hampshire were repealed in 1850.

From about that time military drill ceased in most if not all of the New England states, and no military organizations existed there except an occasional company in cities, whose duties chiefly were in aiding the authorities in preserving order and performing escort duty. While the military power was suffering this decline in the North, it seems strange that political party strife was increasing in intensity, especially during the years just preceding the rebellion, and among the states of the South. The legions of pro-slavery advocates were aggressive and determined, while the anti-slavery element of the country stood firm, unmoved and unsupported by any military power. But after the Civil War began, when they saw the nation's life imperilled, and heard the call for troops, thousands sprang to arms in her defence. The raw recruits of the North, who had scarcely dreamed of war, were soon transmuted into disciplined soldiers.

CHAPTER VII.

Cornish in the Civil War.

It is not necessary to recount the causes which led to the fearful fratricidal strife which deluged our nation in blood, neither the immense sacrifice of lives and treasures required to preserve our national honor and unity. These are all recorded in the archives of the nation's history as a heritage for us, and for millions yet unborn. But the part that the citizens of Cornish took in that eventful period is the work now in hand.

It has never been said that Cornish did not bear her just proportion of the sacrifices and burdens of that crisis, or that she was lacking in true patriotism. Of the eighteen regiments sent from New Hampshire, fourteen of them contained more or less Cornish men, aggregating, including those serving in other organizations connected with the war, men, most of whom served with honor. Thus it will be observed that Cornish sent a very large percentage of her citizen soldiery into the field, beside enlisting many of foreign birth and others to serve in her regiments when they became depleted and reduced by the casualties of war.

The first call of President Lincoln was for 75,000 three months' men, and New Hampshire was required to furnish one regiment of these. This regiment was filled so quickly, that those first enlisting in town, could not find admission to its ranks, therefore, this regiment contained none from Cornish, but those who had enlisted for three months soon had the opportunity of reënlisting for three years in the second regiment soon to follow. The first regiment under command of Col. Mason W. Tappan left the state May 27, 1861, for the seat of war. This regiment had no serious engagement but did guard duty in and around Washington until the expiration of the time of its enlistment, and it was mustered out August 2, 1861.

Second Regiment.

This was the first regiment of three years' men. It was organized at Portsmouth, N. H., in May, 1861, with Gilman Marston as colonel. It was mustered into service early in June, and on the 20th of the same month, with 1,022 officers and men, left Portsmouth for Washington, via Boston and New York. Governor Berry and staff, Ex-Governor Goodwin and many leading men of the state accompanied them to Boston, where they were received with enthusiastic demonstrations. An organization of 1,400 "Sons of New Hampshire" with Governor Andrew and staff, with prominent citizens and military bands escorted the regiment to a banquet prepared for them in Music Hall, where a patriotic address was given by Hon. Marshall P. Wilder. After being reviewed by Governor Andrew on the Common, they left for New York, where they were received by a similar ovation. They reached Washington on the 23d of June. On the 21st of July following, this regiment received its first baptism of blood at Bull Run, Va., the first great battle of the war. Here the regiment had nine killed, thirty-five wounded, four mortally, and sixty-three taken prisoners. Among the latter were two men from Cornish, John L. Rice and Albert L. Hall (See Rolls). Rice was also seriously wounded, left on the field and reported dead, and his funeral obsequies were accordingly held at home. But afterwards he was found to be alive, much to the rejoicing of his many friends.

This regiment saw much hard service and sustained many heavy losses, especially at Williamsburg, Va., and later at Gettysburg, Pa., besides being engaged in many other battles of note, where in every case it reflected honor upon itself and the state.

The rigor of its service and other causes, finally reduced it to about one fourth of its original numbers, and it was mustered out of service early in December, 1865, at City Point, Va., and discharged in Concord, N. H., December 26, 1865. Here they again met a hearty and generous reception.

In the rolls of this, and all regiments hereafter given, it is to be understood that the men were privates and were residents of, or were born in Cornish, unless otherwise mentioned. All transfers and promotions will be noted in connection with the first mention of their names.

Below are given, directly as recorded upon the military rolls of the state, the names and brief records of the men of Cornish in the 2d regiment, in all, 25 names:

Asa M. Benway. Age 26, enl. Apr. 24, 61, disch. disab. June 8, 61, enl. 2d, Sept. 1, 64, in Vt. Cav., killed. Mar. 2, 65, at Waynesboro, Va. Before the engagement he remarked that he should be killed in the first fight in which he engaged. It proved true. He was the only one killed.

John H. Barry, Co. I, b. Plattsburg, N. Y. Age 26, enl. Apr. 28, 61, not must., re-enl. May 21, 61. Captd. July 21, 61, at Bull Run, Va., paroled June 2, 62, disch. July 2, 62.

James A. Cook. Age 47, enl. June 18, 61, from Claremont. Serg. non. com. staff., prom. 2d Q. M. June 9, 62, app. Capt. Com. of Substance July 2, 63, disch. disab. Sept. 8, 64.

John Carroll (sub.) b. Ireland, Co. C. Age 21, enl. Dec. 6, 64, disch. disab. Apr. 7, 65, at Fort Munro, Va.

Edward W. Collins, Jr., Co. I. Age 22, enl. Apr. 27, 61, not must., re-enl. May 21, 61, disch. disab. Aug. 16, 61.

Edward Davis, Co. G, b. N. Y. Age 23, enl. Dec. 1, 63, confined at Camp Hamilton May 9, 64, released July 28, 64, and sent to Bermuda Hundred. No further report.

William Gaines, Co. G, b. N. Y. Age 18, enl. Dec. 1, 63. Furloughed from Hospital Point of Rocks, Va. Failed to return.

Albert L. Hall, Co. I, Age 21, enl. Apr. 28, 61, not must., re-enl. May 21, 61. Captd. July 21, 61, at Bull Run, Va., paroled May 21, 62, disch. July 2, 62.

Burleigh R. Jones. Age 21, enl. Aug. 2, 61, from Hopkinton, Co. B, wd. June 25, 62, at Oak Grove, Va., d. July 1, 62, on Hospital Ship at Hampton Roads, Va.

John Kennison, Co. H, b. Concord, Vt. Age 28, enl. Dec. 1, 63, disch. disab. May 12, 64, at Williamsburg, Va.

Joseph Lumbeck, Co. K, b. Sweden. Age 21, enl. Dec. 4, 63, wd. at Cold Harbor, Va., June 3, 64, app. Corp. Nov. 1, 64, disch. Dec. 19, 65.

Lewis Laurd, Co. K, b. Canada. Age 33, enl. Dec. 4, 63, disch. Dec. 19, 65.

James Lee, Co. H, b. Philadelphia, Pa. Age 18, enl. Dec. 1, 63, disch. Dec. 19, 65.

Timothy Malone, Co. H. b. Ireland. Age 27, enl. Dec. 1, 63, disch. Dec. 19, 65.

Peter Mareau, Co. H, b. N. Y., enl. Dec. 2, 63, deserted Sept. 8, 65, from Fredericksburg, Va.

Stephen Nichols, Co. K, b. Ill.   Age 20, enl. Dec. 4, 63, entered
18th Army Corps and Point of Rocks, Va., Feb. 15, 65,   No
further record appears.

Thomas Perkins, Co. H, b. Wisconsin.   Age 19, enl. Dec. 2, 63,
disch. June 20, 65, at Fort Munroe, Va.

Andrew Pinder, Co. K, b. Ireland.   Age 18, enl. Dec. 4, 63,
disch. Dec. 19, 65.

Clark Allen, Co. K, b. N. Y.   Age 18, enl. Dec. 4, 63, wd. severely
July 5, 64, at Petersburg, Va., disch. May 25, 65.

John L. Rice.   Age 21, enl. Apr. 28, 61, not must., re-enl. May
21, 61, Co. A, wd. and captd. July 21, 61, at Bull Run, Va.,
paroled Jan. 3, 62, exch. and disch. Nov. 18, 62, for promotion,
app. Capt. Co. H, 16th N. H. vols., Nov. 4, 62, must. Dec.
2, 62, volunteered for storming party at Port Hudson,
La., under G. O. No. 49, headqrs. dept. of the Gulf June
15, 63, app. Lieut. Col. Oct. 1, 63, disch. Nov. 25, 65, at New
Orleans, La.

Charles M. Smith, Co. H, b. Hartford, Conn.   Age 19, enl. Dec.
1, 63, d. of dis. Oct. 27, 64, at Fort Munroe, Va.

George E. Tyler.   Age 20, enl. Apr. 27, 61, not must., re-enl. May
21, 61, in Co. I, d. Mar. 6, 63, of dis. at Boston, Mass.

Thomas Welch, Co. H, b. Ireland.   Age 27, enl. Dec. 1, 63,
deserted in face of enemy May 19, 64, at Bermuda Hundred, Va.

William F. Wright.   Age 19, enl. Apr. 28, 61, re-enl. May 21, 61,
must. in Aug. 13, 61, in Co. I, wd. Aug. 29, 62, at Bull Run,
Va., d. from wounds Sept. 27, 62, at Washington, D. C.

John B. Wright.   Age 18, enl. Apr. 28, 61, re-enl. May 21, 61,
must. in Aug. 21, 61, in Co. I, disch. Aug. 23, 64, near Petersburg, Va.

Third Regiment.

This was organized in August 1861, and left the state for Washington on the September following, 1,035 strong.   It was soon sent
to and stationed at Hilton Head, S. C., until April, 1862.   In June
following it was sent to James Island.   Its first sharp engagement
was at Secessionville, S. C., where it lost 105 men.   Returning to
Hilton Head it remained there until April, 1863.   On July 18, 1863,
it was fiercely engaged in the siege of Fort Wagner, where it
lost heavily, as did the 7th New Hampshire.   During 1864 it was
in several serious engagements, and at one time "well-nigh anni-

hilated." With thinned ranks it was finally mustered out, July 20, 1865. Cornish had, at different times, fourteen men in this regiment. Quite a proportion of these were not citizens of the town but were foreign born and hired substitutes.

William Arnie (sub.), Co. B, b. England. Age 21, enl. Oct. 14, 63. No further record obtained.

Elbridge G. Beers, 2d Co. K. Age 18, enl. Aug. 12, 61, d. July 20, 62, in Beaufort, S. C.

Joseph Brady (sub.), Co. I, b. England. Age 29, enl. Oct. 10, 63, sev. wd. May 13, 64, at Drewrys Bluff, Va., disch. disab. July 20, 65.

Dudley Colby, Co. K. Age 27, enl. from Franklin N. H., July 26, 61, disch. Aug. 23, 64.

James A. Douglass (sub.), Co. K. b. Edinburgh, Scotland. Age 20, enl. Oct. 8, 63, wd. Aug. 16, 64, at Deep Bottom, Va., disch. disab. July 20, 65.

Joseph E. Horton, Co. B, b. Taunton, Mass. Age 18, enl. Aug. 19, 62, sev. wd. May 13, 64, at Drewrys Bluff, Va., dis. June 26, 65, at Goldsboro, N. C.

Thomas Langdon (sub.), Co. B, b. N. Y. Age 19, enl. Oct. 14, 63, sev. wd. and d. of wounds May 13, 64, at Drewrys Bluff, Va.

Alcide Lallance (sub.), Co. K, b. France. Age 22, enl. Oct. 10, 63, sev. wd. May 18, 64, at Bermuda Hundred, Va., disch. Aug. 4, 64, at Newark, N. J.

Edward Mitchell (sub.), Co. K, b. Bridgewater, Mass. Age 20, enl. Oct. 10, 63, disch. Nov. 7, 64, at Staten Island, N. Y.

Lewis Maier (sub.), Co. K, b. Germany. Age 22, enl. Dec. 17, 64, disch. July 20, 65.

Thomas Murphy (sub.), Co. C, b. Liverpool, Eng. Age 22, enl. Oct. 10, 63, disch. July 20, 65.

James Reagan (sub.), Co. K, b. Ireland. Age 25, enl. Dec. 27, 64, disch. Apr. 2, 65, at Wilmington, N. C.

Henry Squires, Co. A. Age 25, enl. Aug. 30, 62, disch. disab. Feb. 7, 63, at Hilton Head, S. C.

Sumner B. Tewksbury, Co. K, b. Milford, N. H. Age 21, enl. Aug. 6, 61, disch. disab. Mar. 11, 62, drafted, Oct. 19, 63, and assigned to 5th N. H., disch. from 5th June 28, 65.

Fourth Regiment.

This regiment was organized in August and September, 1861, and started for the seat of war about the 17th of September.

Its services during the first two years were wholly in the South, in Florida and the Carolinas. It joined the army of the Potomac in 1864, and assisted at the siege of Petersburg. It was mustered out at Concord, August 23, 1865.

Cornish was represented in this regiment by four men:

Moses Bohannon, Co. I, b. Danbury, N. H. Age 44, enl. Aug. 23, 64, disch. disab. June 27, 65, at Concord, N. H.

Michael Cane, Co. C, b. Ireland. Age 21, enl. Dec. 21, 64, disch. Mar. 17, 65, at Wilmington, N. C.

David L. M. Comings, enl. Aug. 13, 62, from W. Swansy, N. H., assistant surgeon, d. of dis. at Swansy, Aug. 1, 63.

Lucius Little (sub.), Co. K, b. Lenoxville, Canada. Age 20, enl. Jan. 17, 65, disch. Aug. 23, 65.

Fifth Regiment.

This was organized at Concord September and October, 1861, with Edward E. Cross as colonel. It left the state October 29, and was assigned to a division of the army of the Potomac until the following March and was then transferred to another division, Second Army Corps. It was at the siege of Yorktown and through the peninsular campaign, suffering heavy losses at Fair Oaks, Savage Station, White Oak Swamp and Malvern. A little later it lost one-third of its members at Antietam. At Fredericksburg December 13, 1862, it suffered severely. Of 303 officers and men present, it lost 193, or more than sixty per cent. It was also engaged in the battle of Chancellorville May 1-5, 1863, and also hotly engaged at Gettysburg, Pa., where Colonel Cross was mortally wounded, and where the regiment lost one-half of its numbers then present.

After this, the regiment was sent home to recruit until November, 1863. It then returned to the seat of war, and rejoined the army of the Potomac. It was engaged at Cold Harbor, Va., where it met with great loss. It was also at the siege of Petersburg, at Deep Bottom, Reams Station and others, until April 9, 1865, when Lee surrendered.

It returned to Washington and took part in the final grand review and was mustered out at Alexandria, June 28, 1865.

This regiment won the name of the " New Hampshire fighting fifth." Its record was brilliant, its losses great, its courage never daunted. It had its full share of the stern realities of the bloody field, as well as of the victor's triumph.

Cornish was represented in this regiment by a dozen men:

Edward Avery (sub.), Co. B, b. England. Age 22, enl. Oct. 13, 63, deserted, Oct. 18, 63, at Concord, N. H.

Nathaniel E. Beers, Co. G, b. Hartland, Vt. Age 40, enl. Sept. 27, 61, disch. for disab. Sept. 1, 62, re-enl. Mar. 23, 64, in Co. A, 1st N. H. Cav., captd. June 30, 64, on Wilson's raid, paroled Dec. 15, 64, app. farrier, disch. from Cav. Co. July 15, 65.

Robert H. Chase, Co. G. Age 18, enl. Sept. 27, 61, from Claremont, transf. to Co. C, Mar. 1, 62, captd. at Fair Oaks, Va., June 1, 62, released and afterwards re-enl. Jan. 1, 64, app. Sergt. and Com. 2d Lieut. Co. K, July 1, 64, killed at Reams Sta., Va., Aug. 25, 64.

John Hart (sub.), Co. E, b. Ireland. Age 21, enl. Oct. 13, 63, transf. to U. S. Navy, Apr. 19, 64, as landsman, served on U. S. S. *Matthew*, *Vassar*, *Primrose* and *Princess*, disch. Aug. 21, 65.

John H. Hunter, Co. E. Age 21, enl. Sept. 7, 61, from Newport, N. H., wd. June 1, 62, at Fair Oaks, disch. disab. Jan. 8, 63, at Fort Munroe.

Artemus M. Lewis, Co. G. Age 44, enl. Aug. 24, 62, from Claremont, disch. Mar. 3, 63.

Nathaniel Smith, Co. G. Age 18, enl. Sept. 29, 61, app. Corp., wd. July 1, 62, at Malvern Hill, Va., at Hill, Va., Sept. 16, 62, at Antietam, wd. and captd. June 3, 64, at Cold Harbor, Va., released Feb. 28, 65, disch. Apr. 8, 65, at Concord, N. H.

Stephen L. Stearns, Co. G. Age. 36, enl. Sept. 27, 61, disch. disab. Nov. 2, 63.

Joseph Stevens, Co. G. Age 45 enl. Sept. 27, 61, disch. disab. Jan. 8, 62, near Alexandria, Va.

William Sturtevant, Co. F. Age 36, draf. at Claremont, Oct. 10, 63, disch. June 28, 65.

Cornelius H. Stone, Co. F.   Age 18, enl. Feb. 12, 62, at Man-
chester, N. H., captd. July 26, 63, paroled, and exch., re-enl.,
Mar. 29, 64, sev. wd. June 3, 64, at Cold Harbor, Va., disch.,
at N. Y. City, June 8, 65.
William S. White, Co. G.   Age 21, enl. Sept. 2, 61, disch. disab.
Mar. 26, 63, at Fort Munroe, Va., re-enl. Dec. 29, 63, in 57th,
Mass., disch. July 30, 65.

Sixth Regiment.

The sixth regiment was mustered into service November 30,
1861, with Nelson Converse colonel.   It was stationed at Keene
until Christmas morning when it left the state for Washington.
It was assigned to Burnside's expedition to North Carolina.   In
March, 1862, Colonel Converse resigned and Lieut.-Col. S. G.
Griffin was promoted as colonel, and retained this position until
he was promoted May 11, 1864.

The military records of the services and achievements of this
regiment compare favorably with those of the other New Hampshire regiments.   It was engaged in several prominent battles
of the war and finally was present at the surrender of General
Lee.   It also took part in the grand review at Washington, May
23, 1865.   It was mustered out of service July 17, 1865.   Cornish
had nine men in this regiment.

Soldiers of the 6th regiment representing Cornish:

Patrick O'Conner, Co. D, b. Ireland.   Age 22, enl. Dec. 4, 63.,
disch. July 17, 65.
Richard Craig, Co. H, b. Louisville, Ky.   Age 28, enl. Oct. 28, 61,
app. Corp. Feb. 1, 64, disch. July 22, 64, at Concord, N. H.
Timothy C. Eastman, Co. G.   Age 33, enl. Dec. 5, 61, from Suna-
pee, N. H., d. of dis. Mar. 24, 62, at Roanoke Island, N. C.
Ebenezer Mitchell, Co. G, b. Corinth, Vt.   Age 43, enl. Oct. 7, 61,
disch. for disab. Aug. 11, 62, at Newbern, N. C.
Alvah S. Rawson, Co. G.   Age 18, enl. Nov. 20, 61, re-enl. Jan.
2, 64, in the same reg. and Co., app. Serg., killed July 3, 64, at
Petersburg, Va., while looking over breastworks, bullet entering
at eye.
John Smith, Co. F, b. Ireland.   Age 20, enl. Dec. 4, 63, deserted
Feb. 10, 64, at Camp Nelson, Ky.

Thomas Toole, Co. K, b. Ireland.   Age 20, enl. Dec. 4, 63, captd. Oct. 1, 64, at Poplar Springs Church, Va., released and afterwards app. Corp. July 1, 65, disch. July 17, 65.

Russell Tyler, Co. G.   Age 18, enl. Nov. 22, 61, wd. Dec. 13, 62, at Fredericksburg, Va., re-enl. Dec. 21, 63, in same reg. and Co., wd. at Spottsylvania June 22, 64, and at Petersburg, Va., Apr. 2, 65, app. Corp. Dec. 24, 62, Serg. Dec. 21, 63, 1st Lieut. Mar. 4, 65, disch. July 17, 65.

Henry P. Whittaker, Co. G.   Age 18, enl. Oct. 10, 61, from Goshen, N. H., re-enl. Dec. 27, 63, in same reg. and Co., app. Corp., wd. May 6, 64, at Wilderness, Va., app. Sergt. Aug. 1, 64, 2d Lieut. of Co. I, June 1, 65.

Seventh Regiment.

This regiment was organized in the fall of 1861, in Manchester, N. H., and left the state January 14, 1862.   It was mustered out at Concord, N. H., July 30, 1865.

It contained fifteen men from Cornish:

Charles C. Bartlett, Co. C.   Age 32, enl. Sept. 30, 61, disch. for disab. Jan. 4, 63, at St. Augustine, Fla., re-enl. Sept. 3, 64, in Co. B, 24th V. R. Corps, disch. for disab. June 27, 65, at Washington, D. C.

Thomas Bowen (sub.), b. Ireland. Co. F.   Age 43, enl. Oct. 13, 63, wd. and captd. June 16, 64, at Ware Bottom Church, Va., d. June 18, 64, at Richmond, Va.

George M. Chase, Co. C.   Age 28, enl. Sept. 24, 61, app. Corp. Nov. 15, 61, Sergt. July 18, 62, wd. and captd. July 18, 63, at Fort Wagner, S. C., rejoined reg. July 23, 63, app. 2d Lieut. Co. K, to date July 20, 63, disch. Dec. 24, 64.

Nathaniel B. Dodge, Co. C, b. Barre, Vt.   Age 22, enl. Oct. 9, 61, disch. for disab. Apr. 7, 63, at Hilton Head, S. C.

Newton C. Dodge, Co. C, b. Barre, Vt.   Age 33, enl. Dec. 12, 61, disch. for disab. Nov. 12, 62, at Davis Island, N. Y. Harbor.

Edward A. Downs, Co. I.   Age 23, drafted Sept. 20, 63, from Merrimack, wd. and captd. Feb. 20, 64, at Olustee, Fla., d. of dis. May 25, 64, at Andersonville, Ga.

Marcellus Judkins, Co. C.   Age 21, enl. Sept. 30, 61, d. of dis. Dec. 23, 61, at Manchester, N. H.   The first soldier that d. from Cornish.

Charles Nevens, Co. C, b. Bradford, N. H.   Age 18, enl. Sept. 22, 61, captd. July 18, 63, at Fort Wagner, S. C., d. July 30, 63.

Haldimand S. Putnam.   Age 25, a cadet of West Point, brev. 2d Lieut. Topographical Eng. July 1, 57, app. 2d Lieut. Apr. 1, 61, 1st Lieut. Aug. 3, 61, and Capt. engineers Mar. 3, 63, was Brev. Major July 1, 61, for gallant and meritorious services in Manassas Campaign, Brev. Lieut.-Col. July 10, 63, for gallant services on Morris Island, S. C., Brev. Col. July 18, 63, for gallant service at the assault of Fort Wagner, where he was mortally wd. July 18, 63.

David K. Ripley, Co. C, b. Plymouth, Mass.   Age 44, enl. Sept. 24, 61, d. of dis. Sept. 9, 62, at Hilton Head, S. C.

William Scott, Co. C, b. N. Y. City.   Age 18, enl. Oct. 2, 61, wd. Sept. 7, 63, at Morris Island, S. C., d. of wds. Oct. 5, 63, Fort Schuyler, N. Y.

Benjamin C. Stearns, Co. H.   Age 32, enl. Oct. 21, 61, disch. disab. Sept. 20, 63, d. in Cornish, Aug. 13, 65.

Edward L. Tasker, Co. C.   Age 26, enl. Sept. 23, 61, from Lebanon, N. H., d. of dis. at Beaufort, S. C., Aug. 9, 62.

Orin Watkins, Co. H, b. Townshend, Vt.   Age 38, enl. Oct. 1, 61, re-enl. Feb. 27, 64, in same reg. and Co., deserted May 1, 64, while on furlough.

Andrew P. Wright, Co. C, b. Lebanon, N. H.   Age 18, enl. Oct. 18, 61, killed at Olustee, Fla., Feb. 20, 64.

Eighth Regiment.

This regiment was gathered chiefly from eastern and southern portions of the state, and its service was wholly in the South, chiefly in Louisiana. Cornish had but one representative in it:

Joseph Edmunds, Co. F, b. in Quebec, Can.   Age 20, enl. Nov. 3, 63, transf. to Co. B. 9th Vols., res. Corps, Dec. 20, 64, disch. July 14, 65, at Washington, D. C.

Ninth Regiment.

This regiment was organized in August, 1862 with Enoch Q. Fellows, colonel and Herbert B. Titus, lieutenant-colonel. It left the state on the 25th of the same month for Washington, D. C.

It was assigned to the first brigade, 9th Army Corps of the Army of the Potomac.

On September 14, it had its first engagement of note at South Mountain and on the 17th following at Antietam, and at Fredericksburg on December 13, 1862. Early in 1863, it went south and west as far as Vicksburg, Miss., and was present at the surrender of that city.

The climate of the South seriously affected this regiment, and it soon returned and did service in Kentucky, and afterwards rejoined the 9th Army Corps on the Potomac, where, under Gen. S. G. Griffin it joined with the other New Hampshire regiments, in those grand and stirring events that culminated in the capture of Petersburg and the surrender of General Lee. Soon after this, this regiment was mustered out of service.

Cornish was represented by fifteen men in this regiment:

Henry P. Blood, Co. E. Age 18, enl. Aug. 4, 62, app. Corp., wd. Sept. 30, 64, at Poplar Springs Church, Va., d. of wds. Nov. 8, 64, at Beverly, N. J.

Daniel C. Buswell, b. Lebanon. Age 26, app. Capt. of Co. E, Aug. 10, 62, must. in Aug. 23, 62, as Capt. Had previously, from Apr. 29, 61, served in Co. B, 1st Minnesota Regt. and was disch. to accept promotion.

Albert B. Cressy, Co. G. Age 20, enl. July 23, 62, from Claremont (credited to Newbury), app. Corp., d. of dis. Sept. 14, 64, at Whitehall, Pa.

Charles F. Day, Co. E. Age 18, enl. Aug. 8, 62, app. Corp. was taken prisoner Sept. 30, 64, at Poplar Springs Church, Va., d. at Salisbury Stockade, S. C., or at Libbey, Va., Dec. 25, 64.

Edwin W. Downs, Co. E, b. Enfield, N. H. Age 18, enl. Aug. 8, 62, d. of dis. Aug. 26, 63, at Covington, Ky.

Luman Dudley, Co. G, b. Marlboro. N. H. Age 18, enl. July 25, 62, d. of dis. Jan. 19, 63, near Falmouth, Va.

Dennis C. Hibbard, Co. A. Age 18, enl. Aug. 27, 64, disch. Feb. 3, 65, at Fort Alexander Hayes.

George A. Hutchinson, Co. K. Age 18, enl. from Newport, Aug. 11, 62, d. of dis. Mar. 21, 64, at Camp Nelson, Ky.

James N. Edminster, Co. E. Age 22, enl. Aug. 1, 62, must. in as 2d Lieut. Aug. 23, 62, resigned Oct. 27, 62.

Hollis Knights, Co. E.   Age 23, enl. Aug. 8, 62, disch. for disab. Jan. 25, 64, at Camp Dennison, Ohio.

Oscar D. Robinson, Co. E.   Age 23, enl. July 25, 62, must. in as Sergt., app. 2d. Lieut. Jan. 1, 64, 1st Lieut. Mar. 1, 65, Capt. of Co. E, May 1, 65, disch. June 10, 65.

Sidney C. Spaulding, Co. E.   Age 18, b. Plainfield, enl. Aug. 8, 62, d. of dis. Oct. 4, 63, at Paris, Ky.

George B. Tracy. Co. E.   Age 36, enl. from Lebanon Aug. 8, 62, as Corp., app. Sergt., wd. May 12, 64, at Spottsylvania, Va., d. of wds. June 6, 64, at Washington, D. C.

Ithiel I. White, Co. K.   Age 24, enl. July 31, 62, killed May 12, 64, at Spottsylvania, Va.

Tenth Regiment.

The 10th Regiment had no one in it from Cornish.

Eleventh Regiment.

The 11th Regiment had but two Cornish men, brothers, both born in Cornish, but residing elsewhere:

Edwin Thrasher, Co. H.   Age 21, enl. Aug. 13, 62, from Lyme, N. H., disch. for disab. Dec. 15, 62, at N. Y. City, enl. 2d. Sept. 13, 64, in Co. B, 18th N. H., from Lyme, disch. June 10, 65.

Henry H. Thrasher, Co. C.   Age 21, enl. July 7, 62, des. Dec. 8, 62, at Falmouth, Va., enl. 2d May 3, 64, at New York as a landsman, served on the vessels, *Potomac, M. A. Wood* and U. S. S. *North Carolina*, honorably disch. Jan. 24, 65, from the *North Carolina*.

Twelfth Regiment.

The 12th Regiment contained no Cornish men.

Thirteenth Regiment.

The 13th Regiment contained but one man who was born in Cornish but enlisting from elsewhere:

Amasa Huggins, Co. H.   Age 43, enl. Mar. 31, 65, from Pittsburg, Pa., transf. to Co. B June 21, 65, disch. Dec. 19, 65.

Fourteenth Regiment.

This regiment was organized at Concord in August and September, 1862 with Robert Wilson, colonel. It left the state in

October for Washington and vicinity where it did guard duty generally until March 63. It then, after a furlough of two weeks, sailed and joined the department of the Gulf at New Orleans.

In July it was ordered north and became a part of General Sheridan's Army of the Shenandoah. Here it participated in the fierce battles of Deep Bottom, Winchester, Opequan, Fisher's Hill, Cedar Creek and several others. After this campaign in the Shenandoah Valley, it was again sent to the department of the South, where, in Georgia, it performed provost duty. It was finally mustered out of service at Hilton Head, July 7, 1865.

Cornish was especially interested in this regiment, as it contained twenty-one of her business citizens among its ranks. These all belonged to Co. I. Following is the list:

Reuben T. Benway, b. Plainfield. Age 19, enl. Aug. 20, 62, d. of dis. Nov. 12, 63, at Washington, D. C.

Sylvester M. Bugbee, b. Hartland, Vt. Age 39, enl. Aug. 21, 62, as private, app. Capt. Co. I, Oct. 9, 62, must. in as such, dating Oct. 7, 62, resigned Dec. 17, 62.

Versel E. Burr. Age 34, enl. Sept. 21, 62, d. of dis. Aug. 25, 64, at Fort Munroe.

James H. Chapman, b. Unity. Age 40, enl. Aug. 26, 62, disch. July 8, 65.

Charles B. Comings. Age 21, enl. Aug. 22, 62, app. Corp. July 1, 64, and Sergt. Jan. 2, 65, disch. July 8, 65.

Edward W. Collins, b. Paris, France. Age 44, enl. Aug. 22, 62, disch. for disab. Oct. 5, 63, at Washington, D. C.

Thomas B. Edminster. Age 22, enl. Aug. 21, 62, d. of dis. Dec. 27, 64, at Springfield, Mass.

Walter H. Foss. Age 43, enl. Jan. 4, 64, from Hanover, N. H., disch. disab. Feb. 24, 65, at Washington, D. C.

John B. Hibbard, b. Bethel, Vt. Age 21, enl. Aug. 23, 62, disch. disab. May 28, 63, at Providence, R. I.

Waldo L. Howard. Age 21, enl. Aug. 21, 62, disch. July 8, 65.

Wilbur F. Howard. Age 22, enl. Aug. 21, 62, wd. Sept. 19, 64, at Opequan, lost a leg, disch. Jan. 27, 65.

Harlan P. Hunter. Age 17, enl. Aug. 25, 62, disch. disab. May 2, 65, at Concord, N. H.

Marcus M. Lane. Age 22, enl. Aug. 22, 62, from Plainfield, wd. Sept. 19, 64, at Opequan Creek, disch. June 2, 65.

Alonzo Knights, b. Sharon, Vt.   Age 26, enl. Aug. 21, 62.   Captured Sept. 19, 64, at Opequan, Va., paroled Oct. 2, 64, disch. July 8, 65.

William S. Lewis, b. Hartford, Vt.   Age 29, enl. Aug. 23, 62, d. of dis. Jan. 21, 64, at Washington, D. C.

Theodore Miller, b. Troy, N. Y.   Age 16, enl. Sept. 4, 63, musician, disch. June 8, 65, at Hilton Head, S. C.

Asa W. Richardson, b. Moretown, Vt.   Age 39, enl. Aug. 21, 62, as Orderly Sergt., app. 2d Lieut. Co. E, May 27, 64, 1st Lieut. Co. F, Jan. 4, 65, disch. July 27, 65.

Hiram H. Stone, b. Berwick, Me.   Age 38, enl. Aug. 22, 62, d. of dis. Oct. 6, 64, at Washington, D. C.

George Tasker.   Age 20, enl. Aug. 20, 62, from Croydon.   Captured at Opequan, Va., Sept. 19, 64, paroled Oct. 8, 64, disch. June 8, 65.

Sylvester Tasker.   Age 21, enl. Aug. 20, 62, Corp., killed Sept. 19, 64, at Opequan, Va.

Charles Woodard, b. Plainfield.   Age 20, enl. Aug. 28, 62, disch. July 8, 65.

Fifteenth Regiment.

This regiment contained but one Cornish man:

Simon C. Kelley, Co. K.   Age 24, enl. Sept. 13, 62, from Salem, disch. Aug. 13, 63.

Sixteenth Regiment.

This regiment (as also the 15th and 17th) was a nine months' regiment, organized late in the fall of 1862.   It contained nine Cornish men as follows:

Norman D. Comings, Co. A.   Age 20, enl. Sept. 2, 62, d. Aug. 14, 63, in Mound City, Ill.

George W. Ellis, Co. A, b. Brandon, Vt.   Age 18 enl. Sept. 3, 62, disch. Aug. 20, 63, enl. Dec. 5, 63, in Co. G, 7th Vt. Inf., disch. from 7th Vt. Mar. 20, 63, at Brattleboro, Vt.

Seneca Ellis, Co. A, b. at sea.   Age 45, enl. Sept. 2, 62, disch. Aug. 20, 63, and d. Aug. 26, 63, in town.

Henry Leavitt, Co. A.   Age 22, enl. Sept. 2, 62, disch. Aug. 20, 63.

Joseph Newell, Co. A, b. Ripton, Vt.   Age 18, enl. Sept. 2, 62, disch. Aug. 20, 63.

Lucian Spaulding, Co. A. Age 18, enl. Aug. 13, 62, disch. Aug. 20, 63.

Silas Spaulding, Co. A, b. Peru, Mass. Age 38, enl. Sept. 2, 62, disch. Aug. 20, 63, d. Sept. 20, 63, at Cornish.

John M. Vinton, Co. A. Age 23, enl. Sept. 10, 62, from Plainfield, d. of dis. June 16, 63, at New Orleans, La.

Horace B. Wellman, Co. A. Age 21, enl. Aug. 30, 62, Sergeant, disch. Aug. 20, 63.

Seventeenth Regiment.

The 17th Regiment contained no Cornish men.

Eighteenth Regiment.

The 18th Regiment contained but one man from Cornish:

David B. Hill, Co. E. Age 34, enl. Sept. 22, 64, from Conway, disch. June 10, 65. This regiment was raised for twelve months' service.

Other Branches of Military Service.

Besides the eighteen regiments heretofore mentioned, there were other branches of the military service to which Cornish contributed her share of men. Of the first cavalry furnished for the service from New England, New Hampshire sent in 1861, four companies: I, K, L, and M. These were called the "New Hampshire Battalion of the First New England Cavalry." Company L, contained two men credited to Cornish:

Michael Trodden, b. Ireland. Age 32, enl. Dec. 19, 61. Capt. and paro. Oct. 31, 62, at Mountsville, Va., exch. Dec. 16, 62, des. Dec. 16, 62, at Camp Parole, Annapolis, Md.

James P. Wheeler, b. Newport. Age 18, enl. Oct. 19, 61. Capt. June 18, 63, near Middleburg, Va., released July 23, 63, enl. 2d from Newport June 2, 64. Capt. Aug. 17, 64, at Winchester, Va., d. of dis. Nov. 19, 1864, at Danville, Va.

These four companies of the New Hampshire Battalion returned to Concord in February, 1864, and recruited for a regiment to be called the

First "New Hampshire Cavalry."

Cornish furnished for this regiment nineteen men. A few of these were good and true, but the greater portion being foreigners were "bounty-jumpers," and having little regard for the cause they professed to espouse, rendered but little important service, and after receiving their bounty, deserted on the first opportunity. Following is the list and record:

Alden Barker, b. in N. H.   Age 21, enl. June 29, 64, Co. E, des. at Concord, Aug. 6, 64.

Owen Barker, Co. E, b. Pomfret, Vt.   Age 21, enl. June 29, 64, d. of dis. Nov. 4, 1864, at Camp Stoneman, D. C.

John Burke, b. N. H.   Age 27, enl. Aug. 10, 64, des. Aug. 29, 64, at Camp Stoneman, D. C.

Ezra D. Clark, Co. A, b. N. H.   Age 28, enl. Mar. 19, 64, disch. July 15, 65.

John Conley, Co. F, b. Ireland.   Age 31, enl. Aug. 16, 64, des. Sept. 4, 64, at Camp Stoneman, D. C.

Patrick Conlor, b. Ireland.   Age 22, enl. Aug. 10, 64, des. en route to regiment.

John Dolan, b. Canada.   Age 21, enl. Aug. 11, 64, des. Aug. 27, 64, at Camp Stoneman, D. C.

Horace Dow, Co. A, b. Vt.   Age 28, enl. Mar. 19, 64, disch. June 10, 65, at Washington, D. C.

Alphonso N. Dunbar, Co. C, b. N. H.   Age 18, enl. Mar. 31, 64, des. Apr. 25, 65, at Concord, N. H.

Thomas I. Holbrook, Co. A.   Age 26, enl. Mar. 23, 64, disch. July 15, 65.

George W. Johnson, Co. A, b. Rockingham, Vt.   Age 18, enl. Mar. 9, 64.   Captd. June 30, 64, at Wilson's raid on Welden R. R., Va., escaped same day, disch. July 15, 65.

James B. Kidder, Co. C.   Age 19, enl. Mar. 31, 64, d. of dis. July 7, 64, on transport near City Point.

Isaac H. Kingsbury, Co. A, b. Danville, Vt.   Age 28, enl. 1st from Littleton, N. H., in Co. H, 3d N. H. Vols. July 30, 61, wd. June 16, 62, at Secessionville, S. C. app. Corp. Nov. 1, 62, disch. disab. Aug. 20, 63, at Botany Bay Island, S. C., enl. 2d Mar. 19, 64, and was credited to Cornish, app. Sergt.   Captd. June 30, 64, at Wilson's raid on Welden R. R., and d. of dis. and starvation at Andersonville prison, Ga., Nov. 13, 64.

James McBride, b. Ireland. Age 21, enl. Aug. 11, 64, des. same day at Camp Stoneman, D. C.

Edward Mitchell, b. Ireland. Age 21, enl. Aug. 10, 64, des. Aug. 29, 64, at Camp Stoneman, D. C.

Patrick Munroe, Co. H, b. New York. Age 22, enl. Aug. 18, 64, des. Sept. 4, 64, at Camp Stoneman, D. C.

Oliver P. Smith, b. N. H. Age 19, enl. 1st Dec. 27, 61 from —— in Co. F, 5th N. H. Vols., disch. disab. June 30, 62, enl. 2d Oct. 18, 62, in Co. A, 16th N. H. Vols., transf. to Co. A, 2d N. H. Vols. Apr. 16, 63, disch. Oct. 9, 63, enl. 3d Mar. 19, 64, in Co. A. N. H. Cav., app. Corp. May 1, 64, wd. June 13, 64, at White Oak Swamp, Va., disch. July 15, 65. Credited to Cornish.

Thomas Smith, b. Ireland. Age 22, enl. Aug. 10, 64, des. Aug. 29, 64, at Camp Stoneman, D. C.

George T. Wentworth, Co. K, b. Great Falls. Age 21, enl. Mar. 19, 64, disch. July 15, 65.

Heavy Artillery.

Two companies of this branch were organized in New Hampshire in 1863, serving at Fort Constitution and Kittery Point. In 1864 a regiment of twelve companies was raised in the state of which these two companies became a part. It was employed chiefly in the defence of Washington, and was mustered out June 15, 1865. Eleven Cornish men served in its ranks:

Daniel E. Carroll, Co. A. Age 18, enl. Aug. 20, 64, disch. Aug. 19, 65.

John B. Chase, Co. A. Age 30, enl. Sept. 6, 64, transf. to Cos. B and L, disch. Sept. 11, 65.

Barker B. Churchill, Co. L. Age 43, enl. Aug. 29, 64, transf. to Co. B, Artificer, disch. Sept. 11, 65.

Edgar A. Churchill, Co. L. Age 18, enl. Aug. 29, 64, transf. to Co. B, June 10, 65, disch. Sept. 11, 65.

Edmund H. Cobb, Co. B. Age 42, enl. Mar. 18, 65, disch. disab. Dec. 5, 64.

Erastus O. Cole, Co. B, b. Barnard, Vt. Age 34, enl. Mar. 18, 64, disch. Sept. 11, 65.

Josiah Davis, Co. B, b. Springfield, N. H. Age 34, enl. Aug. 31, 63, app. Sergt, disch. Sept. 11, 65, as Orderly Sergt.

Charles R. Leslie, Co. B.   Age 19, enl. Mar. 18, 64, disch. Sept. 11, 65.

Samuel Merrill, Co. A, b. Hudson, N. H.   Age 43, enl. Aug. 31, 64. disch. Sept. 11, 65.

Sydney K. Richardson, Co. A.   Age 18, enl. Aug. 31, 64, disch. Sept. 11, 65.

Eli B. Stearns, Co. A, b. Highgate, Vt.   Age 36, enl. Aug. 8, 64, disch. Sept. 11, 65.

Sharpshooters.

There was but one man who enlisted in this service from Cornish, while some residents and natives enlisted in it elsewhere as shown later:

Oliver M. Fletcher, Co. F, 2d.   Age 23, enl. Oct. 9, 61, disch. for disability, June 21, 62.

United States Navy.

Clement Antoine, b. Western Islands.   Age 30, enl. Jan. 26, 65, rank, seaman, served on U. S. S. S. *Ohio,* d. Feb. 8, 65, in hospital at Boston.

Patrick Dawson, b. Ireland.   Age 38, enl. Jan. 24, 65, rank, coal heaver, served on U. S. S. S. *Ohio* and *Connecticut,* des. from receiving ship Sept. 9, 65.

Daniel Driscoll, b. Ireland.   Age 22, enl. Jan. 27, 65, rank, seaman, served on U. S. S. S. *Ohio* and *Wachusett,* des. from latter Mar. 4, 65.

John Hayes, b. Philadelphia.   Age 32, enl. Jan. 24, 65, rank, seaman, served on U. S. S. S. *Ohio, Wachusett* and *Hartford,* disch. as Coxswain from the latter Aug. 14, 68.

Charles A. Jackson.   Age 20, enl. Aug. 23, 62, rank, landsman, served on U. S. S. S. *Ohio, Princeton* and *Augusta,* disch. Aug. 4, 63.

Robert H. Jackson, b. N. Y. City.   Age 30, enl. Jan. 24, 65, rank, landsman, served on U. S. S. S. *Ohio, Sea Foam* and *Winnipec,* d. of dis. on the latter Mar. 18, 66.

David Lambert, b. New Brunswick.   Age 24, enl. Feb. 7, 65, rank, seaman, served on U. S. S. S. *Ohio, Kearsarge, Tahoma* and *Yucca,* disch. disab. from receiving ship at N. Y., May 30, 67.

James H. Mitchell, b. Kittery. Me. Age 28, enl. Jan. 24, 65, rank, ordinary seaman, served on U. S. S. S. *Ohio* and *Wachusett*, disch. as sail-maker's mate Jan. 8, 68.

Thomas Rodgers, b. Denmark. Age 29, enl. Feb. 6, 65, rank, seaman. Served on U. S. S. S. *Ohio*, *Kearsarge* and *Frolic*, disch. as quartermaster from the latter Sept. 25, 68.

William H. Smith. Age 19, enl. Mar. 4, 64. Served on U. S. S. S. *Ohio* and *Cherokee*, disch. from receiving ship at Philadelphia, Mar. 12, 65.

William Thomas, b. Barnstable. Age 25, enl. Jan. 26, 65, rank, seaman. Served on U. S. S. S. *Ohio*, *Wachusett* and *Hartford*, disch. Aug. 14, 68.

The following additional list of men were residents or natives of Cornish, who enlisted elsewhere and were credited to the towns where they enlisted. The names and records of a few such have already been given in connection with the branch of service named, and will be counted there in the summary.

Edward F. Chapman, b. Cornish. Age 21, enl. Aug. 22, 61, from Plainfield, 1st U. S. S. S., rank, bugler, disch. disab. Feb. 2, 62, at Washington, D. C., d. Oct. 16, 63, at Plainfield.

Levi L. Chapman, b. Cornish. Age 26, enl. Aug. 22, 61, from Plainfield, 1st U. S. S. S., rank, private, disch. Sept. 8, 64.

Beniah Colby, b. Hill, N. H. Age 55, res. Cornish, enl. Aug. 23, 61, from Franklin, wagoner, Co. H, 3d N. H., disch. disab. May 7, 62 at Edisto, S. C., enl. 2d Aug. 29, 64 Co. C, 24 V. R. C., rank, private, disch. for disab. Aug. 2, 65, at Washington, D. C.

Newell J. Ellis, b. Brandon, Vt. Age 24, res. Cornish, enl. Aug. 15, 64, in Co. G, 7th Vt., private, disch. July 14, 65.

William H. Ellis, b. Brandon, Vt. Age 30, res. Cornish, enl. Aug. 29, 62, in Co. C, 16th Vt., private, disch. Aug. 10, 63, enl. 2d Dec. 1, 63, in Co. G, 7th Vt., at Cavendish, Vt., disch. Mar. 20, 66, at Brattleboro, Vt.

Jason K. Ellis, b. Brandon, Vt. Age 21, res. Cornish, enl. Dec. 28, 63, in Co. G, 7th Vt., private. Lost at explosion of steamer *N. America*, Dec. 22, 64.

Warren H. Fletcher, b. Cornish. Age 23, enl. Oct. 8, 61, from Claremont in Co. G, 2d U. S. S. S., private ———— enl. 2d Dec.

21, 63, from Nashua, N. H., app. Corp., Jan. 1, 62., Sergt.
Apr. 12, 64, 2d Lieut. Nov. 21, 64, transf. to 5th N. H. Jan. 30,
65, app. 1st Lieut Co. F, May 1, 65, assigned to Co. G, June
12, 65, disch. June 28, 65, as 2d Lieut.

Edmund Hardy, b. Cornish.   Age 28, enl.————from————rank,
d. at ———— May 30, 63.

Lewis S. Hoyt, b. Cornish.   Age 32, enl. Dec. 6, 61, from Nashua,
N. H., in Co. G, 2d U. S. S. S., private, disch. disab. Mar. 24, 62
at Washington, D. C.

John H. Humphrey, b. Benson, Vt.   Age 25, enl. Aug. 1, 62, from
Plainfield in Co. E, 9th N. H., private, disch. disab. Nov.
21, 62, at Washington, D. C., enl. 2d Aug. 31, 64, from Cornish
in Co. A, 24th V. R. C., app. Commissary Sergt., July 1,
65, disch. Nov. 14, 65, at Washington, D. C.

Oliver Jackson, b. Cornish.   Age 25, enl. Oct. 2, 61, from Manchester, N. H. in Co. F,   2d U. S. S. S., private, enl. 2d Dec.
21, 63, in same reg. and Co., transf. to 5th N. H. Jan. 30, 65,
assigned to Co. H, June 17, 65, disch. June 28, 65.

John S. Kenyon, b. Cornish.   Age 26, res. Cornish, enl. May 31,
62, in Co. D, 9th Vt., private.   Captd. and paroled Sept. 15, 62,
disch. disab. Apr. 16, 63.

Charles B. Sisson, b. Fall River, Mass.   Age 18, res. Cornish,
enl. Oct. 11, 61, in Co. E, 1st Vt. Cav., rank, saddler.
Captd. May — 62, near Winchester, Va., paroled Sept. 62, enl.
2d Dec. 28, 63, in Co. 3, 1st Vt. Cav., wd. June 13, 64, at White
Oak Swamp Bridge, Va., transf. to Co. A, June 21, 65, disch.
Aug. 9, 65.

William H. Sisson, b. Fall River, Mass.   Age 22, res. Cornish,
enl. Aug. 11, 62, in Co. F, 1st Mass. Cav., private, wd. Sept.
14, 63, at Rapidan Sta., Va., disch. Nov. 7, 64, at Boston, Mass.

David Squires, b. Cornish.   Age 20, res. Cornish, enl. May 31,
62, in Co. D, 9th Vt., private.   Captd. and paroled Sept. 15, 62,
disch. disab. May 26, 63.

William H. Smith, b. Cornish.   Age 24, res. Cornish, enl. Aug.
5, 61, in 16th Mass., musician, disch. Aug. 9, 62.

Charles Tasker, b. Sullivan, N. H.   Age 18, res. Cornish, enl.
Sept. 3, 61, in Co. K, 4th Vt., private, transf. to Co. A, 6th
U. S. Cav., Oct. 30, 62.   Captd. July 3, 63, at Fairfield, Va.,
paroled Aug. 2, 63, disch. Sept. 7, 65, at Frederick, Md.

During the summer and fall of 1863, the demand for recruits exceeded the supply. More men were needed than had volunteered for the service; so the government ordered a draft to be enforced in certain military districts in several states.

The third congressional and military district of New Hampshire, with headquarters at West Lebanon, was ordered to furnish a certain number of men as her quota. Capt. Chester Pike was the Provost Marshal of the district during the war. Acting under the orders of Gov. J. A. Gilmore, he, with his aids, quietly enforced a draft on September 3, 1863, upon all the towns in his district.

The following is the list of men who were drafted from Cornish, in all thirty-seven names, between the ages of eighteen and forty-five:

Newell I. Comings	John M. Deming
George B. Walker	Samuel F. Ayers
Sumner P. Tewksbury	Albert Penniman
Frank S. Edminster	Henry C. Freeman
Frank B. Deming	Lewis Dorman
John B. Chase	William D. Lear
Edwin T. Ayers	S. W. Bryant
Henry Ayers	Eli W. White
Wm. H. Stickney	Lucian O. Williams
Albert Weld	John B. Stevens
Samuel F. Bartlett	Horace L. Bugbee
Edwin H. Smith	Philander W. Smith
Marvin J. Deming	Geo. W. Richardson
Newell J. Ellis	Charles N. Kenyon
Edward Bryant	Julius Dorman
William E. Westgate	Manson Stevens
Frank B. Chapman	Lewis F. Knights
Adolphus G. Vinton	Francis E. Freeman

Martin M. Williams

A part of these men were exempt from service by reason of physical or mental infirmities, while several others purchased a release by the payment of three hundred dollars, or by furnishing a substitute. The balance entered the service.

The foregoing lists probably lack completeness, yet they

conform to the records as received from the state department,
with a few additional names derived from other authentic sources.

The aggregate of all the foregoing lists is 202 men. Of this
number 161 were credited to the town of Cornish and forty-one
were credited to the towns where they enlisted. Of the 161 men
credited to Cornish, several were of foreign birth and were hired
as substitutes or otherwise, to replenish the ranks. A part of
these proved to be "bounty-jumpers" for, after receiving their
bounty, they deserted upon the first convenient opportunity,
as shown by their records.

The town during this crisis was always liberal in the payment
of additional bounties and in providing for the wants of families
of needy soldiers. As a result the town was obliged to hire money
wherever obtainable to meet the requirements of the times.

With a surplus in the treasury of $340 in 1861, the indebt-
edness of the town in 1865 reached the sum of $37,000, then
the war closed, so this proved to be the maximum amount of
the indebtedness of the town. This was gradually liquidated
during the years that followed.

OLD CONGREGATIONAL CHURCH

TRINITY CHURCH, EPISCOPALIAN

BAPTIST CHURCH AT THE FLAT

CONGREGATIONAL CHURCH, AT THE CENTER

FORMERLY METHODIST, NOW UNITARIAN

CHAPTER VIII.

CHURCHES.

A PROMINENT feature in the character of our forefathers was, they were men and women of prayer. In every emergency the mercy-seat was their first and last resort.

"I hear the pilgrims' peaceful prayer
Swelling along the silent air
Amid the forest wild."

Their expectation was from God alone. They hung helpless on his arm, and poured out their fervent believing desires into his ear. Nor did they plead in vain. They had power with God. Eternity alone will fully disclose the influence of their supplications.

They observed the Sabbath with great seriousness. They prepared for its approach by a seasonable adjustment of their temporal affairs. They welcomed its arrival with joy, and spent its hours in the public and private duties of religion. A sacred stillness reigned in their habitations and neighborhoods, well befitting the day of God, and well calculated to raise their affections and thoughts to the eternal rest of Heaven.

The Puritan element and their principles were found in all of the New England Colonies, wherever they settled, and from diaries, letters and other records still in existence, it is evident that the pioneers of Cornish thus recognized their dependence upon a Sovereign power and intelligence. They were sterling men and women, inured to toil for their daily sustenance, training their oftentimes large families as the wise man directs. Few, indeed, were the homes in which the children were not taught the Lord's Prayer, "Now I lay me," and other similar lessons as soon as their infantile lips could lisp the words.

Thus was Cornish settled under very favorable auspices, so far as regards its moral and religious status.

Coming, however, from different communities and from churches of different shades of belief, it could hardly be expected that entire harmony would continue to exist, for, as the population increased, each class or church sought to strengthen its own interests. These conditions served to separate the varying creeds, each from the other, causing more or less acrimony to exist between them.

This state of affairs had a tendency to increase the number of churches and worshiping assemblies of the town. The relations between these different churches, especially at the first, seemed void of that Christian fellowship, so highly commended in the sacred word. Differences of opinion, too, on doctrinal points between different members of the same church, frequently led to bitter disputes and withdrawals. This condition of religious affairs was odious to the feelings of a large number of the citizens of the town. Their better sense sought to prevail, as is shown by the following action of the town:

On May 17, 1790, a call for a meeting of the town was issued, the chief business being to promote the religious unity of the town. The petition was as follows:

"We, whose names are hereunder written, inhabitants of the town of Cornish, do most ardently wish that some plan that is general, Catholic and Charitable may be adopted by the different Churches and the inhabitants at large to unite and form one worshiping assembly and settle the gospel ministry and ordinances among us for mutual good and special benefit of our families and rising generation, and being sensible of the inability of the inhabitants of this town to support several ministers and several different worshipping assemblies, and that we are now losing all the pleasures and advantages of religious society and public worship, and depriving our dear children, and the rising age of those opportunities to cultivate morals & religion which a good and Gracious God has most evidently provided both for us and them, while we are contending, disputing, indulging and promoting separation among us, that some kind, conciliating, effectual measures may be adopted by the inhabitants of this town to unite in the call and settlement of some wise, judicious and prudent gentleman in the ministry. We do unite in a petition to the gentlemen Selectmen to warn a meeting of the inhabitants of this town, to be holden on Wednesday the second day of June (1790) at the old meeting house in this town at one o'clock P. M. then and there to act on this article:

"To take into consideration the general matters mentioned in our petition, and see whether the inhabitants of this town will consent to propose, consider and finally to adopt any measure that may be advisable to effect as general a union in town as may be in supporting publick worship, and hereafter in calling and settling a gospel minister among us, such as that be entertaining and agreeable to the gospel in general.

(Signed)

Daniel Putnam	Samuel Putnam
William Deming	Joseph Taylor
John Vinton	Stephen Child
Eleazer Jackson	Benj. Comings
Abijah Tucker	Seth Deming
William Chase	Nathl. Carpenter
John Morse	Benjn. Jackson
Ebenezer Deming	

CORNISH, May 17, 1790.

"The town met agreeably to the above call and chose a committee to reduce the petition into articles suitable for the town to act upon. The committee were:—Ithamar Chase, Caleb Chase & Lieut. Eleazer Jackson. The meeting was adjourned to June 16th inst. at which time the town again met and considered the petition, and adopted measures well calculated to restore harmony among them. The committee advised, 1st, That the town recommend to the different churches to choose a committee of conference to settle the unhappy disputes existing and agree to submit, in case they do not agree, to mutual arbitration.

"2^d That a 'Union Society' be formed whose purpose shall be to promote as general a union as possible among the churches and the inhabitants of the town; and that a committee be chosen to carry out these plans.

"The report of the committee was accepted, and a committee was chosen consisting of Ebenezer Deming, Lt. Eleazer Jackson and Caleb Chase, for the purpose above mentioned."

As the above record is all that can be found relative to the "Union Society," it is to be inferred that it did not become a success, well intentioned though it may have been.

As years and decades have since passed by, the different denom-

inations have assumed a more friendly attitude towards one
another and not infrequently unite their efforts in a common
cause.

Congregational Church.

The first settlers of the town were largely of the Congregational
persuasion. As subjects of the Crown, the grantees of the town
were required to lay out two hundred acres for the church of
England; two hundred acres for the propagation of the gospel,
and two hundred acres for the first settled minister. The proprietors made ample provision in grants of land for the support
of the gospel ministry dissenting from the church of England.
At their first meeting after the survey and division of the town into
lots, they voted that "there be at least one hundred & fifty acres
of good land laid out in Cornish and set apart towards supporting
a dissenting minister of the gospel in said town." They also
voted at a subsequent meeting "to give one thousand acres of as
good land as then remained undivided, to settle and maintain
a dissenting gospel minister among them."

In 1767, two years after the settlement of the town (which
now numbered thirteen families), measures were first taken to
settle a minister.

The reader need remember that at that early period church and
state had not been divorced. The towns regarded it as their
right to manage all the prudential concerns of the church; to
raise the necessary funds for their support, and employ their
ministers and pay them for their services. So then a minister
was pastor not only of the church, but of the town.

On April 28, 1768, the town met to take action upon settling
its first minister. The proposition was enthusiastically entertained, as the town voted unanimously to extend a call to Rev.
James Wellman, of Sutton, Mass., to become its minister. Several of the families were from the same place and belonged to his
congregation in Sutton. These, therefore, desired that he should
become their pastor in their new settlement.

After the terms regarding his salary had been adjusted, Mr.
Wellman, with his family, moved to Cornish. The citizens
of Windsor, Vt., united with Cornish in this project, with the understanding that he should preach in Windsor one third of the
time, and that one third of his salary for the first five years

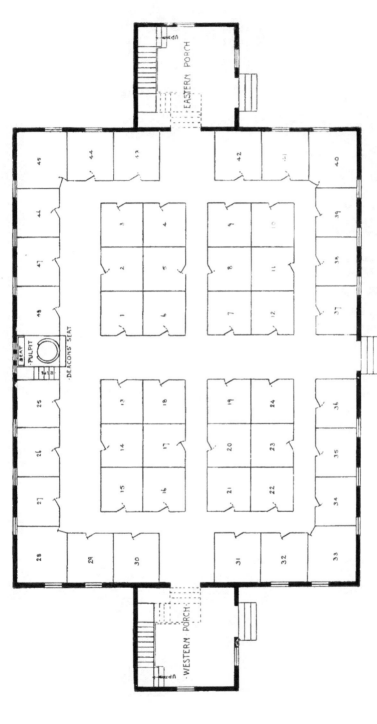

INTERIOR VIEW OF THE OLD CONGREGATIONAL CHURCH ON THE HILL—GROUND FLOOR

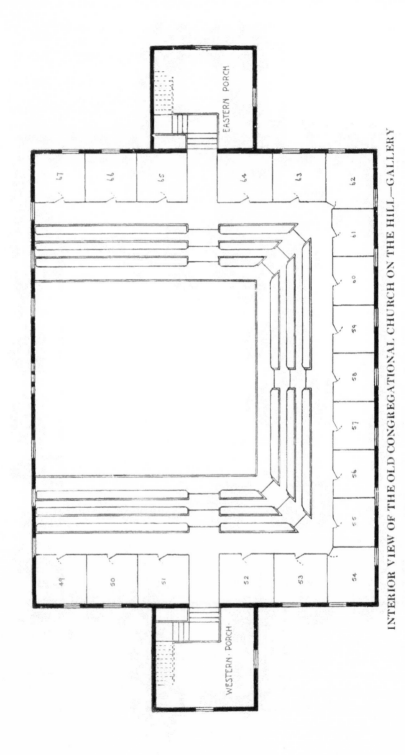

INTERIOR VIEW OF THE OLD CONGREGATIONAL CHURCH ON THE HILL—GALLERY

should be raised there. A council of churches met September 29, 1768, and organized a church, called the "Congregational Church of Cornish and Windsor." At this time it consisted of ten members—six of Cornish and four of Windsor; and Mr. Wellman was installed as minister and pastor of the church and towns of Cornish and Windsor.

The church was formed under a covenant which consisted of the "confession of guilt and inability to do that which is acceptable to God,—the profession of their belief in the Christian religion as revealed in the scriptures,—the scriptures as the Word of God, —the acknowledgment of their obligations to glorify God by a holy and righteous life,—the consecration of themselves and their children to God,—the engagement to walk in love together,— to maintain discipline,—to keep the Lord's Day holy, and attend upon the public worship of God,—to maintain family worship, and to train up all under their care in the paths of holiness and virtue."

Public worship was held in barns in summer, and in dwelling houses in winter, until the fall of 1773 when a meeting house was erected on the banks of the Connecticut River. The people met for public worship clad in garments of home-made cloth,— men and boys with coarse woolen hats and caps, and striped blue woolen or linen frocks and pantaloons. The women were dressed in woolen or linen gowns and checkered blue aprons. In a few instances men gathered for worship on the Sabbath with guns in their hands from fear of the attack of Indians.

Troubles of various kinds soon beset them. It was with difficulty that the pastor's salary was raised. Money was very scarce. The land set apart for ministerial purposes was sold, and the avails expended at the expiration of two years. Dissatisfaction also sprung up in the church respecting the receiving to membership those of doubtful doctrine and practice.

On account of this, six brethren withdrew from the communion, and presented to the church their reasons for so doing November, 1778. Much controversy followed, which resulted in the withdrawing brethren setting up public worship by themselves in 1779.

In the fall and winter of 1780–81, a Reverend Mr. Powers labored among the people in word and doctrine. A revival was the result. Most of the families in the eastern and northern part

of the town were affected by the revival, and many were
converted, yet the dissatisfied brethren did not resume their
allegiance to the church.

Reverend Mr. Wellman and church were much tried by this separate worship and the sanction given it by neighboring ministers.
So the church asked the advice of the Council, December 18,
1780. The Council approved the action, and sustained the complaint of the church. The withdrawing brethren became more
than ever dissatisfied with the condition and character of the
church; and invited a convention of churches in April, 1781, to
examine their grounds of complaint. The convention met and
appointed another session at Lebanon in June, 1781, and sent a
summons to Reverend Mr. Wellman, to appear before them.
The summons was treated with a measure of contempt by Mr.
Wellman and his church. He, however, sent a message to the
convention, denying its jurisdiction and refusing to appear
before them, giving six reasons therefor. This evidently prejudiced the convention against Mr. Wellman and his church, as
results afterwards showed.

The convention proceeded, and in its report severely censured
the pastor and church for their action, and "openly declared
that they could not recognize said church as a church of Christ,
and that they felt themselves in duty bound to withdraw communion and renounce fellowship with them in the special
ordinances of the Gospel until they shall be restored to our charity by visible repentance."

This church was never again received to the fellowship of the
other churches. Reverend Mr. Wellman continued to preach until October, 1785, when the churches of Claremont and Charlestown convened in council at Cornish and dissolved the pastoral
relation of Reverend Mr. Wellman to the church and town.

Thus terminated the existence of the First Congregational
Church in Cornish. Her light went out in darkness after a brief
existence of seventeen years and six months. The number of
members received to full communion during this time was sixty-
four. To half-way communion, forty-two.

The town had been divided (in June, 1781), into east and west
parishes by an act of the Legislature upon petition of the citizens
of Cornish to that effect. Attempts were afterwards made to
establish two separate churches,—one in each parish. The

Windsor association at first recommended this plan, but afterwards, October 14, 1800, retracted their former decision. A church was partially erected in the northwestern part of the town in 1787, but was never fully completed. Another was erected near the center of the town in 1788. The former was located on or near the farm of Nathaniel Johnson, and the latter on the John Morse farm, situated south, and several rods below the site where the Center Church was afterwards built. This latter was styled the "East Church."

On December 1, 1790, a council was convened at the Northwest Meeting house, and Rev. Benjamin Bell was installed for the term of five years as pastor of the two churches in Cornish, beside preaching in Windsor. His services in Cornish were to be rendered at the Northwest Meeting house. The brethren of the East Church remonstrated and would not unite with their brethren of the Northwest Church. These two branches or churches soon began to realize the reproach they were bringing upon the Gospel of Christ by their visible estrangement from each other. Reverend Mr. Bell closed his labors in Cornish in April, 1795; and the two divisions or churches began to meet in conference, and proposals for reunion were made by each and reasonably considered. Such confession and acknowledgments were rendered by individuals of both sections that a mutual agreement was made to unite in one body. This was publicly done December 13, 1795. Although thus *formally* united, they were *not* all of one heart and one mind.

In the fall of 1797 and the winter following, Rev. Siloam Short, a faithful and earnest minister of the Gospel, labored among them. The Holy Spirit descended in great power upon the church and community. This brought the church together, and also to its right mind, doing the very thing that brethren, ministers, councils, and associations had failed to accomplish. When "*God spake it was done.*" The church came up from its dark state "beautiful as Tirzah." The brethren were humbled in their own sight. They came together of one accord. Four successive days they spent in prayer, in confession one to another and to the church, and in asking and receiving forgiveness of one another and the church. Converts unto righteousness were multiplied, and seventy-six were added to the church as the result of this gracious visitation of the Holy Spirit.

9

The following year (1799), the church, now apparently united, and harmonious, erected a large and commodious house of worship upon the hill near the center of the town. It was the general place for worship for the greater part of the inhabitants of the town, with an average congregation of nearly eight hundred, and in some instances nearly or quite a thousand souls.

On September 24, 1800, Rev. Joseph Rowell was ordained and installed pastor of the church, which relation he maintained until April 1, 1828, when he was dismissed. The church enjoyed three precious seasons of revival during his ministry, and 157 individuals were converted and added to the church. (See Rowell.) November 29, 1828, Rev. Joseph W. Clary was installed pastor of the church for five years. He was born in Rowe, Mass., in 1786; graduated at Middlebury College in 1808; studied theology at Andover, Mass., and was installed pastor of the Congregational Church in Dover from 1812 to 1828. His ministry in Cornish was blessed by two revivals, one in 1829 and the other in 1831, and seventy-six were gathered into the church. He was dismissed in October, 1834.

On October 1, 1835, Rev. Alvah Spaulding was installed pastor of the church, which relation he maintained until February 7, 1865, when he was dismissed. Several seasons of revival were enjoyed during his pastorate. (See Spaulding Gen.) During his pastorate, the peace and harmony of the church was again disturbed. The meeting house on the hill was becoming old and uncomfortable, especially for the winter season, and the subject of locating and building a new house of worship absorbed the minds of the people. The church did not, and would not, agree upon the location of the new house of worship. Some wanted it built southwest of the church hill, while the larger number chose the interval lying north of the same. The majority prevailed, and the new meeting house, the present building, was built in 1841.

This action resulted in a division of the church, and the withdrawal of the minority from its fellowship. This included several families of influence and caused a sore loss to the church.

After a while the church seemed to recover from the effects of this trial; and her history since then has afforded few striking events, but rather a prolonged chapter of blessings.

Soon after the close of Reverend Mr. Spaulding's pastorate,

Rev. Philander Bates became "acting pastor," serving the church nearly five years, or until December 28, 1870. He was born September 26, 1810, and died April 19, 1873. He was a graduate of Amherst College.

In May, 1871, Rev. Charles M. Palmer, from Harrisville, became pastor of the church. His connection with it ended in March, 1873, when he received a call from the church in Meriden, which he accepted. (See Palmer Gen.)

On December 17, 1874, Rev. James T. Jackson of Danbury, was ordained and installed pastor. In this capacity he served the church nearly twenty-two years, until failing health induced him to ask for a dismission. This was granted, and he removed to Merrimac, Mass., March 12, 1896. (See Jackson Gen.) His union with the church was a very happy and pleasant one both for pastor and people. Social and kind-hearted, he, with his equally gifted wife, endeared themselves to the people of their charge, as well as to all others by their kindly ministrations. The Old People's Visit (which see), since so famous and popular, was originated by this worthy couple in August, 1877. Since the close of Reverend Mr. Jackson's pastorate the church has had no settled pastor, but only short terms of service, by "acting pastors." Chief among these were the Reverends Silas G. Tucker, Maurice J. Duncklee, Perley Grant, J. E. Heath, A. J. Bailey of Meriden and D. T. Davies.

It was on November 6, 1781, in the midst of solemn services incident to such occasions, that men of God, having due authority therefor, pronounced this "East Church of Cornish," a "Church of Jesus Christ." On November 9, 1881 (the sixth, being on Sunday), in the midst of Rev. James T. Jackson's pastorate, the church again assembled and celebrated its centennial with thankfulness and joy. Invitations had been extended to all former pastors, officers and members then living, and a very generous response was manifested. The season was a very enjoyable one,—a real home-gathering occupying the day and evening. The history of the church was given by the pastor and also by Rev. Joshua W. Wellman. Letters were read, and reminiscences of great interest were given, interspersed by religious exercises and choice selections of music appropriate to the occasion.

The Second Division.

The outcome of the minority that withdrew from the parent Congregational Church furnishes an interesting, though brief and sad chapter.

After the location of the present meeting house had been settled upon in 1841, and active measures adopted for building the same, a large and important portion of the church in the southern and western parts of the town felt aggrieved, and decided they could no longer remain in fellowship with the other portion. The "high hills" of separation arose between them. It was a grief to each portion, and especially so to the minority, but the "die had been cast," the new house was being erected and these, feeling themselves ostracised from the main body, took counsel and agreed to associate themselves together and set up worship by themselves. Accordingly they called a meeting on June 4, 1841, and chose a committee to prepare articles of association. These were soon reported, and also a code of by-laws, all of which were adopted, and the new organization assumed the name of "The First Congregational Society of Cornish." Public-spirited men among them, at their own expense, erected a parsonage with vestry attached, during the first year. This they located near the junction of the two roads leading towards Windsor. This is the church parsonage building of the present day.

On the September following they took united action about building a new meeting house (42 x 56) on ground in the rear of the new parsonage, to be completed on or before November 1, 1842, and chose the necessary committee to carry out their plans.

The house was completed within the specified time. The pews were all engaged or sold and the horse sheds erected during the year. The avails from the sale of the pews were insufficient to meet the expenses incurred, thus leaving them considerably in debt. This they were never able to fully liquidate.

In 1843, they invited Rev. Rufus A. Putnam of Epsom to preach for them. Opposition from outside was soon manifested, but he was employed nevertheless, and preached for them until October 18, 1846, when he was dismissed.

The Sullivan County Association, having jurisdiction over all the Congregational churches in the county, had never looked with favor upon this offshoot from the main body. It was their mind that the members who withdrew in 1841 should have acquiesced with the will of the majority, hence their opposition to another and separate church in Cornish.

On the other hand, the new organization felt its cause to be *just*, and so moved vigorously forward, as if there was no opposition. October 15, 1845, they met for the purpose of organizing a *church* to be connected with their society. This was affirmed by an unanimous vote and committees were appointed to perfect all necessary arrangements; they afterwards appointed November 11, 1845, as the day for convening a council and organizing the church. The numbers of the council present were not sufficient, therefore the event was postponed until December 10, 1845, when the council was present, and the church was organized and pronounced a religious church of Christ, and in fellowship with the churches of Christ. The first called meeting of the church was on January 29, 1846, when they voted that their name should be: "The Evangelical Congregational Church in Cornish."

The second meeting of the church was March 20, 1846, when it was voted that, under existing circumstances, it was advisable that the church receive to its membership all those having no letters of dismission from the parent church, as that body had refused to acknowledge them as a separate body.

About this time the Sullivan County Association assumed a more determined attitude against them. In the *Congregational Journal* of May 12, 1846, an account was published of the Association's proceedings against them stating that they refused to acknowledge this new church as one of their body. Its doom, as a church, was now sealed. *It was compelled to die.* This action of the Association called forth a lengthy and vigorous protest from the church, in which they set forth in a very able manner their grievances and claims; but all to no use. The powers were against them. The following October, Reverend Mr. Putnam and wife were dismissed from the church, and no other preacher succeeded him, only as an occasional one may have chanced to render a service.

"Loving the Gates of Zion," the people often assembled in their new and beloved house of worship, sometimes having the benefit of preaching, but oftener otherwise. In this way matters continued until the 26th of December, 1850, when they voted "to give letters of recommendation to any and all of their members, desiring to unite with any other Evangelical Church.

This was the last meeting of the "Evangelical Congregational Church of Cornish."

"The First Congregational Society of Cornish," associated with said church, continued to exist (only in name) a little longer. Its last recorded meeting was held March 7, 1853, and signed by Jesse O. Wyman, clerk. The house was then closed.

Baptist Church.

Among those who first came to Cornish were individuals who believed in the principles and practice of the Baptist denomination. These principles or tenets briefly stated, are:

(1) "Liberty of conscience. (2) That civil magistrates have no authority from God to regulate or control religion. (3) Baptism by immersion."

Reverends Jedediah Hibbard, Job Seamans, Abiel Ledoyt and several other missionary preachers of this persuasion occasionally visited the town, and aided in laying the foundation of a church of this order.

The church was duly organized July, 1789, in a barn owned by Moses Barrows, situated about forty rods southwest of the summit of "Furnald Hill" and about one mile northwest from where the church now stands. There were but nine members, Jonas and Zilpha Richardson, Moses and Elizabeth Barrows, Samuel and Rebecca Meekers, Nathaniel Dustin, Elizabeth Thompson and Charity Barrows. An addition of six members was made during the following year.

It was organized by Rev. Jedediah Hibbard, who became its first pastor. He held this position until 1796, preaching but a part of the time in Cornish, as his duties as a missionary preacher often called him abroad.

No records of the church have been preserved earlier than June 24, 1791. On this date the following votes were passed:

"1st That Bro. Richardson act as moderator to govern s^d. meeting.

"2d Chose Moses Weld, standing Clerk.

"3d Chose Samuel Hibbard, Deacon.

"4th Chose Elder Hibbard, standing moderator.

"5th Voted that Deacon Hilliard act as moderator in the absence of Elder Hibbard.

"6th Voted to Commune the third Sunday in every second month."

On the 17th of September, 1791, the following record was made:

"1st Voted to join the Woodstock Vt. Association, with their consent.

"2d Chose Elder Hibbard, Deacon Hilliard, John Weld and Moses Weld messengers to said association.

"3d Chose Moses Weld to write a letter to the association from the church."

Their union with the Woodstock Association was effected, and they remained connected with it until 1828.

"On Sunday ye 2^d of October, 1791, the church pas^d. the following vote: Chose Elder Hibbard, Dea. Samuel Hilliard and Bro. Moses Weld to sit in Council at Croydon on the 12th of October inst. for the purpose of installing Elder Abiel Ledoyt as pastor of the Baptist Church in Croydon."

July 3, 1792, the church expressed their "approbation that Dea. Samuel Hilliard should improve his gift in public."

"On Sept. 20, 1792, John Weld was chosen deacon and Moses Weld as leader in singing. At the same time a committee was chosen to confer with the Plainfield Baptist Church in regard to supporting preaching together."

"May 3^d, 1794, voted to raise twenty pounds for preaching, each man paying according to his property."

"December 19, 1794, voted that the meetings be held at the center meetinghouse during the pleasure of the church."

During several of the first years, the church held its meetings in various places, generally in the families of its members; sometimes in the Center Church, and sometimes, in warm weather, in barns and groves. A building of one roof, standing near Arunah Burnap's house on the Flat, and bearing the unpoetical name of "Salt Box" was used for a considerable time as a house of worship.

March 4, 1797, a committee was appointed to confer with the Newport Baptist Church about joining it as a branch of said church. This project failed of success.

After the close of Elder Hibbard's labors with the church, Dea. Samuel Hilliard performed the duties of a preacher, rendering acceptable service for some time, at one time receiving forty dollars compensation therefor.

In the year 1798 there was a great spiritual awakening in Cornish and Plainfield through the ministry of Rev. Siloam Short, an evangelist. Many were added to both Congregational and Baptist churches during this season.

On the 26th of December, 1798, the church voted to provide the first utensils for communion service at the expense of the church and chose Dea. John Weld to procure them.

February 13, 1799, the church voted "that it is the opinion of the church that we are not able to support preaching statedly the ensuing year." A vote on February 27, 1799, was passed to attempt to unite with the Congregationalists in joint worship, each paying their proportion for preaching. After careful consideration, this project was abandoned and the vote was reconsidered July 11, 1799. Differences of opinion on this matter caused some alienation of feeling but on June 9, 1800, it was voted "to bury all unkind feelings and walk together in fellowship and brotherly love."

Thus every attempt to unite with other religious bodies failed.

In the year 1801, when numbering about thirty members, the church invited Elder Ariel Kendrick, who was about closing a pastorate in Salisbury, to become their pastor. He accepted their invitation and came and continued as pastor for nearly twenty years. After this, still remaining in town, he supplied the pulpit in the interim between two or three succeeding pastorates. He was a humble and unpretentious preacher, but well versed in Scripture and sound on the tenets of the sect. During his pastorate, the church enjoyed three seasons of revival,— thus strengthening her graces and adding many to her numbers. (See Kendrick Gen.)

In the year 1803, during the second year of Elder Kendrick's ministry, the church erected a new meeting house on the hill at the Center of the town, in close proximity to the Congregational Church (already erected there in 1799). It remained there until the summer of 1818 when, for various reasons, it was taken down and removed to its present location on Cornish Flat. The dedication sermon of 1803 and the re-dedication sermon of

1818 were both preached by Rev. Aaron Leland of Chester, Vt., from the same text: Gen. 28:17. Following the erection of the church in 1803, the records show a term of prosperity and peace. Officers were chosen and measures adopted that promoted the welfare of the church.

In June, 1805, it was voted "to provide clothing for the poor, so they could all attend meeting."

After due consideration about introducing a bass viol into the church choir, it was voted to do so March 19, 1810.

September 2, 1810, "it was voted the duty of every family to maintain the worship of God in their families."

In 1811 an unpleasantness occurred involving both pastor and people. It was due to the pastor's interference in the domestic affairs of some of his parishioners. Although well intended, it wrought some bitterness, but it afforded a good lesson of wisdom for future guidance. From this time until the autumn of 1816, the church seemed to gain but little either in numbers or spirituality. But after the disastrous season of 1816, when Nature failed to reward the husbandman for his toil, the minds of the people were disposed to receive blessings from beyond the reach of frost and drought. Under such conditions, a work of grace began which lasted several months. During this time large numbers were converted, thus showing that "man's extremity is God's opportunity." During this revival about forty souls were added to the church.

In the year 1819 a still greater work was wrought, and the records show a list of sixty-four names added during the year.

On January 6, 1821, the church dismissed several of its members to assist in organizing a Baptist Church in Claremont.

Sometime during the year 1821 (date not definite), Elder Kendrick resigned the pastoral care of the church. From this time until June 29, 1826, the church had no pastor. Several different preachers came but evidently none of them were chosen.

On this last-named date, the church invited Elder Simeon W. Beckwith to become their pastor. He came and rendered very acceptable service, endearing himself to all the church and community, but death claimed him the following year on May 22, 1827. His remains rest in the cemetery at the Flat. A tablet was inscribed to his memory by the Free Masons of which fraternity he was a beloved member.

On August 30, 1827, the "First Baptist Society" of Cornish was organized and incorporated. This continued in existence, exercising its functions until February 15, 1904, when, as laws had been passed empowering churches to become corporate bodies, and to manage their own financial affairs that formerly had devolved upon the society, the society was of no further use, and on this date ceased to exist.

Early in the year 1828 Rev. Gibbon Williams, who was born March 13, 1797, in Monmouthshire, Eng., became pastor of the church. A solemn and impressive preacher and of agreeable manners, he proved an excellent pastor and the attachment between him and the church was very strong.

The Woodstock Association, of which the church was a member, was divided about this time, and a new one formed on the east side of the Connecticut River called the "Newport Baptist Association," and the Cornish church became a member of this body in September, 1828. During this year a parsonage was provided, in which was a room furnished for a vestry for social meetings. This building still remains standing at the west of the cemetery on the Flat.

In April, 1829, a donation of five hundred dollars was received from Dea. John Weld, the income of which was to be annually expended for preaching. Elder Williams closed his labors in Cornish, January 1, 1833, after a successful ministry of five years.

During Elder Williams' pastorate, a great revival occurred which is thus described by Mrs. Marcia L. Fletcher, an eye-witness, and also "one of them." It had its beginning in the old red schoolhouse at the "City," so called. She says: "The few isolated disciples there realized that a very large class of young people there were giving their early years to worldly pleasures and felt something must be done to save them. With fervent prayers they felt that works must unite with faith. So they requested Elder Williams to hold a meeting at the schoolhouse on a Sabbath evening at 'early candle light.' The appointment was given, although the pastor's faith at first was weak, thinking the effort would prove abortive. But to his happy surprise, the house was filled with a very attentive audience composed largely of young people. This strengthened his faith, so he appointed another meeting. This was in the autumn of 1830. The Woodstock Baptist Association was holding its anniversary with the

Windsor Baptist Church of which Elder Leland Howard was pastor. It was customary to send some of the ministers assembled to hold meetings in the neighboring districts in the evening of the first day of the session. So Elder Packard of Mt. Holly, Vt., was sent over the river to preach in the 'city' schoolhouse. The house was filled to its utmost capacity and a powerful sermon delivered from Gen. 24: 58. On returning to Windsor, he said to Elder Howard: 'There is going to be a revival over in Cornish and you had better go over and hold meetings there.' 'I will when there is a moon,' said Elder Howard. 'Don't wait for a moon,' replied Elder Packard, '*the Holy Spirit is there*.' From that time meetings were held two and three times a week by Elders Williams and Howard through the winter of 1830-31. Young people would walk several miles even on dark nights to attend the meetings. The climax was reached on a certain evening at a dwelling house, when, aided by brethren from Claremont, the Holy Spirit came in power. Old and young, strong men in the meridian of life, yielded to the sweet influences of the Spirit and it was estimated that nearly three hundred were converted during that revival. 'Those happy hours. How sweet their memory still!' It was a marked feature that very few of those professing conversion at this revival ever returned to the transitory pleasures of the world, thus evidencing a genuine work of grace in their hearts."

In the autumn of 1833 Oliver Barron became pastor. He was a good man of strong mind and convictions and of great energy, possessing that independence which led him sometimes to unnecessarily attack the opinions of others. His labors, however, were blessed by the addition of nearly one hundred souls. Among the years of these great revivals, there arose a class styling themselves "Universalists" that advocated tenets quite at variance with those of the other churches of the town. It is not known that they ever formed any organization in town, although they employed preachers and held many meetings. By consent they often used the meeting houses for their services.

Reverend Mr. Barron strenuously denounced them, giving them no quarter. On a certain Sabbath during his pastorate, these Universalists and the Baptists each claimed the use of the Baptist meeting house for the same hour of service. It became understood that the party first taking possession of the pulpit, after the unlocking of the doors, should occupy it for their service. After the doors were opened a rush was made for the pulpit by two strong men, representatives of each party, the Universalist leading. Just as they reached the "deacons' seats" at the foot of the pulpit, the hindmost man pushed the other into these seats, and, passing on, took possession of the pulpit. So that day they had Baptist services, but how profitable they were spiritually, the writer cannot say.

In 1837, after a pastorate of four years, Elder Barron closed his labors in Cornish. He was succeeded the same year by Rev. David Burroughs, who was born in Lyndeborough, N. H., August 10, 1810. He was a man of acknowledged ability and was greatly beloved by many.

About this time the anti-slavery movement was deeply agitating the people of the North, and the majority of the church, with their pastor, was in sympathy with it, while some entertained opposite opinions. For this cause a bitterness arose between brethren, resulting in the withdrawal of some from the church. The pastor's strong denunciation of slavery begat opposition in the community outside, as well as inside the church. Even the air was at times polluted with the ungracious epithets of "nigger," "black abolitionist," etc., but the pastor never failed to calmly express his humane convictions.

Some mischievous individuals bedaubed the white doors of the church with black paint, and on a certain Sabbath morning the pastor ascended the high pulpit stairs and found the pulpit already occupied by a black ram. He retraced his steps down the stairs and occupied the deacons' station as a pulpit for that forenoon. He made no allusion to the matter in his discourse, but the black occupant above, occasionally responded during the service, beside occasionally rising and standing on his hind legs, looking over the pulpit at the audience and causing much amusement for the children and the less seriously disposed part of the congregation.

In the summer of 1897 the writer enjoyed a pleasant correspondence with Elder Burroughs, who was then eighty-seven years of age. He wrote that near the beginning of his pastorate in Cornish, the weekly prayer-meeting became so reduced that often only two beside himself were present, namely: Arunah Burnap and Alvin Comings. "These brethren had faithfully remembered their covenant vows and so mutually agreed, if possible, *ever* to be present. Thus they 'held on' until they saw a grand awakening and nearly a hundred souls added to the church."

Elder Burroughs' pastorate in Cornish ended in the winter of 1841–42. He died August 30, 1898, aged eighty-eight, having spent sixty-five years of active labor in the ministry.

August 22, 1843, the church called Nahum P. Foster to preach for them. He accepted the call and was ordained May 29, 1844. His pastorate in Cornish continued until December 9, 1854, over ten years. He was a man of fine talents, pleasing personality and an agreeable preacher. His union with the church was a pleasant one. About thirty members were added to the church during his term of service. He was also a physician of skill, practicing medicine in connection with his ministerial labors. He was born in Fitzwilliam, N. H., February 10, 1814, and died in New London, Conn., May 6, 1876.

In 1845–46 the meeting house was remodeled. The old-time galleries, square pews, high pulpit and sounding board were removed. These gave place to the present audience room on the second floor with a vestry underneath.

In 1846 a new parsonage lot was secured near the meeting house and the present set of buildings were erected.

In January and February, 1856, revival meetings were held, conducted by Rev. John Peacock, evangelist, and about twenty united with the church as the result; sixteen of these were baptized February 17, 1856.

Rev. Phinehas Bond was the next pastor beginning in February, 1856. His pastorate closed in May, 1858. "He was an earnest, devoted man."

In December, 1858, Rev. D. P. Deming was secured as pastor. His term of service lasted seven years. His motto was, "owe no man anything but to love one another." Reducing this to practice, with the coöperation of the brethren a long-standing debt against the society was liquidated. The services of Elder Deming were very acceptable to the church and community. He was strictly evangelical and always in sympathy with those needing sympathy. This was his mother church. (See Deming Gen.) His services to the church ended December, 1865.

The Sunday school, which hitherto had been active only during the warm seasons, decided in 1860 that hereafter it should be active at all seasons of the year. This decision has ever since been complied with.

During the fall of 1866 and winter and spring following, Rev. John A. Baskwell preached for the church, but did not settle as pastor. He, however, rendered acceptable service.

November 17, 1867, Rev. Halsey C. Leavitt of Swanton, Vt., became pastor of the church. He was born in Gouverneur, N. Y., September 27, 1827, and died in West Rutland, Vt., January 2, 1885. He was an earnest and energetic preacher and worker. As a leader in social meetings he had few equals. His biographer says he was "judicious and careful" and as a preacher he was "scriptural, spiritual and faithful." During his ministry of five years in Cornish the church enjoyed the presence of the revival spirit in good degree much of the time. Two or three seasons of revival resulted in numerous conversions. His memorandum makes mention of eighty additions to the church, sixty-six baptisms, six hundred and nine sermons, twenty-five communion services, thirty-five marriages, fifty funerals and conducted over one thousand prayer meetings; all of these services rendered within the five years. His union with the church was a great blessing to it.

On January 6, 1872, the church, through the efforts of Elder Leavitt, procured a new bell. It was suspended in the church tower February 17, 1872. The old bell, procured in 1818, had become cracked and unfit for use. The inscription on the new bell, as furnished by the pastor was, "Praise God in His Holiness." Elder Leavitt left Cornish Church for Newport Baptist Church in December, 1872.

Rev. Gideon S. Smith succeeded Elder Leavitt, beginning his labors in February, 1873. He continued with the church until February, 1875. He was a conscientious and faithful preacher, but ill health rendered it advisable for him to resign.

Prior to 1875 all of the pastors of the church preached sermons in both forenoon and afternoon on each Sabbath. Beginning in May of that year, they have since rendered but one sermon on each Lord's Day, except at an occasional evening service.

In May, 1875, Rev. George A. Glines came from Hudson and was pastor of the church until May, 1880. In 1890 he was recalled and served the church another five years, ending in 1895. Owing to failing health he then retired from the ministry. He was born in Moultonborough, September 17, 1827, and died in Claremont, July 6, 1907. As a preacher he rendered very acceptable service. Between his two terms of service Rev. J. K. Chase from Rowley, Mass., preached one year ending September 1, 1882. Also Rev. Dennis Donovan preached two and one-half years, ending in June, 1886. After the close of Rev. G. A. Glines' second pastorate in 1895, Rev. Charles E. Gould came and preached three years, closing in September, 1898. On July 30, 1899, Rev. Charles V. French became pastor until October, 1901. After this the pastor of Meriden Church, Rev. Thomas Adams, supplied the pulpit nearly two years. His services were followed by those of Rev. James Nobbs, who remained pastor a little over a year. He was followed by the present incumbent, Rev. T. C. Russell, who came in June, 1906.

At the present writing (1909), the church, at the age of one hundred and twenty years, presents a great contrast to that of former years. Death has continued to remove her strong pillars of spirituality and of finance, until few are left to bear the burden. Few, too, have been the numbers that for many years past have been added to her membership. We will glance backward and present a portion of her history of more cheerful aspect.

The decade showing the greatest degree of prosperity of the church was from 1830 to 1840. We present a few items:

1830. Church numbered at opening of year, 111.
        Baptized 124, 74 of whom united with the church in Cornish and the rest in Windsor.
1831. Church numbered 180. Raised for benevolence, $160.
1832. Church numbered 184. Raised for benevolence, $195.
1833. Several gold rings contributed.
1834. Sunday school, 200. Volumes in library, 300.
1835. Baptized into church, 87. Church now numbered 257. Sunday school large. Home missions, $37.06.
1836. Church numbered 251. Library, 400 volumes. Sunday school, 200, with 20 teachers.
1837. Church numbered 229.
1838. Sunday school, 250. Teachers, 30. Volumes in library, 400. Donations liberal for all purposes.

1839.   Church numbered 320.   Sunday school, 275.
        Teachers, 30.   Volumes in library, 400.
1840.   Church numbered 277.

About seven hundred have been baptized into the church,
while many have been received by letter, making about eight
hundred different members since the organization of the church.
The present number is thirty-two resident and nine non-resident.

Evangelists at different times have labored in the church.
Prominent among these were Revs. Siloam Short, John Peacock,
Edward A. Whittier and Otis L. Leonard.   Their efforts always
seemed to prove a blessing to the church.   Sometimes the revival
spirit would be manifest through the earnest prayerful labors of
the pastor aided by the faithful members of his charge, and also
by neighboring ministers.

It is noteworthy that two of the church clerks served each
twenty-seven years in succession, Dea. Arunah Burnap from
1831 to 1858 and Dea. Henry E. Rich from 1858 to 1885.

Ten men have gone out from the church as preachers of the
gospel: George H. Hough, Thadeus Gage, Sanford Gustin, Reuel
Lothrop, Calvin Baker, Daniel, Stillman and Horace Richardson,
Charles H. Green and D. P. Deming.   These were all men of
fidelity and devotion to their calling.   They have all passed away.
Stillman Richardson died when just ready to enter the ministry,
but the others filled the measure of useful lives in the work.

Mr. Hough went as a missionary to India, becoming a companion of the immortal Judson in his sufferings and his joy.   Of
Horace Richardson a writer says: "True to Christ and his word,
he wrought well, was of beautiful spirit, and leaves to church
and family the legacy of an unsullied character."   The biographer of Daniel F. Richardson makes mention of "high scholarly
attainments; of several successful pastorates; of his release from
a palsy just before his death, and his rapturous joy as he then
crowned the Savior, Lord of all."   Of Charles H. Green a
writer says: "Of pure and amiable character whose daily walk
with God, rendered his society like rays of sunshine, and his
labors were blest."   His last words were, "He whom I have
preached as the sinners' hope is now my own."   (See Green Gen.)

It is interesting to notice that during the early history of the
church its members were *required* to attend divine service, and

be severely called to account for any absence therefrom. The modern sentiment hardly sustains this policy. But who shall declare the right?

The Newport Baptist Association, of which this church is a member, has met with the church in annual session nine different years: 1833, 1837, 1846, 1849, 1857, 1860, 1869, 1885 and 1896. The New Hampshire State Convention has met there but once, June, 1844.

The church and society have received the following legacies:

1834. Dea. John Weld, $500, the income only to be used for preaching.

1835. Ebenezer Weld, $1,200, the income only to be used for preaching.

1885. Mr. and Mrs. Henry Gould, new pulpit, with chairs, Bible and all furnishings complete.

1886. A library association, 168 volumes for adult readers.

1887. Daniel G. Deming, one half of the yearly income from his estate after his decease in 1887.

1899. Miss Sarah A. Bryant, about $300, the income only to be used for preaching.

1901. Henry Gould, $2,200, under the trusteeship of the New Hampshire Baptist State Convention, the income of which shall annually be expended for Baptist preaching on the Flat. With this he also bequeathed and devised that his present home, with all its furnishings, should at his decease become the home of the pastor of the church and his family, during his pastorate.

1902. Mrs. Sarah Gould, about $300, the income only to be used for preaching.

In 1883 the old-time open belfry was changed to the closed tower of the present day. This was slated as was the entire roof of the church.

There never has been a baptistry in the church, but on all occasions requiring it, ponds or brooks have been resorted to. August 25, 1889, a committee was chosen to make arrangements for a centennial meeting of the church. Accordingly centennial exercises were held in the church in September, 1889; a sermon was preached by Rev. N. F. Tilden of Lebanon. A history of the church was prepared and read by Rev. George N. Green, who

10

was then a resident supply for the pulpit. A poetic "Reminiscence of Cornish Flat Forty and Fifty Years Ago," by Mrs. Susan (Baker) Kenerson was read. The occasion was of great interest to all present.

By virtue of a law previously enacted, the church was incorporated February 1, 1904.

Episcopal Church.

The existence of the First Congregational Church had terminated. Its remaining members were not of one heart and mind. They had apparently abandoned the jurisdiction of the old church and were absorbed in building up two separate places of worship further north and east. (For record of these see Cong. Hist.) The southern and western parts of the town therefore were left unsupplied with religious services. The old meeting house formerly occupied by Mr. Wellman's Church now stood empty. That section had become missionary ground, and open to embrace the doctrines and services of any evangelical church.

During Reverend Mr. Bell's pastorate over the North Church in the fall of 1791, Philander Chase, the youngest son of Dea. Dudley Chase, entered Dartmouth College. While there he accidentally came across a "Book of Common Prayer,"—a rare book in those days. Instead of carelessly looking the book over and throwing it aside, he carefully and prayerfully studied it, and compared its forms and ordinances with the Word of God. The more he examined it, the more forcibly it appealed to his sense of what constituted the true way of worship.

These ideas he communicated to his parents, relatives and friends. To these, *truth* was the great desire of their hearts. They desired something stable and sure in worship and belief. This prayer book seemed to them as a new light to guide them towards a more satisfactory form of worship than they had heretofore experienced or witnessed. These considerations, joined to well-authenticated claims to apostolic successions in the ministry, were the principal reasons that induced the parents, relatives and neighbors of Philander Chase, to conform to the doctrine and practices of the Episcopal Church. Then again, these individuals had been, in a measure, instructed in the new forms of worship, by distinguished clergymen of the Episcopal order who occasionally had visited Cornish and other towns along the river. Prominent among these gospel preachers was Rev. John C. Ogden, afterwards their first pastor or rector, and Rev. Bethuel Chittenden, brother of a governor of Vermont. The visits of this latter gentleman were especially prized by these earnest seekers after the truth.

Their numbers increased until they deemed it advisable to meet and organize as a society. This was done, and they held their first meeting on December 16, 1793, in the old Congregational Church. They drew up the following "Instrument of Association":

"We the subscribers, inhabitants of the town and Neighborhood of Cornish in the state of New Hampshire, wishing to enjoy the Benefit of public religious worship and instruction for ourselves and families, do hereby associate ourselves together for that purpose as members and friends of the Protestant Episcopal Church, Agreeing with each other to conform to such future rules and regulations as in the circumstances of this society, parish, or church we shall agree upon—from time to time in Legal regular meetings, by a majority of votes, for the purpose of the same.—

"And we further agree to attend upon the public offices of religion, for the present under the ministry of the Rev^d. John Cozens Ogden as frequently as he can officiate among us at the old meetinghouse in said Cornish.—

"In witness whereof we have set our hands this sixteenth day of December 1793."

At the same meeting it was "Voted by a majority of the subscribers to this parish, that M^r. Ithamar Chase and Jonathan Chase, J. P. be appointed as Wardens until Easter next.—

"Be it known that the above votes were passed and that fourteen persons also signed this subscription, paper or Instrument of Association in our presence on the day above mentioned, test^d. by John Cozens Ogden, Presbytere the Episcopal Church and missionary in New Hampshire.

"Voted that this meeting be adjourned unto Monday the 21st day of April next.

ITH. CHASE } Wardens."
JONA CHASE J. P. }

The Monday after Easter Sabbath has ever since been observed by the church as the date of their annual business meeting.

On their second meeting April 21, 1794, a committee was chosen to petition the General Court of New Hampshire for an act of incorporation under the name of *Christ's Church*. For some reason the committee failed in the discharge of their duty, and so the matter was postponed until the following year, when the committee was again instructed to renew their petition and forward their project to completion.

The General Court was in session at Hanover on the first Wednesday of June, 1795. The committee then presented their petition. On the 16th of June it came before the court, which ordered a time for hearing later, when, if no objections appeared, their prayer would be granted. The bill passed both the House and Senate December 24, 1795, and the church was incorporated under the name of *Trinity Church*, which name it has since borne. John Prentiss at this time was speaker of the House, Ebenezer Smith, president of the Senate, and J. Taylor Gilman was governor. The incorporation of the church was recorded April 9, 1796, by Nathaniel Hall, registrar. This same year the clerk and wardens were directed to request Gen. Jonathan Chase to give a deed of the common land where the old meeting house now stands.

On August 10, 1801, the church took measures in conjunction with other Episcopal churches of New Hampshire for the formation of a district or diocese embracing this church. Delegates were appointed and sent to Claremont to a convention assembled there for said purpose and also to another convention at Concord. On May 25, 1802, the diocese was formed and a constitution prepared to be adopted by its several churches. This was unanimously adopted by Trinity Church on November 1, 1802.

By the terms of the grant of Cornish lands, the minister who first settled in town, had the benefit of two hundred acres of land, the first Congregational Church receiving this benefit by reason of their priority. The Episcopal Society, however, had its glebe lands; but coming a little later, found them mainly occupied, and in some cases improved by those occupying them and who were reluctant to relinquish them. This gave rise to disputes concerning titles, and even lawsuits occurred before they could be recovered. But proper measures were taken and satisfaction finally obtained.

The old meeting house, built in 1773, was needing repairs, and it did not fully meet the wants of those now worshiping there. Something must be done; either to make extensive repairs or to pull down the old house and build a new and larger one. The latter policy was unanimously adopted. A plan for a new house had been drafted and submitted by Philip Tabor, a carpenter and builder. With this plan all were well pleased. Accordingly a meeting was convened on November 2, 1801, to take action on the matter. A committee was appointed "to sell the pews of the old house and appropriate the avails for building s⁴. house." A committee to purchase lumber, and solicit and collect donations was also appointed. The donations of timber and other material were liberal. The work was delayed, however, and the old house stood until after the business meeting of the society on April 2, 1804. It was, however, taken down during that year.

An article appeared in the town warrant of April 15, 1805, which was "to see how much money the society would raise to complete the house," but for some reason the article was "passed over." During the years 1806–07 the records are silent regarding the progress of the work, or the raising of means to carry it forward. It is supposable, however, that the work was progressing during those years, for in the spring of 1808, the society "warned" its first business meeting to be held in Trinity Church, which is the edifice of today. Probably the reason why so much time was spent in building was the scarcity of funds needful to speedily accomplish the work. The income from their lands at this time came in slowly, being jeopardized in litigation and the society was awaiting the outcome.

The new house was located upon the site of the old one, and it "was to be 36 x 44 feet, with two porches and a belfry, with a steeple, and of a suitable heighth."

It has numbered among its worshipers a class of noble and gifted men and women whose influence has been potent in all the affairs of the town.

The attendance has never been of the fitful and overflowing kind, but rather of a steady, quiet order that is befitting and favorable to the worship and service of the Highest.

The church has not at all times supported a rector of her own, but has received the ministrations of those from Windsor and Claremont and other churches near at hand. Rev. George

Leonard is the most notable exception as he was a resident of the town, and officiated as rector eighteen years. The records make mention in their order of Reverends Ogden, Chittenden, Barber, Montague, Felch, Leonard, Smith, Staples, Wright, Flanders, Randolph, Jones, Douglas, Goddard, Ticknor and perhaps others. The services rendered by these worthy men, beside the visits of the Bishop and others, have enabled them to maintain services a large part of the time.

In 1816 the church made an appeal to Bishop Alexander V. Griswold for aid, on the plea that their predecessors had disposed of lands rightfully belonging to *them*, and now wished these lands might be redeemed by subscription. Following this, the same year, the church was successful in securing donations, and decisions in law against those holding glebe lands, which gave them much encouragement.

June 4, 1822, the clerk of the society, Capt. Bela Chase was voted as disqualified to hold office, or even membership in the church owing to his joining the Catholic Communion with his family. He was accordingly dismissed.

According to the records, the society has held its annual meetings from 1793 to the present time, a period of 116 years, with the exception of the years from 1875 to 1895. The causes given for these omissions are the same as those applying to all the other churches in town, viz.: 1st, the decline in population being accompanied by a corresponding decline in church membership; 2d, the present generation, as a rule, do not attach the importance to the service of God that their fathers and grandfathers did.

In closing we append the interesting event of the consecration of Trinity Church in the language of the record.

"To the Rt. Revd Carlton Chase D. D. Bishop of the Diocese of New Hampshire,
  Rt. Revd Sir.
"We the undersigned, Wardens of Trinity Church Cornish respectfully request you to consecrate our house of worship to the service of Almighty God.
 "Cornish, Jan. 11, 1846.

       "John L. Putnam }
              Wardens.
       "Israel Hall }

 "A true record, Attest, John L. Putnam Reg^r "

"Diocese of New Hampshire.

"In the name of God, Amen.

"Whereas, it hath pleased Almighty God to put it into the hearts of His servants, the people of the Parish of Trinity Church in the town of Cornish in said Diocese to erect and devote a house to His great and glorious name, and whereas the officers of said Parish have moved and requested that the same may be publicly consecrated to Him according to the usages of the Protestant Episcopal Church in the United States:—Now therefore be it known that I, Carlton Chase, by the grace of God, Bishop of said Diocese in virtue of my holy office, do this day dedicate and solemnly consecrate to God, and to the sacred purposes of the Gospel, this the aforesaid house under the name of Trinity Church, forever separating it from all unhallowed, worldly and common uses, and requiring and enjoining that henceforth it shall be wholly and exclusively devoted to the solemn uses and services of the blessed religion of Jesus Christ, according to the Doctrine, Discipline and worship of the Protestant Episcopal Church.

"In testimony whereof I have hereunto set my hand and seal this eleventh day of January, in the year of our Lord, one thousand eight hundred and forty six.

"CARLTON CHASE [Seal]

"A true Record, Attest, John L. Putnam, Reg^r"

Methodist Episcopal Church.

This church was organized November 5, 1838. There were but few members during the first years of its existence, as it was at a time when the other churches seemed to "cover the ground." The doctrines of the Wesleys, however, presented a charm for those who valued an earnest and aggressive, rather than a steady and formal mode of worship.

Rev. John G. Bennett was the first stationed preacher in 1840. As he was a man of earnest piety, joined to other gifts of no mean order, he was enabled to give quite an impetus to the new sect in town.

Rev. Amos Kidder, appointed in 1843, was the next preacher. The additions at first were slow and prospects not very encouraging. Meetings were held in schoolhouses and in private resi-

dences.   The old brick schoolhouse on the Flat was used several
seasons as a house of worship.   Here the first and second meetings
of the quarterly conference were held, July 1 and September 21,
1843.   Jared Perkins was the presiding elder.

During a space of six years, from April 24, 1844, to July 10,
1850, no record of the church is found.

The "Evangelical Congregational Church and Society" had
built their neat and commodious meeting house, but they had been
frowned out of existence as a church, thus leaving their meeting
house and parsonage without an occupant.   It was in some
respects a blessing to the Methodist Society to have the privilege
of occupying the meeting house and pay rent therefor.

Another fortunate thing for the Methodists was this: Many of
the members of the former church that were anxious to affiliate
with some earnest religious body, united themselves with the
new order and became a very important factor with them.
More than half of the members of the former church were
thus absorbed in the Methodist Church.   All were thus greatly
encouraged and regarded it as an interposition of Divine Providence in behalf of all concerned.   From this time the church
took fair rank with her sister churches in the district, and most of
the time supported a local preacher of her own.   Her members
increased, and in various ways the Good Providence seemed to
overshadow them.   The preachers assigned were men of God
and wrought good works, as several revivals evidenced.

Up to 1860, the meeting house in which the Methodists wor-
shiped belonged to the former pew owners.   On April 22 of this
year, a committee was appointed "to negotiate for the mortgage
on the church and parsonage, for the benefit of the Methodist
Church."   On February 5, 1861, the committee rendered a partial
report, sufficient, however, to encourage them to persevere in the
undertaking.

April 27, 1866, a meeting "to excite an interest in favor of a
transfer of the property to the Methodist Church" was called,
and further committees were appointed and instructed.

On March 25, 1867, the committees announced that they had
secured a "good and sufficient deed of the church and parsonage
property within the last quarter" (the date of the deed being
February 21, 1867), on condition that $200 should be ex-
pended for the repairs of the meeting house.   These terms were

mutually agreed upon. Having thus acquired possession, they immediately appointed a committee for the performance of the necessary repairs on the church. In less than three months the committee reported the repairs completed, and on the 27th of June, 1867, the dedicatory services were held. The trustees formally presented the house for dedication in the following words: "We present this building to be dedicated to the service and worship of Almighty God." Rev. W. H. Clark, presiding elder of the Claremont district, had charge of the services and preached the sermon. The dedicatory prayer was offered by Reverend Mr. Dearborn of Vermont, followed by a voluntary, the doxology, and benediction.

The years 1868–69 were years of gracious outpouring of the spirit and blessing upon the church; perhaps they were the best of all the years of the past. The records of these years are as follows:

Members already belonging.........................   63
Added by baptism during year   18
                                                      ————
                                                        81

Church property valued at.......................... $1,500
Parsonage property valued at   500
                                                      ————
                                                      $2,000

These were years of apparent prosperity.

In 1872 the church reported many and extensive repairs, and also the purchase of an organ at a cost of $106.

After the Methodist Camp Meeting had been established at Claremont Junction, this church took a lively interest in it, and, owing to its nearness, most of the members attended its annual meetings.

In August, 1873, a committee was appointed to select a location among many others, for a tent or building on the camp grounds. A site was selected, agreeable to the minds of all, north of, and near, the preacher's stand. A building committee was at once appointed. Mr. Benjamin S. Lewis, of the committee, had charge of the work, while many ready and willing hands were there to aid, and the house was ready for occupancy in season for the meeting near the close of the month, and was filled to overflowing night

and day throughout the meetings much to the satisfaction and
apparent blessing of all who attended. These seasons of interest
at the camp ground meetings continued several years, until, the
church, through decline failed to pay its camp ground rent, and
thus forfeited its right there and the building was removed. In
April, 1875, the society rented its vestry to Cornish Grange, who,
wishing it enlarged for their use, agreed to pay the church fifty
dollars towards enlarging it, and five dollars per year for the
rent of the same. They have occupied it ever since.

The following is the list of preachers, in their order, that have
been sent to Cornish, and have mainly resided here during the
term of their appointment:

John G. Bennett, Amos Kidder, Lorenzo Draper, John Clough,
Richard Newhall, N. S. Bentley, P. Wallingford, John H. Griffin,
George F. Wells, B. P. Spaulding, John S. Parker, C. F. Merrill,
C. H. Leet, Edward Francis, Josiah Hooper, in all, fifteen. Of
these Richard Newhall received a second appointment, and
Lorenzo Draper received three appointments to the church.
Besides these, several others, chiefly from Claremont, have
supplied the pulpit.

Thirteen presiding elders have had the watch care of this
church. These, in their order, were: Jared Perkins, Silas
Quimby, C. N. Smith, Newell Culver, A. C. Manson, Elisha
Adams, John Thurston, W. H. Clark, James Pike, M. T. Cilley,
G. J. Judkins, O. H. Jasper, and ———— Robbins. Since August,
1891, there is no record of any business meeting of either the church
or society. Occasional services may have been held, but no
record of them is found. In looking over the history of this
church for sixty years, and beholding it, from its small beginning
grow to a healthy, happy and prosperous church, and then see it
suffering a slow decline, almost to the stage of extinction of name
and being, we behold a picture not pleasant to contemplate.
Various causes have contributed to this. The death and removal
of many of the principal members, and the age and infirmity of
the few remaining, and the fact that, as in all other churches
of the town, very few of the young are falling into the ranks, to
fill the places thus made vacant, are the chief causes of the decadence of all of our churches. Yet they have all wrought well in
their day, and perhaps all have fulfilled their mission.

Perfectionists, Millerites, etc.

In the early forties of the last century a revolution among the moral, political and religious questions then existing, seemed to be the order of the day. Old doctrines that had heretofore been received with moderation were reëxamined and received with fresh inspiration, and became subjects of absorbing interest to the many who embraced them. The minds of the people were inclined as never before, to entertain *intense* views, on many subjects. Especially did this apply to the doctrines of Sanctification and the Second Advent.

A number of young men from Claremont, having become deeply impressed by the Scriptural requirements regarding heart-purity, came to Cornish and held meetings in the homes of those whose doors were open to receive them. These styled themselves "Perfectionists," claiming Scriptural authority both in doctrine and name. This doctrine was received with avidity by many of the good citizens of the town.

Soon after this, the doctrine of the Second Advent of Christ as preached by William Miller, swept over New England. This, too, received many adherents in our town, and of necessity gave an increased impetus to the former movement. Mr. Miller believed and preached that the world's history would end in 1843; great excitement prevailed among many, believers in his doctrine were thereby incited to liberality and self-sacrifice. Means were readily secured, and a house of worship was erected by the Perfectionists on a tract of land deeded them by Hiram C. Fletcher, said deed bearing date, August 12, 1840.

After Mr. Miller's prophecy regarding the end of the world in 1843 had proved a failure, and "the end was not yet," many, who were ardent believers in both doctrines, were disheartened. Services dwindled and finally ceased; the house of worship became unused and finally closed.

The town, at this juncture being in need of a house in which to hold its meetings, came into possession of said meeting house of the Perfectionists, and have since used it for all its public meetings.

Whatever the result of these extreme views may have been, we are bound to credit those entertaining them with honesty and sincerity. Possibly the results may be greater, grander,

and more far-reaching than human judgment can determine.
At any rate, they led to a more prayerful and considerate study
of the Bible, especially in regard to the Second Advent.

Thus we see that every body of Christ's disciples that have
lived and associated in Cornish, have had its joyful, hopeful and
happy rise; its seasons of substantial prosperity in accomplishing
its mission, followed by periods of decline, ending, in some
cases, in its death. These monuments of perished hopes lie all
around us. The historian would willingly, yet mournfully,
inscribe to their memory the foregoing records of the former
churches of Cornish.

Independent Parish.

Soon after the opening of the present century, it was found
that the Methodist Episcopal Society of Cornish had become
nearly extinct, and the church edifice was partly in ruins. A
commendable desire prevailed among the citizens of that section
to revive religious services, and to repair the house of worship.
Rev. P. J. Robinson, pastor of the Unitarian Church in Windsor,
was invited to hold services there in 1902. This movement was
attended with a good degree of success. The ladies of the vicinity
organized a society called the "Woman's Alliance," and accomplished much for the benefit of the parish. The organization of
a church there was effected March 30, 1905, under the name of
"The Independent Parish." A constitution and by-laws were
adopted; a full quota of officers was chosen from a membership
of nearly fifty members, and Rev. P. J. Robinson was chosen as
pastor, who served until December, 1905. A petition asking fellowship with the "American Unitarian Association" was presented
and was duly granted. The committee of the parish now nego-
tiated with the remaining trustees of the former Methodist
Episcopal Church, for a lease of the church building for a term of
twenty years, with the condition that they make certain necessary
repairs on the church. This was accordingly done, and the church
edifice was thoroughly refitted. Contributions for this purpose
had been generously made: By the Unitarian Association, $200;
F. A. Kennedy, $200; Woman's Alliance, $180; and other gifts,
aggregating $700 in all; besides special gifts of value for furnishing
the interior of the house by Mr. and Mrs. W. C. Houston and
Mr. and Mrs. A. E. Lang.

In its new order and dress, the church was again dedicated, December 3, 1906. Rev. Sidney Snow preached the dedicatory sermon. He had served the church from December, 1905, until the spring of 1906, when Rev. J. E. Locke came and preached until August, 1907. He was followed by a year's service from Rev. H. L. Buzzell, who was succeeded by the present pastor, Rev. R. S. Barrow, who began his services in the fall of 1909.

"The Independent Parish of Cornish is dedicated to the worship of God, and to the cultivation of that spirit which was in Jesus Christ; and it has no other creed. It is now affiliated with the Unitarian Church at Windsor, whose pastor serves both parishes."

Pentecostal Nazarene.

During the season of 1908, a few members of the Baptist Church at the Flat became desirous of establishing meetings by themselves at South Cornish. Obtaining letters of dismission from the parent church, they organized a church at that place, and Benjamin F. Lindsay was ordained as its pastor. It was first organized as a Freewill Baptist Church. While earnestly seeking after the most acceptable forms of worship and spiritual development, Brother Lindsay came in contact with the sect of "the Pentecostal Nazarene." Its doctrines and practices appealed forcibly to his convictions, and the little church, through his influence, readily espoused the doctrines of the sect. It became identified with the denomination, and Rev. Mr. Lindsay was solemnly ordained as pastor, October 25, 1908.

Meetings have been sustained there ever since with a good measure of satisfaction on the part of all concerned. The meetings have been held chiefly in the schoolroom of School Division 10.

It needs the prophetic eye to determine the final results of this movement. It is to be hoped, however, that the moral and religious influences emanating from this little church, will be a potent factor for the uplifting and spiritualizing of many.

CHAPTER IX.

THE early settlers of Cornish were generally educated men and women according to the standard of their times. They came from towns where they had enjoyed the privileges of established schools and, therefore, well appreciated their value.

According to well-authenticated tradition the first schools of the town were assembled around the firesides and under the supervision of intelligent and painstaking parents. Next in importance to the preaching of the Gospel, they regarded the education of their children; therefore, as soon as possible after the pioneers had organized a town, they assembled in town meeting and adopted such measures as they deemed best and voted to raise money for the support of schools.

The reservations in favor of schools, provided by the grants, proved an insufficient source of revenue; therefore additional means were soon needed. Then again, the meager income from these lands was, at first, necessarily so slow in coming, that some children might die in ignorance before getting any benefit from it. For many years after its settlement, the town, like many others, was supreme in authority on all matters relating to schools. This was due to the absence of all state law regarding it. So the early schools of Cornish were not the creation of legislation, but were of spontaneous growth.

The town's records for the years 1785–90 show its action on the subject as follows: On March 22, 1785, the town voted to divide the town into school districts, and raised £30 for schooling. Previous to this time there were no district limits and parents could send their children to school wherever they chose. On March 14, 1786, the town voted to raise £100 for schooling. At this time there were but two school districts in town.

March 13, 1787, voted to raise £80 for schooling purposes.

March 12, 1788, voted to raise £100.

March 24, 1789, voted to raise £30.

SCHOOL HOUSE. DIVISION 6. CORNISH FLAT

SCHOOL HOUSE DIVISION 11.

SCHOOL HOUSE. DIVISION 1.

SCHOOL HOUSE. DIVISION 7.

March 24, 1790, voted the subject of dividing the town into school districts be referred to the selectmen, who should also select sites for the locations and erection of schoolhouses.

The history of the schools of a town in New Hampshire is divided into three epochs. During the first, or voluntary period, which ended in 1827, the schools, as we have shown, were established and maintained, and schoolhouses were erected by the town. During all this time there were but few and imperfect statutes. The proceedings of the several towns were so constant and uniform that a system was formulated and established without the regulation and compulsory influence of law. It was preëminently a town system.

By the statute of 1827, and subsequent amendments, school districts became corporations with authority to choose their own officers, to own school lots, to build schoolhouses and to have a general control of their schools. The towns were instructed to raise money for school purposes, and to choose a committee for supervision. *This*, the second epoch, extended from 1827, until the abolishment of school districts in 1885.

During this second epoch, the town attained its highest point in population,—over 1,700. Also the number of school districts in town reached their maximum,—sixteen in all. These had been numbered in the order of their need and organization. Numbers 1, 2 and 3 extended the entire length of the town, on the Connecticut River where settlements first took place. Numbers 4 and 5 on the hills east and north of the last, where hardy pioneers had decided to settle. No. 6 on an interval in the northeast part of the town where a mountain stream spread, that invited manufacturers. Numbers 7, 8, 9 and 10 following the intervale south and southwest with the adjacent hillsides, reaching to the north line of Claremont. No. 11, west of these last, embracing the territory east of the river districts and No. 4.

The whole town was now embraced within the eleven districts already organized. The five other districts were afterwards formed by the division of districts already established. This was done to better accommodate the children of settlers remote from school privileges. No. 12, formerly embraced in No. 6, was formed by those who settled farther up the mountain stream east of the Flat. It bore the unpoetical name of "Poppy Squash." No. 13 was formed in 1828 from the southern por-

tions of districts 9 and 11, and bordered on the north line of
Claremont. No. 14 embraced the southeast corner of the town,
large in territory, but sparse in population, except a portion of
it called the "Hemp yard." No. 15 was a small, sparsely settled
district, lying east of No. 1, on "Root Hill," not conveniently
accessible either to Nos. 1, 11, or 13, which lay contiguous. No.
16 embraced the northeast corner of the town. It formerly
belonged mainly to Grantham and was annexed to Cornish in
1844. This district was thereafter called "Texas."

After 1840, the population of the town began slowly to decline,
and this decline continued steadily throughout the remainder of
this epoch for forty-five years, or until 1885. During this time the
town lost about seven hundred of its former inhabitants, so that
its population at this date was only about one thousand. There
were fewer families and these had become smaller, and the number
of school children was correspondingly less. Some of the hill farms
had become abandoned; dwellings had been torn down and removed; and the general trend of the remaining population had
been to the village, or to more accessible lowland farms. It is
easy to see what the effect of these changes would be upon
school districts located on the hills and mountain sides remote
from the more populous centers.

The districts in town that first suffered from the lack of patronage were the last ones formed, namely: Numbers 12, 13, 14, 15
and 16. In some of these a single short term of school was taught
during the year, and sometimes none at all. The scholars were
so few that it was not always deemed advisable to open a school
during the year, as the expense *per capita* would be so much. The
number of scholars in most of the other schools was much less
than formerly. To illustrate: The enrollment of the scholars in
town in 1851 was 385 between four and sixteen years of age; 80
attended school over sixteen years of age; 465 in all attending
school. In 1886 the enrollment was 165 in all, according to
the report of these two years.

The causes that have contributed to this change are many.
While the population of the country has steadily increased, many
of the earlier settled towns of New England have shown a great
decline. The increasing tendency of the young men and women
of recent years to avoid the severe manual labor of their ancestors;
the attractions of the great West with its labor-saving machinery;

the innumerable professions and trades which offer better wages
at a less expense of muscle, oftentimes coupled with the charms
of city life,—all these and many other causes have been, and
are still, at work luring the young men from the rugged hillsides
to lives of fancied enjoyment elsewhere; and meanwhile several
schools of Cornish had become extinct, and those that remained
were but the skeletons of once active and populous schools.

Similar results were manifest in many other towns of our state,
some exhibiting even a greater falling off than Cornish.

These conditions invited discussion among the leading educators of the state

The people generally had become attached to the district
system, and had enjoyed the benefit and pleasure of district
rivalry and of local control, and although the system had become
imperfect in that it denied equal privilege to all scholars; still they
were unwilling to admit of any change. They deemed it a sacri-
lege for any lawmaker to meddle with an institution so dear to
them as the *district school system.*

But the time had come for a change. A more elastic system
was needed. The districts would never have voted it. The
leading educators in the state must take the matter in hand, or
the district system with its inequality of privilege would continue
with a tendency towards worse conditions. The town system
seemed to be the only solution of the problem. Therefore, it was
duly presented to the legislature; its claims as a panacea for the
existing evils fully demonstrated, and the law was adopted in
March, 1885. This closed the second epoch of the history of
schools in New Hampshire.

With the town system, was inaugurated a new era in the history of the schools of New Hampshire. The little petty republics
or districts of the town were all abolished and fused into one district. The several district officers heretofore chosen by them
were needed no longer. The control of all affairs, both prudential
and educational, was vested in three well-selected individuals
called a "school board," or "board of education." These had
power to temporarily locate and maintain schools wherever, in
their united judgment, it was thought best; to hire teachers and
provide all the needful requirements of the schools; and to super-
intend the same. Scholars living remote from the established
schools were provided with means of conveyance to the nearest

11

suitable school, and the new law provided for the raising of additional funds for this purpose. In this way equality of school privileges could be secured for all the scholars of the town better than was possible under the former system.

The term *district* as applied to the small local schools, was abandoned, and that of *division*, substituted therefor, as they were now but divisions of the one town district.

Notwithstanding all the advantages the new law offered, it was at the first stubbornly opposed by the majority of the voters of the town, who even instructed their representative in 1886, to use his utmost influence to have the new law repealed, but all efforts in that direction failed, as a matter of course. It was now the aim of the school board during this storm of opposition to exemplify the merits of the law to the best advantage, by judicious management. Their plans in this respect were to a large extent successful, and so the unfriendly feeling in opposition to the new law gradually subsided. The general verdict of public opinion a few years later was that the system is an advance step in the cause of education.

Schoolhouses.

There have been sixteen schoolhouses; one for each of the old districts in town. Each of these, in their years of prosperity were filled with interesting and intelligent children. As before stated, after the decline in population, the houses, especially in the back districts or divisions, began to suffer from need of repairs; notably those in divisions 12, 14, 15 and 16. Limited repairs from time to time had been bestowed upon these houses, but they had gradually grown more unfit for use, and extensive repairs were really impracticable. The new system was prepared to solve this problem. The scholars in these divisions were so few that the school board decided to convey them to other and more central schools, and the houses in those four divisions were removed or sold.

In nearly all of the old districts, the original houses have given place to houses of newer and improved pattern. The old brick schoolhouse at the Flat, which so many years served the village school of sometimes nearly a hundred scholars, was, in 1878, superseded by one of more imposing and modern type, on another site. Several of the other districts had a similar experience a few years before under the old system. After the town system was adopted, a new house on a different site was built in division 10; and also one soon after, south of the last, near the Claremont line. This last has received the number 12, as the former house of this number had been torn down.

At the present time (1909) there are thirteen schoolhouses in town in which schools are kept. Owing to the limited number of scholars, schools are not maintained in all of them at the same time, but when there is no school in a division, those scholars are to receive the benefit of another school in an adjoining division, thus increasing their school privileges.

Under this head the following suggestions are pertinent: *Schoolhouses* are in *themselves educative.*

It is a law largely governing our existence that we are what we have been made by our environments.

It is not alone the spoken precept, neither is it the printed page, but both of these, in conjunction with the object lessons of life with which we come in contact, that mould the character of men and women. This is emphatically true while young. The knowledge that children obtain of life, at first, is principally obtained through their visual organs. The objects they then come in contact with are continually shaping the future of their lives. A large portion of their early life is spent in the schoolroom. Every object within and without, contributes its mite to the characters forming there.

Thus the *schoolhouse* is a silent yet eloquent preacher. If the schoolhouse and its environments are unsightly from any cause, or constructed out of proportion, cheerless and uncomfortable, the effect in embryo is stamped on the young mind that is ever seeking to adapt itself to its surroundings. It finally succeeds by becoming of like character. For such a house, a pupil educated there, has no affectionate regard or even respect in after years.

On the other hand, let the schoolhouse and all its surroundings be neat and orderly; let an air of comfort pervade the room and everything around, within, without, give evidence of good taste and refinement; introduce the child into such environments and note results. Its attractiveness is winning. He delights in his surroundings. They become a part of his nature. His character is forming with a love for all that is desirable and good, and in after years, next to the parental home of his childhood, will he remember the old schoolhouse with unspeakable affection.

The value of proper educational privileges and surroundings cannot be overestimated, as they have to do with the choicest elements that enter into the trifold organism of man, as the immortal Daniel Webster has well said:

"If we work on marble, it will perish; if we work on brass, time will efface it. If we rear temples, they will crumble into dust; but if we work on immortal minds; if we imbue them with principles, and with the just fear of God and love of our fellowmen, we engrave on these tablets something which will brighten to all eternity."

High Schools.

Not until near the close of the nineteenth century has Cornish been favored by any legacy or fund for the establishment of a high school within her borders, or in any way made appropriations to favor those desiring high school privileges.

The need of a school supplementary to the district or division school has always been recognized by all progressive students. Hence from time to time private funds have been contributed for the establishment of brief terms of school in town for advanced scholars. These have been a great aid to many, especially to those whose finances were limited. After receiving these additional school privileges many have left the schoolrooms for the activities of business. The advantages of such additional schooling needs no proof.

Such schools have usually been held in the most eligible schoolrooms of the town, principally at the Flat; and in some instances in suitable private dwellings. Usually, these terms have been sandwiched between the summer and winter terms when the district schools were not in session. Teachers of advanced qualifications have been employed. These have generally been selected from some academy or college. The last terms of high school in Cornish before the town system was adopted were held in district No. 7, in 1880–81, conducted by Miss Emily Leavitt (now Mrs. C. F. Huggins), a teacher of large experience, assisted by Rev. James T. Jackson. These were very successful terms.

In addition to the local privileges already named, the advanced scholars of the town have, since 1813, been favored by the near

WILLIAM W. MERCER.

presence of an academy at Meriden. This academy has been a great boon to several scores of students from Cornish who have attended there, and have been fitted for college and otherwise prepared for the business of life. (See Kimball Union Academy.)

As adjuncts of the high school as well as of the district school, singing schools, writing schools, and even spelling schools, have played an important part in the education of our youth. All these occasions are remembered as seasons of pleasure and profit.

By the provisions of a will made by William W. Mercer of Cornish, who died September 19, 1895, a sum of nearly seven thousand dollars was left to the town on certain conditions. The income from this fund is to be devoted to the aid of worthy students of both sexes from Cornish, who, having passed the town schools, desire an academic or high school education.

The town warrant of March 10, 1896, contained this article: "To see if the town will vote to accept the provisions of the will of William W. Mercer, and take action in regard to said legacy."

At the meeting, the town voted to accept the legacy and to comply with the conditions of the will. The income has been expended agreeably to said will. Through this means a large number of worthy students from Cornish, who have attended Kimball Union Academy have received more or less aid from said income. Several students have been enabled thereby to pursue their studies longer, much to their advantage.

School Supervision.

From the settlement of the town until 1809, the selectmen were the sole guardians of the schools of the town. Upon them devolved the locating of the schools, the hiring of teachers and providing for schools and superintending the same.

As the population increased, and also the number of schools, it became evident that another set of officers should be chosen to have the entire charge of the schools, and thus relieve the selectmen of this duty. These were usually to be chosen by the people and were styled "Inspectors of Schools." This title was continued until 1827 when a law was passed defining their duties, and changing their title to that of "Superintendents of Schools." This title continued until 1885, when it was again changed to that of "School Board."

The law of 1827 also provided that each district should be independent in all its local affairs, and that a prudential committee
be chosen by each district, whose duties would be the hiring
of teachers, the maintaining of schools and having a general
care of them. In this way, the superintending committee was
relieved of all the financial concerns of each and every district
in town, their only province being that of determining the qualifications of the teachers employed, and a general supervision
of their schools while they were in session. This was under the
district school system which ended in 1885. Since this date
the supervision of schools, together with the duties of the prudential committees have devolved upon the school board.

The following is a list of the supervisory officers of the schools
of the town as far as can be gathered from the records.

For the list previous to 1809, the reader is referred to the list
of the selectmen of that period. Then a record begins as
follows:

Inspectors of Schools.

1809　Harvey Chase.
　　　Rev. Joseph Rowell.
　　　Rev. Ariel Kendrick.
1810　Rev. Joseph Rowell.
　　　Timothy W. Hall.
　　　Newton Whittlesey.
1811　Rev. Ariel Kendrick.
　　　Rev. Joseph Rowell.
　　　Wm. Whittlesey.
1812　No record.
1813　Rev. Joseph Rowell.
　　　Eleazer Jackson, Jr.
　　　Hon. Ithamar Chase.
1814　One person for each school,
　　　name not given.
1815　Rev. Joseph Rowell.
　　　Rev. Ariel Kendrick.
　　　Eleazer Jackson, Jr.
1816　Rev. Joseph Rowell.
　　　Rev. Ariel Kendrick.
　　　Wm. Whittlesey.
1817　Wm. Deming.
　　　Rev. Joseph Rowell.
　　　Rev. Ariel Kendrick.

1818　Eleazer Jackson, Jr.
　　　Rev. Joseph Rowell.
　　　Rev. Ariel Kendrick.
1819　Newton Whittlesey.
　　　Rev. Joseph Rowell.
　　　Rev. Ariel Kendrick.
1820　Eleven persons, one from each
　　　district; names not given.
1821　Twelve persons, one from each
　　　district, names not given.
1822　Newton Whittlesey.
　　　Rev. Ariel Kendrick.
　　　Rev. Joseph Rowell.
1823　No record.
1824　No record.
1825　Eleazer Jackson.
　　　Arunah Burnap.
　　　Benj. Chapman.
1826　Newton Whittlesey.
　　　Rev. George Leonard.
　　　Rev. Joseph Rowell.
1827　Newton Whittlesey.
　　　Rev. George Leonard.
　　　Rev. Joseph Rowell.

After 1827 no record of these officers appears on the records of the town until 1843. During a part of these years, superintendents were probably chosen, but their names and the records of their doings have not been found. During several of these years votes were passed showing that the people desired to dispense with the services of the superintendents.

Superintendents of Schools, 1843-85.

1843	Harvey Chase.	1856	William Balloch.
	Rev. Alvah Spaulding.		Lyman Hall.
	Elijah Boardman.	1857	William Balloch.
1844	Rev. Oliver H. Staples.	1858	William Balloch.
	Rev. Alvah Spaulding.	1859	Adophus G. Vinton.
	Elijah Boardman.	1860	Adolphus G. Vinton.
1845	Rev. Alvah Spaulding.	1861	Elihu H. Pike.
	Rev. N. P. Foster.	1862	Rev. D. P. Deming.
	Eleazer Jackson, Jr.	1863	Rev. D. P. Deming.
1846	Rev. N. P. Foster.	1864	Henry Ayers.
	Rev. Alvah Spaulding.	1865	George W. Hunt.
	Rufus A. Putnam.	1866	George W. Hunt.
1847	Elijah Boardman.	1867	George W. Hunt.
	Lyman Hall.	1868	George W. Hunt.
	Harrison Leslie.	1869	George W. Hunt.
1848	Lyman Hall.	1870	Henry M. Day.
	Elijah Boardman.	1871	Henry M. Day.
	Chauncey P. Jenney.	1872	Rev. Charles M. Palmer.
1849	Chauncey P. Jenney.	1873	Rev. Benj. P. Spaulding.
	Eleazer Jackson.	1874	Rev. Benj. P. Spaulding.
	William Balloch.	1875	Rev. James T. Jackson.
1850	Eleazer Jackson.	1876	Rev. James T. Jackson.
	Chauncey P. Jenney.	1877	Rev. James T. Jackson.
	William Balloch.	1878	Rev. James T. Jackson.
1851	Lyman Hall.	1879	Emily Leavitt.
	Elijah Boardman.	1880	Emily Leavitt.
	Carlos F. Huggins.	1881	Martha W. Day.
1852	Rev. Alvah Spaulding.	1882	Martha W. Day.
1853	Rev. Alvah Spaulding.		Herbert Deming.
1854	Rev. Alvah Spaulding.	1883	Herbert Deming.
1855	Rev. Alvah Spaulding.	1884	George L. Deming.
1856	Rev. Alvah Spaulding.	1885	George L. Deming.

Members of the School Board.

The following is a list of members of the school board since the town district system was adopted. The law was passed in **1885.** On the March following (1886), the first members were elected. The law provided that one of the members of the board should be elected for three years, one for two years, and one for one year, and that thereafter, ordinarily, one member was to be elected annually to supply the place of a retiring senior member:

1886	Chester Pike.	1898	Maurice J. Duncklee.
	Herbert Deming.		Frank J. Chadbourne.
	W. H. Child.	1899	Frank J. Chadbourne.
1887	Chester Pike.		Ella I. Richardson (Mrs. S. K.).
	Herbert Deming.		Maurice J. Duncklee.
	W. H. Child.	1900	Frank J. Chadbourne.
1888	Chester Pike.		Ella I. Richardson.
	W. H. Child.		Jennie L. Lear (resigned).
	Herbert Deming.	1901	Ella I. Richardson.
1889	W. H. Child.		George L. Deming.
	Herbert Deming.		Josiah Davis.
	Stephen A. Tracy (resigned).	1902	George L. Deming.
1890	Herbert Deming.		Josiah Davis.
	George L. Deming.		Amy I. Hilliard.
	W. H. Child.	1903	Josiah Davis.
1891	George L. Deming.		Amy I. Hilliard.
	W. H. Child.		Rebecca Bartlett.
	Albert E. Wellman.	1904	Fred C. Pardy (appointed).
1892	W. H. Child.		Alice O. F. Young (Mrs. W. E.).
	James W. Fitch (appointed).		George L. Deming.
	Samuel Putnam.	1905	Alice O. F. Young.
1893	James W. Fitch.		George L. Deming.
	Samuel Putnam (resigned).		Fred C. Pardy.
	Herbert Deming.	1906	George L. Deming.
1894	Frank J. Chadborne (appointed).		Fred C. Pardy.
			Herbert Deming.
	Herbert Deming.	1907	Fred C. Pardy.
	W. H. Child.		Herbert Deming.
1895	Herbert Deming.		George L. Deming.
	W. H. Child.	1908	Herbert Deming.
	Frank J. Chadbourne.		George L. Deming.
1896	W. H. Child.		Margaret Beaman.
	Frank J. Chadbourne.	1909	Elwyn W. Quimby (appointed).
	Rebecca Bartlett (Mrs. D. D.).		
1897	Frank J. Chadbourne.		Fred C. Pardy (appointed).
	Rebecca Bartlett.		Herbert Deming.
	Nellie F. Gould (Mrs. Chas. E.) (resigned).	1910	Fred C. Pardy.
			Herbert Deming.
1898	Rebecca Bartlett.		Eben M. Johnson.

In concluding the subject of the schools of Cornish, we would say that a chapter might well be devoted to the teachers of the schools during the several epochs of the town's history, but it would be a colossal undertaking to obtain a full list of those who have taught in town. Over seven hundred different teachers have had charge of the schools in Cornish since 1850. Prior to this date, extending back to the settlement of the town, a space of nearly eighty-five years, probably there were as many more.

In passing this great number, it is proper to say, that among their ranks have been enrolled many who were eminently adapted to their calling, and who have given abundant evidence of their fitness by being repeatedly employed in the work. Some of these completed nearly a half century of teaching service here in town.

It is also a matter of justice to make honorable allusion to a large number who were natives of Cornish, who have gone out and taken high rank as teachers and have spent, and are spending, their lives in educational work. Of such, Cornish may well be proud. A partial list of these may be found in the following article prepared from the records of Kimball Union Academy by Mrs. Marion W. Palmer.

Kimball Union Academy.

An important factor in the educational history of Cornish is its proximity to Kimball Union Academy. To this school, distinguished during its existence for thorough mental training and high moral standards, Cornish has sent many of her sons and daughters. Indeed, the school itself may be said to be a child of Cornish, for Mrs. Kimball, the wife of the founder was a daughter of Moses Chase, one of the pioneers of Cornish, and was in full sympathy with her husband in the founding of the school, and, according to tradition, advised him in making it his residuary legatee. She gave freely of her counsel and her means to the school, enabling the board of trust to open the Female Department in 1839, which proved an important extension to the original design. From the year 1816 when we find the name of Levi Cobb, a farmer, upon the rolls until 1880 we may count up ninety-eight from Cornish who graduated or nearly completed the full course at Meriden. Of these sixteen became ministers, six physicians, four lawyers and a large proportion of the ninety-eight, both men and women, were teachers for a longer or shorter time. Beside these there is a still larger number who attended this school for a few terms, and from it received a touch of blessing which enabled them to do a better work in the world than could otherwise have been theirs. This work may be as important and count for as much in the great day of reckoning as that of those who went to higher schools and thence into professional life.

We cannot overestimate the worth of education and religious culture in the home, nor can we bring together for review these homes, scattered as they are, far and wide, but we are thankful that Cornish has had these households and that she has sent her children forth to reproduce them through our own and other lands. It would be a labor of love to give a history of these ninety-eight mentioned, and recount the work they have done; but that would require volumes and the hand of a master. It is, indeed, a delicate task to select any names from so many that have done well, but we cannot refrain from mentioning a few individuals and families who have received especial benefit from the institution:

Rev. Levi H. Cobb, D. D., winning as a preacher and teacher and efficient in his work for the Church Building Society.

The Leavitts, who went out from their Cornish Flat home and for two generations have been eminent and successful preachers of the gospel.

The Wellmans, through the influence of this institution have sent out one, eminent as a preacher, another as a physician and several teachers of rare merit.

The Rowells, a brother and sister going as missionaries to the Hawaiian Islands, and another brother, a clergyman prominent in religious work.

The Tracys, one of whom published four arithmetics and became professor of mathematics in Lansing, Mich., and teacher in several other places.

The Wymans, one becoming much noted for his musical gifts, while others of the name excelled as teachers.

The Spauldings, one of whom, the son of one who for thirty-six years was pastor at the "Center," became a distinguished preacher of the gospel.

The Harringtons, one of whom became a clergyman and was a power in all religious work.

Champion S. Chase, whom the great West knew as the mayor of Omaha and very eminent in political and social circles.

The Powers, a name almost synonymous with *good teachers,* while others have adorned the legal profession, and the halls of Congress have listened to the voice of one of this name well known as a devoted alumni of K. U. A.

Nor would we omit to mention the apostles of healing: *Ford, Jackson, Comings, Fletcher,* and others who have attained high standing in their profession.

Others might be particularly mentioned as the *Halls,* the *Comings,* the *Chases,* the *Richardsons,* the *Stones,* the *Fletchers,* the *Robinsons,* and scores of others might be named upon whom Kimball Union Academy has set her seal of honor and influence.

The following is a list of the Cornish graduates of K. U. A. from the opening of the school in 1813 to 1880:

	CLASS.		CLASS.
Jonathan Leavitt	1818	Samuel W. Rowell	1845
Thomas Hall	1819	Levi Henry Cobb	1850
Jeffries Hall	1824	William K. Fletcher	1852
Moody Chase	1825	Abbie B. Cobb	1853
Moody Harrington	1827	Emily S. Leavitt	1854
Daniel F. Richardson	1827	William H. Child	1856
Calvin Tracy	1827	Frances L. Wyman	1856
Levi N. Tracy	1830	Lysander T. Spaulding	1857
Daniel C. Rowell	1833	Marcia L. Kelley	1857
George R. Rowell	1833	Cordelia I. Richardson	1857
Horace Richardson	1833	Horace B. Wellman	1859
John D. Ford	1835	Caroline M. Powers	1859
Horace Hall	1835	Marion W. Powers	1859
George C. Chase	1836	D. Story Fletcher	1860
Benjamin N. Comings	1837	Erastus B. Powers	1860
George P. Comings	1838	Sarah J. Walker	1860
Truman Rickart	1838	Ellen M. Spaulding	1861
Jonathan Wyman	1838	Oscar D. Robinson	1862
Francis B. Chase	1839	James N. Edminster	1862
Albert Chase	1840	Flora M. Clark	1866
James C. Jackson	1840	Alice V. Powers	1867
William A. Stone	1840	Samuel L. Powers	1870
Benjamin C. Chase	1842	David L. Spaulding	1871
Joshua W. Wellman	1842	Martha W. Day	1872
Dudley T. Chase	1844	Albert K. Smith	1873
Joseph Rowell	1844	Wallace L. Bugbee	1880

List of Graduates from Cornish after 1880 to present, omitting dates.

Carrie M. Deming.
Edmund B. Chadbourne.
Lizzie S. Chadbourne.
Emily N. Tracy.
Nettie G. Williams.
Edmund B. Hunt.
Arbella A. Johnson.
Ada P. Wellman.
Nellie J. Johnson.
George D. Austin.
Henry S. Richardson.
Ida L. Child.
Charles Alden Tracy.
Clarence C. Walker.
Mary Ellen Goward.
Nellie Lucy Wyman.

Ina Eliza Hilliard.
Perley L. Barton.
Cora May Andrews.
Claude H. Deming.
Clyde Leroy Deming.
Leroy Harlow.
Charles S. Richardson.
Herman L. Walker.
Harry D. Witherell.
Hubert I. Deming.
Harold A. Fitch.
Charlotte A. Davies.
Annie Rena Howard.
Mildred Lucile Hunt.
George E. Hunt.

Time would fail us to mention all who have attained distinction nor would we place the work of those named above others who are not mentioned. In humble spheres and quiet homes the real work of the world is done. In the schools of Cornish, and in the lyceums of the olden day, many by the hands of others received blessing from Kimball Union, who had never been within her walls.

All good is not in the past. Cornish since 1880 has sent her usual quota to Meriden, graduating thirty. As the years go by, these also will come to places of influence and, even now, some are worthy to be remembered with the illustrious of the past.

CHAPTER X.

Town Officers.

During the first twenty years after the organization of the town, ending with the election of 1787, the town annually elected *five* selectmen.

Ever after this year, beginning with 1788, the number of selectmen annually elected has been *three*.

SELECTMEN.	YEARS OF THEIR SERVICE.
Samuel Chase	1767, 1768, 1769, 1770, 1771, 1772, 1773, 1774, 1775, 1785.
Elijah Cady	1767, 1769.
Jonathan Chase	1767, 1768, 1769, 1775, 1777, 1779, 1780, 1787.
Dudley Chase	1767.
Moses Chase	1767, 1768, 1771, 1772, 1773, 1777, 1778, 1782, 1784.
Dyer Spaulding	1768, 1769, 1770, 1771, 1772, 1773, 1777, 1788.
Daniel Putnam	1768.
William Richardson	1769, 1770, 1771.
Nathaniel Walker	1770.
John March	1770.
Elias Cady	1771, 1773, 1774, 1778, 1782.
Samuel Chase, Jr	1772.
Jonathan Huggins	1772, 1774.
Joseph Vinton	1773, 1774.
Daniel Waldo	1774.
Samuel Comings	1775, 1776, 1781.
Thomas Hall	1776, 1778, 1781.
William Ripley	1776, 1777, 1778, 1780, 1782, 1783, 1784, 1786, 1787.
Thomas Chase	1777, 1789.
Stephen Cady	1778.
Eleazer Jackson	1778, 1781, 1783, 1795, 1800, 1804, 1817, 1818, 1819.
Abel Spaulding	1779, 1780.
Ebenezer Deming	1779.
Stephen Child	1779, 1780, 1784.
William Paine	1779, 1780.
John Huggins	1781.
Daniel Chase	1781, 1783.
Reuben Jirauld	1782, 1783.
Benjamin Comings	1782, 1789.
Caleb Chase	1783, 1799.

SELECTMEN.	YEARS OF THEIR SERVICE.

John Weld............1784, 1791, 1792, 1793, 1794, 1807, 1809.

William Deming........1784, 1788, 1796, 1797.

Ichabod Smith.........1785, 1786.

Ebenezer Brewer........1785.

Samuel Chase, 3d.......1785, 1787.

John Morse............1785, 1786.

Elias Bingham.........1787, 1788, 1807, 1808, 1811.

Andrew Tracy..........1787.

Moody Hall............1789, 1790, 1791, 1792, 1793, 1794, 1796, 1798, 1799, 1801.

Benjamin Dorr.........1790, 1796, 1797, 1799.

Ithamar Chase.........1789, 1798, 1799, 1800, 1801, 1802.

David Reed............1791, 1792, 1795, 1802, 1803.

James Ripley..........1793, 1794, 1800, 1801, 1802, 1803, 1804, 1805, 1808, 1809, 1810, 1816, 1817, 1818.

Joseph Chapman........1795, 1797, 1798, 1799, 1804, 1805, 1806.

Moses Weld............1799, 1805, 1806.

Joshua Wyman..........1803, 1811, 1812, 1813, 1814, 1815.

Samuel Putnam.........1806, 1817.

John Lovell Kimball.....1809, 1810, 1818.

Newton Whittlesey......1810, 1812, 1813, 1814, 1815.

George Cook...........1811, 1812, 1813, 1814, 1815, 1816.

Timothy W. Hall.......1816.

Jonathan Wyman........1817, 1820, 1822, 1823, 1824, 1828.

Solomon Wellman, Jr.....1819, 1820, 1821, 1822, 1823, 1824.

Eleazer Jackson, Jr......1820, 1821, 1825, 1826, 1829, 1830, 1831, 1832, 1839, 1840, 1842, 1843, 1844.

Benjamin Chapman......1821, 1822, 1823, 1825, 1826.

John Weld............1821.

Joseph Huggins........1824, 1846.

Arunah Burnap.........1825, 1826, 1841.

Seth Johnson..........1827.

John L. Putnam........1827, 1829, 1830, 1833, 1836, 1839.

Sylvanus Bryant.......1833.

Benjamin Comings, Jr....1828, 1837, 1840, 1842.

Obed Powers...........1834, 1835.

Leonard Comings.......1828.

Israel Hall...........1834, 1835, 1837, 1838, 1841, 1843, 1844, 1845, 1846, 1848, 1849, 1850, 1851, 1852, 1855.

Rufus Day............1829, 1830.

William S. Deming......1836, 1840, 1842, 1845.

Simon Coburn..........1831, 1832.

William F. Comings.....1831, 1832.

Amos Richardson.......1833, 1834, 1835, 1839.

Stillman Jackson.......1837, 1838.

Reuben Davis..........1838.

Ebenezer Cole.........1845, 1847, 1853.

SELECTMEN.	YEARS OF THEIR SERVICE.

Joshua B. Wellman......1842, 1843.
John Johnson..........1846.
James W. Bradley.......1847, 1849, 1850.
John T. Freeman.......1847.
Hiram Little............1844, 1848, 1849, 1850, 1853, 1854.
Joseph B. Comings.......1836, 1848, 1855, 1856, 1857.
George W. Weld.........1850, 1852, 1854.
James M. Davidson......1851, 1852, 1856, 1857, 1858, 1873, 1874, 1875.
Gilbert Hilliard.........1851.
Joshua B. Wyman.......1853, 1854.
Willard Heywood.......1855, 1856.
Chester Pike...........1857, 1858, 1859.
Lemuel Martindale......1858, 1859, 1860, 1866.
George D. Kenyon.......1859, 1860, 1861.
William Balloch.........1860, 1861, 1862, 1863, 1865.
Hiram A. Day...........1861, 1862.
Norman A. Deming......1862, 1863, 1864, 1875, 1876, 1877, 1881, 1882, 1883.
Benjamin S. Fletcher.....1863, 1864.
Henry Gould............1864, 1865.
Jonas Hastings..........1865, 1866, 1867.
Stephen A. Tracy.......1866, 1867, 1868, 1871, 1872.
Louis T. Chase.........1867, 1868, 1869.
Norman E. Hebard......1868, 1869, 1870.
Dana N. Morgan........1869.
Charles E. Jackson.......1870, 1871, 1872, 1873, 1885, 1886, 1887, 1888, 1889.
Seth Cole...............1870.
William C. Hart.........1871, 1874, 1875, 1876.
Edward O. Day.........1872, 1873, 1874, 1876, 1877, 1879, 1880, 1882.
Orville B. Williams......1877, 1884.
Carlos F. Huggins.......1878.
Elias S. Leavitt..........1878, 1879.
Chauncey P. Jenney......1878, 1879, 1884.
Benjamin T. Harlow.....1880, 1881, 1882.
Philander W. Smith......1880, 1881.
William Tandy..........1883, 1889.
Edward T. Ayers........1883.
William E. Westgate.....1884, 1885, 1886.
Albert E. Wellman.......1885, 1886, 1887.
Jacob Beal..............1887.
Charles H. Andrews......1888.
James W. Fitch.........1888, 1889, 1890.
George L. Deming.......1890, 1891.
William W. Balloch......1890, 1891, 1892, 1893, 1894, 1896, 1897, 1898, 1899, 1900, 1901.
Charles H. Deming......1891, 1892, 1893, 1894.
Clayton B. Hilliard......1892.
Edgar A. Churchill.......1893, 1894, 1895, 1896, 1901, 1902, 1904.

SELECTMEN.   YEARS OF THEIR SERVICE.

Edwin G. Kenyon . . . . . . .1895.
Frank C. Jackson . . . . . . .1895, 1896, 1897.
Levi R. Dole . . . . .1897, 1898, 1899.
Edwin O. Goward . . . . . .1898, 1899, 1900.
Eben M. Johnson . . . . . . .1900, 1901, 1902, 1903.
Fenno B. Comings . . . . . .1902, 1903.
James B. Chadbourne . . . .1903, 1904, 1905, 1906, 1907, 1908.
Erwin W. Quimby . . . . . .1904, 1905, 1906, 1907, 1908, 1909.
Robert A. Austin . . . . . . .1905, 1906, 1907, 1908.
Fred N. Weld . . . . .1909, 1910, 1911.
Norman C. Penniman . . . .1909, 1910, 1911.
Charles S. Lear . . . . .1910, 1911.

YEAR.	TOWN CLERKS.	YEAR.	TOWN CLERKS
1767	Daniel Putnam.	1798	Moses Weld
1768	Jonathan Chase.	1799	Moses Weld.
1769	Daniel Putnam.	1800	Samuel Putnam.
1770	Daniel Putnam.	1801	Samuel Putnam.
1771	Daniel Putnam.	1802	Samuel Putnam.
1772	Daniel Putnam.	1803	Samuel Putnam.
1773	Daniel Putnam.	1804	Samuel Putnam.
1774	Daniel Putnam.	1805	Samuel Putnam.
1775	Daniel Putnam.	1806	Samuel Putnam.
1776	William Ripley.	1807	Samuel Putnam.
1777	William Ripley.	1808	Samuel Putnam.
1778	William Ripley.	1809	Newton Whittlesey.
1779	John Morse and William Ripley.	1810	Newton Whittlesey.
1780	John Morse.	1811	Newton Whittlesey.
1781	John Morse.	1812	Newton Whittlesey.
1782	Thomas Chase.	1813	Newton Whittlesey.
1783	Thomas Chase.	1814	Newton Whittlesey.
1784	Caleb Chase.	1815	Newton Whittlesey.
1785	Caleb Chase.	1816	Newton Whittlesey.
1786	Caleb Chase.	1817	Newton Whittlesey.
1787	Caleb Chase.	1818	Newton Whittlesey.
1788	Caleb Chase.	1819	Newton Whittlesey.
1789	Caleb Chase.	1820	Newton Whittlesey.
1790	Moses Weld.	1821	Stephen Cole.
1791	Moses Weld.	1822	Stephen Cole.
1792	Moses Weld.	1823	Stephen Cole.
1793	Moses Weld.	1824	Stephen Cole.
1794	Moses Weld.	1825	William Whittlesey.
1795	Moses Weld.	1826	William Whittlesey.
1796	Moses Weld.	1827	William Whittlesey.
1797	Moses Weld.	1828	William Whittlesey.
		1829	William Whittlesey.

YEAR.	TOWN CLERKS.	YEAR.	TOWN CLERKS.
1830	John S. Blanchard.	1871	Timothy A. Gleason.
1831	John S. Blanchard.	1872	Timothy A. Gleason.
1832	John S. Blanchard.	1873	Timothy A. Gleason.
1833	Eleazer Jackson.	1874	Timothy A. Gleason.
1834	John T. Freeman.	1875	Timothy A. Gleason.
1835	John T. Freeman.	1876	Timothy A. Gleason.
1836	John T. Freeman.	1877	Timothy A. Gleason.
1837	John T. Freeman.	1878	Samuel M. Green.
1838	John T. Freeman.	1879	Orlando Powers.
1839	Orlando Powers.	1880	Samuel M. Green.
1840	John T. Freeman.	1881	Samuel M. Green.
1841	John T. Freeman.	1882	Samuel M. Green.
1842	Orlando Powers.	1883	Samuel M. Green and John C. Boynton.
1843	Elijah Boardman.		
1844	John T. Freeman.	1884	John C. Boynton.
1845	John T. Freeman.	1885	John C. Boynton.
1846	John T. Freeman.	1886	John C. Boynton.
1847	John T. Freeman.	1887	John C. Boynton.
1848	John T. Freeman.	1888	John C. Boynton.
1849	Orlando Powers.	1889	William H. Sisson.
1850	Orlando Powers.	1890	William H. Sisson.
1851	Orlando Powers.	1891	William H. Sisson.
1852	Orlando Powers.	1892	William H. Sisson.
1853	Orlando Powers.	1893	Paul Davidson.
1854	John T. Breck.	1894	Paul Davidson.
1855	John T. Breck.	1895	Paul Davidson.
1856	John T. Breck.	1896	Paul Davidson.
1857	John T. Breck.	1897	Paul Davidson.
1858	John T. Breck.	1898	Paul Davidson.
1859	John T. Breck.	1899	Paul Davidson.
1860	John T. Breck.	1900	Paul Davidson.
1861	John T. Breck.	1901	Paul Davidson.
1862	John T. Breck.	1902	Paul Davidson.
1863	John T. Breck.	1903	Paul Davidson.
1864	John T. Breck.	1904	Paul Davidson.
1865	John T. Breck.	1905	Paul Davidson.
1866	John T. Breck.	1906	Paul Davidson.
1867	Arunah Burnap.	1907	Paul Davidson.
1868	Daniel Chase.	1908	Paul Davidson.
1869	Daniel Chase.	1909	Paul Davidson.
1870	Daniel Chase and T. A. Gleason.	1910	Paul Davidson.

YEAR.	MODERATORS.	YEAR.	MODERATORS.
1767	Samuel Chase.	1770	Samuel Chase.
1768	Moses Chase.	1771	Samuel Chase.
1769	Samuel Chase.	1772	Moses Chase.

12

YEAR.	MODERATORS.
1773	Samuel Chase.
1774	Samuel Chase.
1775	Samuel Chase.
1776	Samuel Comings.
1777	Moses Chase.
1778	Moses Chase.
1779	Moses Chase, Esq.
1780	William Ripley.
1781	Samuel Chase.
1782	Moses Chase.
1783	William Ripley.
1784	William Ripley.
1785	Samuel Chase.
1786	Samuel Chase.
1787	Samuel Chase.
1788	Moses Chase.
1789	Jonathan Chase.
1790	Jonathan Chase.
1791	William Ripley.
1792	William Ripley.
1793	Jonathan Chase.
1794	Jonathan Chase.
1795	Dea. Reuben Jirauld.
1796	William Deming.
1797	Capt. Caleb Chase.
1798	Capt. Caleb Chase.
1799	Capt. Caleb Chase.
1800	William Deming.
1801	Ithamar Chase.
1802	Ithamar Chase.
1803	Ithamar Chase.
1804	Ithamar Chase.
1805	Ithamar Chase.
1806	Ithamar Chase.
1807	Ithamar Chase.
1808	Ithamar Chase.
1809	Ithamar Chase.
1810	Ithamar Chase.
1811	Ithamar Chase.
1812	Thomas Chase.
1813	Harvey Chase.
1814	Ithamar Chase.
1815	Harvey Chase.
1816	Caleb Chase.
1817	Harvey Chase.
1818	Caleb Chase.
1819	Harvey Chase.

YEAR.	MODERATORS.
1820	William Whittlesey.
1821	Harvey Chase.
1822	William Whittlesey.
1823	Eleazer Jackson, Jr.
1824	Eleazer Jackson, Jr.
1825	Eleazer Jackson, Jr.
1826	Eleazer Jackson, Jr.
1827	Eleazer Jackson, Jr.
1828	William Whittlesey.
1829	Newton Whittlesey.
1830	Eleazer Jackson, Jr.
1831	Eleazer Jackson, Jr.
1832	Eleazer Jackson, Jr.
1833	John L. Putnam.
1834	Sylvanus Bryant.
1835	Eleazer Jackson, Jr.
1836	John L. Putnam.
1837	Newton Whittlesey.
1838	Eleazer Jackson, Jr.
1839	Eleazer Jackson, Jr.
1840	Eleazer Jackson, Jr.
1841	Harvey Chase.
1842	Harvey Chase.
1843	Eleazer Jackson, Jr.
1844	Eleazer Jackson, Jr.
1845	Israel Hall.
1846	Eleazer Jackson, Jr.
1847	William R. Kimball.
1848	William R. Kimball.
1849	Sylvanus Bryant.
1850	Sylvanus Bryant.
1851	Sylvanus Bryant.
1852	Sylvanus Bryant.
1853	Samuel P. Thrasher.
1854	Edward D. Baker.
1855	Ebenezer Cole.
1856	William R. Kimball.
1857	Sylvanus Bryant.
1858	Bradley Burr.
1859	Bradley Burr.
1860	William Balloch.
1861	William Balloch.
1862	William Balloch.
1863	Chester Pike.
1864	Chester Pike.
1865	Chester Pike.
1866	Chester Pike.

YEAR.	MODERATORS.	YEAR.	MODERATORS.
1867	Chester Pike.	1885	Chester Pike.
1868	Chester Pike.	1886	Chester Pike.
1869	Chester Pike.	1887	Chester Pike.
1870	Chester Pike.	1888	Chester Pike.
1871	Chester Pike.	1889	William Balloch.
1872	Chester Pike.	1890	George L. Deming.
1873	Chester Pike.	1891	George L. Deming.
1874	Chester Pike.	1892–94	Chester Pike.[1]
1875	Chester Pike.	1894–96	Chester Pike.[1]
1876	Chester Pike.	1896–98	Chester Pike.[1]
1877	Chester Pike.	1898–00	George E. Fairbanks.[1]
1878	Lemuel Martindale.	1900–02	George E. Fairbanks.[1]
1879	Chester Pike.	1902–04	George E. Fairbanks.[1]
1880	Chester Pike.	1904–06	George E. Fairbanks.[1]
1881	Chester Pike.	1906–08	George L. Deming.[1]
1882	Chester Pike.	1908–10	George L. Deming.[1]
1883	Chester Pike.	1910–12	William W. Balloch.[1]
1884	Chester Pike.		

While a province under the dominion of Great Britain the colonists could assert no self-governing rights, hence no representatives were chosen until after the Declaration of Independence. Even after this event the records show no representation to the General Court of New Hampshire until 1782. There had, however, been a Provincial Congress organized at Exeter, July 21, 1774. This held several sessions, and on December 21, 1775, it assumed the prerogatives of a legislature and adopted a temporary constitution. Under this, from 1776 to 1783, inclusive, the members of the legislature were elected for the term of one year, and convened on the third Wednesday of December following. The town of Cornish did not choose to be represented there until 1782. On this and the following year, she chose and sent her representatives.

In 1782 Cornish was classed with Plainfield and Grantham, and sent one representative. In 1783–84 she was classed with Grantham alone and sent two representatives each of these years. Under the state constitution, which became operative in June, 1784, the legislature was elected on the second Tuesday of March for the term of one year, and convened on the first Wednesday in June. Cornish had chosen her representatives on the March preceding, and these were there.

[1] Elected for two years.

For reasons not now known, the representative for 1785 was recalled. Cornish remained classified with Grantham until and including the session of 1787. After this, to the present time, she has been represented by but one person. From 1784 to 1878, inclusive, the legislature was elected on the second Tuesday in March of each year and convened on the June following.

Beginning with the session of 1879, the members of the legislature were elected on the first Tuesday after the first Monday in November for the term of two years, and convened biennially on the first Wednesday in June following, until and including the session of 1889. Since, and including the session of 1891, the legislature has convened biennially on the first Wednesday in January, the members having been elected on the previous November. Thus the elections occur on the even years, and the sessions are convened on the odd years.

The town has been represented by the following men:

YEAR.	REPRESENTATIVES.	YEAR.	REPRESENTATIVES.
1782	Abel Stevens.[1]	1802	Ithamar Chase.
1783	Moses Chase.[1]	1803	Ithamar Chase.
	William Ripley.[1]	1804	Ithamar Chase.
1784	Moses Chase,	1805	Ithamar Chase.
	William Ripley.[1]	1806	James Ripley.
1785	Rep. recalled.[1]	1807	Ithamar Chase.
1786	Dudley Chase.[1]	1808	Ithamar Chase.
1787	Moses Chase.[1]	1809	James Ripley.
1788	Gen. Jonathan Chase.	1810	James Ripley.[2]
1789	James Wellman.	1811	Capt. Daniel Chase.[2]
1790	James Wellman.	1812	Capt. Daniel Chase.[2]
1791	James Wellman.	1813	Caleb Chase, 2d.[3]
1792	James Wellman.	1814	Caleb Chase, 2d.[3]
1793	James Wellman.	1815	Caleb Chase, 2d.[3]
1794	Capt. Daniel Chase.	1816	Newton Whittlesey.[3]
1795	Capt. Daniel Chase.	1817	Newton Whittlesey.[3]
1796	Capt. Daniel Chase.	1818	Newton Whittlesey.[3]
1797	Ithamar Chase.	1819	Newton Whittlesey.[3]
1798	Ithamar Chase.	1820	Eleazer Jackson, Jr.[3]
1799	Ithamar Chase.	1821	Eleazer Jackson, Jr.[3]
1800	Ithamar Chase.	1822	Eleazer Jackson, Jr.[3]
1801	Ithamar Chase.	1823	Eleazer Jackson, Jr.[3]

[1] Classed with towns.

[2] Elected March; convened December.

[3] Elected in March for one year, until and including 1878; convened in June for one year, until and including 1878.

YEAR.	REPRESENTATIVES.	YEAR.	REPRESENTATIVES.
1824	Eleazer Jackson, Jr.[1]	1865	Joshua B. Wellman
1825	Eleazer Jackson. Jr.[1]	1866	Seth Johnson.
1826	Benjamin Chapman.[1]	1867	Seth Johnson.
1827	John L. Putnam.[1]	1868	Joseph B. Comings.
1828	Benjamin Chapman.[1]	1869	Joseph B. Comings.
1829	Benjamin Chapman.[1]	1870	James M. Davidson.
1830	John L. Putnam.[1]	1871	James M. Davidson.
1831	John L. Putnam.[1]	1872	Sylvanus W. Bryant.
1832	John L. Putnam.[1]	1873	George D. Kenyon.
1833	John L. Putnam.[1]	1874	George D. Kenyon.
1834	Sylvanus Bryant.[1]	1875	Stephen A. Tracy.
1835	Sylvanus Bryant.[1]	1876	Stephen A. Tracy.
1836	Could not elect, did not send.	1877	Charles E. Jackson.
1837	William S. Deming.[1]	1878	No election in March.
1838	William S. Deming.[1]		Philander W. Smith elected
1839	Reuben Davis.[1]		in November.
1840	Henry Breck.		
1841	Henry Breck.	1879	Session.[4]
1842	Reuben Davis.	1880	Dr. Geo. W. Hunt.[2]
1843		1881	Session.[3]
1844	Orlando Powers.	1882	Hiram A. Day.[2]
1845		1883	Session.[3]
1846	Benjamin Chapman.	1884	William Tandy.[2]
1847	Amos Richardson.	1885	Session.[3]
1848	Ebenezer Cole.	1886	Chester Pike.[2]
1849	Ebenezer Cole.	1887	Session.[3]
1850	Ebenezer Cole.	1888	Albert E. Wellman.[2]
1851	Ebenezer Cole.	1889	Session.[3]
1852	Joseph Wood.	1890	William H. Sisson.[2]
1853	Joseph Wood.	1891	Session.[4]
1854	Elijah Boardman.	1892	Edward O. Day.[2]
1855	Elijah Boardman.	1893	Session.[4]
1856	Israel Hall.	1894	William E. Westgate.[2]
1857	Israel Hall.	1895	Session.[4]
1858	Alvin Comings.	1896	William W. Balloch.[2]
1859	Alvin Comings.	1897	Session.[4]
1860	Arunah Burnap.	1898	Frank C. Jackson.[2]
1861	Arunah Burnap.	1899	Session.[4]
1862	Chester Pike.	1900	Josiah Davis.[2]
1863	Chester Pike.	1901	Session.[4]
1864	Joshua B. Wellman.	1902	Winston Churchill.[3]
		1903	Session.[4]

[1] Elected in March for one year, until and including 1878; convened in June for one year, until and including 1878.

[2] Elected in November.

[3] Convened biennially in June.

[4] Convened biennially in January.

YEAR.	REPRESENTATIVES.
1904	....Winston Churchill.[1]
1905	....Session.[2]
1906	....Herbert Deming.[1]
1907	....Session.[2]

YEAR.	REPRESENTATIVES.
1908	....Erwin W. Quimby.[1]
1909	....Session.[2]
1910	....Fenno B. Comings.[1]
1911	.....Session.[2]

[1] Elected in November.
[2] Convened biennially in January.

CHAPTER XI.

Societies.

Grand Army of the Republic.

This society was organized during the winter of 1865–66 at Springfield, Ill. The first post was established in Decatur, Ill., in 1866. Its ritual is secret. All soldiers and sailors of the United States army and navy who served in the Civil War between April 12, 1861, and April 9, 1865, are eligible for membership, provided they have had an honorable discharge from said service.

Its object and purpose is fraternal association and fellowship, as well as the perpetuation of the memories of that fearful struggle by those who were engaged in it, and also to exercise a kind guardianship and care of the widows and orphans of their deceased comrades. The movement became immensely popular and nearly all the veterans of the North joined it. Its membership increased, so that in 1893 it numbered 407,781. Posts were established in most of the towns in the North wherever there was a sufficient number of the veterans to warrant it. The veterans of Cornish and Plainfield established the "William H. Bryant" Post No. 63, which holds its meetings alternately at each place. It was organized June 21, 1887, and was named in honor of William H. Bryant, adjutant of the Fourteenth New Hampshire Regiment of volunteers, who died in the service.

Their principal public exercises, aside from the burial of deceased comrades, are associated with the beautiful and impressive ceremonies of "Memorial Day," on May 30 of each year, when they meet to decorate the graves of their former comrades with national emblems and flowers. Forty years have so decimated their numbers that but a handful now remain. These are still faithful to the memory of their heroic dead. Of the great majority who have passed on it may be said:

> "On fame's eternal camping ground
> Their silent tents are spread,
> While glory guards with solemn round
> The bivouac of the dead."

Soldiers' Aid Society.

Among the noblest and most humane institutions ever founded
were those of the Sanitary and Christian Commission, organized
during the War of the Rebellion. The horrors of war, in all their
detail, had been precipitated upon our nation. This national
crisis demanded the immediate presence of troops in large numbers to preserve the life of the nation. These were hurried forward to the theater of strife wholly unprepared to meet the fearful
conditions that were sure to be their portion. The government
at this period had made no provision for the amelioration of the
condition of her soldiery beyond their blankets, uniform and
rations. The new recruits from homes of comfort and plenty
were forced to endure hardships that soon told upon their physical
as well as their moral constitutions. Sickness became prevalent
in camp. Sanitary laws were few and poorly administered and
suffering increased. To these conditions were added the victims
of strife on the battlefield. These could not receive the kindly
attention they needed, for aside from the surgeon's services, there
were none to minister to them as they needed.

The government at first seemed blind to these conditions
owing, perhaps, to its anxiety to swell the number of its defenders.
When this state of things became known, a wail of sympathy
arose from the entire North. This soon took forms of organization called the Sanitary Commission and the Christian Commission; the one having special reference to the health and physical
welfare of the soldiers, and the other providing as well for
their moral and religious needs.

Hand in hand these two agencies of love and mercy followed the
fortunes of our soldiery throughout the entire war. The women
of the North, without exception, espoused the cause of their
fathers, husbands and brothers, and were first and foremost in
all plans and labors to relieve their necessities and mitigate their
sufferings. Nearly every village and hamlet of the North had its
organization, and meetings were often held to raise funds and
prepare articles for the comfort of their dear ones in the army.
Beside the preparation of bandages and scraping of lint, the ladies
prepared articles for sale and at times held fairs or festivals when
these articles were sold, oftentimes realizing considerable sums
to aid them in their benevolent work.

Cornish was wide awake on the subject and was well organized with a large band of faithful, sympathetic and efficient workers. They sent a good many packages to the "boys in blue" whose hearts were cheered thereby; and none watched with deeper interest the fortunes of the war than did the good women of Cornish. Just previous to the close of the war they held one of their festivals for the benefit of the soldiers. The event was successful and a goodly sum was raised. As the boys soon "came marching home" this money was not needed and so was never sent them. A portion of it was afterwards expended for a chandelier for the Baptist Church, and the balance of it, with other money remaining in their treasury, amounting in all to $176.80, was devoted to the purchase of the soldiers' monument in 1889. (See Soldiers' Monument.)

"Cornish Colonization Society."

Early woven into the fabric of our national life was the institution of slavery. It began with the importation of a cargo of slaves into Virginia in 1619, and it was gradually introduced into the other colonies. It seemed to flourish at its best in the southern colonies or states and soon became an important factor in the society of those states.

Meantime a sentiment unfavorable to it began to develop in the colonies, especially in the North. The Revolution, as a movement for liberty, declaring all men free and equal, joined with this humanitarian spirit, helped to increase the anti-slavery sentiment. The northern states soon abolished slavery, or provided for its gradual extinction. Abolition societies were formed, but these accomplished but little more then to intensify the sentiment already aroused.

In 1816, an organization entitled the National Colonization Society was formed at Princeton, N. J., and immediately reorganized at Washington, D. C., its principal object being to encourage the emancipation of slaves and to obtain for them a place outside of the United States to which they might emigrate. Branches of the society were soon established in almost every state. About 1830 the agitation against slavery took on a more ardent phase, and henceforth for thirty years, slavery was the most absorbing of political themes.

On February 7, 1840, a branch of the Colonization Society was organized in Cornish, and the following preamble was adopted:

"The deplorable condition of the African race, whether bond or free, calls for the sympathy of the philanthropist, and the prayers of the Christian. To these we rejoice to learn has been added a portion of active benevolence. To this charity we desire to lend our feeble aid, and to promote and encourage the object, we hereby associate ourselves together under the name of *Cornish Colonization Society,* and adopt as the basis of our operation the following.

"Constitution."

This constitution consists of seven articles, drawn up much after the common form and somewhat lengthy:

Article 1st explains more definitely the object of the society and as being auxiliary to the National or American Society, and that funds by them collected should be paid over to the State Society, which was also auxiliary to the National.

Article 2d tells who are eligible and how to join the society.

Article 3d prescribes the officers and their duties.

Article 4th relates to the meetings of the society.

Article 5th relates to funds and manner of raising them.

Article 6th relates to specific duties of the treasurer.

Article 7th relates to alterations and amendments.

The above preamble, together with the constitution, was adopted on the last-mentioned date, and was signed by the following individuals:

James Ripley	James R. Wellman
J. L. Putnam	Joshua Wyman
Alvah Spaulding	John Hall
Eleazer Jackson	Harvey Chase
Amos Richardson	Harvey Smith
H. H. Comings	Israel Hall
Reuben Davis	Ebenezer Cole
Nathan S. Luther	George D. Kenyon
Edwin Leslie	John Johnson
Sophia Richardson	

This organization was evidently effected at the home of Dea. Amos Richardson, as the foregoing record was found among his papers. We have been unable to find further records of the doings of this branch of the society, or when it ceased to exist. It was evidently begotten in the spirit of true philanthropy and perhaps accomplished its humble part in the praiseworthy work of its mission.

Temperance.

"Oh, that men should put an enemy in
Their mouth to steal away their brains! that we
Should with joy, pleasure, revel and applause
Transform ourselves to beasts."—*Shakespeare.*

During the first half century after the town was settled the use of ardent spirits was well-nigh universal. Every family kept it on hand the entire year as a beverage or as a treat for occasional guests. It was especially indispensable in the field during the haying and harvesting seasons. Marriages, and even funerals, were occasions that called forth liberal potations of the stimulating draught.

Liquors in those days were purer and contained less alcohol than at the present time; else such free use would have wrought more direful results. Delirium tremens was then unknown, yet the drink habit had baneful results. Then, as now, its use begat idleness and deprived a man of his reason, and led him to spend his time and money with convivial friends at taverns or elsewhere. In this way many a man lost his farm because his earnings largely went for strong drink.

In process of time adulteration of liquors began to be practiced, producing a cheaper but more poisonous drink, the use of which produced effects more dreadful than formerly. Delirium tremens then began to appear and the mad-house opened its doors more frequently as the result of its use. During the entire period previous to about 1825, temperance societies and temperance advocates were unknown. It is true, however, that germs of temperance principles were apparent from time to time, as shown on the records of the town, by certain votes passed, excluding the sale of liquors in the vicinity of the house on town meeting days and other such occasions.

About the time of the date above named, the effects and extent of the use of ardent spirits, as then manufactured, were becoming fearful and alarming. Their use was increasing, with a corresponding increase of drunkenness and crime. These conditions received the attention of thoughtful and considerate men, who began to devise ways and means to check the growth of the evil.

No legislation of importance, as yet, had interposed to ward it off. The voice and arguments of eloquent public speakers were now called into requisition. In this way a healthy sentiment was created in opposition to the general use of intoxicating beverages. Minor and local organizations were formed and pledges were passed through the community, receiving many signatures of men, women and children. In this way the minds of the people were prepared to embrace the Washingtonian movement which swept over the North in the early forties. This was a total abstinence society, organized at Washington, D. C.,— hence its name. It was formed solely in the interests of temperance and good order. It is said that a branch of this organization was formed in Cornish, but the records of it have not been found. It was during this period that the lines became definitely drawn between the temperance forces and those who still favored a free manufacture and sale of liquors, and these lines have been maintained ever since.

In 1855–58 and 1877 laws were passed by the state prohibiting the manufacture and sale of spirituous liquors except for medicinal and mechanical purposes. These laws were not allowed to lie still, but have been modified more or less by nearly every Legislature since. The distinctive feature of prohibition, however, has been retained.

In 1903 a local option amendment was attached to the law. This was a system of "high license" granting certain individuals the right to sell under certain restrictions, the rates being regulated by a commission, according to the circumstances in each case. In order to render the amendment operative, it required a majority vote of the town to render it so. The supporters of high license won each year until November 3, 1908, when, by a bare majority, the promoters of temperance won the day, and, at this writing (1910), the town still remains "dry."

Diversity of opinion has ever existed among the so-called temperance people in regard to the manner of suppressing the evil. Some advocate absolute prohibition by stringent legislation. Others would allow a limited manufacture and sale, having it strictly limited by law to medicinal and mechanical purposes, meanwhile endeavoring to educate the public mind against its excessive use.

The only temperance organization in Cornish, of which any record can be found, was a branch of the "Sons of Temperance" that was organized on Cornish Flat, November 20, 1866. The distinctive features of this order were secrecy and absolute prohibition. It was instituted by the deputy of the "State Grand Division," aided by a large delegation from the Claremont Division. About thirty members were initiated at the first meeting, and the new division started off under very favorable auspices. Its membership subsequently increased until about eighty members were enrolled.

They fitted up a hall for their use in the basement of the Baptist Church at an expense of nearly two hundred dollars. Meetings were regularly held. Literary exercises bearing on the subject of temperance constituted a prominent feature of each meeting which doubtless contributed in establishing a healthier one in favor of the cause of temperance.

This organization, however, had but a brief term of existence— only about two years. The by-laws of the order requiring total abstinence applied as rigidly to the use of new cider as to the fermented article. This was an unforeseen temptation, and several members, unwittingly or otherwise, were found to have violated their pledge and were thereby amenable to the laws and were subjects for discipline. This proved a bombshell to the division, causing discipline and disaffection, and led to a decline of interest from which it never rallied.

Its furniture and fittings, together with a small debt, were all surrendered to the Baptist Society, since which time the hall has been used as a church vestry.

Patrons of Husbandry—The Grange.

This is a secret association devoted to the promotion of agricultural interests. It was first organized in Washington, D. C., December 4, 1867. A sentiment was beginning to be entertained by the agricultural masses that their rights and privileges and voice in legislation were somewhat restricted as compared with those of other vocations. They began to realize, too, that they fed the world, and that they were entitled to reason-

able consideration in governmental affairs. No organization had
heretofore existed among them having any such end in view. Its
purpose, therefore, was to arouse the farmers to a sense of their
privileges and to restore dignity to their occupation by placing
it at once on a level with the other callings and professions. So
jealous were its first promoters that none were admitted to the
privileges of the order but farmers and their families. Pro-
fessedly it was non-partisan, yet it has exerted great political
influence on many important questions of the day.

With such an end in view, the order became quite popular, so
that in 1875 it numbered 1,500,000 members. Local organizations of the order were formed in nearly every section of the
country.

Unlike some other secret societies, the Grange bids the female
sex welcome to all its meetings, and confers equal rights and
honors upon them in all its deliberations.

On March 25, 1874, the Cornish Grange was organized
at the Methodist vestry by Dudley T. Chase, then master
of the New Hampshire State Grange. There were twenty-five
charter members. A large number of the farmers and their
wives joined them in the seasons following. They continued to
hold their meetings in the vestry until the following summer
when the Grange took possession of the commodious quarters
then used by the Methodist Church.

The charter members of the Grange were: Samuel Putnam,
Nettie L. Putnam, Dana N. Morgan, Julia A. Morgan, Henry A.
Weld, Eliza A. Weld, Albert Weld, Lucy C. Weld, Lemuel
Martindale, Rebecca W. Martindale, George D. Kenyon,
Lizzie Q. Kenyon, Charles E. Jackson, Judith C. Jackson, Amos
Richardson, Jane S. Richardson, Philander W. Smith, Almina S.
Smith, Charles B. Comings, Lucretia B. Comings, James M.
Davidson, E. D. Austin, Charles Williams, Charles D' Nevens,
Curtis H. Blake.

The first officers of the Cornish Grange were: Samuel Putnam,
master; Lemuel Martindale, overseer; Dana N. Morgan, lecturer; Charles D. Nevens, steward; Charles E. Jackson,
assistant steward; George D. Kenyon, chaplain; Henry A.
Weld, treasurer; Charles B. Comings, secretary; Philander W.
Smith, gatekeeper; Nettie L. Putnam, Ceres; Eliza A. Weld,

Pomona; Julia A. Morgan, Flora; Lucy C. Weld, lady assistant steward.

July 6, 1874, the National Grange granted its charter, which was received and recorded by the New Hampshire State Grange July 15 following.

DUDLEY T. CHASE, Master.

CHRISTOPHER C. SHAW, Secretary.

During the first few years of Cornish Grange the interest in the order was sustained, and its membership increased. This was largely due to the financial and social advantages it offered. As in other Granges it voted to purchase and make sale of staple groceries especially for the benefit of its members. This proved in some instances quite a saving to those who patronized this mode. Its social features were highly prized; affording, as it did, an opportunity for farmers and their wives to meet twice each month and enjoy an hour or two of pleasant social intercourse.

But however prosperous or promising a social, political, or even religious organization may be at first, a law in nature seems to order a change and it is permitted to suffer a decline. Cornish Grange afforded no exception to this. After a brief period of prosperity the interest decreased and the attendance of its members grew less. In this condition, though slightly varied, it remained about fifteen years, or until 1895, when it apparently received a fresh impetus and new members were added to the order. As many of the new members and also some of the old ones resided nearer Cornish Flat than to the hall of Cornish Grange, the idea of a new grange being organized at the Flat seemed to meet with much enthusiasm. Accordingly, a petition for a new grange was presented to the State Grange. The petition was favorably received and James W. Fitch, then deputy of the district, was instructed to organize a grange at the Flat. This took place on the evening of August 29, 1896, in schoolhouse hall. The name of the new grange was Park Grange No. 249.

For several months the meetings were held in the room where organized, but during the season of 1897 the Grange purchased the "Bachelor" house across the street just above the cemetery. This building was entirely remodeled by removing all inside partitions and reducing all the rooms into one, which was refitted into the present commodious hall.

The list of the charter members of Park Grange was as follows: John S. Andrews, Willis J. Coburn, Rev. Charles E. Gould, Mrs. Charles E. Gould, Dr. George W. Hunt, Miss Martha A. Harrington, Edmund B. Hunt, Mrs. Edmund B. Hunt, William H. Harlow, Mrs. William H. Harlow, Frank C. Jackson, Mrs. Frank C. Jackson, John B. Moore, Mrs. John B. Moore, Norman C. Penniman, Mrs. Norman C. Penniman, William H. Sisson, Mrs. William H. Sisson, Alfred S. Sisson, Mrs. Alfred S. Sisson, Arthur P. Thrasher, Mrs. Arthur P. Thrasher, Mrs. Minnie Spaulding; twenty-three in all.

These were organized by electing John S. Andrews, master;* Frank C. Jackson, overseer, and Willis J. Coburn, lecturer, beside a full list of other required officers.

On the 17th of September following, eight members of Cornish Grange received demits, and at the next meeting of Park Grange were received into its membership.

From its start to the present (1908) this Grange has enjoyed a fair degree of prosperity and continued growth. Its present numbers are 110. In addition to its social features it has made a specialty of choice literary exercises with music which have been for the enjoyment and edification of its members, and the Grange is reputed to enjoy a good standing among others of its kind, as evinced by many testimonials for excellence of work and literary accomplishment from state officials.

Cheshire Lodge of Free and Accepted Masons.

Cheshire Lodge of Free and Accepted Masons was first organized in Plainfield. Daniel Cole, David Read and others of Plainfield petitioned the Grand Lodge on October 26, 1814, for a new lodge to be called "Mt. Moriah Lodge." On the following day the grand master, Edward J. Long, considered the petition and ordered that the prayer of the petitioners be granted, and empowered them to assemble and perfect themselves in the several duties of Masonry, make choice of officers, make regulations and by-laws . . . according to the ancient customs of the order; but inasmuch as there was a lodge at

* Deceased March 2, 1898, while master.

Canaan already named "Mt. Moriah Lodge," that the lodge at Plainfield be called "Cheshire Lodge No. 23," and that the privileges thus granted be and remain in full force until the next meeting of the Grand Lodge. On January 25, 1815, the Grand Lodge assembled at Portsmouth and confirmed its former action and the grand master appointed William H. Woodward a deputy to go to Plainfield and install the first officers and present them their charter, which was finally done on the 24th of May, 1815.

Thus propitiously started, the lodge increased in numbers and its members, for a time at least, were quite constant in their attendance, the lodge took fair rank among the other lodges of the state, and favorable mention of it was generally made by Grand Lodge deputies up to 1832, a period of seventeen years. The lodge had ever labored under one serious inconvenience that contributed much to the ill-fortune that befell it. The members of the lodge chiefly lived at opposite ends of the town, nearly six miles apart and the place of meeting was at the west end. The members at the east end began to think their privileges were not equal to those of their brethren of the west part, and desired some change. They, however, tried to compromise the matter by meeting alternately at each end of the town. This action of the lodge did not meet the approval of the Grand Lodge, and so the practice was abandoned.

After 1832 the interest in the lodge seemed to decline. They failed to be represented in the Grand Lodge. They also ceased to work, and soon after, ceased to meet.

On June 9, 1840, the Grand Lodge, then in session, declared the charters of twenty-six lodges forfeited, including that of Cheshire Lodge, and ordered them to be recalled, which was accordingly done. The Grand Lodge, unwilling, however, to thus lose its subordinates, sent a committee to the jurisdiction of Cheshire Lodge on June 8, 1841, to see if any hopes remained of the revival of the lodge. But so far as known the committee accomplished nothing.

For nearly twenty-two years the lodge remained dormant, its charter being surrendered; consequently, there was no gathering of its members.

The opening of the Civil War seemed to create a fresh interest in the order which was quite general throughout the northern states. The former members of Cheshire Lodge who were then

13

living, still retained their love for the order and desired to see
the lodge again revived. A petition from these brethren was
sent to the Grand Lodge asking for a renewal of the charter
and that the lodge might be restored to the rights and privileges
belonging to a lodge of Masons. The Grand Lodge saw fit to
grant their petition, and on the seventh of May, 1862, they
convened at the dwelling house of Dr. Charles C. Beckley in
Plainfield, when officers of the lodge were elected and installed.
A good degree of enthusiasm prevailed, giving promise of the
productive results which appeared in the succeeding years.

After the revival of the lodge in Plainfield it soon became
apparent that a change in its location would promote the interests
of the lodge by accommodating a larger number of its present
and prospective members. During the summer of 1862 the
lodge held all its meetings in Plainfield, but on the eighth day of
September following, it was voted to remove the lodge to Cornish
Flat, and that its next meeting, in October, be holden there.
Permission for this removal had been previously obtained of the
Grand Lodge through its deputy, and on October 13, 1862,
Cheshire Lodge held its first meeting on Cornish Flat in Union
Hall (since called Hampshire Hall). Here it convened at all of its
stated communications until July 25, 1863, inclusive. Meanwhile
the lodge had previously engaged and fitted apartments for its
use in the upper story of the store of John T. Breck, and on
the latter date it was voted to occupy the new hall at the
next regular meeting. This was accordingly done on August
22, 1863. Since this date the lodge has held all of its communications in this hall. Like all kindred organizations, the
lodge has had its seasons of prosperity and its periods of
decline of interest; but it has ever since maintained its rank
and standing among other lodges of its order. Its jurisdiction
embraces the towns of Cornish and Plainfield. Its membership
has ever been composed of representatives of most of the good
families of these two towns.

CHAPTER XII.

MANUFACTURING INDUSTRIES.

NOT unlike every other New England town, Cornish has had her quota of domestic industries and her share of men to carry them on.

Nature here has not been as favorable to the manufacturing of goods on a large scale as in some towns favored with greater water privileges. Yet such privileges as have been afforded have been utilized to the best advantage.

During those years when the people were dependent upon goods manufactured in their own homes, workmen of every trade were at hand preparing the same for use. Coopers, tailors, shoemakers, weavers and spinners and other workmen were then in demand in every home.

Now all these are among the things of the past, and the people have but little use for them, as the goods once manufactured by them can be obtained "ready-made" in the markets and at cheaper rates, and, perchance, of better quality than formerly. For the same reason carding and fulling mills have gone out of business. Two prominent ones formerly did a good business in town: one in the west part of the town operated by Walter Mercer, and one near the Flat operated by Eldad Coburn. Each of these were active many years, greatly to the advantage of the community, and bringing profit to their owners.

When every family made its own shoes, it was necessary that tanners should prepare the leather for the shoemaker. So with the departure of the shoemaker goes the tanner, both to the larger central places where at their trade they may find more steady employment and greater profit.

There were several tanneries in town some of whose sites can scarcely be located. The last one to abide in use was at the Flat, owned and operated many years by Alvin Comings. The Weld families also carried on this industry to considerable extent, also the Comingses, in the early days of the town.

Blacksmiths, carpenters and wheelwrights still remain, although many of the articles heretofore made by them are procured from the larger factories and at a better advantage. A larger percentage of the labor of these artisans now is that of repairing.

For many years carriage building was a large item of industry at the Flat. Hiram Little, a skilled workman, employed a few men and for many years produced carriages that were second to none then in use; some of these are in use at the present time. Henry Gould also carried on a similar business there. Each of these men had successors in their shops who continued the business for a longer or shorter period; but these industries have departed, and even the buildings then used by them have been torn down and the sites almost obliterated.

Brick has been made in several places and several houses have been erected in town from the product of the kilns. Four of these kilns are known to have been in use. Brick was formerly made on the Henry Bartlett farm not far from the site of his present house. A limited amount was made on the Joshua Wyman farm and the Wyman houses were built from the brick made there. On the mountain farm of Capt. William Atwood brick was made. In the southwest part of the town on the farm owned by Leonard Harlow, brick has been made in large quantities. This kiln is still used occasionally. Other places for making brick have probably existed, but they are slumbering in the memories of the past.

Gristmills were counted of prime importance. The first of these erected in town was by Jonathan Chase on a brook on his allotment. This constituted a center for many miles around for farmers to bring their grain to have it ground for use in their families. This mill was built during the fall of 1765, soon after the town was settled. It was operated by Mr. Chase until 1773 when it came into the possession of Samuel Comings. He and his children, and others of the same name and their successors, continued to successfully operate this mill and other mills adjoining it for more than a century. This was long known as "Comings' mills." It was burned in 1894, but was succeeded by another doing a moderate amount of business.

Dea. John Chase had for many years a gristmill in connection with his sawmill which accommodated several families in that neighborhood.

A gristmill east of the Flat, for two or three generations,

did a large amount of business. Beside ordinary grinding like Comings' mill, it was fully equipped for the bolting of wheat flour. This mill recently became disused and now (1907) is in a state of ruin and decay.

B. S. Lewis built a gristmill about 1850 but operated it only a few years; also Bryant's mill, in the west part of the town, was for many years successfully operated as a gristmill until it burned.

The last gristmill erected in town is on the estate of the late C. C. Beaman, Esq. This is still active, doing the needful work for the estate and some for the neighborhood. It is the only gristmill now doing any business in town. The sites of some of these already named can scarcely be located; others may have existed, but none are left to tell their story.

The decadence of gristmills is mainly due to a great change that has taken place in the commercial world.

The great West is, to a large extent, now feeding the East with wheat and corn. These are raised and manufactured in the West and come to us ready for our consumption, so that many farmers think they can buy cheaper than they can raise the grain and get it ground near home, and so as a result, the eastern mills have been suffered to decay.

The sawmills of Cornish are interesting to consider. The great necessity for lumber for building purposes incident to the rapid settlement of the town, and the difficulties of removing large logs long distances, induced many to utilize every sufficient stream of water, by building a dam and erecting a mill as near their home as possible; consequently, the number of sawmills was greater than that of other mills.

The first sawmill in town was a companion to the first gristmill, both built and owned by Col. Jonathan Chase. This, like the gristmill, passed into the possession of the Comingses who carried it on through their lives. A succession of owners have since operated it, and it is still active and doing a good amount of business. Below this mill, nearer the river, was another sawmill also built and used by Colonel Chase. This was used considerably in its day, but it has long since disappeared.

At the Flat have been two sawmills. The lower one near the head of the street was rebuilt in 1832 by Abel Jackson, who operated the same a number of years, but it was in turn succeeded by others. This mill has recently been taken down and the site has nearly reverted to its natural state. The upper mill, now standing, was built and operated by Jonathan Wyman who came from Pelham, N. H., to Cornish in 1794. This mill is partially active, doing a moderate amount of business, but it is evidently doomed to destruction like all of the adjoining buildings whose industries were formerly active but have now passed away. This mill has passed through the hands of several owners, chief among whom was Henry Gould who built a fine dam of granite and otherwise substantially repaired the mill, as well as the gristmill which he also owned.

An important sawmill was that of Dea. John Chase which was built about the first of the last century. It was burned in March, 1847, but rebuilt that season. It has done a large amount of business, but is now dismantled and ready for destruction.

A sawmill, not long since, stood on the brook in "Slab City," owned and operated during its last years by James F. Tasker. Nothing of this mill is now left but huge walls of stone. The same may be said of a sawmill once standing on the Ichabod Smith farm, which did a good amount of business. On the mountain streams farthest east were three mills: one in the "Hempyard," and one in the "Poppy Squash" neighborhood, having long since ceased to exist. The other in school district No. 8, belonging to Edward O. Day, is still standing, but not used as a mill.

The kind of saw used in all the old mills was the upright kind, attached to a pitman shaft that was fastened to the crank of the water-wheel beneath. There were two sawmills in town that had the circular saw substituted in place of the upright saw.

Portable sawmills, run by steam or gasoline, with circular saw, have recently been established in several places for brief periods, doing a large amount of business. These have contributed to the decline and decay of stationary mills that are dependent upon water power alone.

Remains of other sawmills, and also of various other kinds of mills, comparatively unimportant, are pointed out by the "say-so" of men; but if they have a history it has become buried in the past, and of no use to the present generation. Slight evidences there are in some of these cases, but we can record nothing reliable concerning them.

Abel Jackson, a millwright, said, during the last years of his life, that he had built and assisted in building nineteen mills in town, and that Cornish had had thirty different mills. We are unable to locate as many as that, but are sure that the principal ones have been mentioned.

Another industry of considerable interest to some and of credit to the town, was the gun manufactory of David H. Hilliard. As a manufacturer of rifles he had no superior. His reputation for making a first-class shooting piece went far and wide, and orders came to him from the Far West. He employed several expert workmen for years and tested with accuracy every piece himself, so that his reputation was thoroughly sustained. But age came on and he was obliged to relinquish the business which soon after declined, and has never been revived. He died in 1877, aged 71.

Creameries.

About the year 1878 the art of separating the cream from milk was discovered and brought into practice. It has proved to be an invention or discovery of immense value to the farmer, his wife and to the world at large. The slow and tedious process of making butter by hand has prevailed from time immemorial. This old process involved a large expenditure of muscle and time, both of the husbandman and of his good wife, who was usually regarded as the butter-maker of the family. By the new invention this burden is mainly lifted from her shoulders; and on a larger scale, with greater results, the work is performed by machinery.

It was a new and novel idea that milk subjected to rapid rotation should have a tendency to separate, throwing the cream into one mass, and leaving the impoverished milk by itself. This is accomplished by means of a large circular bowl containing the milk that is caused to revolve at a high rate of speed. The De Laval Separator was the first in use, but was soon followed by others.

This invention or discovery spread like wildfire and separating stations and creameries were soon established throughout the chief dairy sections of the country.

In 1888 a coöperative creamery company was organized at the Flat under the name of the "Cornish Creamery." A building was erected near the Flat which was opened for business September 3, 1888. This plant has prospered ever since, dis-

CORNISH CREAMERY.
Bert E. Huggins, Superintendent, 1910.

HILLSIDE CREAMERY.

tributing annually between ten and fifteen thousand dollars among its several patrons.

On the following year the "Hillside Creamery" was organized, and a building erected in Cornish near Windsor Bridge. This creamery immediately went into operation and has done a thriving business ever since. Its locality is very favorable, as it receives much patronage from the farmers of Vermont living in the vicinity of Windsor.

The power employed to operate each of these creameries is supplied by an engine. These are immense labor savers. Hand separators, or separators on a smaller scale, are used by some individual farmers in preference to using the coöperative plant, as they save the farmer the time and trouble required in carrying milk to and from the creamery.

Blacksmiths.

This class of artisans, to a limited extent, have found employment in town ever since its settlement. As elsewhere stated the manufacture of iron goods has largely been assumed by factories, so the labor of the blacksmiths now is chiefly that of repairing and fitting. This, together with the shoeing of horses, renders him one of the most indispensable members of the community. A great number of these have lived and worked in different parts of the town. It would be impossible to recall all of them. A brief mention of a few of the most prominent must suffice.

Daniel Putnam, whose services in the Revolutionary War also included that of blacksmithing, came back to town and worked at this trade more or less during his life.

Charles Chase worked at this trade most of his life, serving the citizens of the town, especially those living along the river. John Fellows, near the south central part of the town, was also one of these serviceable men for many years.

At the Flat was Capt. William Atwood. He came from Pelham, N. H., to Cornish in 1811. He built the brick shop that is still used as a blacksmith shop. He did a large business in this line, employing several different young men who became skilled workmen in the trade. He continued at this until age and infirmity compelled him to retire. This shop has since been used by scores of men of this trade, and the property has changed owners several times. Prominent among those who have each spent years of service in this shop are: Stillman Coburn, Samuel Sherburne and Charles T. Sturtevant. At, or near each of the mills east of the Flat, shops have been located, but these have recently disappeared with the decay of the mills. William Atwood, Jr., worked at this trade on the hill east of the Flat, and afterwards built a shop on the site now occupied by Cornish creamery. This shop was used many years and then was torn down. Several blacksmiths who have wrought as such in town might be named as: Daniel Hamblett, Henry Gould, Ariel K. Spaulding, John Watson and others.

Harness Making.

Harness making has never been driven from the town by the competition of larger manufactories. With first-class workmen at this business, the idea has always prevailed among the people, that a better and more durable article may be obtained by employing home skill, than from the markets of the ready-made goods, hence these home harness makers have generally found steady employment at their trade. So far as known, the principal of these in town have been located at Cornish Flat. Walter Stone, when a young man, built a shop and went into the business in the same building now used by Mrs. Louis Peaslee as a millinery shop. He continued many years in the business until in advanced life he left town for Webster, Mass. He was succeeded soon after by John M. Couch who came from Plainfield in 1845. He remained here nine years and then removed to Holyoke, Mass. His oldest son (by a second marriage), John L. Couch, continued in town doing a thriving business for a number of years. He left town in 1864, and later removed to St. Johnsbury, Vt. Mervin G. Day, one of Mr. Couch's workmen, succeeded him, and carried on the business a few years. After Mr. Day had left town, William H. Sisson established himself in the business. With characteristic energy and thorough workmanship, he has built up a thriving trade in this line. First-class workmanship always commands patronage, and Mr. Sisson, in his business, affords no exception to this rule.

CHAPTER XIII.

Census Data of Cornish.

During the administration of Gov. Benning Wentworth, the British government made efforts to have a census of the Province of New Hampshire taken, but they proved of but little account by reason of ineffective laws and insufficient funds. In 1767, under the supervision of the selectmen of the towns, the first census was taken. This is presumed to be nearly correct. The following is the report given by the selectmen of Cornish:

Men unmarried from 16 to 60	17
Men married from 16 to 60	21
Boys 16 and under	36
Men over 60	0
Females unmarried	37
Females married	22
Population of Cornish in 1767	133

The second census of the Province of New Hampshire was taken in 1773. The record of it was for many years lost, but afterwards was found by Senator A. H. Cragin of New Hampshire in the Congressional Library. It was then copied and sent to the New Hampshire Historical Society.

The order for this census came from Gov. John Wentworth to the selectmen of Cornish, under date of October 15, 1773, and resulted in the following enumeration:

Unmarried men in town 16 to 60	28
Married men 16 to 60	36
Boys 16 and under	52
Men over 60	1
Females unmarried	60
Females married	35
Widows	1
Total in 1773	213

Sam'l Chase, ⎫
Jon'th Chase, ⎬ Selectmen.
Elias Cady, ⎭

The third census was taken in obedience to an order from the Provincial Congress of New Hampshire, under date of August 25, 1775. At this time it had ceased to be a province of Great Britain and was about to become an independent state. The following is the Cornish record:

Males under 16 years of age	83
Males from 16 to 50 not in army	77
Males above 50 years of age	9
Persons gone into the army	4
All females	136
Total	309
Firearms in town fit for use	53
No. of lbs. of powder in town	20

And this last is "privit" property.

Cornish, October ye 30th, 1775.

Personally appeared Sam'l. Chase Esqr. and made solemn oath that he had acted faithfully and impartially in taking the above numbers according to the best of his discretion, before me,

DANIEL PUTNAM, Town Clerk.

The fourth census of New Hampshire was taken after it had become a state, through an act of the Legislature in the year 1786. The following are the returns from Cornish:

Males of all ages	312
Females	293
Total	605

To L. E. Thompson,
Secretary to the State of New Hampshire.

WM. RIPLEY, \
ICHABOD SMITH, } Selectmen.
JOHN MORSE, /

No other census was taken until an act of Congress approved March 1, 1790, came into effect.

This act provided for a more extensive and elaborate enumeration than those preceding it.

The constitution of 1787 required that the representation of each state in Congress should be in proportion to its population, and therefore it was necessary to provide for enumerations, and that such enumerations be made decennially. The first was made in 1790, and in each decade since the enumeration has been increasingly elaborate.

In 1790 the enumeration for Cornish was as follows:

Heads of families in town	161
Males under 16 years of age	258
Males 16 years or over	238
All males (white)	496
All females (white)	484
Colored	2
Total population of Cornish in 1790	982

The following shows the *definite* list of the population of Cornish at this time:

Heads of Cornish Families in the Census of 1790, also Number in Each Family.

	Males 16 and over including head.	Males under 16.	Females all ages including head.		Males 16 and over including head.	Males under 16.	Females all ages including head.
Aplin, Oliver	2		2	Chase, Caleb, 2d	1		4
Ayers, Thomas	1		3	Chase, Daniel	2	1	4
Backus, Simon	1	3	5	Chase, Dudley	2	1	4
Barrows, Moses, Jr	2	1	2	Chase, John	2	1	2
Bartlett, John	3		3	Chase, Jonathan	4	2	7
Bartlett, Joseph	1	1	1	Chase, Joseph	1	1	3
Bartlett, Nathaniel	1	1	3	Chase, Joshua	1	1	1
Bingham, Elias	1	6	2	Chase, Moses	4	2	4
Bingham, Elisha W	1	2	1	Chase, Moses, Jr	1	2	2
Bingham, Jonathan	1	1	1	Chase, Nahum	1	1	4
Bryant, Israel	1		1	Chase, Peter	2	2	5
Bryant, Sylvanus	1	4	2	Chase, Samuel	1		1
Cady, Elias	2	1	5	Chase, Samuel, Jr	4	3	10
Cady, Nicholas	1	2	3	Chase, Simeon	2	1	3
Carpenter, Nathaniel	1	3	3	Chase, Solomon	3	3	4
Cate, Eleazer	1		1	Chase, Stephen	1		3
Cate, James	1	1	1	Chase, William	1	1	1
Chase, Caleb	1	2	6	Child, Stephen	2	2	6

	Males 16 and over including head.	Males under 16.	Females all ages including head.
Choate, William	1	2	5
Cobb, Ebenezer	1		2
Cobb, Francis	1	3	3
Coburn, Asa	1	4	2
Coburn, Dudley	2	2	2
Coburn, Merrill	1	2	5
Cole, Benjamin	1	1	2
Cole, John	1	3	2
Colton, Caleb	1	2	5
Cotton, Bybye L.	2	1	1
Comings, Benjamin	2	5	4
Comings, Samuel	4	2	6
Comings, Warren	1		1
Curtis, Nathaniel	1	1	2
Davis, David	1	4	2
Deming, Ebenezer	3		2
Deming, William	2		1
Dorr, Benjamin	1	1	2
Dunlap, Robert	1	1	4
Dustin, Nathaniel	1	3	3
Fairbanks, Abel	1	6	1
Fitch, Hezekiah	1	2	2
Fitch, Samuel	2	1	5
Fitch, Zebadiah	1	4	4
French, Ephraim	1	2	6
Ferguson, John	2	2	2
Furnald, William	1	5	1
Gibbs, Eliakim	1	3	3
Hall, Benjamin	1	5	3
Hall, Moody	3	2	2
Hall, Nathaniel	1	2	3
Hall, Thomas	1		1
Hall, Thomas, Jr.	1	2	1
Hambleton, Joseph	1	3	3
Harlow, James	1	3	2
Harlow, Robert	1		1
Haskell, John	1	1	5
Hildreth, Joel	1	2	1
Hildreth, Samuel	1	1	2
Hilliard, Luther	2		3
Hilliard, Samuel	3	2	3
Huggins, David	1	1	8

	Males 16 and over including head.	Males under 16.	Females all ages including head.
Huggins, Jonathan	2	2	5
Huggins, Nathaniel	2	3	2
Huggins, Samuel	3	3	3
Hunter, James	2	1	1
Jackson, Benjamin	1	3	3
Jackson, Eleazer	2	4	2
Jackson, Michael	1	2	5
Jackson, Perez	2		1
Jackson, Stephen	1		4
Jerould, Reuben	2		4
Johnson, Abel	1	1	3
Johnson, Abraham	2		3
Johnson, Jesse	1		3
Johnson, Joshua	2		1
Kimball, Edward	1	3	3
Kimball, Eliphalet	2		2
Kimball, Eliphalet, Jr.	1		1
Kimball, Lovell	1		3
Lucas, John	1	1	4
Lucy, Thomas	1	1	2
Lucy, William	1	2	4
Luther, Caleb	1	5	4
McCauley, Samuel	1		1
Machries, Samuel	1	1	3
Morse, Jeremiah	1		1
Morse, John	1	2	5
Nutter, Thomas I.	1		1
Page, Joshua	1	3	5
Paine, William	1	6	4
Parker, Stephen	1	1	2
Pike, Samuel	2		2
Plastridge, Caleb	1	5	3
Pratt, Stephen	1	1	1
Putnam, Daniel	3		5
Record, Lemuel	1	2	2
Reed, Benjamin	1	1	2
Reed, David	2	4	2
Reed, Elisha	1	2	3
Reed, Jonathan	1	1	4
Richardson, Jonas	1	2	3
Ripley, William	3		3
Roberts, Absolom	1	2	2

	Males 16 and over including head.	Males under 16.	Females all ages including head.		Males 16 and over including head.	Males under 16.	Females all ages including head.
Roberts, Daniel	1	2	4	Tracy, Andrew	3	3	4
Shapley, Jabez	2		4	Tucker, Abijah	3	1	3
Shapley, Thomas	1	1	3	Tucker, Chester	1	1	1
Smith, Benjamin	1		4	Vial, Abraham	1		1
Smith, David	2		3	Vincent, Richard	1		1
Smith, Ichabod	1	3	2	Vinton, John	2	3	4
Smith, Joseph	1	1	2	Weld, John	3	4	5
Smith, William	1	2	2	Weld, Moses	1	1	6
Spaulding, Abel	2		4	Weld, Walter	1	2	3
Spaulding, Andrew	3		4	Wellman, James	2	1	2
Spaulding, Dyer	3	1	2	Wellman, James, Jr.	3	2	3
Spaulding, Darius	1	3	2	Wellman, Solomon	1	1	1
Spaulding, John	1	1	5	Whiting, Nathan	1	2	3
Spicer, Jabez	1	4	3	Whitten, John	2	2	9
Stone, Josiah	1	4	3	Wickwire, Samuel	1		4
Tabor, Phillip	2		2	Williams, Benjamin	2	1	4
Taylor, Joseph	1	1	5	Wilson, Robert	1	1	3
Thomas, Samuel	1	2	4	Woodward, Joshua	1	1	3
Thompson, Caleb	1	1	2	Wyman, Jesse	2	2	3
Thompson, Loring	1	2	4	Young, Thomas	1		4
Thompson, Thomas	2		5				

In addition to the above were two colored people; one in the family of Oliver Aplin, and the other in the family of Dudley Chase.

The following shows the population of Cornish and that of four adjoining towns on each decennial census since and including that of 1790—in all, twelve censuses:

Census	Cornish	Plainfield	Claremont	Croydon	Newport
1790	982	1024	1423	536	779
1800	1268	1435	1889	984	1266
1810	1606	1463	2094	682	1427
1820	1701	1460	2290	1060	1679
1830	1687	1581	2526	1057	1913
1840	1726	1552	3217	956	1958
1850	1606	1392	3606	861	2020
1860	1520	1620	4026	755	2077
1870	1334	1589	4053	652	2163
1880	1156	1372	4704	608	2612
1890	934	1173	5565	512	2623
1900	962	1114	6498	372	3126

The following shows the growth of territory, and increase of population of the United States since 1790:

1790	17 states, beside territories	3,929,214
1800	21 states, beside territories	5,308,483
1810	25 states, beside territories	7,239,881
1820	27 states, beside territories	9,638,453
1830	28 states, beside territories	12,866,020
1840	30 states, beside territories	17,069,453
1850	36 states, beside territories	23,191,876
1860	42 states, beside territories	31,443,321
1870	47 states, beside territories	38,558,371
1880	47 states, beside territories	50,155,783
1890	49 states, beside territories	62,622,250
1900	52 states, beside territories	76,303,387

The center of the population in 1900 was near Columbus, Ind.

Following is the population of New Hampshire at each census beginning with 1790; also her representation in Congress at these periods. Before 1790, it was three.

Year	Population	Representation
1790	141,885	4
1800	183,858	5
1810	214,460	6
1820	244,161	6
1830	269,328	5
1840	284,574	4
1850	317,976	3
1860	326,073	3
1870	318,300	3
1880	346,991	2
1890	376,530	2
1900	411,588	2

CHAPTER XIV.

Cemeteries of Cornish—Casualties.

Cemeteries of Cornish.

It has been said that a contemplation of the soul's immortality cannot be exercised too much or too often. Amid the busy events of life this subject receives little thought. Reminders that our bodies are mortal are on every hand. In no place will our minds be brought to these contemplations more than at the graves of our friends. It behooves us, then, to turn aside and often visit the hallowed ground where they repose and to beautify and make attractive the places of their sepulture. The consciousness, too, that *we* are not to be forgotten and that our surviving friends will erect over our remains tokens expressive of their love, will rob the grave of many of its terrors.

It was customary during the early years of the town for many of the people to bury their dead upon their own farms and in many cases to erect no tablet to their memory, save, however, placing a common stone at each end of the grave. In process of time the mounds and stones would disappear. The hands and aching hearts that tenderly laid their dear ones to rest, they, *too*, have mouldered away. In this way the records of many have doubtless been lost.

The expediency of having common burial lots set apart by the town was soon recognized and practiced.

There are eleven cemeteries in town, which have been used as common burial places. *Three* of these have been abandoned as out of the way and counted unsuitable for the purpose, being far from present traveled highways, and in pastures almost inaccessible. A few years since the town, recognizing the requirements of the law regarding the care of cemeteries, enclosed each of these with a wire fence. These are some of the oldest burial places in town and of great interest to the genealogist. They are (1) on "Kenyon Hill" containing five gravestones and twelve graves unmarked. (2) On farm of Charles W. Comings. This was once a popular burying place, but has

14

long since been disused. It contains thirty-seven tablets, and at
least fifteen mounds unmarked. Several persons of note in the
town's history lie buried there. (3) On the Daniel Weld farm, now
owned by Freeman A. Johnson. This contained at least twelve
gravestones and about twenty-five mounds unmarked. But the
vandal propensity of some lawless scamps has destroyed or
broken all the gravestones in the lot except one, thus affording a
strong argument supporting "total depravity," at least in this
case.

The other eight cemeteries are as follows:

(1) At Trinity Church. This contains the earliest dates of
burial in town. Twin sons of Col. Jonathan Chase were buried there in August, 1768, followed by their mother who died
November 25, 1768. These are the first recorded burials in
town. In this yard there are 213 well-marked graves, and at
least a dozen mounds unmarked.

(2) "Mercer" burial ground up the river. This contains
dates of burial nearly as early as the last. It contains 264 well-
marked graves, and about fifty mounds, at least, that have no
headstones.

(3) Cornish Flat. The most numerous of all; containing
320 well-marked graves and about forty mounds that are
unmarked.

(4) South Cornish. Contains 247 headstones and thirty-eight
mounds unmarked.

(5) "New Cemetery" (Childs'). This was first opened in
November, 1870; yet it contains 147 well-marked graves, and
sixteen mounds unmarked.

(6) Huggins' Cemetery. On the hills in north part of the town.
It contains 116 well-marked graves and eight mounds unmarked.

(7) Comings Mills' Cemetery. Contains 215 marked graves
and about fifteen mounds unmarked.

(8) Center Cemetery: back of Congregational Church. This
contains 60 well-marked graves and six unmarked.

The above figures were correct in 1898. Some changes have
occurred in them since, as a matter of course. Those above
termed "unmarked" refers to well-defined mounds, evidently
graves. It is not claimed that these mounds indicate *all* that are
buried in those yards, for many may have been buried there, and

their graves become wholly obliterated, but though unknown to us, God remembers them *all*, and none will be lost.

The eight principal burying grounds of the town are usually kept in good order. Sextons are appointed for each yard who perform the labors of sepulture and also have a general care of the grounds. Five of these yards have been enlarged beyond their original limits, to meet the requirements of the town. And the "New Cemetery" was rendered necessary chiefly by the crowded condition of the Flat Cemetery.

There are also a few private or family burial lots in town, well known and generally well cared for. The aggregate of decedents in all these burial lots in town are nearly as follows: about 1,700 well-marked graves, and over 250 nameless mounds, making nearly 2,000 whom it is known have been buried in the soil of Cornish.

The writer has personally visited every known grave in town and copied every inscription with date of death and also copied many of the epitaphs. (These latter were much more in vogue a century ago and more voluminous than at the present time.) He has also visited burial lots in towns adjoining for the same purpose— the obtaining of needful data. The full list of all heretofore mentioned, amounts to 2,140 names. Most of these names and dates appear in the genealogical records of the several families of Cornish.

This thought has often occurred to the writer when contemplating this army of the dead. What a vast amount of mental anguish and suffering is represented here in "God's Acre" especially on the part of surviving friends! How many hearts have bled in sorrow! How many tears have been shed on this hallowed ground when dear ones have been torn from families and the earth has hidden them forever from view! It is the "wailing place" for all living, and hence a sacred place, and a profitable place for reflection. Here we may learn that:

" We are the same our fathers have been;
  We see the same sights our fathers have seen;
  We drink the same stream and view the same sun,
  And run the same course our fathers have run.

" The thoughts we are thinking, our fathers would think;
  From the death we are shrinking our fathers would shrink;

To the life we are clinging, they also would cling;
But it speeds for us all like a bird on the wing.

"They died! Aye! they died; and we things that are now,
Who walk on the turf that lies over their brow,
Who make in their dwellings a transient abode,
Meet the things that they met on their pilgrimage road."

Casualties.

The following list may not be a complete one, but it includes all the names gleaned from the various sources at hand. It does not, however, include any fatalities of war or of sudden attack of disease, but simply of those whose lives have suddenly terminated by some accident.

1767.　First recorded accidental death in town was Tisdale Dean of Claremont, who was killed at the Chase (or Comings) mill. No particulars ascertained. He had previously married Lucy Spaulding of Cornish. Was buried on the banks of Connecticut River. This death is also said to be the first in town from any cause.

1773.　Daniel Chase Putnam, son of Daniel and Anna (Chase) Putnam, was drowned in the Connecticut River.

1785.　Benjamin Swinnerton of Cornish was drowned in the Connecticut River while attempting to swim it in company with an Indian.

1798.　May 27, Harvey S. Deming, two years of age, son of Alpheus and Hannah (Taylor) Deming, was drowned in a water cistern. The household cat coming in very wet caused search for the missing boy and he was found as stated. It was supposed that in attempting to throw the cat into the water he lost his balance and together they fell into it.

1801.　June 3, John Bulkley Paine, aged thirteen, son of Capt. Samuel and Lucy (Hall) Paine, and living with Gen. Jonathan Chase, was drowned in the Connecticut River.

1812.　June 10, Daniel Atwood, son of William and Elizabeth (Hall) Atwood, aged four years, was instantly crushed to death by falling in front of a cart, the wheel passing over him.

1814. April 4, Lucinda Hilliard, aged five, daughter of Amos and Sarah (Huggins) Hilliard, while playing with some beans, accidently inhaled one, causing almost instant death.

1823. February 5, Lucy (Hilliard) York, wife of William York, went on foot visiting a neighbor. A heavy snowstorm came on. Not returning at a seasonable hour her family started for her and found her dead and partially buried in the snow. She was sixty years of age.

1837. March 4, Rebecca M. Tasker, aged thirty-four, was drowned in Cold River on her way to town, by the upsetting of the stage while crossing the river at Walpole. A sister, Hannah (Tasker) Chesley, was drowned at the same time and place.

1842. June 25, Edwin H. Lothrop, aged eighteen, son of Francis and Sarah (Huggins) Lothrop, fell from the roof of Dea. Ripley Wellman's house, striking on his head, killing him instantly.

1846. June 25, Henry ———, a colored boy, aged seventeen, in the employ of Dea. Benjamin Comings, was killed on the highway by being run over by a team he was driving.

1847. Savory Gile, living at the "Hempyard," fell upon his scythe, cutting his knee so badly that he soon after died of blood poisoning. Age not known.

1848. July 27, four members of the family of Dea. Andrew Dodge were killed by the blowing down of a house during a fearful storm of wind and rain. (For further particulars see Dodge Gen.) It was the greatest calamity that ever happened in town.

1853. December 11, Hiram Coburn of Cornish was drowned in New York, aged twenty-nine.

1854. March 26, Jonathan E. Tasker, aged thirty, fell from a building near Windsor bridge, receiving injuries terminating fatally.

1856. July 4, Edna L. Weld, aged three, daughter of John and Anna (Bartlett) Weld, fell through a hole in a bridge in the "City," striking on the rocks below, fracturing her skull. She died on the following day.

1856.   July 26, Carter O. Strong, aged nineteen, was drowned
         while bathing in mill-pond at the "City" in the even-
         ing; probably was taken with the cramps. Was a mem-
         ber of the family of the Kenyon brothers.

1857.   July 19, a little daughter of Israel Foster Weld, aged two
         years, was killed by a cart body falling upon and crush-
         ing her.

1858.   February 5, Arthur M. Wyman, aged thirteen, son of
         Milton Wyman, was sliding in the field near his school-
         house, when his sled struck a pile of frozen manure,
         breaking it, and a portion of it was driven into his body
         several inches. From the effects of this he died after
         a few hours of extreme suffering.

1865.   March 18, John C. Shedd, a boy of fourteen years, was
         drowned in a freshet.

1866.   October 22, Mary Treat, only child of Edward Kimball,
         aged two years and six months, fell into a pail of scald-
         ing water, from the effects of which she soon died.
         Sorrow stricken, the parents left town.

1869.   December 16, Lizzie M. Deming, aged two years, only
         child of Marvin J. Deming, inhaled a beechnut into her
         lungs, causing instant death.

1870.   February 17, Willie H. Chase, aged eight years, son of Henry
         S. Chase, while at play in the barnyard, was accidentally
         hit on the head by a piece of frozen manure, which
         soon caused his death.

1871.   April 11, a little daughter of Martin M. and Sarah A.
         (Bugbee) Williams, aged three years, fell backward into
         a pail of hot water, soon causing death.

1872.   August 31, Henry W. Sturtevant of this town, aged
         twenty-one, son of Nahum C., was killed on the Boston
         and Albany Railroad.

1872.   October 7, the house of Abner Lull was burned to the
         ground, and Mrs. Lull, aged seventy-eight, perished in
         the flames. Mr. and Mrs. Lull came to town in 1860,
         settled on the Gilman Chase farm, where they remained
         until her death.

1874.   February 21, Mrs. Jennie E. (Sisson) Raymond, aged
         twenty-one, daughter of John F. and Emily A. (Smith)
         Sisson, accidentally shot herself fatally, while toying

with a loaded pistol, while on a visit to South Woodstock, Vt. Some have entertained suspicions of suicide, but proof is wanted to establish it.

1874. August 5, Frederic L. Wood, aged nearly seven, son of Lyman D. and Susan A. (Flowers) Wood, fell from a loft in the barn, striking on his head, breaking his neck.

1875. March 23, Peter Coult, aged twenty-six years, a woodchopper in the employ of George Jackson, was killed by a falling tree.

1875. September 4, Bertie E. Shedd, aged five years, son of Reed and Electa Shedd, was drowned in the Connecticut River.

1875. December 15, Jedediah Huntington, aged fifty-six, while drawing wood, was instantly killed by falling in front of his load of wood, the sled passing over him.

1878. January 27, George F. Badger, aged twenty-five, son of Rufus and Clarissa Badger, having frozen his feet a day or two previously, died of lockjaw.

1878. April 18, Asa Jenney of Meriden, aged sixty-eight, was instantly killed on Cornish Flat by being thrown from his carriage, his head striking a stone. The horse had become frightened and suddenly turned around.

1878. May 8, Nettie H. Read, aged thirteen, daughter of Harvey S. Read, was terribly burned by her clothes taking fire, so that she died in a few hours. She was looking over the ruins of a building just burned.

1879. November 28, Levi F. Stone, aged fifty-one, a painter, died. He was previously found in his barn partially unconscious with a broken skull, from the effects of which he died. Foul play suspected, but nothing conclusive has ever been obtained.

1882. September 20, Henry Allen Bugbee, son of Benjamin Franklin and Almira (Williams) Bugbee of Cornish, was killed at Lebanon on the railroad.

1885. April 25, Orville B. Williams, aged fifty-four, while plowing in his field, was kicked in the head by a horse. He lived but a few hours.

1885. September 10, Caleb B. Williamson, aged sixty-seven, was instantly killed by being thrown from his carriage

against a wall just north of the residence of Dea. P. C.
Hardy, formerly the Daniel Chase. Esq., residence.

1887.   March 22, Lyman H. Hunter, formerly of Cornish, aged
thirty-four, died from injuries received in Claremont
from a stick of wood hurled by a circular saw. Was
then living in Claremont.

1888.   June 23, Franklin H. Curtis, aged ten years, son of Hartley K. Curtis, was fatally kicked by a horse that he
was attempting to feed in the stall. He lived but a
short time after the injury.

1891.   June 26, Alfred C. Chadbourne, aged fifty-nine, died from
the effects of a severe cut from a scythe received a few
days previous, terminating in blood poisoning.

1897.   April 13, Peter Emery, aged sixty-nine, died from the
effects of a severe cut in the foot received March 25,
followed by blood poisoning. He lived on the Stearns
place south of George Jackson's.

1905.   December 3, William Harvey Harlow, aged fifty-two, died
from the effects of a fearful fall the day previous. The
buildings of Wilbur Quimby being on fire, efforts were
made to arrest the fire by tearing one building away.
Mr. Harlow, with axe in hand, ascended a ladder to
mount the roof, and when about fifteen feet from the
ground the ladder broke, precipitating him backward
to the frozen ground. He struck upon his head and
shoulders breaking his back, while the axe followed
cutting him severely in the face. Injured beyond all
medical aid, he sank away and died early in the following morning. His loss was deeply deplored.

1910.   July 24, Leonard Smith of Cornish was drowned in the
Connecticut River, while bathing.

While no murder has ever stained the records of the town,
events have transpired that have given rise to divisions of opinion regarding the possibility of such guilt. The case of Levi F.
Stone, November 28, 1879, affords one of these.

Another is concerning the tradition of a traveling man with
a grip-sack of unknown contents and value, who spent a few days
in the home of John Morse. On a certain night, it is said, he left
the Morse home, intending going to the home of Antipas Marble.

Afterwards it was learned that he never arrived at the Marble home, and that he had entirely disappeared from among men. The facts becoming known, aroused suspicions, and gave rise to much unhappy conjecture and excitement among the good people of Cornish. A public hearing on the case was held, but no further facts were brought to light than above stated, and so the case was dismissed. The public, however, was hardly willing to abandon its suspicions. So it is said that buildings were searched, ground dug over, etc., but nothing further was found implicating any one in the case. The traveler was never seen again and his disappearance has ever been shrouded in mystery. The above comes to the writer from various sources as a dateless tradition, except that it occurred during the first quarter of the nineteenth century.

CHAPTER XV.

PAUPERISM—COUNTY AFFAIRS.

Pauperism.

"For the poor shall never cease out of the land; therefore I command thee, saying: Thou shalt open thy hand wide unto thy brother, to thy poor, and to thy needy in thy land."—*Deut. 15:11.*

THE settlements upon the frontiers of New England towns were peopled by rugged, self-supporting families. The prevailing conditions did not invite the aged and infirm, therefore, these at first, seldom removed from the older towns unless attended by relatives who were able to provide for them a comfortable support. For these reasons, with few exceptions, only the industrious, able-bodied husbandman, the mechanic and a few professional and business men were found among these early settlers. A commendable sentiment of good fellowship prevailed in all the towns and between the families. The interest of each family was the interest of the whole community, and the interest of the whole community seemed to embrace the welfare and comfort of every family, so that the people considered any poor or unfortunate individual among them as one of themselves, and therefore were inspired to alleviate their wants. Every misfortune or accident was followed by some substantial expression of sympathy. If a farmer was sick at seed-time, his fields were prepared and planted by generous hands, and if he failed to recover until the close of harvest, he found his crops secured and his granaries rejoicing with the products of willing labor. These neighborly offerings were a school of charity. Under this beautiful system, few public laws were needed to regulate the expressions of charity to the needy, and in such a community there were but few, if any, who were reckoned as paupers.

This state of affairs could not and did not continue unchanged a great many years. As the population increased the number of

those needing help increased in a somewhat larger ratio, and
consequently methods of rendering aid have undergone some
change. The private, humane methods of the earlier years, to some
extent, gave place to those of public expression through the selectmen. These, however, at the first, generally treated each case
considerately according to the circumstances and necessities
of the needy. The methods of relief were as numerous as were
the poor. Sometimes their taxes were abated; sometimes
their rent was paid by the town; sometimes a cow was bought
by the town and loaned to the needy family; sometimes the
firewood, or a stipulated amount of clothing or provision were
provided.

While private charities were not debarred, the town was
careful each year to adopt some system and to make appropriations for the support of its poor. In some cases the town would
render a partial support to some not wholly dependent. Con-
tracts were often made with families to keep certain of the
poor at a stipulated price. This method soon degenerated
into the inhuman practice of "selling the poor at auction,"
or consigning them to homes at the lowest possible price; in
this way, some of the poor might fare well, while in other cases
it might be otherwise.

Cornish has passed through the experience of each of the fore-
named methods. Tradition is replete with praises of the "good
old times" when neighbors loved each other, but times have
changed. It might seem to some that charity had lost its hold
upon the human affections, and that individuals and communities were more selfish than formerly and not as regardful of
the needs of the unfortunate. Then, too, it is not easy to dis-
possess the mind that poverty in itself is in a greater or less degree
criminal. Those entertaining this impression seem to be forgetful
of the words of the Master, who said: "Ye have the poor with
you always, and whensoever ye will, ye may do them good."
It is often unfortunately the case that the friends and near
relatives of dependent ones are removed by death and then those
who have been lovingly and tenderly cared for are left to the
care of those who have little interest in them. All these things
have had weight in the molding of methods for providing for those
needing help. Instead of their receiving the kindly ministrations at home as in the early years, many of the poor are collected

in homes with overseers employed over them whose duties are to provide for their chief necessities and furnish employment for such as are able to work.

On April 11, 1780, is a record of the selectmen furnishing homes for certain poor persons. This is the first recorded action of the town upon the subject.

The next record speaks of the town voting to "sink" all taxes against certain poor persons; and also provided for the care of Miriam Roberts, a poor woman. On March 8, 1791, the town voted to "abait" the town tax of sundry individuals who were unable to pay them. August 25, 1794, the case of poor Miriam Roberts again came before the town, when it was voted that "the selectmen take care of her till winter, and then convey her Killingly" the cheapest way they can! What was meant by this vote is not clear. Perhaps the recorder intended to write Killingly, Conn., but the record is as here given. At any rate her case does not appear again in the records.

October 10, 1805, the town voted that the selectmen provide a "house of correction" for the poor of the town. We can hardly believe the town intended to provide a home of the character as implied by the modern interpretation of the above term. But if so intended, one may infer that the class of paupers alluded to were a set of "toughs" that needed "correction."

March 10, 1807, the town voted the selectmen take care of the poor of the town "to the best advantage." Inasmuch as this had been their duty, it would imply that they provide homes for the poor chiefly with reference to its cheapness.

The town also voted March 14, 1809, that the selectmen post notices on the several meeting houses of the town, regarding any pauper in order to receive proposals for their support.

March 11, 1817, the subject of building a house for the poor was considered and referred to a committee who were to report at the next annual meeting. There is no evidence on record of any report being made on the following year, and the records are silent upon the subject until March 12, 1822. Then it was voted "that the selectmen be a committee to enquire into the expediency of purchasing a farm for the support of the poor of the town and report at the next annual meeting." Again the town records are silent as to the action of the aforesaid committee for a full decade, or until March 13, 1832. At this time the town accepted a report of a committee respecting purchasing the real estate then occupied by Rebecca Tasker and Betsey Huggins, for such purpose. This plan for some reason not given failed to materialize.

The example of many neighboring towns had in the meantime been adopted by Cornish: That of constituting and denominating the selectmen as "overseers of the poor."

On March 11, 1834, it was voted that the overseers of the poor contract with one or more persons on such terms as might

RESIDENCE OF FREEMAN A. JOHNSON.
Formerly the Home of the Town's Poor.

be consistent with the interests of the town and humane treatment, and requiring bonds as to the latter clause ensuring *humane treatment*. A selectman moved a recommittal of plan to a special committee for later report, which was accordingly done.

The following year, March 10, 1835, the committee on pauperism reported that the selectmen take into their special consideration the subject of the support of the town's poor; and that in their judgment a farm be purchased for the caring of said poor.

On March 8, 1836, the town voted to choose a special committee to look out for a farm and buildings suitable for the care of the poor of the town. John L. Putnam, William S. Deming and Joseph B. Comings were chosen as said committee. During this year, it is gratifying to notice these benefactions of the town, viz: (1) Voted the town furnish Thomas Lewis with a cow or its equivalent in money. (2) Voted the town loan twenty-five dollars to Peletiah Martindale to enable him to visit the eye infirmary in New York.

There is no record of any action of this special committee during this, or the following year, but doubtless their efforts resulted in the action of the town the next year. On March 13, 1838, an agent was chosen to contract for a suitable farm and buildings for the purpose, and Benjamin Comings was chosen as said agent. He contracted for and purchased the farm and buildings of the Dea. John Weld estate, more recently owned and occupied by his son, Horace Weld. Mr. Comings reported the expense of the farm, terms of payment and the town fully endorsed the action of its agent in this purchase, and then voted to choose a committee to prepare a code of rules, rates and regulations for the management of the town farm and its occupants. Said committee were Benjamin Comings, Benjamin Chapman and Simon Coburn. This committee on the following year (1839) submitted an exhaustive and elaborate code consisting of eighteen articles. These were readily adopted by the town, and the name of "Cornish Alms House" was given to the paupers' new home. Jonathan Wakefield and wife were the first superintendents chosen by the town to have charge of it. They were succeeded by others who served in the care of the unfortunate poor of Cornish. They were required annually to report their doings in full to the town, even the daily condition of each inmate, amount of labor performed by them, etc. This excellent and careful supervision was a source of mutual gratification both to the citizens of the town and to its unfortunate poor.

This method of management continued for nearly thirty years when a change of the pauper laws of New Hampshire took place, enabling towns, so choosing, to place the burden of pauper support upon the counties to which they belonged. Accordingly a test vote was called for in Cornish on March 12, 1867. The question was, "Is it expedient to abolish pauper settlements in town and throw their entire support upon counties?" The result of the vote in Cornish, as elsewhere, was in favor of this measure.

A county farm for Sullivan County was established at Unity and most of the paupers of Cornish were removed to it during the year. This institution, under the care and management of the county commissioners, provides a home for the county paupers similar to that the towns afforded. The town continues a temporary or partial support to those who need assistance for a season, but those whose necessities demand permanent assistance are humanely supported at the county farm.

The abandonment of the town farm property for pauper use necessitated its sale. This took place on December 1, 1868. The proceeds of this sale amounted to $6,358.26, which was reported to the town on the following March.

A fund of two thousand dollars for the worthy poor of Cornish was left by the will of Jacob Foss of Charlestown, Mass., who died June 22, 1866. (See sketch.) The town received the legacy on the following September, less a revenue tax. This fund is to be securely invested and its income to be annually devoted to the partial support of any worthy poor in town.

On June 14, 1889, Edward D. Kimball of Mt. Auburn, Mass., a native of Cornish, gave the town the sum of three thousand dollars for the same object and on the same terms as did Jacob Foss. The interest from these two funds has proved a great blessing in ameliorating the condition and circumstances of many worthy individuals and families at home, who might otherwise have been conveyed to the county farm.

The following is a list of paupers from Cornish who have died at the county farm since its establishment: Benjamin Edminister, 73 years old, died January 8, 1862; Charles Lucy, 45 years old, died November 3, 1877; John Bell, 69 years old, died May 5, 1877; William Lane, 78 years old, died December 25, 1878; Eliza Forehand, 57 years old, died May 15, 1883; George Babcock, 72 years old, died June 1, 1884; Catherine Chase, 73 years old, died June 13, 1896; Caroline Jackson, 68 years old, died March 20, 1897; Elihu Russell, 87 years old, died March 22, 1897; Albert Kelley, 79 years old, died March 22, 1899; Frank Newman, 84 years old, died January 28, 1900; Albert Spaulding, 45 years old, died July 22, 1901; Edgar Geer, 27 years old, died September 8, 1907.

A peculiar, though rare type of pauperism, that once existed was the traveling mendicant. Their sustenance they begged from door to door. No laws, as now, at that time restrained them. They were dependent wayfarers, not from choice but from accident. Not tramps, in our modern sense of the word, neither thiefs, "hobos" nor "yeggs," but creatures of fortune, or rather of misfortune. To perpetuate the memory of one of this type, we would refer to a familiar personage called "Old Haines," or "Crazy Haines," who from the twenties to the seventies of the last century, wandered through many of the towns of New England, and always included Cornish in his trips. Some, doubtless today, will remember his tall, grim figure, clothed in tattered black garments, originally shaped for judicial or ecclesiastical dignitaries, with corresponding stove-pipe hat, or hats telescoped together. In memory of this man, Prof. David H. Lamberton of Morrisville, Vt., has inscribed the following touching memorial:

"Old Haines."

'Tis not of a Cornish man at all, these words of remembrance bear,
That is, he neither was born nor bred, around here anywhere.
He only straggled through the town, as seasons came and went,
If not in spring, why then in fall, while fifty years were spent.

His name was "Haines," or just "Old Haines," as boys, now men, recall,
And these same boys remember, too, that, when they were young and small,
The mother's threat to have "Old Haines" carry them off in his pack—
Would bring more good from a mischief-brew, than a switch or slipper's
    whack.

He begged his way and clubbed the dogs, that barked up and down his path,
Or angered sore by taunting gibe, he'd swear in a mighty wrath,
Yet country folk along the roads, wherever his wanderings led,
Rarely denied his spoken need for food or a shake-down bed.

"Old Haines" in stature was tall and thin, and erect in the red man's mold
And despite the mark of a vagabond, there was a hint of a lineage old—
A sign of blood that never had begged, a glint of a spirit in strife—
And a remnant of youth that had promised more than a useless waste of
    life.

His story, however, no man can repeat, as his silence upon it was strict,
But the older folk who had known him long, declared him a sad derelict
On the Sea of Love, where a woman's guile had left him adrift and astray,
A bourneless, masterless, rudderless craft, where currents unchartered have
    sway.

Full many a year since the vagrant "Haines" roamed over these Cornish
    hills
Has sped its way down the flight of time, leaving measure of good and of ills,
And not only he, but his class, no more begs at doors of the dwellings of men,
For Charity's kinder to playthings of Fate nowadays than her habit was then.

Somewhere in a mendicant's grave his frame has crumbled away into dust
The same as others 'neath marble shafts, who in life only threw him a crust,
But the Reaper of all has garnered his soul, however benighted it trod
Companionless ways in an unfriendly world, unwelcomed till lastly with God.

A vagrant was "Haines," yet alas, it is true, he was scarcely more vagrant
    than we,
Who chase our own phantoms and dream our own dreams, of successes that
    never can be,
The difference is really far less than it seems, when gauged by Eternity's span,
For of all that is gained and of all that is lost, there's a balance Divine in the
    plan.

County Affairs.

Previous to March 8, 1769, there were no county divisions in
New Hampshire. The sessions of the Legislature and the courts
for the adjustment of all legal matters were held at Portsmouth.
At that time the state or province was divided by act of the
Legislature, into five counties, that were named by the governor:
Rockingham, Hillsborough, Cheshire, Strafford and Grafton.
The three counties first named were organized in 1771 and their
officers appointed. The organization of Strafford and Grafton
counties was not long delayed. A message from the governor
under date of May 28, 1772, to the council and assembly, recommended the establishing and organizing of these two counties,
which took place about eight months later. These five counties
embraced the entire limits of the state. Subsequently, from time
to time, other counties were created and their boundaries defined
by the Legislature. Cheshire County extended north from the
line of the state of Massachusetts about sixty-five miles to the
south line of Grafton County, and east from the west bank of
the Connecticut River about twenty miles to the west lines of
Hillsborough and Merrimack Counties, making an area three times
as long as it was broad. It contained thirty-eight towns. The
county courts were held alternately at Keene and Charlestown.
At each of these places a jail and other necessary buildings
were erected.

15

To better accommodate the business of the northern part of the county, on December 8, 1824, the Legislature passed an act that the May term of the supreme court should be removed from Charlestown to Newport. This was only a partial relief. The inconveniences for the transaction of the business of the county were so great that it became apparent the only remedy was the erection of a new county. In June, 1826, the question of a division of Cheshire County came before the Legislature. On the twenty-third, by an appropriate act, the question of division was to be submitted to the several towns of Cheshire County; and also the question whether Newport or Claremont should become the shire town of the new county. A good deal of discussion followed, but the result of the election was: first, a vote to divide the county, and second, that Newport be the county seat of the new county.

The trial vote on the subject in Cornish took place on March 13, 1827, when, by calling for the yeas and nays, the vote stood: 128 yeas and 10 nays. On July 5, 1827, the county was incorporated, to take effect on the following September. The county was named in honor of John Sullivan, one of New Hampshire's most distinguished patriotic soldiers, whose name was reverenced by the people of the state.

The new county comprised the towns of Acworth, Charlestown, Claremont, Cornish, Croydon, Grantham, Goshen, Langdon, Lempster, Newport, Plainfield, Sunapee, Springfield, Unity and Washington—in all, fifteen towns.

Sullivan County is about thirty miles long from north to south, and about twenty miles wide from the somewhat irregular line of Merrimack County on the east to the Connecticut River as its western boundary. The general inclination of its surface is towards the west, thus furnishing a water-shed for the Connecticut River. The highest point of land in the county is that of Croydon Mountain which has an elevation of 2,789 feet above sea-level. From its summit a large portion of the county can be seen.

The scenery of Sullivan County is picturesque and delightful, though less imposing than that of the northern portions of the state. Along the Connecticut River are some of the best farms of the state.

The population of Sullivan County in 1890 was 17,304. In 1900 it was 18,009, having made a gain of 705 during the decade. The removal of the courts from Charlestown to Newport necessitated the erection of new buildings at the latter place. The old jail at Charlestown continued to be used, however, by the county until April 1, 1842, when it was burned by Hicks, a notorious robber who was then confined there. A new jail was then erected at Newport at a cost of $3,300. A meeting of the town of Newport was held January 13, 1825, when it was voted to raise the sum of $2,000 to assist in building a new court house, the balance of the funds needed for the purpose were to be furnished by individual subscription. By the eleventh of February, 1826, the building was ready for occupancy. This building continued to be used as a court house until 1873. The increasing population and consequent increase of court matters, had awakened the citizens to the fact that the old building was insufficient to meet its present and increasing requirements; so steps were taken in 1872 towards the erection of the present commodious town hall and court house. This was soon erected at a cost of nearly $40,000. A county safe building was erected in 1843, which still continues to be used.

CHAPTER XVI.

CORNISH BRIDGE—BLUE MOUNTAIN PARK.

The Cornish Bridge.

BY concurrent acts of the Legislatures of New Hampshire and Vermont, the former passed in January, 1795, and the latter a little later, the toll-bridge company which maintains the bridge across the Connecticut, known to the people of Cornish as "the Windsor Bridge," was chartered under the corporate title of "The Proprietors of the Cornish Bridge." The charter was granted to Jonathan Chase, to whom had been granted in the year 1784 by the New Hampshire Legislature, a charter for a ferry across the Connecticut between Cornish and Windsor near the point where the bridge now stands. The original subscription agreement for shares of stock in the bridge company bears the date of the thirteenth day of April, 1796, and is signed by Jonathan Chase and by the following other subscribers: Nathaniel Hall, Ithamar Chase and Dudley Chase of Cornish, Nathaniel Leonard, Amasa Paine, Stephen Jacob, Isaac Green, Nathan Coolidge, Caleb Stone, Zebina Curtis, Allen Hayes, Samuel Shuttlesworth, Stephen Conant, Jonathan H. Hubbard, Freeman Hopkins, Ebenezer W. Judd, Nahum Trask, Abiel Leonard, William Leverett, William Sweetser, Abner Forbes and John Leverett of Windsor, Benjamin Page of Hartland, Vt., and by the firms of Jones & Tuttle and George Bull & Company, both of Hartford, Conn. These subscribers, together with Benjamin Sumner of Boston, who did not sign, became the first proprietors. The subscription list also bears the signature of E. Brewer, but he does not appear to have become a stockholder. Jonathan Chase was by far the largest stockholder and Benjamin Sumner the next. Most of Jonathan Chase's conveyances of stock to his fellow-proprietors were witnessed by Nathan Smith and Philander Chase and acknowledged before Dudley Chase, justice of the peace. From the foregoing it appears that the promoters of the enterprise included in their number, in addition to the influential Chase family of Cornish, the leading professional men and merchants of Windsor.

The first meeting of the proprietors was held at the house of Nathaniel Hall, innholder, in Cornish, on May 4, 1796, pursuant to a notice dated April 14, 1796, published in the *New Hampshire and Vermont Journal of Walpole*, and signed by Jonathan Chase, Esq. At this meeting Jonathan Chase was moderator and was elected the first president of the company. The proprietors also chose at the same meeting the following other officers: Abiel Leonard, clerk; William Leverett, treasurer; and the following board of directors: Jonathan Chase, Esq., Nathaniel Hall, Nathaniel Leonard. Perez Jones, Caleb Stone, Ithamar Chase and Jonathan H. Hubbard.

The first bridge constructed by the company was built in 1796 at a cost of $17,099.27, a sum which, as the proprietors admitted, "in consequence of the unexpected rise of labor, provisions and the materials necessary for such a work," was "far beyond their expectations." This bridge was probably uncovered and supported by three piers between the abutments. It lasted until the spring freshet of 1824, which carried it away. The second bridge was presumably of similar design and was built in 1824. Some of the old toll-house journals, kept during the life of the second bridge, throw much light on the times. For instance, the records from December, 1824, to about 1840, which were kept in great detail, show to what a vast extent sheepraising was carried on. This was before the railroad had touched Cornish. Then the Cornish Bridge was a truly great artery for commerce. Sheep and cattle in great numbers passed over the bridge from the North and West on their way to market. On the Sabbath day, October 23, 1825, there crossed the bridge, 450 sheep; on the 24th, 838 sheep and 259 cattle; on the Sabbath day, October 30, 328 sheep; on the 31st, 200 sheep and 108 cattle; on November 7, 920 sheep and 236 cattle; on December 4, 470 cattle. The record for that year was about 9,500 sheep and 2,600 cattle. The droves went to market chiefly in the autumn and early winter. The records for the years 1837 to 1841 show the total numbers of sheep and cattle as follows:

YEAR.	SHEEP.	CATTLE.
1837	13,233	2,420
1838	14,084	2,208
1839	12,229	1,705
1840	11,451	2,657
1841	11,513	2,988

The largest drove in one day which the writer has found recorded was on September 30, 1833, when 1,000 sheep crossed.

In the years 1825 to 1836 Skinner's stage, Pettes' stage and the Concord and Lebanon stages were regular patrons of the bridge. Colonel Nettleton's Boston stage was using the bridge in 1826. Charles Bell, Jeremiah Hubbard and Joel Nettleton were stage drivers in the early thirties and in 1836 Paran Stevens' stage was crossing. The toll-gatherer of the period from 1825 to 1836, one Colonel Brown, found time to record in the journal his comments on the weather and to mention events of interest. In the year 1825 there seems to have been a great drought. Among the toll-gatherer's repeated and sad observations on dry weather, smoky air and no rain, we find on August 12: "Many fields Corn dried up and Cut up for Cattle." On September 23 he recorded: "Mill Brook so low the Mills have stood still for 3 months." On October 7: "In many places in Mill Brook there is no water." But a "powerful" rain came on October 27, so that on October 29 he could record: "Rafts and Boats run on the Connecticut." Earlier in the same year, February 16, there was a "Convention for navigating the Vally of the Connecticut River," which, with the help of the October rain, may have caused the appearance of the rafts and boats. But historically the most interesting item of the year was noted on Tuesday, June 28, when "Marquis Fayette passed with his Suit." On September 14, 1826, there was a "Muster at Cornish." On September 13, 1831, there was a "Wolf Hunt," followed the next day by "Calvenistick Convention."

In 1849 the second bridge was lost by flood and that year a third bridge was contracted for. This bridge had but one pier and was a covered lattice bridge of the same type as the present, and stood until the night of March 3 and 4, 1866, when its turn came to be carried away. The contract for the erection of the present bridge, "to be constructed after the plan and in all respects equal to the late one built by Brown and others," bears date, April 3, 1866, and is signed by James F. Tasker of Cornish

and Bela J. Fletcher of Claremont as builders, and on the part
of the proprietors by Allen Wardner, Alfred Hall and Henry
Wardner. The bridge was framed on the meadow to the north
of Bridge Street in Windsor village and put in place before the
end of the year. The length of the bridge is upwards of 470 feet,
and each span about 220 feet between supports.

Besides the names of members of the Chase and Hall families,
some of the other familiar Cornish names to appear upon the
bridge company's books are Davis, Wood, Balloch, Fitch and Weld.

While toll-gates have never been popular institutions with the
public at large, it may fairly be said that this particular bridge
company has served the public well and has furnished, at not
unreasonable rates, adequate means of communication between
Cornish and Windsor for about one hundred and thirteen years.
During that period no part of the cost of building or maintaining any of the company's several bridges has fallen on the towns,
counties or states. On the contrary the company has borne all
of such costs and has been a large taxpayer in Cornish and
Windsor besides. Of late there has been much talk of a free
bridge and a good deal of claptrap has been written and spoken
on the antiquated system of supporting bridges and roads by
tolls. It is true that the system is old, but it is obviously fair;
and the appeals for its abolition derive their greatest vitality
from that instinct in human nature which desires to get something for nothing. If Cornish, in having a toll-bridge, is old-
fashioned and behind the times, her people can bear in mind
that in New York City the great Brooklyn and Williamsburgh
bridges are toll-bridges, that four toll-bridges cross the Ohio at
Cincinnati, that the Mississippi is spanned by a toll-bridge at
St. Louis and by another at Hannibal; that there is a toll-ferry
across the Potomac at Washington, and that every one of the
fourteen ferries from New York City to New Jersey is operated
only for tolls and by private capital.   H. S. WARDNER.

Blue Mountain Park.

This is a large tract of land situated on either side of and
including Croydon and Grantham mountains. It embraces
portions of Croydon, Cornish, Plainfield, Grantham and Newport.

It contains about 24,000 acres, being in size equivalent to a
primitive township. The town of Croydon contributes a larger

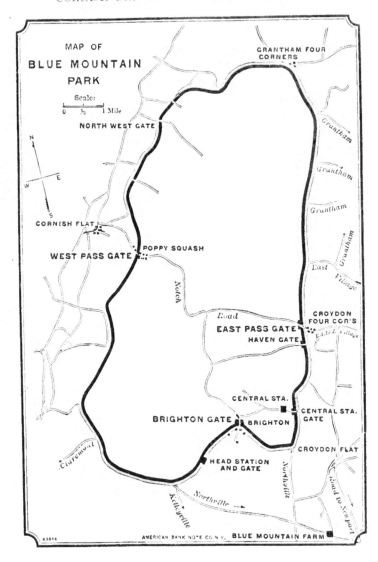

MAP OF
BLUE MOUNTAIN
PARK

Scale:
0   ½   1 Mile

NORTH WEST GATE

CORNISH FLAT

WEST PASS GATE

POPPY SQUASH

GRANTHAM FOUR CORNERS

Grantham

Grantham

Grantham

Grantham

East Village

Notch

Road

CROYDON FOUR COR'S

EAST PASS GATE

HAVEN GATE

Ea. to E. Village

CENTRAL STA.

BRIGHTON GATE   BRIGHTON

CENTRAL STA. GATE

CROYDON FLAT

Claremont

HEAD STATION AND GATE

Northville

Road to Newport

Kelleyville   Northville

AMERICAN BANK NOTE CO. N.Y.   BLUE MOUNTAIN FARM

percentage of its territory to the park than any other town, while
Cornish contributes a strip along her entire eastern boundary
amounting to about 2,800 acres.

Before the park was established, the land all belonged to individual owners and consisted of a large number of upland farms,

while higher up above them were timber lots belonging to individuals generally more remote, who used their lots each year to obtain their supply of lumber. Mr. Austin Corbin, the prime promoter of the enterprise, conceived the idea of purchasing these farms and woodlands, and by fencing, converting them into a forest game preserve. He had become aware that the noble buffalo of the country were fast becoming extinct, and that other animals of note were about to share the same fate, which aroused him to the sublime project of preparing an asylum wherein a few at least of these valuable animals might be preserved from the avarice, cruelty and greed of man. It was perfectly characteristic of the man to do this. Few others would or could dare embark in an enterprise of such dimensions, but Mr. Corbin enjoyed the satisfaction a little later, of having it said that he had the largest and best appointed fenced game preserve in the United States.

Under Mr. Corbin's direction, Mr. Sidney A. Stockwell began the purchase of the farms and timber lots in 1886. The purchases were completed sometime during the following year. A wire fence was erected enclosing the entire purchases excepting irregular portions of some farms that could not well be embraced within it. The length of the fence is a little less than thirty miles and it is about eleven feet high. The fence is strengthened at the base by a lining of wire netting, and also by iron stays midway between the wooden posts. A telephone wire passes around the entire length of, and above the fence, for the convenience and coöperation of those having the care of the park.

An association was formed and incorporated in 1888, with Mr. Corbin at its head. In 1890 Mr. Corbin began to introduce game into the park. This at the first consisted of about thirty buffalo, one hundred and forty deer, embracing four varieties, thirty-five moose, one hundred and thirty-five elk, and fourteen wild boar, a few Himalayan goats and six antelope.

All the game, but the moose, has done well, except during one severe winter, when there was a great loss among the elk and deer. Since that time they have been fed in winter by cutting browse for the deer and elk, and feeding the boar with corn.

To avoid being overstocked, large numbers of the animals

have been sold to zoölogical parks and gardens and to other parties. At present (1908) there are about one hundred and sixty-five buffalo, five hundred deer, fifty elk, and four hundred to five hundred boar, also a few moose and red deer.

A proprietary game club was started in 1899 with a lease of five years. The members, men from New York, Boston and Washington, were allowed certain shooting privileges. The club was successful and they propose soon to start another.

The sudden death of Mr. Corbin in 1896 very naturally effected a greater or less change in the management of the affairs of the park. This is especially shown in the sale and removal of immense quantities of lumber from it. This action on the part of the association possibly gives rise to emotions of regret among those who admire Nature as seen in the full-fledged forest. Nevertheless, the association maintain that their action is under the direction and sanction of the Forestry Bureau at Washington.

The present directors (1908) are Mrs. H. M. Corbin, Mrs. Isabella C. Edgell, George S. Edgell, Austin Corbin, Jr., William E. Chandler, A. N. Parlin, William Dunton and A. C. Champollion.

CHAPTER XVII.

"CITY FOLKS" IN CORNISH.

You have long called them the "City Folks" of "Little New York," these strangers who have bought land in Cornish. For a time the phrase "City Folks" set up a barrier that surely no right-hearted man could approve, whether he were from the country or from a town. But that antagonism is passing and the words, now too old to be displaced, carry with them only good-humored reference to the origin of the possessors.

The coming of the "City Folks" began over a quarter of a century ago in as much to be expected a fashion as any immigration could possibly have been conceived. Mr. William M. Evarts of New York married Miss Helen M. Wardner of Windsor, Vt., and eventually made his home in her town in 1843. Their oldest daughter, Miss Hettie Evarts, became the wife of a rising young New York lawyer, Mr. C. C. Beaman. So in 1884 it was quite natural that the young people should cross the river to Cornish, where they bought land of Mr. Chester Pike for a permanent country home, adding to their property from time to time until now the Beaman family owns almost two thousand acres hereabouts.

Shortly after his arrival, Mr. Beaman, in turn, tendered what had been the William W. Mercer place, with its old brick house, "Huggins' Folly," to his New York friend, the sculptor, Mr. Augustus Saint-Gaudens. For the first few years the latter preferred to rent the land, but eventually in 1891 Mr. Beaman's offer to sell was accepted, and from then to the time of his death the sculptor spent untold energy in beautifying his home. Through these two men came all the others attracted to our town.

During these early years it required a nine-hour train ride to reach Cornish from New York; and nine hours seemed infinitely further then than now. So, probably, despite the influence of the two "founders" the "colony" would have failed to make its beginning when it did had not the peace and dreamlike ripe-

ness of the hills, with their dark clumps of trees and their river
winding south before the mountain, called strongly to these
artists who desired a simple living. No country at a distance
can compare with Cornish. No country near at hand can equal
it. Go north toward Hanover—it is flat. Go east over the
Corbin Game Preserve—it is covered with scrubby bushes.
Go south toward Claremont—it is sandy, with a dearth of
intimate detail. Go west behind Ascutney—the barren pastures are but scantily shaded by trees. Yet sadly enough through

RESIDENCE OF MRS. C. C. BEAMAN.

their very coming, the beauty of out-rolling pasture slopes,
dotted with round-topped maples and quartz out-crops, is beginning to lose its charm. For as the "City Folks" have bought
the mowings and the pastures and have no longer tilled them
or allowed stock to graze upon them, the land which they admired,
through their own neglect, is rapidly reverting to that unshorn
appearance from which they fled.

Those who bought first were simple in their tastes. Mr.
Saint-Gaudens worked upon his commissions in a dilapidated
barn, hastily provided with a north light; Mr. George deForest

Brush of New York, the painter, spent a summer in an Indian
tepee at the foot of Mr. Saint-Gaudens' mowing, and later
returned for several years to rent from Mr. Beaman the modest
house on the old "Big Tree Farm" just over the Plainfield line,
north of what was then Mr. John Freeman's property; while
Mr. Thomas W. Dewing, another charming painter of New
York, in 1885 bought a portion of the one-time Mercer farm
from Mr. Beaman and lived there in the midst of a rambling

MRS. C. C. BEAMAN'S CASINO.
Said to be the First Framed House Constructed in Cornish.

confusion of small buildings. These were the original "City
Folks."

In 1889 came Mr. Dewing's great friend, the mural decorator,
Mr. Henry Oliver Walker of New York, who bought land from
Mr. Chester Pike on the Plainfield stage road. Mr. Walker's
modest house, wholly hidden from the highway, is perched bird-
like on the edge of a fascinating ravine. His recognition as an
artist, which he gained for himself at about the time he painted
his "Lyric Poetry" in the library of Congress, has continued
in such other compositions as "The Pilgrims on the Mayflower,"
in the Massachusetts State House.

Very shortly after Mr. Walker, came his intimate friend, Mr. Charles A. Platt, who settled just south of him, also on some of the Chester Pike land. From his house Mr. Platt may see the blue silhouette of Ascutney rising above his grove of tall pines, with such a singular composition of lines as to suggest Italy. During those early years Mr. Platt was a landscape painter and an etcher. But later, when he took up the career of an architect, this view gave him his cue to decorate Cornish slopes with pseudo-

"HIGH COURT," RESIDENCE OF MR. NORMAN HAPGOOD.

Italian buildings and to crop the heads of our native white pines that they might pathetically imitate the fashion of the trees in southern Europe.

In 1892 Mr. Platt in turn brought his friend, Mr. Stephen Parrish of Philadelphia, who, strangely enough, has been the only man to build a house on the north slope of a hill, out of sight of the much-prized mountain, purchasing his property from Mr. S. A. Tracy. Mr. Parrish is a man who was able to take up painting at the age of thirty and make a success of it; for certainly success includes creating delicate landscape paintings mostly for one's own pleasure.

At about this time, too, in 1890, Mr. Dewing's friend, Miss Emma Lazarus of New York, set up her home, "High Court," on the western edge of the Austin farm. While the next year Mr. William C. Houston of Boston bought from Mr. Beaman what had been part of the Williams place, above the old Mercer mill, and Mr. Henry Prellwitz, a landscape painter from New York, and Mr. Arthur Whiting, a musician from the same city, took portions of the southern slope of Mr. Edward Bryant's land.

Meantime, while these newcomers had followed in the footsteps of Mr. Augustus Saint-Gaudens, the Beaman family in turn had brought their allotment, for Mr. Alfred Bullard of Roxbury, Mass., in 1886, leased Mr. Beaman's farm, "Chaseholme." Miss Charlotte Arnold and Mrs. Clendenen Graydon of New York began to rent "The Butternuts," formerly belonging to Mr. William Mercer, from Mr. Beaman. Mr. and Mrs. Fraser Campbell of New York since 1890 have occupied the cottage next to it, which belongs to the Beaman estate, and Mr. Frederick Todd and his family from Roxbury, Mass., in 1895 established themselves in a new house belonging to Mr. Beaman near at hand.

Thus was formed the group of the first period of ten years, a sociable, unsophisticated group, whose chief entertainment centered in Mr. Beaman's Saturday night balls in his "Casino," an old building which he had moved to close by his residence. From 1895 on, however, the Cornish "Little New York" began to assume a more fashionable atmosphere, with somewhat pretentious elements creeping in, until close to 1907 when the "boom" reached its final height. Of course Cornish could never have attained the elaborate limits of the country around Lenox, Mass., or Dublin, N. H. Those regions are controlled by bankers or business men, who back their original purchases by large fortunes. While here, with scarcely an exception, most of the residents, after the fashion of artists, live to the extent of their incomes. It is strange, indeed, that this genuinely rich element has never crept in, yet such is the fact, with the exception of the late Dr. George Hayward of Boston, who in 1901 bought the old Eggleston place, just over the Plainfield line, and of Mr. Albion E. Lang of Toledo, Ohio, who in 1905 bought land of Mr. Frank J. Chadbourne, just north of Doctor Hayward's. Rather, the newcomers have given the region a literary turn which is supplanting the artistic one, for the only painters and sculptors here now are Mr. and Mrs. Kenyon Cox, Mr. Stephen Parrish, Mr. Henry C. Walker, Mr. and Mrs. Louis Saint-Gaudens, Mr. William H. Hyde, Mrs. Homer Saint-Gaudens, with, across the Plainfield line, Mr. Herbert Adams, Mr. Maxfield Parrish and Mr. and Mrs. Henry B. Fuller, with a welcome summer transient or two such as Mr. James Wall Finn.

Mr. and Mrs. Kenyon Cox of New York, in 1896 bought land

"ASPET," RESIDENCE OF MRS. AUGUSTUS SAINT-GAUDENS.

from Mr. John Freeman and set up their house in a picturesque spot between woods and fields where the ground falls away toward a creek brawling beneath the antiquated dam of the one-time "Freeman's Mill." Mr. Cox is a mural decorator of scholarly and earnest workmanship, a leading American in his craft. Perhaps the most popular of his canvases, and the one so frequently seen reproduced, is his painting of "Hope and Memory." In it is represented a tall dark-clad figure, whose step lingers as she turns her face backward to the visions of the past, sharply contrasted to the lightly garbed, joyous-faced companion whose

16

hand she holds. Mrs. Louise Cox, the painter's wife, is best known by her intimate pictures of children.

Mr. Louis Saint-Gaudens came directly through his brother, Mr. Augustus Saint-Gaudens, when in 1903 he bought a few acres of land from Mr. William E. Westgate. Shortly after this he purchased in Enfield, N. H., an old hip-roofed Shaker Meeting House, which he had moved to its present site and wherein he now lives. Mr. Saint-Gaudens has long been a sculptor of thorough and consistent work, in which he is greatly helped by his wife.

Mr. William H. Hyde of New York bought the larger part of Mr. Dewing's place in 1905, since, unfortunately, the latter artist became disgruntled with Cornish at the end of that first period and, as he expressed it, "trekked North" in search of pastures "new" where picture hats would no longer spoil his keen enjoyment of unsophisticated landscape. Mr. Hyde is a portrait painter of some reputation in New York City.

Mrs. Homer Saint-Gaudens, like Mrs. Fuller, is a miniature painter. Mrs. Saint-Gaudens and her husband lived for a time on a tiny lot of land purchased of Mrs. C. C. Beaman, just to the east of the home of Mr. Augustus Saint-Gaudens and are now established in the old home of Mr. Frank Johnson.

Mr. Herbert Adams, Mr. Frederick Maxfield Parrish and Mr. and Mrs. Henry B. Fuller have not really resided to any extent in Cornish, though the town may well claim them as a part of the community. Mr. Adams came here through the influence of Mr. Augustus Saint-Gaudens, whose faithful admirer he has always been, following Mr. Brush at Mr. Beaman's "Big Tree Farm" in 1894, and remaining there until 1904, when he built upon some land which he had purchased from Mr. Elmer DeGoosh in Plainfield. Mr. Frederick Maxfield Parrish, son of Mr. Stephen Parrish, in 1898 bought land from Mr. Charles Williams and thereon erected for himself "The Oaks," his charming home. His delightful magazine illustrations and his recent decorations need no further mention here. Mr. and Mrs. Henry Brown Fuller of Boston built upon land which they had bought from Mr. Solomon Stone. Mr. Fuller has established himself as a painter of much poetic imagination, while Mrs. Fuller is generally accorded the position of the first miniature painter in America.

The change of the center of interest of this peculiar community from painting to literature, developed most naturally through two of its artists, Mr. Charles A. Platt and Mr. Kenyon Cox. Mr. Platt became interested by writing a book upon Italian Gardens, wherein he shows his perspicuity and good taste. But with Mr. Cox literature was a much more serious business. For besides being a decorator of recognized power, he has long proved his merit as an art critic, holding an established place on *The Nation*, and publishing occasional books. His thorough and learned essays combine an understanding of his subject

"HARLAKENDEN HOUSE." RESIDENCE OF WINSTON CHURCHILL.

with an excellence of style that could only be equalled by one other man in the country, the late Mr. John LaFarge. Mr. Cox and Mr. Platt then formed a connecting link between the older artists and the more recent apostles of writing for the sake of literature alone.

The first of this latter class, Mr. Louis Evan Shipman, and Mr. Herbert D. Croly, both men of New York, came to Cornish in 1893. For that and the following summer they and their families hired the square, wooden, white-painted, century-old farmhouse set about with elm trees, then belonging to Mr.

Frank L. Johnson, and now the home of Mr. and Mrs. Homer
Saint-Gaudens.   But at the end of that period they had become
sufficiently enamored with the beauties of the landscape to
establish themselves permanently. Mr. Shipman in 1902
bought the John Gilkie farm in Plainfield.   In the past he has
staged, among other plays, "D'Arcy of the Guards," a comedy
of delicious and healthy temper, and dramatizations of Mr.
Winston Churchill's novel, "The Crisis."   Mr. Croly, however,
remained near to where he originally spent his summers, buying
some pasture land in 1897 from Mr. Edward Bryant. There,
with the help of Mr. Platt, he set up his white dwelling among
the tumbling hillocks and blue-green clusters of pine trees.
And there he has spent the past seven years producing his most
scholarly work on American sociology, called "The Promise of
American Life."

The next author to come to Cornish, brought by Mr. Shipman,
was Mr. Winston Churchill of St. Louis. He decided to buy
at once, and in 1898 purchased from Mr. Leonard Spaulding
and Mr. John Freeman some five hundred acres of woodland and
valley mowings.   From here Mr. Churchill has taken close interest in local affairs, and written a large part of "The Crisis,"
"The Crossing," "Coniston," and "A Modern Chronicle."

After Mr. Churchill, there appeared in the vicinity a man
laboring in quite a different department of the literary world,
that of journalism, Mr. Norman Hapgood, biographer, and
editorial writer of *Collier's Weekly*, who purchased from Miss
Emma Lazarus in 1902, "High Court," her dwelling designed
by Mr. Platt in the Italian manner and situated on the crest of
one of the foothills that line the valley.   Mr. Hapgood is well
known for his unbiased and unprejudiced attacks on what seems
bad in American politics and American customs.

Following him came an author of still other literary tastes, the
poet and dramatist, Mr. Percy MacKaye of New York, who in 1904
leased a little brown-colored house, "The Snuff Box," tucked into
a corner of the estate of Admiral William M. Folger, who had
bought his land from Mr. Charles Gilkie in 1898. Mr. MacKaye
remained in "The Snuff Box" until 1906 when he rented what
has been the old "Wells" house, now on the estate of the late
Dr. George Hayward. Mr. MacKaye hopes some day to make
this place his permanent dwelling. Mr. MacKaye displays a

fertile sense of poetry and wealth of imagination, which he
devotes his days to expressing in dramatic form. His "Scare-
crow" produced by Mr. Henry B. Harris, has been probably his
most successful drama. Previous to this Mr. MacKaye has
produced "Jean D'Arc," played by E. H. Sothern and Julia
Marlowe; "Sappho and Phaon," performed by Bertha Kalish
under the direction of Harrison Grey Fiske, and the comedy
"Mater" also produced by this same manager.

On the heels of Mr. MacKaye there arrived in "The Snuff

RESIDENCE OF MR. C. A. PLATT.

Box" Mr. Langdon Mitchell of Philadelphia, a dramatist of
established reputation, who had been living for a time in
Mrs. Elizabeth Perkins' house in Windsor, Vt. Mr. Mitchell
appeared before the public about ten years ago with his production of "Becky Sharpe," a dramatization of Thackeray's novel,
"Vanity Fair." Others of Mr. Mitchell's best plays are his
extraordinarily clever translation of "The Kreutzer Sonata,"
and a piece produced by Mrs. Fiske a few years ago known as
"The New York Idea," a satire on divorce.

A third dramatist in this community, Mr. Philip Littell, lived

for four years in what is known as the Beaman "Turnpike House,"
where he finished a charming adaptation of William J. Locke's
novel, "Simple Septimus," played for a time by Mr. George
Arliss. Mr. Littell has returned this year to live in Mr. Churchill's "Farm House."

Two other writers of younger years remain, Miss Frances
Duncan, an essayist on horticultural subjects who has installed
herself in the old "Cherry Hill" farm leased from Mrs. C. C.
Beaman; and myself.

Finally, to complete the list of Cornish "City Folks," mention
should be made of Mr. George Rublee of New York City, who
in 1907 bought the Houston place; Misses Elizabeth and
Frances Slade, who in 1903 built a house upon the pasture
land purchased from Mr. William E. Westgate; the Misses
Emily and Augusta Slade, who also in 1903 made their home
upon land obtained from Mr. Lyman Bartlett; Miss Frances
Arnold of New York, who has leased the old Mercer cottage
from Mrs. Beaman; and Mr. and Mrs. Herbert C. Lakin of
New York, who now live in "Chascholme," belonging to Mrs.
Beaman.

So much for the actual Cornish colony. But there still
remain a few others in Plainfield who are so closely connected
with the "City Folks" in this town that their names should not
be overlooked. They are Mr. William Howard Hart of New
York, who in 1907 bought land of Mr. G. F. Lewin; Mrs.
Geohegan, who built a house upon land once belonging to the
Eggleston farm; Mr. and Mrs. John Elliott of Boston, who bought
land from Mr. John DeGoosh and Mr. Walter Williams; Miss
Edith Lawrence and Mrs. Grace Lawrence Taylor, who in 1899
went to live upon land purchased from Mr. William W. Taylor;
Mrs. M. C. Davidge of New York, who purchased the "Old Kings-
bury Tavern" just outside of Plainfield from Mr. Charles Empey;
Miss M. E. Wood, who now occupies the "Big Tree Farm"
which she leased from Mrs. Beaman in 1903; and Mr. and Mrs.
Robert Treat Paine, now living in the E. S. Shinn house on the
old Westgate farm.

Such is the extent to which the "City Folks" have grown,
adding by the money they have brought with them to the prosperity of the community. Moreover, as time passes, it is pleasant to realize that a kindly spirit has sprung up between those

who have bought in Cornish and those who have sold, a spirit
which did not exist ten years ago. For though, since the beginning, a desire to be friendly has lain dormant in farmers and
"City Folks," yet the difference of inherited ideas has made it
hard for the two groups to recognize the good qualities in one
another and to tolerate their quite unconscious stepping on one
another's toes. This maturing friendship should be all the
more prized, since despite the fact that "Little New York" has
reached its growth, yet the persons who have come, unlike the

RESIDENCE OF DR. A. H. NICHOLS.

residents in many other summer places, have come to stay. Year
by year their dread of frozen water pipes, the lack of proper
heating, or hired help has dwindled, and year by year the "City
Folks" remain later in the fall and venture back earlier in the
spring. Already there are eight of these men who vote in this
town and who remain here for the greater part of the year.
They are Mr. William E. Beaman, Mr. Winston Churchill, Mr.
George Rublee, Mr. Stephen Parrish, Mr. Herbert D. Croly,
Mr. Percy MacKaye, Mr. Louis Saint-Gaudens and myself.
And, as time goes by, more of those who come and go, and who,

therefore, are careless of the needs of the town, will join the ranks of those who stay and who are vitally anxious for the good of the community.

The remaining shyness which exists in both groups will surely wear away in the near future. Many of the "City Folks" would be only too glad to lend their best efforts in town and school meetings or in the Grange, if they had the chance which they are somewhat too diffident to ask for. Many of those who have always been here, while glad to welcome the "City Folks" into their circles, dread risking the snub which they feel might follow the offer. And year by year the barriers are falling. The fire of 1909 on the edge of Mr. James Bryant's pasture did infinitely more good than harm; for the burned portion was of small consequence, whereas the acquaintance bred by sitting all night in the rain together guarding the smouldering embers, taught both farmers and "City Folks" that men are just men. No one wishes another fire, yet when a few more good reasons have appeared to throw the "City Folks" in spite of themselves into the arms of those who belong here, the change for the increased happiness of the town of Cornish would be immeasurable.

HOMER SAINT-GAUDENS.

CHAPTER XVIII.

Town Buildings—Soldiers' Monument—Libraries.

Town Buildings.

During the earlier years the town seemed to claim jurisdiction over all the religious interests within its limits. The town built the houses of worship. The town employed the preachers to minister in them. The liabilities of the town included the settlement and support of the minister, as well as all church buildings and repairs on the same.

At first there seemed to be no diversity of opinion regarding this matter. Church and state were "at one." A wonderful harmony existed, as nearly all of the early settlers were in habitual attendance upon divine worship. In process of time differences of opinion arose on doctrinal tenets. Then divisions followed. Loyalty to a common cause weakened. Each faction became more independent of the other. The town, too, gradually relinquished her responsibility of the churches and separation between town and church authorities became final, and the church or churches became independent of all town action. The intelligent interpretation of the Constitution of the United States also contributed to this latter state of things.

As the town had enjoyed the privilege of using the houses of worship for her public business, under restrictions, the practice still continued. Oftentimes meetings for town business were called at dwelling houses, but ordinarily were "warned" to meet at the meeting houses. The meeting house "on the river," and later the old Congregational Church "on the hill" near the center of the town were the places where the town usually met for the transaction of its public business. A building especially for this purpose was much needed. The old Congregational house on the hill continued to be used by the town a few years after divine worship in it had ceased, but it was becoming unsuitable even for that, and so about 1844 it was taken down.

About 1840–41 the people of Cornish, as elsewhere, were stirred by a wave of religious enthusiasm. During this time

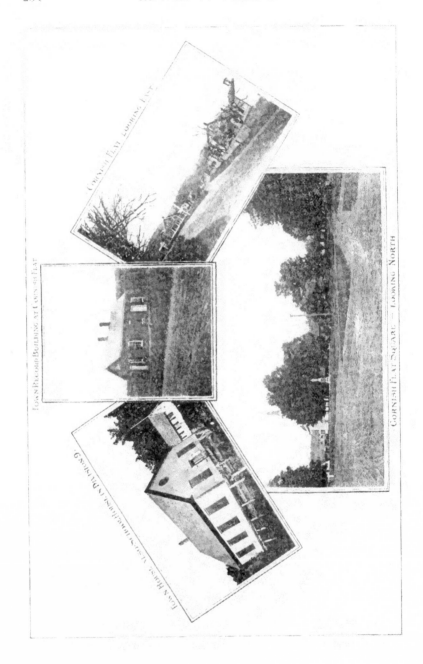

CORNISH FLAT — LOOKING EAST

TOWN RECORD BUILDING AT CORNISH FLAT

CORNISH FLAT SQUARE — LOOKING NORTH

BARN HORSE AND STOCK HOUSE IN PASTURE.

the "Perfectionists" (which see) built a house of worship which after a few years became disused. At this opportune time the town purchased this building and suitably fitted it up for the use of the town. Since that time it has been used for the holding of annual and other town meetings. All such meetings are now "warned" to meet at the *"Town-House."* Its location is nearly central, and is readily accessible, and is generally counted as suitable for the needs of the town.

While the town was generally well satisfied with the town house as a place for a full meeting of the town, there existed a pressing need of a place to safely deposit the accumulating records, books, papers, etc., belonging to the town. With every change of town clerk these valuables were shifted to a new home, incurring more or less risk of damage and loss.

A large safe was provided by the town for the most valuable portion of its documents; but this afforded only a partial solution of the difficulty, as its capacity was insufficient for its requirements, and this cumbrous article had to migrate to the home of the newly elected clerk, there to remain until his successor was chosen. Then, again, a convenient room for the selectmen to meet in for the transaction of the town's business was much needed. It had been their custom from the first to meet at hotels or private dwelling houses for this purpose. Realizing this state of affairs the town felt justified in inserting in the warrant for town meeting March 9, 1886, the following article: "To see what sum of money, if any, the town will vote to raise and appropriate for the building of a suitable place for the safe keeping of the town-records agreeable to Chapter 74 of the General Laws."

The article was favorably considered by the town at this meeting and it was then voted to raise the sum of $800 for the erection and finishing of a small brick building, containing all needful safety vaults, library cases, etc., with a commodious selectmen's room in front, with all necessary furnishings. Labor soon commenced, and during the season the building was made ready for occupancy. The records, books, etc., were then lodged there in safety. The safe, before named, also found a permanent resting place in the selectmen's room. This safe had been purchased for the town by virtue of a vote passed March 12, 1872, when the town voted to raise $300 for the purchase of a safe.

It was bought of the American Steel Safe Co. for said sum. It may be of interest to record that while the safe stood in the store of Boynton Brothers (George H. Boynton being then town clerk) that an attempt was made by some burglars to force it open. They drilled through the outer door of the safe and attempted blowing it open with explosives, but fortune did not favor their designs so they abandoned the job and got nothing.

An annex to the rear of the Record Building was made in 1895, at an expense of about $450, furnishing the only "lock-up" belonging to the town. Its chief use has been to accommodate certain moneyless traveling gentry, called tramps, with cheap lodgings, crackers and cheese moistened with "Adam's Ale," all at the expense of the town. Sometimes this institution receives its share of patronage, but has no constant boarders.

Soldiers' Monument.

The town warrant of February 22, 1889, for the meeting to be holden on March 12 following, contained the following article: "To see what action the town will take in relation to a soldiers' monument, and raise money therefor."

The same article in substance had appeared in previous warrants, but had been set aside through the indifference and opposition of a majority of the town. A goodly number of the minority, however, were in hearty sympathy with the project, and were intent that something should be done. Prominent among these were Joseph B. Comings, Hiram A. Day and William H. Sisson,-- the latter a soldier of the Rebellion, and the other two, fathers who had each given to their country's cause, a son who had been buried in graves far from kindred and home.

These men continued to agitate the subject, making investigation as to resources, etc., and received such measures of encouragement as to induce them to cause the above article to be again inserted in the warrant. At this meeting the article obtained a favorable hearing, and the sum of two hundred and fifty dollars was voted by the town for the purpose, and a committee of three men was chosen to take the matter in charge, secure further pledges, obtain a suitable design, and make a contract for the construction and erection of the monument. The doings of this committee appear in their report in the town report of March 13, 1890, which is as follows:

"Your committee appointed to raise funds and take charge of all things pertaining to a soldiers' monument, would report as follows: Having a sufficient sum pledged outside of the 'Soldiers' Aid Society' money, and the amount voted by the town which in our opinion warranted the making a contract, due, after receiving and carefully considering the proposals and designs of bronze, marble and granite companies, decided to accept the proposals of the Sunapee Granite Co. to erect a monument made of cut granite according to a design furnished by us, to be surmounted by a statue of a soldier at 'Parade Rest,' said statue to be cut from granite and to be six feet in height above base, model furnished by them. The name, company and regiment of all the soldiers who died in 'The War of the Rebellion,' who were counted on the quota of the town, to be inscribed on the polished die, and a suitable inscription on the base, and contracted with said company to furnish the monument complete above the foundation for $900.00. The foundation was furnished by the committee, the labor and all expense of said foundation, except the cement used, were furnished by contribution. After considering the different places proposed for location, we decided to accept a plot of ground sixteen feet square and approaches thereto offered by the Baptist Church and Society in the south end of their park on Cornish Flat, and a lease was taken of said plot in the name of the town for ninety-nine years.

"We would at this time acknowledge the obligations we are under to Hon. William M. Evarts of New York, who so generously contributed toward the expense; and to C. C. Beaman, Esq., of New York, who so kindly furnished the design (except the statue), for the monument, and contributed largely towards the expense, and to both of them and their friends for their valuable advice and suggestions in regard to material, plans and location, and to the citizens generally who have given of their time and money so liberally, and helped your committee make the monument a success."

SOLDIERS' MONUMENT, CORNISH FLAT.

The committee acknowledge the receipt of the following sums of money for the monument:

From Town Treasurer	$250.00	
Soldiers' Aid Society	176.80	
Hiram A. Day	100.00	
Joseph B. Comings	100.00	
Hon. Wm. M. Evarts	50.00	
C. C. Beaman, Esq	50.00	
Henry Gould	50.00	
All other persons	112.25	
Deficit afterwards voted by town	19.85	
		$908.90
Total expenses were:		
For monument	$900.00	
Cement for same	8.90	
		$908.90

WILLIAM H. SISSON, ⎫
STEPHEN A. TRACY, ⎬ Committee.
ALBERT E. WELLMAN, ⎭

The monument stands in the south end of the park on Cornish Flat, placed due north and south, surmounted by statue facing south. On upper base, below the die is inscribed:

"Erected by the town and grateful friends in memory of the sons of Cornish who fell in defense of the Union.
"A. D. 1861–1865."

Upon the four equal sides of the die of the monument the following names of soldiers are inscribed, who died in the service:

NORTH SIDE.

Henry P. Blood, Co. E, 9th N. H. Inf.
David K. Ripley, Co. I, 7th N. H. Inf.
Edwin W. Downs, Co. E, 9th N. H. Inf.
Luman B. Dudley, Co. G, 9th N. H. Inf.
William S. Lewis, Co. I, 14th N. H. Inf.
William Scott, Co. G, 7th N. H. Inf.
Versal E. Burr, Co. I, 14th N. H. Inf.

SOUTH SIDE.

Marcellus Judkins, Co. G, 7th N. H. Inf.
Charles F. Day, Co. E, 9th N. H. Inf.
Charles Nevens, Co. G, 7th N. H. Inf.
John Gilbert, Co. F, 3d N. H. Inf.
Edmund B. Chadbourn, Co. G, 5th N. H. Inf.
Ithiel J. White, Co. K, 9th N. H. Inf.
James P. Wheeler, Co. L, 1st N. H. Cav.

EAST SIDE.

Col. Haldimand S. Putnam, Col. 7th N. H. Inf.
George E. Tyler, Co. I, 2d N. H. Inf.
Andrew P. Wright, Co. C, 7th N. H. Inf.
William Wright, Co. I. 2d N. H. Inf.
Hiram Stone, Co. I, 14th N. H. Inf.
Sylvester Tasker, Co. I, 14th N. H. Inf.
Alvah S. Rawson, Co. G, 6th N. H. Inf.

WEST SIDE.

Thomas B. Edminster, Co. I, 14th N. H. Inf.
Norman D. Comings, Co. A, 16th N. H. Inf.
James B. Kidder, Co. G, 1st N. H. Cav.
Asa M. Benway, Co. E, 1st Vt. Cav.
Reuben T. Benway, Co. I, 14th N. H. Inf.
Sidney C. Spaulding, Co. E, 9th N. H. Inf.
Elbridge G. Beers, Co. K, 3d N. H. Inf.

Libraries.

The town has ever manifested a willingness to supply its inhabitants with what reading matter the times could afford. The churches invariably supplied their Sunday school libraries with religious reading, as far as their means would allow. Such libraries began their existence nearly coeval with religious service in the churches and have been maintained ever since as an important factor of church service.

During a part of the thirties and until nearly the middle of the nineteenth century, a circulating library for adults called the "Cornish Social Library," was maintained in town, much to the pleasure and edification of the people. The records of this library have not been found, and whatever of such there was, is doubtless lost.

In 1861 a Sabbath school library association was formed on the Flat. It was especially to purchase and preserve religious books for adult reading for which there seemed to be a strong demand. The number of its volumes was about one hundred sixty. This association, with its original plan, was maintained twenty-five years, when all restrictions were removed, and its books were all donated to the church library and placed under the same restrictions as the juvenile Sunday school library of the Baptist Church.

A law was passed by the Legislature of 1891, providing for the establishing of libraries in each of the towns of New Hampshire where they did not already exist.

Section 23, chapter 8 on Free Public Libraries, Laws of 1891, is as follows:

"The board is hereby authorized and directed to expend, upon the application of any town having no public library owned and controlled by the town, a sum, not exceeding one hundred dollars for books, for such town entitled to the benefits of these provisions, such books to be used by the town for the purpose of establishing a free public library and the commissioners shall select and purchase all books to be provided."

The above board of commissioners consisted of four persons of the state appointed by the governor. No town was entitled to the benefit of the law until such town had accepted its provisions at a regularly called meeting of the town.

The law also provided that a board of library trustees, three in number, should be elected by each town, one for three years, one for two years and one for one year, whose duties should be to provide for the care and circulation of the books and to judiciously expend all appropriations made for books.

The law also required of each town making application for the library, an appropriation by such town of a certain sum of money additional, to be expended for books and maintenance of the library.

After the enactment of the law in 1891 the town appeared comparatively indifferent regarding it. An article, however, appeared in the town warrant of March 8, 1892, as follows: "To see if the town will elect a board of library trustees, and appropri-

17

THE STOWELL FREE LIBRARY AT CORNISH FLAT.

A Gift to the Town from Hon. George H. Stowell.   Erected 1910-11.

ate the money necessary to receive the gift of one hundred dollars worth of books from the state."

The article was postponed at this meeting, but it appeared again on the warrant of 1893. At this meeting the article shared the same fate as on the preceding year.

At the meeting on March 13, 1894, the town voted to accept the proposition of the state agreeably to the foregoing law. During this year the necessary money was raised; the hundred dollars worth of books were received from the state, and the new free library began its life. It was thought best to divide the library for the convenience of its patrons, leaving half at the Flat and half nearer Windsor, with privilege of exchanging the same at any time. The library has been in successful operation ever since.

During the season of 1909, Hon. Geo. H. Stowell of Claremont, who was a native of Cornish, made known his intentions of erecting a valuable library building in his native town and, when completed, of presenting the same to the town under the name of "Stowell Free Public Library."

Mr. Stowell's preference for a site for said building favored Cornish Flat, as it was the center of his activities when young. He is proposing to expend the sum of six thousand dollars on said building and its furniture.

The town unanimously voted (March 8, 1910) to accept the proposed legacy, and to furnish a site whereon to build; and the work began in early spring and was carried on during the season, and, excepting the interior, was nearly completed before the close of the year 1910, the date this record closes.

CHAPTER XIX.

MISCELLANEOUS — CLIMATIC EXTREMES — HOTELS — STORES — CENTENNIAL — POST OFFICES — TOWN REPORTS — INDIANS — SHOWS — ASCUTNEY MOUNTAIN — PRESIDENT'S VISIT — OLD PEOPLE'S ASSOCIATION.

CLIMATIC EXTREMES.

The Cold Winter of 1779-80.

THE winter of 1779–80 was the most severe that had ever been known in this country. It is said that the cold extended south so that Chesapeake Bay was covered with solid ice from its head to the mouth of the Potomac. At Annapolis the ice was five to seven inches thick, so that loaded teams passed over it. Snow was so deep in all New England that nearly all roads were closed for several weeks. People traveled only on snow shoes. Travel had not been so much obstructed for forty years.

—*Boston Chronicle*, Jan. 28, 1780.

The Dark Day of 1780.

The nineteenth day of May was remarkable for its uncommon darkness. The morning was cloudy, attended with a little rain. Between ten and eleven o'clock the darkness increased and began to assume the appearance of evening. Fowls went to roost, and cattle collected around the barnyards, as at the approach of night. Before noon it became so dark as to be difficult to read without a candle; and lights were necessary at dinner and to transact the ordinary work of a family through the afternoon. The evening was enveloped in total darkness. The sky could not be distinguished from the ground. All these circumstances caused much consternation throughout New England. A little before midnight the clouds began to separate and the vapors to disperse and some glimmerings of light appeared. The next morning was cloudy but not unusually dark.

The theory generally accepted as to the cause of this phenomenon was this: For several weeks previous there had been

extensive fires in the woods, and the westerly winds had driven
the smoke and cinders, with which the air was charged, all over
this part of the country. On the morning of the nineteenth,
the wind came in various directions but principally from the
eastward, and brought with it a thick fog. These opposite
currents meeting, stopped the progress of the clouds and formed
several different strata of them. Owing to their number, breadth
and density they became almost impervious to the light of the
sun. The atmosphere was likewise filled with clouds of smoke
and cinders, as well as with vapors which gave it a dirty,
yellowish hue. Pieces of burned leaves were continually falling.
The darkness extended throughout New England and was observed several leagues at sea.

The traditions of this day have often been repeated within
the memory of the writer, and these also state that the phenomenon gave rise to fears in the minds of many that the end of
the world had come, and that these fears were not fully allayed
until Nature had resumed her wonted appearance on the following day.

The Year 1816.

But few, if any, now living retain any remembrance of the
year 1816. But the hardships of that year were by those
immediately concerned forcibly impressed upon the succeeding
generation. The year is designated as "the year without a
summer." In New England it went by the phrase, "eighteen
hundred and starve-to-death" and also as "the cold summer of
1816."

It was phenomenal in every sense, being unlike any other year
of modern, or even of any known ancient record. The sun's
rays seemed to be destitute of heat, and all Nature was clad in a
sable hue. Men and women became frightened and imagined
the "fire in the sun" was being extinguished, and that the world
was about to come to an end. Ministers took the phenomenon
as a text for their sermons. The winter of 1815-16 was not
unlike that of other years, and did not indicate the character of
the weather that subsequently prevailed.

January was mild, so much so that artificial heat was but
little needed for comfort. This continued until near the middle
of February, when a "cold snap" occurred, followed by more mild

weather. There was nothing unusual in the climatic conditions
of March.

April was the first manifestation of this strange freak in temperature. The early days of April were warm and bright; but
as the month drew to a close, the cold increased, until it ended
in ice and snow with a very low temperature.

May was a month of bitter disappointment to those who delighted in balmy days, opening spring and budding flowers.
Almost every attempt of the husbandmen to start the usual
crops, was attended by frosts and a blackened waste. Corn
was killed, and the fields again made ready for a second
planting; but the people's disappointment was complete when
they found ice formed to the thickness of half an inch in the
pools.

June, usually the month of roses and other bloom, was this
year a month of desolation. Frost and snow were common.
A few intervening warm days permitted some crops to partially
develop a growth, and then be followed by a frost or snow.
Various kinds of fruit were nearly all destroyed. One day this
month, snow fell to the depth of ten inches in New Hampshire
and Vermont. Matters were beginning to assume a serious
aspect.

July was accompanied by frost and ice and it is said that those
who celebrated the "glorious Fourth" found an abundance of
ice handy for immediate use on the next morning. This caused
the good people to look grave. This month, Indian corn was
finally destroyed in all but the most favored locations, and but
a small quantity escaped.

August came, and with it the expectation and hope that the
cold weather would end, but in this they were disappointed.
Ice formed even thicker than during the previous month and
almost every green plant was frozen. The scanty corn was
cut for fodder. The little that was ripened in sheltered localities
and states was worth almost its weight in silver, and farmers
were compelled to obtain corn grown in 1815 for seed used in
the spring of 1817, at a cost of five dollars per bushel.

The next month was ushered in, bright and warm, and for a
week or two the almost frozen people began to thaw out. It
was the mildest weather of the year, and just as the people got
ready to appreciate it, the cold winds with Jack Frost came,

and hardened and whitened everything in their path. On the sixteenth of September, ice formed one fourth of an inch thick, and winter clothing was brought forth and wrapped around shivering humanity. By this time people had given up all hopes of seeing flowers bloom or hearing the birds sing, and so they began to prepare for a hard winter.

October kept up the marvelous record of its predecessors. Scarcely a day did the thermometer register higher than 30 degrees. November was also extremely cold. Sleighing was good nearly all the month, but when December came, the spell seemed broken, and, strange to say, this month was the mildest and most comfortable month of the year.

As a matter of course, breadstuffs were the highest ever known and it was impossible to obtain many of the common vegetables at any price.

The writer has often heard the circumstances of that year mentioned by those who experienced them, and therefore believes the foregoing account is no exaggeration.

Tornadoes or Cyclones—1821, 1848.

Cornish has been slightly visited by two, at least, of these troublesome events. The first one, in 1821, was the larger, and the most destructive generally. It seemed to form not far north and west of Cornish, passing over the north part of the town in a southeast direction, striking Croydon Mountain. Here it destroyed nearly every tree on hundreds of acres. Passing over the mountain, it finally spent its force about Wendell Harbor (now Sunapee) where it did considerable damage.

The cyclone of 1848 was of less dimensions. It started and followed nearly the same course as the other, sweeping down through "Dodge Hollow," overturning many trees and destroying one house with disastrous results. (See Dodge Record.)

Snow-Crust of 1862.

During the winter of 1861-62 a large amount of snow fell, somewhat larger than usual. Slight thaws, followed by freezing, had hardened each successive layer of snow during the winter and thus formed a solid icy mass about three feet deep, firm enough to hold any team in safety. A good deal of teaming business was safely done upon the surface of this crust for several weeks. This vast body of snow and ice was very slow in melting, and therefore remained until late in the season. As late as the middle of April, teams could be driven over it in safety, it being at that time about two feet in depth and still retaining its solidity. Many an enjoyable morning sleigh ride over this crust was taken in April, riding over fields and even fences, avoiding the highways as much as possible, as there was no sleighing there.

There were scarcely any spring rains this year to hasten the melting of the snow, but the increasing warmth of the sun soon caused the snow to disappear, while underneath it the green grass had finely started. Some now living can easily recall the events of this season.

Floods—July 19, 1859.

The circumstances of this flood are vivid in the mind of the writer. They resulted from a succession of very heavy thunder showers occurring on the afternoon of July 19, 1850. These show-ers were almost continuous, lasting from 2.30 p. m. until nearly six o'clock. The rain poured in torrents most of this time. The effects were very marked and sudden. The brooks were swelled to unheard-of dimensions. Intervales and meadows were soon under water. Bridges were carried away. Acres of grass just ready for cutting were ruined. Some brooks were diverted from their original channel. The upper sawmill at the Flat, with its dam, gave way. The water with the timbers coming down, caused the lower dam also to give way, and the débris was all carried down stream and deposited on the meadows below. The damage to highways and bridges in Cornish by this freshet, amounted to nearly four hundred dollars.

Floods—March 3 and 4, 1866.

This was a veritable thaw and spring freshet. Water was high in all the brooks. Those pouring their waters into the Con-necticut River caused the ice to break up. This dammed the water of the river at Cornish bridge. The latter could not stand the pressure, and gave way, and the bridge all went down stream. The other damage in Cornish was only trifling. A new bridge (the present one) was erected the following season. (See Cornish Bridge.)

Floods—October 4, 1896.

A succession of heavy rains occurred on this day that caused the water to rise as high as was ever known by any persons of that time. This rain was more general throughout New England than was the flood of 1850. The damage was great and widespread. Brooks became small rivers and swept off many of the bridges crossing them. Roads were washed and many of them rendered impassable for a time. These conditions were similar in all of the surrounding towns, but the damage was chiefly confined to highways and bridges.

Hotels.

During the first half of the nineteenth century there was necessarily much more business on the highways than now. All the merchandise for the country stores, all the surplus products of the farm, all the products of the mills, passed over the highways for long distances, to reach their destination by the slow and tedious agency of horse power. All thus traveling over the roads were obliged to stop wherever night overtook them. This made necessary a large number of public houses or taverns. The leading thoroughfares were thickly dotted with them in all New England towns. These houses were always open to receive and entertain teamsters and all other travelers. Here they usually found comfortable quarters both for themselves and for their teams, with ample refreshments and lodgings for both. These taverns were the news centers of the town. Here the post-riders always stopped, bringing occasional letters and newspapers; and later the stage coach, bringing in the same, together with passengers with the latest news. Every weekday night here congregated travelers and teamsters, and many residents of the town, and discussed the general news of the day, as well as the local happenings, not forgetting meanwhile to test the quality of the landlord's grog whenever they felt so inclined. These were generally counted as "gay old times." They still linger in the memory of a very few aged persons. The writer well remembers, when a boy, of hearing the old men of those days speak of the good times they had enjoyed in the old-time taverns.

But within the last sixty years, these things have greatly changed. The advent of the steam car on the railroad has revolutionized the modes of travel and the conveyance of merchandise. Long-distance travelers now go on the cars from center to center, and so have no use for these country hotels. For this reason taverning on the old plan has almost entirely disappeared in all the New England towns. In Cornish the houses heretofore thus devoted to the use of the public have been converted into private dwelling houses. The number of these which were in town, and the number of their landlords or owners can be told only by much research that does not warrant a sufficient compensation for the effort; but it is known, however, there were many of them. Several houses now standing are pointed out as having once been public houses. There are but two that now remain in use in town: one near Windsor bridge, and the other at the Flat. In each of these the entertainment feature has been made secondary to that of the saloon, usually attached to each.

Stores.

One of the most essential members of a community is the vender of goods necessary for the use of the people. A good many different persons at different times have been thus employed in different parts of the town. No sooner was the town settled than a need was felt that at some convenient place a ready supply of needful articles could be procured. Apprehending this need, Col. Jonathan Chase opened the first store in town on his premises on the river. This store continued to do business for a good many years. As the population of the town increased eastward from the river, other places were opened for the sale of goods in several parts of the town. Citizens of the town residing near Windsor have gone there to procure their supplies and do their trading because more convenient. The greatest trading center finally located at Cornish Flat, where a store was opened some time prior to the opening of the nineteenth century. This has ever since been considered a trade center of the town,— all the time having one store and much of the time two of them. Among the most prominent merchants who have been longest in trade there have been, Esq. Daniel Chase, Capt. William Atwood, Newton Whittlesey, Henry Breck, Orlando Powers, and Breck & Powers, John T. Breck, Lafayette H. Smith, Timo-

thy A. Gleason, Boynton Brothers, George W. Hunt and others.
For about twenty-five years George E. Fairbanks has kept a
store of general merchandise at South Cornish. This has been
a great accommodation, especially to many living in that section
of the town.

Centennial Anniversary.

March 14, 1865, an article appeared in the town warrant
which read: "To see what measures the town will adopt, and
how much money the town will vote to raise for the purpose of
celebrating the present year, the anniversary of the settlement
of the town which took place June, A. D. 1765."

When the subject came before the town for their action, the
advocates of the movement were not in sufficient numbers to
warrant further action, and so the subject was indefinitely
postponed, much to the regret of the minority.

It appears that on May 31, 1865, the town, or a self-appointed
committee, attempted to rally the citizens to reconsider their
former action and they met for this purpose at the town house;
but little enthusiasm was manifested and so the project was
abandoned.

Post Offices.

In all the earliest years of the town, before the advent of the
steam cars or even the stage coach, a place was appointed for
the reception and distribution of mail in some convenient home
on the river road. This of course was named Cornish Post Office, as
for a time it was the only post office in town, receiving the entire
mail designed for the people of Cornish.

It is well to note the fact that the quantity of mail in those days
was much less in proportion to the population than at present.
Letters were a greater rarity and sent at greater cost. Magazines
and newspapers were few in number and but few taken; hence,
the post-riders on their weekly or semi-weekly rounds were not
heavily loaded with mail.

As the population of the town spread eastward and northward,
it became quite inconvenient for the citizens of the newer
parts of the town to obtain their mail from the Cornish post
office. For this reason a post office was opened at Cornish
Flat which for many years was the chief receiving and dis-

tributing center for the largest part of the town. This office, with that on the river, handled all the mail of the town until after the middle of the last century, when, owing to the nearness of the Cornish post office to that of Windsor, the office of the latter seemed to absorb the former, and the citizens of West Cornish were obliged to go to Cornish Flat or to Windsor for their mail. This order of mail service was unsatisfactory to the western and middle parts of the town, yet it continued until 1878, when a petition by George E. Hilliard and others was presented to the post office department, for a post office at the "City" (so called) to be called "Cornish Center Post Office." The petition was granted and the office was opened July 1, 1878, in the house of Mr. Hilliard, and himself appointed post-master. He held the office until his death, March 31, 1904. After this his widow was appointed and served until June 15, 1908, when she resigned. On September 15, 1908, the office was discontinued by reason of the establishment of new postal routes under the law creating rural free delivery routes. During the thirty years this office was in operation, it was a great convenience and received a good share of patronage.

In 1879 another post office was established in the southern part of the town on the mail route from Cornish Flat to Claremont. It was called "South Cornish Post Office." It was granted on petition of George E. Fairbanks and others, and Mr. Fairbanks was appointed postmaster. This office, under the same management, continued twenty-nine years, or until June, 1908, when it was discontinued, being supplanted in part by the rural free delivery routes.

In 1879 another petition was sent to the post office department for an office at the geographical center of the town. This fact gave prestige to the scheme and the project was favorably entertained, and another office was opened there January 1, 1880, near the Congregational parsonage, bearing the name of "Cornish Post Office." The name of "Cornish Center Post Office," which had been applied to the office two miles nearer Windsor, has sometimes been mistaken for this office at the Center.

The town, therefore, has been favored with four contemporaneous post offices for more than a fourth of a century, ending in 1908, at which time three of them gave way to rural free delivery, while the other at the Flat, is still active (January 1, 1909).

Town Reports.

In 1850 the first annual Cornish town report was printed for distribution among the inhabitants of the town, and they have been issued yearly ever since. The first year it was simply a sheet, but has been in pamphlet form each year since.

All records of the town prior to the above date were recorded by the town clerk in the ordinary book of records and were kept in his office.

A law enacted in 1886 requires the town clerk to make a full record of the vital statistics of the town each year. Since that year this report has been prepared and appended to the other town report.

Indians.

Previous to the settlement of Cornish, the Indians had apparently receded to other sections, chiefly towards Canada, therefore they figure but little in the early history of the town. Occasionally some friendly Indians have appeared for a brief period, but owing to their roving habits and their natural dislike of agricultural pursuits, none ever became permanent citizens of the town. Nothing now remains of them in New England except in tradition or song, or the sweet names they left on mountain, lake or stream.

Shows and Exhibitions.

The citizens of Cornish are no exception to the mass everywhere who are fun loving, and seeking after the new, the curious and exciting things of the world. These proclivities are innate and are ever seeking their gratification. Large and pretentious shows have not been attracted to the town, owing to the sparseness of the population, and the smallness of the village, hence, the people of the town have generally resorted to adjoining towns, more populous, to attend shows and "see the folks."

For several years the circus and kindred shows were debarred from showing in the State of Vermont, while at the same time they were permitted in New Hampshire. This gave occasion for them to exhibit on "Cornish Street," near Trinity Church. The proximity of this place to Windsor gave opportunity for many from the Vermont side to attend.

The only circus that ever made a showing at Cornish Flat

was there August 11, 1851. It drew quite a crowd for so small a place.

School exhibitions have sometimes furnished interesting entertainments. Some of these have displayed a good deal of merit, reflecting favorably upon those who have taken part in them.

Ascutney Mountain.

Situated outside the town, and outside the state, and "beyond the river," even its mention seems out of place. Yet, in truth, it comes in for its share of honorable mention among the associations of Cornish.

This noble mountain has greeted the eyes of thousands who have lived in town that have since passed on to greater heights. Like a faithful sentinel it has stood with unchanged face looking down into the affairs of our town. Before Cornish had any history to record, it stood in silent majesty by her side. Would that it had been a chronicler of all the events that have been enacted within the radius of its vision! then the historian of today would have abundant material wherewith to accomplish his work. This mountain rears its lofty head 3,320 feet above the level of the sea. The traveler to its summit is richly paid for his toil by the view he obtains of the surrounding country on every side. For this reason foot paths, and even bridle paths have been prepared that the tourist may enjoy a day's outing on its summit.

O life-long companion of our days, we've watched thee from our homes;
We've seen thee mid summer's bloom and winter's cheerless gloom;
Our homes, they change; our dear ones pale in death;
Our earthly aspirations are creatures of a breath,
But thou, O Mount, remain unchanged.
Thine attitude, thy friendly presence still remains
To cheer us on our way.
Mid all the changing scenes dost thou look down
With unchanged, benignant face, and fresh inspiration give.
No wonder then we love thee. No wonder we're here today[1]
To breathe into thine ear the words of adoration pure.
What shall we render thee in token of our love
But tribute to our *God* who reigns above,
Whose handiwork thou art?
Thy beauteous form was moulded by His hand,
Thy nakedness was covered by a mantle green,

[1] September 5, 1908.

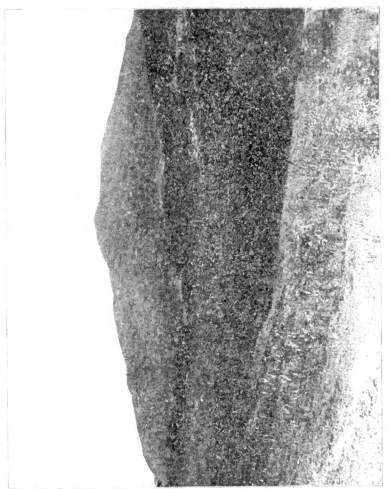

ASCUTNEY MOUNTAIN FROM CORNISH HILLS.

Woven by the same.
We've never heard thee boast, there is no need of that,
Thy silent majesty is ample thy glories to repeat.
In reverence would we bow before thy shrine, O lovely Mount.
We would enjoy thy presence for a day,
And leave thee to thy solitude again.—But ere we go,
Permit thine admirers to ask thee questions profound:—
What are the secrets locked in thy bosom pure?
What tales of weal and woe hast thou been a silent listener to?
When didst thou first rear thy lofty head
Above the chaos of the plain?
Why didst thou appear in our lovely valley *alone*,
Rather than among thy kindred of the verdant hills?
Was it that thou shouldst receive adoration full by being alone?
When will thy watch-care cease, thy silent vigils end?
Ages have seen thy beauty, and basked in thy shadows,
And thy face remains the same.
The rains of summer and the snows of winter
Have swept over thy summit.
If thou hast rejoiced, we have not known it.
If thou hast sorrowed, the breezes of Nature hast wiped
The tears from off thy face.
Is *eternity* written on thy brow?
Are thy years without end?   . . .
We will not pause for answer, for thou hast *none* to give.
Thy Maker alone can answer.
But today, thou art *ours*. We will enjoy thee as one of the gifts of His boun-
teous hand.

                                                    W. H. CHILD.

President Roosevelt's Visit to Cornish.

During the closing days of August, 1902, President Roosevelt
made a tour through Maine, New Hampshire and Vermont.
Thursday, August 28, he was at the Agricultural Fair at Newport,
N. H. The day following he spent his time in hunting in the
noted game preserve of Blue Mountain Park, and spent the
night there in the club house in "Central Station." Leaving
this place about 8 a. m., on Saturday (30th), the presidential
party crossed the mountain and arrived at Cornish Flat about
10 a. m., where many citizens from this and adjoining towns
had assembled from curiosity and to do him honor.

The event had been anticipated to some extent by the citizens,
therefore some preparations were made to give him a fitting
reception so far as the circumstances would permit. The school

children and other young people, having been taught the "Flag Drill," which consists of a graceful salutation, in unison, of our national flag, accompanied by a pledge of loyalty to it, were stationed at the expected time in front of the soldiers' monument awaiting the coming of the president. On his arrival at this spot, the procession halted, the salute and pledge were rendered under the tutelage of Dr. G. W. Hunt. All the children then presented Mr. Roosevelt with a fine bouquet of flowers, banking his carriage almost to overflowing.

These tributes to the flag and himself, the presence of a body of the Grand Army ranged by the monument of their deceased comrades, all together presented a scene deeply impressive and evidently gratifying to the president, as he gave visible evidence of deep emotion. He then spoke substantially as follows:

"I want to thank you for what you have done, and for the very kind and graceful way in which you have greeted me this morning. I cannot think of anything that augurs better for the country, than in just such a typical old American town as this, to have the school children drawn up before a monument like that (pointing to the soldiers' monument), in the town which was the birthplace of Salmon P. Chase, and to have them look towards *you*, the veterans of the great Civil War, *you* who have proved your truth by your endeavor, and to see in you an example of what they are to be when they grow up.

"I believe in preaching, but I believe in practice a good deal more, and it has been given to you, my friends of the great Civil War, to practice in the four years when the life of the republic was at stake, the virtues which we so earnestly ask that our children shall learn— virtues that count in war as well as in peace. Of course, there are exceptions, but ordinarily the man who is a first-class soldier in war has got in him the stuff that will make a first-class citizen in time of peace. The men, who, in this beautiful country of yours, till the soil, make their living here and breed up American citizens have to show the same fundamental righteousness, and the same virile virtues that you did in time of war.

"It is not enough, Gentlemen, to *mean* well either in battle or in civil life. You not only had to *mean* well, but had to *do* well, and it is the same in civil life.

"I think there is but one class of people who deserve as well

18

as the soldiers, and these are they who teach their children of
the present, how to be the masters of our country in the future.
I thank you."

After his speech the president shook hands with the members
of the Grand Army and a few others, and then he and the rest of
his party left the teams that had brought them to the Flat, and
entered other carriages prepared to receive them. Two of
these were each drawn by six horses and one four-in-hand team
was driven by Winston Churchill of Cornish. The president
chose the latter team and the party left for Windsor, Vt., where
Mr. Roosevelt was to appear before an agricultural fair then in
progress. As the party left the Flat they were enthusiastically
cheered by the crowd they left behind. Accompanying the
president were his secretary, George B. Cortelyou; Senator
Proctor and Ex-Governor Dillingham, both of Vermont;
ex-Senator Chandler of New Hampshire, and others, constituting the president's bodyguard. The day was fine and the
occasion one of interest to all present.

Old People's Association.

This institution apparently found its origin in the kindly
hearts of a beloved pastor and wife who were ever on the alert
to render a cheerful and happy service to all about them. In
their family resided an aged widow, a native of the town and
relic of a former prominent family. They planned, with her
consent, to invite to the parsonage a goodly number of the
elderly people of the town, chiefly ladies, many of whom she had
not met for many years.

The time appointed for the visit was on Wednesday, August
15, 1877. The day was a beautiful one, and the gathering a
complete success. Eighteen of the aged people were present.
The pleasure incident upon the reunion of so many aged people,
so long separated, was almost beyond expression. They seemed
to forget they were old people, and again became boys and girls
as of long years before. The occasion was one of thorough enjoyment to all present, and afforded them one of the happiest days
of their lives. The writer's mother, then seventy-six years of
age, was one of those present, who stated on her return home that
she "never had so good a time in her life," as she had met some
she had not seen since girlhood. As the party was about to

disperse, the question arose: "Shall we meet again?" "Yes, YES," was the eager and unanimous response. "But when?" By advice of the pastor, Rev. James T. Jackson and his worthy wife, it was decided they again meet on the Wednesday nearest the 20th of August on the following year.

The second meeting, in 1878, was in the Center Church, and

REV. AND MRS. JAMES T. JACKSON.

seventy-five were present, "a social, happy company," followed by a picnic dinner in the vestry. On August 20, 1879, they met again, and one hundred and fifty were present. At this time it was voted to become an organization with the pastor as acting chairman, a secretary and a committee, and that the day of meeting hereafter should be on the Wednesday nearest the 20th of August of each year.

On August 18, 1880, more than two hundred were present. On August 17, 1881, more than three hundred were present. Thus the "visit" increased in favor and apparently became a permanent institution, and has held its convocations every year since with unfaltering interest. The numbers present, aside from those already noted, have varied from 300 to 800 every year. Sons and daughters of Cornish have come from nearly every state in the Union. It is a somewhat remarkable fact that every day of meeting has been clear and beautiful for the thirty years prior to 1907.

The first four years of its records were kept by Albert E. Wellman; the next two by George L. Deming, and since 1882 by W. H. Child.

The meetings have been of a thoroughly social nature. The pleasure of reunion with so many natives and former residents of the town has furnished a happy feast every year. The elderly people of adjoining towns have delighted to join in all the festivities of the occasion. There has been no necessity of a set programme in advance to advertise the occasion, as every year so many have come from abroad who have contributed to the interest and enjoyment of the occasion by their presence and cheery remarks. The forenoon of each of the days is wholly informal and devoted to meeting and greeting the incoming guests. The dinner hour over, they assemble in church, where the exercises are more formal. These have always been prefaced by brief religious exercises, followed chiefly by reminiscent addresses from visitors, the whole being interspersed with appropriate songs and other music.

The meeting of August 21, 1907, though fewer were in attendance than usual owing to unfavorable weather conditions, was possessed of its usual interest. Choice songs were rendered and interesting addresses given by several. We append a brief one by E. Wellman Barnard, Esq., of Springfield, Vt., a son of Cornish, who was present.

"*Mr. Chairman, Ladies and Gentlemen:* I am happy in the knowledge that I first saw the light of day on a New Hampshire hill in the good old town of Cornish. Like its namesake over the sea, around it hovers rich memories of the best records of human impulse and mental and moral effort, and like other choice spots on earth's surface, it has an atmosphere peculiarly its own, where mind and matter seem to come into close communion, giving a greater power to each production of thought and purpose.

"I believe it has been fairly settled that the Old Home idea originated *right here*, and this thirty-first anniversary is an earnest demonstration that it was not a passing fancy with Cornish people. Your persisting in it has brought about wonderful results, results you could hardly have dreamed of at the outset. The idea itself has encircled the globe, and the Old Home habit has taken strong hold of many communities in other lands beside our own. States now vie with each other in sending out Old Home literature and invitations. It also fosters the restoration and preservation of old-time structures, holding them out as visual reminders to adorn historic pages. It is well to preserve the relics of other times and days so the mind's eye and the visual eye may together grasp the full meaning of the long ago they represent. Old Home days mean something to all the families of New England, in that they preserve the relics of the past and intensify our regard for her institutions and for each other. I have all faith in a great future for upper New England. The cloud-capped granite hills of New Hampshire and the green hills of Vermont have a use in the annual routine of this nation. Ere long this territory will become the "Mecca" of tired brain. Men and women of art and literature, students of science and people of leisure will find solace in this beautiful landscape where hills in billows roll, and doubtless will make permanent homes among us. I need not remind you that Cornish has a big start in this direction, and today Cornish needs no political designation in the Hall of Fame. Long may she hold her proud position and be a magnet to draw benefits to surrounding territory."

It is proper to mention that the prime object of the institution was the annual reunion among themselves of the aged people of Cornish and vicinity; hence its first name: "Old People's Visit." Soon the relatives and friends living abroad esteemed it a privilege to meet with their aged relatives in town. In this way the idea of *family reunions* on this day sprung up and added a prominent feature. In this way, too, the home-gathering spirit was fostered, and the importance of the occasion was increased, while it still retained its original name.

The sentiment spread to several other towns where similar organizations were formed with very gratifying results.

In 1899, after Cornish had enjoyed its "visits" for twenty-two years, His Excellency, Gov. Frank W. Rollins, who knew a good thing when he saw it, a man of generous impulse and kindly spirit, conceived the idea of a state organization based upon the identical principles embodied in the Cornish Old People's Visit. It was received by the state with great favor and added much to the name and fame of him who promulgated it from his high position. Instead of there being a *single day* devoted to reunion, *a week* was to be devoted to it, and one of its days to be used for a public gathering. This new organization took the name of "Old Home Week." The new name, with a slight variation in its form, constitutes the only difference, while the spirit and purpose in both remain the same.

CHAPTER XX.

LAWYERS— PHYSICIANS.

Lawyers.

A LIST of natives of Cornish, who have devoted their lives to the practice of law elsewhere, would be a lengthy one. It is not proposed to make mention of these. Many of them, however, receive brief mention in the records of the families from which they sprung, and also a few, among the records or biographies of *Cornish* men (which see). Mention here is made of only those who gave a greater or less portion of their lives to the practice of law in town.

The modern, up-to-date lawyer was an unknown quantity during the early years of the town. Justices of the peace had the handling of all cases of litigation between man and man, as well as the execution of necessary documents in the transfer of property, and all other business now devolving upon the modern attorney.

Judge Samuel Chase seemed to head the list of these. Coming to town in advanced life, bringing with him the rich experience of many years of such service in Sutton, Massachusetts, he was the acknowledged authority for, and executor of, such business as came before the early inhabitants of the town. His younger brother Moses was also found eminently capable of discharging a similar service. Doubtless other men beside the two named, rendered such service.

Of the second generation, the name of Harvey Chase, Esq., first presents itself. His is the first publicly recorded name of an attorney-at-law that lived in town, who had chosen the law as a profession.

Harvey Chase was born in Cornish, November 13, 1778. He was the son of Esq. Moses and Hannah (Brown) Chase, a lawyer of fair abilities and success, yet never attaining the distinction that some others of his name did. He was a graduate of Yale

College in 1800. He led a quiet life in town, dividing his time between the duties of his profession and those of agricultural pursuits. He lived in Cornish near Windsor, Vermont, where he obtained considerable patronage in his legal business.

He married Eunice Dana and by her had four children. (See his genealogy.) He died February 18, 1857.

Alonzo B. Williamson was born December 20, 1815, in Woodstock, Vermont. He studied law in Claremont with P. C. Freeman, Esq., and was admitted to the bar in 1837. He first practiced law in Claremont a few years. He then came to Cornish Flat where he established himself for about two years in the practice of his profession. These years were 1843 and 1844.

Not finding the field as lucrative and promising as he had hoped, and having received an appointment as postmaster at Claremont, he returned to Claremont where he spent the remainder of his life. Here he was postmaster, county solicitor, state senator, etc. He was a person of good ability, a respectable advocate, and quite a politician. Habits of intemperance somewhat interfered with his business during his later years. He married Sarah Ann Blake of Bellows Falls, Vermont, and had three children. He died March 19, 1860.

Edward Dimick Baker was born in Meriden, April 21, 1827. He availed himself of several years of study at Kimball Union Academy. He was a very successful teacher until he gave his attention to the study of law. He read in Enfield and Concord and was admitted to the bar in Sullivan County in July, 1851. Soon after this he opened a law office on Cornish Flat, where he continued in practice until October, 1855, when he removed to Claremont, where he spent the rest of his life.

Soon after his settlement in Cornish, he married, November 12, 1851, Elizabeth Ticknor of Plainfield, who after this was his life-long companion. They had no children. In social and legal standing, in prospering in his profession, and in securing an ample competence, he seemed to have made his life a success. He died February 1, 1895, at the age of nearly sixty-eight.

During his four years of practice at Cornish Flat, his business was comparatively light. This was due to several causes: a sparse population; the dislike of cases of litigation, by the staid people of the town, and the habit of patronizing petty justices on ordinary matters, thereby saving expense. These circumstances were not in harmony with the aspirations of the young, ambitious lawyer, so he decided to leave the town and go to Claremont, where his life record was chiefly made.

Physicians.

The following is a list of all the physicians who have practiced in town since its settlement.

The list may not include a few, who, for a brief period, have made a trial settlement and then left the town. Quacks of all kinds are excluded, but only men of principle and honor are included.

Neither does the list include natives of Cornish, who having chosen the profession, have gone forth and made a name and fame elsewhere.

The larger portion of those named have a family record in the genealogical department, to which the reader is referred for additional information. Repetition has been avoided as much as possible. Still, in order to do justice to each department, some repetition has been tolerated.

ISAAC ALDEN.

Dr. Isaac Alden for a few years was a practicing physician in Cornish and Plainfield, but was never prominent in his profession. Of a modest and retiring disposition, he never won his way to great distinction. He was, withal, a man of many virtues, a safe counsellor and had many friends both in and outside of his profession. He was established as a physician in Orange and Chelsea, Vermont, before coming to town, but never acquired an extensive practice. As a lover of nature, he took great pleasure in farming and gardening pursuits, so that he, in his later years, gradually let his medical practice subside and gave his attention more to the cultivation of the soil. (See Alden Gen.) He was born February 11, 1770, and died August 25, 1845.

DR. JOHN S. BLANCHARD.

Dr. John S. Blanchard was born August 10, 1805, in Canaan, New Hampshire. He attended medical lectures at Dartmouth College, afterwards studying with Doctors Smith and Muzzey, the latter granting him his diploma. He located and first began to practice at Cornish Flat in 1829, immediately succeeding Dr. Aaron Pierce. He continued here in practice until about 1843 (?) when he removed to Meriden that his children might receive the benefit of the academy there. He still continued in practice at Meriden several years, as his health would permit, until his death in 1861.

Of the old school of medicine, he was counted a successful practitioner, and well skilled in his profession. He was much interested in all educational enterprises, and assisted several young men to obtain an education. He was a kind and indulgent parent and very anxious that his children should always be under Christian influence. Politically he was a Democrat, and was postmaster while at the Flat.

In 1832 he married Louisa Jackson of Cornish who survived him several years. (See Blanchard Gen.)

ELIJAH BOARDMAN.

Dr. Elijah Boardman graduated at Dartmouth College in 1818 and from the medical department in 1831. While pursuing his studies (he taught school many terms with excellent success, several of them being in Cornish) he formed pleasant associations that led him to choose it as his life home. He had previously studied medicine with Doctor Cole of Cornish, and later commenced practicing in the same town. Doctor Boardman was a man of fine scholarly attainments, modest and reserved, conscientious and distrustful of his own abilities, even though possessed of a mind richly stored with a knowledge of men and things. This lack of self-confidence probably was no aid to him in attaining those higher ranks of eminence in his profession to which he was justly entitled. But he had the full confidence of all who knew him and was reckoned a safe counsellor and an excellent family physician. He was a friend to everybody and everybody was his friend. It was a common saying regarding him, that he was never heard to speak disparagingly of any one.

He was born in Norwich, Vermont, July 24, 1794, and died in Cornish, January 27, 1880. (See Boardman Gen.)

DR. ELIJAH BOARDMAN.

JOSEPH CHAPMAN.

Dr. Joseph Chapman is said to have been one of the first doctors in town. He was born in 1757, and died in 1810. *Records* concerning him are somewhat meager, but the *traditions* preserved by his descendants evidence him as a man of influence and culture for those times. Of his medical equipment little can be gleaned, but his success in the profession is confirmed by the united testimony of his posterity. Being settled upon a large farm, it is to be inferred that farming supplemented the practice of his profession, and that in both branches of his calling he was successful.

EBENEZER BREWER CHASE.

Dr. E. Brewer Chase, son of Lebbeus Chase, was born November 30, 1815. The preparation for his profession is not known, but he was accounted quite skillful in his profession, and had a fair share of patronage, especially in his neighborhood along the river. Although strictly moral, he possessed a spirit of independence that rendered him somewhat indifferent to the criticisms of others. This led him to be careless as to his speaking, manners and dress. These circumstances did not contribute to the popularity of which he was really deserving. He died January 21, 1855. (See Lebbeus Chase Gen.)

SOLOMON CHASE.

Dr. Solomon Chase was born in Sutton, Massachusetts, September 1, 1742. He left Sutton when of age, came to Walpole, New Hampshire, where he studied medicine and after receiving his diploma, practiced there until 1773 when he rejoined his relatives and settled in Cornish. He was the first physician known to settle in town; and his entire life was devoted to his profession, unless we except an appointment as captain over a company of militia, but in this case he soon changed the sword for the medical saddle-bags.

During the Revolution, he received appointments from headquarters and was made surgeon-general in the Continental Army for several years. Sometimes he had the charge of the sick and wounded of three regiments (another account says two brigades), which duties he faithfully rendered, reporting satisfactorily to his commanders. These commissions are matters of national history.

On his return home he resumed his practice and so continued until extreme age. His descendants refer to him with pride and pleasure. He was, without doubt, a physician and surgeon that met every need the community required. He died November 1, 1828. (See Chase Gen.)

STEPHEN COLE.

Dr. Stephen Cole studied medicine with Drs. Roswell Leavitt of Cornish and E. E. Phelps of Windsor, Vermont, they granting him a license to practice. Afterwards he received an honorary

degree from Dartmouth College. After his preparation was
complete he made his first trial settlement at Huntsburg, Vermont. This place he soon left, returning to Cornish in 1813,
where he remained seventeen years, or until 1830. After leaving
Cornish he continued practice, and finally settled in Peru, New
York, where he died in 1876, at the advanced age of 89 years.
While a resident of Cornish, he acquired a host of friends. He
was accounted a physician of skill and judgment, and enjoyed
a good patronage. (For family record, see Cole Gen.)

ISAAC DOTON.

Dr. Isaac Doton was born August 18, 1790. He studied
medicine first with Dr. Asa Crosby of Sandwich; attended
lectures at Hanover in 1814 and began practice in 1815. He settled in several places; came to Cornish in 1839 and remained here
four years. Leaving town in 1843, he settled in Bradford, New
Hampshire, and Lowell, Massachusetts, and Manchester, New
Hampshire, where he died August 18, 1865. He was a physician
commanding the respect and confidence of the people of Cornish,
and had a good practice while here. (See Doton Gen.)

NAHUM PARKER FOSTER.

The introduction of this noble man into Cornish was brought
about by his accepting a call to preach in the Baptist
Church in 1843. He came as a candidate for the ministry
and was ordained on the Flat, May 29, 1844. His medical
training had been previously obtained, and also considerable practice. He had attended lectures at Dartmouth
College, and from it received his diploma in 1834. During the
entire time of his pastorate in town he was also actively engaged
in medical practice,—"healing the bodies as well as the souls
of his fellowmen." This, of course, gave rise to some criticism
resulting in diverse opinions, but Doctor Foster was a man of
uncommon gifts, and seemed able to be a master in both branches
of his calling. As a preacher he was eloquent and entertaining.
As a doctor of medicine he seemed not a whit behind his fellows.
He had many warm friends and admirers in both professions, and
among the general public. His pastorate in town as also his
medical practice ended in 1855, when he left for other fields of
labor, chiefly in Massachusetts and Connecticut.

Near the close of his life he made an extensive tour of Egypt and Palestine. On his return he gave many addresses relating to those countries. He was born February 10, 1814, and died in New London, Connecticut, May 6, 1876.

LYMAN HALL.

Dr. Lyman Hall was born in Croydon, December 9, 1805, and died in Cornish, May 24, 1862. He studied medicine and

DR. LYMAN HALL.

graduated from the medical department of Dartmouth College in 1832. After two brief settlements, first at Mt. Desert, Maine, and also at Blue Hill, Maine, he came to Cornish in November, 1844, and spent the rest of his life here. As a physician, he had a good practice, was always genial and mirthful and therefore beloved and highly respected. As a citizen he was well informed, reliable and ranked well among his townsmen. He took much interest in the schools of the town and was repeatedly chosen as school superintendent. At his decease a far-reaching community mourned his loss. (See Hall Gen.)

GEORGE W. HUNT.

Dr. George W. Hunt had the honor of rendering the longest term of service in town of any of his profession. For nearly forty-five years he was the "beloved physician" of Cornish and adjacent towns. He came to town in August, 1862, and his public services ended with his death, March 3, 1907. Doctor Hunt was born in Georgia, Vermont, May 20, 1828. He was

DR. GEORGE W. HUNT.

a graduate of Castleton Medical College. Afterwards, in 1868, he received the honorary degree of M. D. from Dartmouth College. He enjoyed a fine standing, not only among his fellow physicians, but among all classes of society to whom he rendered professional services. His skill was acknowledged by all and, to a large extent, he enjoyed the confidence and respect of the community. He had been in town but a few months when he decided to make it his life-home, and built for himself a fine residence on the Flat.

He contributed much to the social and intellectual status of the town. Deeply interested in all educational subjects, he has been superintendent of schools and a zealous promoter of all up-to-date methods. He was a man of broad views, large understanding and intensely optimistic in all his beliefs. As a politician, he was a Republican, and as such represented the town in the Legislature of 1880. (See Hunt Gen.)

HENRY KETCHUM.

Dr. Henry Ketchum came to Cornish Flat in 1899 and stayed about two years, and then settled elsewhere. He appeared to be well skilled in his profession, but lack of patronage, and the loss of his only child, apparently discouraged his remaining longer in town.

ROSWELL LEAVITT.

Just previous to the opening of the nineteenth century, in 1799, Doctor Leavitt with his young and accomplished bride came from

RESIDENCE OF D. J. SPAULDING.
Built by Dr. Roswell Leavitt, 1804-05.

Charlemont, Massachusetts, to Cornish. They both came on horseback. Here they had purposed to establish their home, but the reason of their choice is not now known. The preparation for his life-work, too, is not found on record, but he came to

Cornish thoroughly equipped to take high rank among those of his profession. He soon found himself in the midst of a lucrative practice, and enjoying the society of many friends. Prosperity seemed to attend him and his good wife who contributed not a little to his good fortune. He built the capacious and imposing brick house near the Flat, now (1908) owned and occupied by Darwin J. Spaulding—but earthly good fortunes are liable to reverses and so with Doctor Leavitt. A severe fit of sickness nearly wrecked him. Occasional fits of insanity seized him, and in one of these he terminated his heretofore useful life by hanging himself while yet in the prime of life, at the age of forty-two years and ten months. He left an enviable name, a host of friends and a posterity who have taken high rank. (See family record.)

C. W. MANCHESTER.

Dr. Constant Wood Manchester was the son of Dr. John and Susan (Wood) Manchester. He was born in Plainfield, New Hampshire, April 20, 1831. When a small boy, his father moved to Morristown, Vermont. He lived there a few years, then moved to Royalton, Vermont, where he grew to manhood. Choosing the medical profession, he studied medicine with his father, also with Dr. H. H. Whitcomb of the same town. He attended lectures at Dartmouth Medical College, also at Burlington, Vermont, where in June, 1858, he graduated. In August of the same year he commenced the practice of medicine at Cornish Flat. He lived there until August, 1860, then moved to Meriden, where he successfully practiced his profession until February, 1874. He then moved to Lebanon, where he resided and practiced until he died August 4, 1892. While residing in Cornish in May, 1859, he married Miss Amelia Chamberlain of Royalton, Vermont. In March, 1861, a son was born to them, an only child, Dr. Frank Constant Manchester, now a practicing physician in Grafton, New Hampshire.

AARON PIERCE.

Dr. Aaron Pierce was born in Barnard, Vermont, November 23, 1787. Choosing the medical profession attended lectures at Dartmouth College, where he obtained his diploma. After completing his course he married Sarah Hough of Lebanon. He

19

chose Cornish as his first field of labor. So with his new bride
he settled on Cornish Flat in 1819. He remained here ten years
or until 1829, when he left town, and was succeeded by Dr. John
S. Blanchard. While here Doctor Pierce was adjudged a good
family physician, and won the confidence and good will of the
people in a large degree. For reasons unknown to the writer,
Doctor Pierce saw fit to close his services here and go to other
fields of labor. He established himself first at Weathersfield,
then at Irasburg, and finally at Barton, Vermont. In this latter
place he lost his wife, Sarah, in 1842, and in 1844 he married
Mary Billings of Lebanon who survived him nearly twenty
years.

Doctor Pierce was tall and of commanding presence, with
strong convictions and forceful manners. It is said that after
leaving Cornish he was licensed to preach, which he did with great
success in connection with his medical practice. He died in
Barton, Vermont, June 1, 1860. (See Pierce Gen.)

S. T. SHAW.

Dr. S. T. Shaw came to town from Claremont and settled on
a farm for a few years, dividing his attention between his profession and his farm. He was accounted a fair practitioner and
had a measure of success.

NATHAN SMITH.

The record of Doctor Smith sounds like a romance. Fortune,
coupled with his own exertions, seemed to open to him paths that
led to distinction and renown. How well he walked them, the
results of his life-work show. While Rehoboth, Massachusetts,
may claim the honor of his birth, Cornish claims the honor of
discovering his worth.

He never left the plow until twenty-eight years of age. He
then began laying the foundation for his future usefulness. After
four years of initiatory practice in Cornish as one of the best of
physicians, his record, as copied from Dartmouth College records,
is as follows:

"Nathan Smith, M. B. Harvard, 1790; A. M. 1798; M. D. 1801;
also Harvard, 1811. B. 13 Sept., 1762, Rehoboth, Mass. Prof.
Theos. and Pract. Med., 1798–1813; also Anat. and Surg. 1798–1810;
Prof. Theos. and Pract. Med., Surg. and Obst., Yale, 1813–29. Prof.

Theos. and Pract. Med., Bowdoin, 1820–25.   Lecturer, Med. and
Surg., Univ. of Vt., 1822–25.   D. 26 July, 1828, New Haven, Conn."

The savor and influence of Doctor Smith's career were entailed
upon his descendants and inspired them for like exalted positions
in life. (See his genealogy; also the records of his two eldest sons
and their children.)

DR. NATHAN SMITH.

ROBERT THORNBURGH.

Dr. Robert Thornburgh was born in New York City and
studied medicine there. This was supplemented by attending
several courses of lectures at Dartmouth Medical College, so
that he acquired a thorough fitting for his work. He opened
an office on the Flat where he practiced about two years with

excellent success. Receiving an appointment from the government as a surgeon in the United States' employ, he left Cornish
and has been stationed in the Marine Hospital at Manila, P. I.

EBENEZER WRIGHT.

But little is now known of Dr. Ebenezer Wright. He married
a daughter of the Rev. James Wellman in 1781. He lived near
the Cornish line in Plainfield and practiced in both towns.
Tradition speaks of him as a well-qualified and successful physician. He died October 28, 1798. (See Wellman Gen.)

CHAPTER XXI

"Lives of great men all remind us
We can make our lives sublime,
And departing, leave behind us
Footprints on the sands of time."

CHARLES C. BEAMAN, ESQ.

FEW men, not natives of Cornish, have seemed more interested in its affairs, and have won the love and respect of their townsmen more than did Charles C. Beaman, Esq.

He was a lawyer by profession and practice, and as such first settled in New York City. He had become associated with the eminent Wm. M. Evarts of the same city, whose summer home was at Windsor, Vt.

In his association with this family, Mr. Beaman had become enamored, not only with the cultured and winsome daughter of Mr. Evarts, but also with the beautiful lands lying over the river in Cornish nearly opposite the village of Windsor. Here he determined to locate a summer home, and to this end he purchased extensively. He revived and adopted "Blow-me-down" as the name of his new estate. Here he built in 1883 the present delightful residence, since occupied in summer by himself and family.

During his residence in Cornish he ever had a keen eye to substantial material improvements. It was through his efforts that "Hillside Creamery," since such a boon to many farmers, was started and carried to complete success. The arched stone bridge over Blow-me-down Brook on his estate, one of the finest stone structures in town, stands as a monument to the enterprise and benevolence of Messrs. Beaman and Evarts, the town, however, paying the cost of a wooden bridge. Near the bridge he erected a dam and grist-mill for the use of the general public.

His benevolence embraced liberal sums for the improvement of highways in town,—for the erection of the schoolhouse in Division 10, for the beautiful Soldiers' Monument at the Flat, beside numerous other gifts, as no worthy cause ever appealed to him in vain. As a final gift, he bequeathed a thousand dollars, the interest of which is to be expended for the erection and maintenance of guide-boards in town.

The love and interest Mr. Beaman had for his adopted town was contagious among his numerous friends of the city. As they visited him and his family in their Cornish home, they saw the charms of the locality—the beautiful river, the mountain view, the verdant meadows, the wood-crowned heights, the pure air and gushing springs of water.

Several of these friends were induced to follow Mr. Beaman's example, and came and purchased, not primitive land, but estates that had been occupied and improved since the first settlement of the town. (A more extended account of these modern settlers in town is given elsewhere. See, also, Beaman Gen.) To Mr. Beaman, therefore, belongs the honor of being the pioneer and promoter in this movement which has effected so great a change in the social status of the town.

As was his usual custom he retired in the fall of 1900 to his city home for the winter, where he was taken sick with pneumonia and on the fifteenth day of December following he passed away from earth.

Judge Henry E. Howland of New York, a dear friend of Mr. Beaman, bestowed upon him the following tribute:

"Nature casts men in various forms, but rarely does she give to the world a more thoroughly finished product than Charles C. Beaman, for there were combined in him all those qualities that command the respect and win the love of men—strength and gentleness, marked ability, a high sense of duty, kindly thoughtfulness for others, geniality of temper, brilliant wit, and unfailing generosity. With these, he won his way to distinction in a community where there is no royal road to success, and where rivalry is fierce and unceasing."

The incidents in his career are like a finished romance. It is a story which every father can place before his boys and ask no better of them than to copy it.

It is said that genius consists in seizing upon opportunity, and his career justifies the assertion.

After graduating at Harvard in 1861, where he made a marked impression, he entered the Harvard Law School and in 1865 was awarded the first prize for his essay on the "Rights and Duties

of Belligerent War Vessels." It was well written, displaying discriminating judgment and an admirable knowledge of international law, and when published in the *North American Review*, attracted the attention of Senator Sumner, who thereupon appointed him his secretary and clerk of the Committee on Foreign Relations in the Senate. In 1868 he began to practice in New York, and in 1871 he published his book on the "Alabama Claims and their Settlement." He was then appointed examiner of claims in the Department of State, an office which he filled with signal ability. He was appointed by the President solicitor of the United States before the Tribunal of Arbitration at Geneva, a selection due to his knowledge of the subject, and to the influential gentlemen connected with the commission who realized his ability. At Paris he soon showed that he knew more about the details of claims than any one else, and was in constant consultation with Messrs. Cushing, Evarts and Waite, the counsel for the United States. Mr. Evarts was accompanied by his family, and Mr. Beaman there made the acquaintance of his daughter, Miss Hettie Sherman Evarts, whom he subsequently married.

After the conclusion of the arbitration he represented many of the claimants in establishing their claims, and of course received substantial regard for his services.

Thus Mr. Beaman's opportunity came by the chance choice of a subject for a prize thesis, and he so well availed himself of it that it brought him position, his wife, and a fortune.

He practiced his profession in partnership with Edward N. Dickerson, a distinguished patent lawyer, until 1879, when he became a member of that firm of notable lawyers composed of Wm. M. Evarts, Charles F. Southmayd and Joseph H. Choate. By the retirement of its senior members, he was at the time of his death practically at its head, and as such, entrusted with the largest and most important business interests as counsel for great railway lines, for important corporations and leading capitalists whose operations were world wide. How well he administered these weighty trusts, all who were brought in contact with him will freely admit.

His trained legal mind, sound judgment, far-reaching sagacity, fair conclusions, conciliatory spirit were effective and convincing and brought him high reputation and successful issues to his clients.

With all this engrossing professional work pressing upon him, he was always a leader in any movement for the public good, social, charitable or political, unsparing in his efforts and regardless of himself.

But it is for his personal qualities that he will be best remembered. He was one of the cheeriest men that ever drew the breath of life, bubbling over with boyish enthusiasm, gifted with an irrepressible humor.

"Whose wit in the combat as gentle as bright,
   Ne'er carried a heart-stain away on its blade."

Buoyant, fascinating, pervading the very air with his contagious sympathy, he was the center of every social gathering, and the best man at a dinner table for raillery, repartee and brilliant passage at arms in conversation.

"He made a July day short as December,
   And with his varying childness cured in us
   Thoughts that would thick our blood."

He was responsive in his sympathy with suffering and sorrow, quick in his emotions, gracious in his universal benevolence, gentle and tender with every young thing, and the very soul of hospitality, which, as hundreds of his friends will long remember, he dispensed with a lavish hand at his estate of Blow-me-down, which he loved so well. He was a grateful, affectionate son, a loving husband, a devoted, thoughtful father, a kind and helpful neighbor and a noble man. It seems impossible to think of him as dead. No man could have left a larger gap, for he brightened his world while in it and it is poorer for his going. He died as he had lived, like a Christian gentleman, knowing that his end was near, in the full possession of his faculties, with a message on his lips, he said: "Give my love to all my friends. I don't think I have many enemies," in which every one who knew him will concur.

Although the summons came to him in his prime, the measure of his life was as full as if it had rounded out the psalmist's term of human existence up to the limit beyond which all is vanity, and he came to his eternal rest as one who

"Bends to the grave with unperceived decay,
   While resignation gently slopes the way;
   And, all his prospects brightening to the last,
   His Heaven commences ere the world be past."

COL. LYSANDER HERBERT CARROLL.

Born in Croydon, October 8, 1835. Received his education in the schools of Cornish. At the age of seventeen engaged with Francis Robbins of Sutton, selling stoves in Sutton and sur-

LYSANDER H. CARROLL.

rounding towns. At the age of twenty-two purchased the business of Mr. Robbins and continued the same until 1865, when he removed to Concord, where he engaged in the stove and hardware business under the firm name of Carroll & Stone, a very lucrative business which he followed for six years.

During the next twelve years he conducted the popular dining rooms of Piper & Haskins in Concord. In 1875 he was appointed colonel on Governor Cheney's staff, and with them represented New Hampshire in the United States Centennial Celebration at Philadelphia in 1876.

In 1876 he was chosen to bear the votes of the New Hampshire presidential electors to Washington on the election of President Hayes.

For two years he acted as transfer agent of the mails at the Concord depot. In 1879 was appointed by President Hayes postmaster at Concord, which position he occupied under two administrations. During his second term he inaugurated Concord's present free delivery system. After this, until 1895, he was associated with and a director in the banking house of E. H. Rollins & Sons. In 1895 and 1896 he was a member of the Legislature from Ward 6, Concord, and in May, 1899, was appointed labor commissioner, which position he still holds (1910).

Colonel Carroll is an active member of the South Congregational Church, Concord.

As a Republican he has been active in political campaigns since 1856; a member of the Republican state committee for over thirty years and a Knights Templar Mason.

He has two daughters: Jennie B., the wife of Horace J. Davis, member of the Davis Paper Manufacturers at Contoocook; Ella B., the wife of Edward M. Nason, keeper of the state house at Concord; and one son, Charles Herbert, a popular conductor on the Boston & Maine Railroad, married Annie Wilkins of Manchester.

CHAMPION S. CHASE.

Champion Spaulding Chase was born in Cornish, March 20, 1820. He was the son of Deacon Clement and Olive (Spaulding) Chase.

His education consisted of the primary education afforded by the district schools of Cornish, supplemented by several terms at Kimball Union Academy.

He was a teacher for several terms in the common schools and also an assistant teacher in the academies of Amsterdam and West Hartwick, N. Y.

He then studied law in Buffalo, N. Y.; was admitted to the bar in 1847, at Canandaigua, N. Y., and opened his first law office at Racine, Wis., on May 1, 1848, the same day of his marriage to Sophronia Butterfield of Homer, N. Y.

He remained at Racine until the opening of the Civil War. Previous to that event, in 1851, he was admitted to practice in the

United States Supreme Court at Washington, D. C. In 1856, he was a delegate to the National Republican Convention at Philadelphia, which nominated John C. Fremont as a candidate for the presidency, and the same year he was elected to the Wisconsin State Senate for two years, during which time he, as chairman of the judiciary committee, supervised the revision of the statutes of the state.

For several years he was a member of the board of education of Racine and two years was chairman of the board.

During the Civil War he rendered a variety of valuable services during a period of four years. He was commissioned paymaster in the Union Army for a while; was on special duty in the West and Southwest; was at the sieges of Knoxville, Mobile and Vicksburg and afterwards had headquarters at New Orleans for nearly two years. He, at this time, was brevetted lieutenant colonel for meritorious services in the Gulf Campaign. He was honorably discharged in January, 1866. The same year he went to Omaha, Neb., the year before Nebraska was admitted to the Union as a state, and upon its admission, he was the first attorney-general of the state, and in 1869, was appointed a regent of the State University of Nebraska for six years.

In 1874 he was elected mayor of Omaha, and also in 1875, 1879 and 1883, for two years each, in all seven years, ending in 1885. While mayor, Colonel Chase received, and officially and socially entertained, a large number of distinguished people. Among them was the king of the Hawaiian Islands, the emperor of Brazil, the governor-general of Canada, also President Hayes and Mrs. Hayes, General and Mrs. U. S. Grant, besides Generals Sherman, Sheridan, Custer and others.

In Masonry, he was eminent commander of Mt. Calvary Commandery, Knights Templar, of Omaha, and generalissimo of the state commandery. He was also identified with the G. A. R. and the S. A. R. and other similar organizations. It was a complimentary act on the part of the Legislature of Nebraska that they should name one of their counties, *Chase* County, after him, and also one of the towns in said county was called *Champion*.

As a public speaker, Colonel Chase achieved a large reputation and his services as such were sought in many parts of the West. Many of his speeches and addresses have been published. Notably among them was one delivered in the Wisconsin Senate in 1857 in opposition to the extension of slavery.

Colonel and Mrs. Chase had but one child, a son, Champion Clement, born February 25, 1860, in Racine, Wis., who continues to reside in Omaha, and is now the editor and proprietor of the *Omaha Excelsior*.

Mrs. Chase died in Omaha, January 3, 1882. He again married. He died in Omaha, November 3, 1898, from the result of a fall. To the last he was devoted to the memories of his native town, often expressing his loyalty and love for it.

Impressive funeral obsequies were held by the several societies to which he belonged; the various city officials joining the cortege, while the chiming bells contributed their solemn notes to the occasion.

DUDLEY CHASE.

Dudley Chase, son of Dudley and Alice (Corbett) Chase, was born in Cornish, December 30, 1771. He entered Dartmouth College when but sixteen years of age, in the autumn of 1787, and graduated from it in the class of 1791. He then gave his attention to the study of law and was admitted to the bar in 1794. He began its practice in Randolph, Vt. This place was his home during the remainder of his life except as public duties called him away. The town of his adoption became so identified with his name, that he was familiarly known as "Judge Chase of Randolph." Successful and eminent at the bar as a jurist, as well as a safe legal counsellor, he won the confidence of his clients, thereby opening the way to broader fields.

He was the state attorney for Orange County from 1803 to 1811. The Legislature of Vermont recognizing his fitness elected him to the United States Senate in 1813, which position he held four years, completing the unexpired term of his predecessor. After this he was judge of the Supreme Court of Vermont from 1817 until 1821. Several times he represented his town in the state Legislature, and was speaker of the House in 1823 and 1824. In 1825 he was again elected to the Senate of the United States for the full term, ending in 1831. After the expiration of this term he retired from political life to more quiet duties in his adopted town. Of his services while in the Senate much might be written expressive of his ability, high moral integrity, and

sound judgment, but his history during those ten years in the
Senate is found in the nation's records of those times.

While a member of the Senate he was approached by his
nephew, Salmon P. Chase, who at that time desired his influence
in procuring a clerkship in some department of the government. Judge Chase was doubtful about the expediency of his
nephew's wish, so he took a half dollar from his pocket, and
offering it to him said: "If you wish to make a success in life,
buy a spade and go to work." This was a cooler to the ardent
aspirations of the nephew, who of course indignantly refused
the money and went away somewhat disheartened at the
apparent unfeeling attitude of his uncle. Judge Chase was
never charged with nepotism and by this transaction showed
that, as in his own case, if one is to obtain offices of honor
and trust, he is to *earn* them by showing himself worthy
of them, as he had done, and *not* receive them through the
recommendation of friends.

Chief Justice Chase in his last visit to Cornish in 1866, in
speaking of the circumstance, jokingly said in the hearing of the
writer, "I guess I made a mistake in not taking the half
dollar, for, if I had taken it, I might have been president of the
United States."

Judge Chase's success as a lawyer and statesman was known
all over the country, and his honesty as a man and citizen was
never questioned. One wonders what this pure and noble man
would think of the "log-rolling" too often practiced by the
politicians of today!

He was also a great stickler for the dignity of the court.
Under his rule, no "boy's play" among the lawyers of the
court was tolerated, and everything tending towards levity was
frowned from his presence. Trifling cases were not suffered to
find a place on his docket, but were ordered settled at some
other tribunal than his.

After his retirement from political life, he devoted himself
to the duties of his profession, and also to the improvement
of his home in Randolph. As in his political life, so in all his
domestic matters, he was the exemplar of thoroughness in everything he did. He was the best farmer, had the best fences,
best and most beautiful garden, and he built the finest house
in that section of the country, planted the finest orchards,

raised the finest fruit. He also planned for the best and widest roads in Randolph.

In earlier life he married Olivia Brown. They had no children of their own, but they adopted or supported twelve children, educating the boys and giving the girls a portion at their marriage.

Olivia died in January, 1846, and Judge Chase died the following month. Their ashes repose in the old cemetery at Randolph Center, Vt.

ITHAMAR CHASE.

Ithamar Chase was born September 27, 1762, in Sutton, Mass. He was but three years of age when, with his mother, he came to Cornish Like other boys of the early days, but little is left on record concerning him. It is said, however, that he early gave evidence of an energetic business talent. He prepared for, and entered Dartmouth College and there pursued his studies for some time, but for reasons unknown to the writer, he left college and went soon after to Keene, N. H., at, or a little before his majority. It does not appear how long he stayed there, or the business he followed, but he won the heart and hand of Janette, the beautiful and gifted daughter of Alexander Ralston, at that time the wealthiest, and one of the most influential men of Keene.

Soon after their marriage, he, with his wife, returned and resided in Cornish. Here he spent the best part of his life. Here most of their children were born. Here, enjoying the confidence of all of his townsmen, relatives and friends, he received at their hands the best official gifts in their power to bestow. He was justice of the peace, and chief legal counsellor for the town and vicinity.

While residing in Cornish it is related that a certain couple came to him to get married. It was in the evening of the day of the annual town meeting. Mr. Chase had been moderator and had also administered the oath of office to nearly all officers chosen that day, and being wearied with the duties of the day, he was sitting in his easy chair in front of the large fireplace "toasting his feet," and in this attitude fell asleep. A knock at the door was answered by Mrs. Chase, who, upon learning their business, came to Mr. Chase, and, jogging him, told him there was a couple at the door wanting to get married. In a half-conscious condition he told his wife to bring them in. She complied with his request and they stood beside him. "What do you want?" asked Mr. Chase, rather gruffly. "To get married," they replied. "Well then, hold up your right hands." They did so, and he administered the usual qualifying oath of office, making a little variation in the latter clause, and pronounced them husband and wife, to their apparent satisfaction. They paid their fee and went on their way rejoicing and he returned to his slumbers.

After the death of his father-in-law in 1810, he, with his family, returned to Keene, and here spent the brief remainder of his life. He took charge of the Ralston Hotel and also of the management of the estate. He also engaged in the glass manufacturing business. This, however, did not prove a financial success.

He was a member of the council for the State of New Hampshire for several years, ending in 1816.

He was a prominent Free Mason, and was the first master of Hiram Lodge in Claremont. Subsequently his name appears on the rolls of the first Royal Arch Chapter in Keene.

He never sought eminence but, rather, was one of those robust characters that always prove equal to all the labors and duties that are imposed upon them. It is of this type of men that leaders are ofttimes born, as was proved in the present case.

But his busy life work ended August 11, 1817. Being a zealous member of the Protestant Episcopal Church, and in harmony with his desire, his funeral was conducted according to the rites of that church. It was the first funeral of this order ever solemnized in Keene. It was largely attended and created a deep and favorable impression on behalf of the church. Reverend Doctor Strong of Greenfield, Mass., officiated. Mr. Chase was buried in Keene.

On his tombstone is written:

> "And now, Lord, what is my hope?
> Truly my hope is ever in Thee."

GEN. JONATHAN CHASE.

Jonathan Chase was born in Sutton, Mass., December 6, 1732. He was the son of Judge Samuel and Mary (Dudley) Chase. He came to Cornish in 1765 at the time the town was settled. Al-

though young, he devoted himself actively to the interests of the
new settlement in every way. He became an extensive land
proprietor, a farmer and surveyor. He opened the first store
ever kept in town, which continued many years. After buildings
were erected, he also kept the first inn. In the absence of any
public place of meeting, his doors were ever open for all the meetings of the colonists for any purpose whatever. Several of the
first town meetings were held there. His counsel and means
were freely bestowed on all progressive measures. He built,
owned and operated the first sawmill and gristmill in town.

The influence of the French and Indian War and other stirring
events of those times evidently tended to develop in him a martial
spirit, fitting him as a military leader, for he soon became a bold
and efficient organizer and leader of the militia of Cornish and
vicinity. It soon became evident that he possessed an admirable
fitness for leadership, as on August 30, 1775, by act of the assembly,
he was commissioned colonel of the territorial regiment consisting
of the towns of Hanover, Lebanon, Lyme, Orford, Cornish and
Plainfield.

All the able-bodied men of these towns between the ages of
sixteen and fifty were enrolled, subject to drill and call to service
whenever and wherever needed. At first the terms of enlistment
were short, simply meeting the requirements of each campaign.

The full account of the military services rendered by Colonel
Chase during the Revolutionary War are omitted here, but they
find brief mention in the records of that eventful period. It is
true, however, that during the war his military record at all times
and under all circumstances reflected honor upon himself and the
town of his adoption. He manifested his fitness as a commander
in many ways. He was bold and fearless though not rash or
arbitrary and of fine physical proportions. He was beloved by
his men and fellow officers who quickly responded to his orders,
while he in turn as quickly responded to the orders of his superior
officers, and whenever a fearful crisis was imminent, his cool and
deliberate counsel was sought and heeded. He served during
all the short campaigns in the North until the theater of war was
removed to the South and West whither he followed its fortunes
for sometime afterwards.

After the war was over, in 1788, he was appointed brigadier-
general on Governor Langdon's staff. In 1789 he, under the same

rank and title, was appointed on Governor Pickering's staff.   By virtue of these appointments, and supported by a splendid military record of the past, his claim to the title of *general* was undisputed, this title he ever afterwards bore.

Not alone in the counsels of war, or on the battlefield, was General Chase a power.   In the general affairs of the town he was active in all measures for the development of its resources. The offices of the town were often tendered him.   Some of these he accepted while he refused others.   He was selectman nine years; three years town treasurer.   Three years he served as moderator, and represented the town in the Grand Assembly in 1788.   In the opening of new highways in town, General Chase was the leading spirit.   He established the first ferry across the Connecticut River between Cornish and Windsor.   This was done in 1784, and it continued in use until 1795.   (See Cornish Bridge.)

An examination of his public papers and private records shows he had a wonderful business capacity and sound judgment.   While many have gone out from the town and been mighty in influence in other places, probably no resident of the town ever consulted her interests more effectively during his day than did he.   To him the town has been, and still is, indebted for much of the prestige she has enjoyed.   Though no grand monument marks his final resting place, yet the record of his works furnishes a monument that will abide.

The activities and exposures incident to a pioneer life, his military campaigns and hardships connected with them, together with the burden of his responsibility to his adopted town, all left their impress upon his naturally robust constitution, and in the midst of his seeming usefulness he died January 12, 1800.   He was twice married and had eleven children.   (See his family record.)   The slab over his remains bears this inscription:

"One of the early settlers of the town, filling a variety of offices with honor to himself and advantage to the public."

DR. MAURICE J. CHASE.

Dr. Maurice J. Chase, a son of Benjamin C. and Eliza (Royce) Chase, was born in Cornish, March 4, 1826.

When quite young, less than four years, his father died, and he went to live with his grandmother until he was twelve years of

20

age. After this he went forth into the world to make his own living as best he could.

Favorable impressions concerning the medical profession were early stamped upon his mind, and in all his youthful years, he never faltered in his aim nor was tempted to abandon his early choice.

During this period of his life he resorted to a variety of commendable occupations to secure a livelihood. Of vigorous health and praiseworthy ambition, he did not shun any of the labors incident to the farm or shop. He worked on farms, chopped wood, and made himself generally useful. Besides this he availed himself of all the educational advantages his time and means would allow. As soon as he was of sufficient age and qualification he taught school winters, clerked in stores, etc., never losing sight of his main purpose in life,—to secure an education along medical lines. After leaving the district school he attended Kimball Union Academy for some time. In 1845 he went to Hanover and began the study of medicine under the late Dr. Dixi Crosby. Here he took two full courses of lectures, and also a full course at the medical school at Woodstock, Vt. On June 17, 1850, he counted himself equipped for life work in his profession. At this time he found himself in debt about four hundred dollars, but by diligence in his practice and prudent saving this was soon liquidated. He commenced his practice in Truro and South Boston, Mass. But he soon became convinced that there were broader fields of usefulness in the West, so he removed to the State of Indiana in 1854. He remained here but two years and then removed to Malcomb, Ill. In July of 1859 he located in Galesburg, Ill., which place he ever after made his home. More than forty-five years he spent in active practice of his profession in this town. He was one of the prominent figures of his profession, not only in Galesburg, but in the surrounding country. He was distinguished for his self-sacrificing spirit in behalf of his suffering patients. His professional idea of ethics was to allow himself no rest until every effort and power of his had been exerted for the aid and relief of those in sickness and suffering. In this way Doctor Chase earned an honorable distinction in his practice. For careful and painstaking treatment his reputation was acknowledged among his patients and fellow practitioners. His clinical instruction was full and complete, and his diagnosis of thousands of cases all stand as proofs of his ability. As a physician, therefore, his labors were crowned with success, and much of this has been attributed to the sympathy which he felt and expressed for his patients. Care and attention in Doctor Chase's treatment were counted quite as important as medicine.

Before going to Galesburg—while living in Indiana—his own child became seriously ill. Being then but a young practitioner he called in several older medical advisers, without any successful results. The death of the child under the circumstances convinced him of the errors of the old Allopathic school of medicine, and thereafter he became a convert of the new Homeopathic school, of which he was the most successful exponent in that section of the state.

In religious belief, Doctor Chase was a Universalist, but as such was never aggressive. The religious tenets of his faith were exemplified in his family and among the many patients of his extensive practice.

As a politician, he was a Republican, but never took an active part in the movements of his party. While not active as a politician, there was one question upon which he had strong pronounced views, and this was the *liquor question*. With this he would effect no compromise. Never was there a more uncompromising foe of the liquor traffic than was Doctor Chase; and during his entire practice he lived up to his convictions and never prescribed liquor as a medicine. Doctor Chase was united in marriage, March 15, 1849, with Lucy F. Crocker at Falmouth, Mass. Four children were the result of this union, two of whom died in infancy. The others are residents of Galesburg, Ill.

Doctor Chase remained active in his profession until the spring of 1905. At this time he lost his favorite driving horse which proved quite a shock to him. This ended his practice away from home, yet he continued to minister to such as called upon him until the first of May, 1906, when as the result of a fall down stairs he was compelled to take to his bed from which he never rose. He died September 7, 1906, but was survived by his wife whose loving companionship he had enjoyed more than fifty-seven years.

From the Galesburg *Daily Republican Register* of September 7, 1906, we append the following:

"In the death of Dr. J. M. Chase, the city loses another of its strong, capable, and forceful men whose lives have been stamped on the community.

"He was a thorough student of his chosen work. In certain lines he was very proficient. His skill in treating the ailments of childhood was pronounced. He seemed to have an intuitive knowledge of what to do. He appeared to comprehend the language of their complaints, and the children loved him.

"Doctor Chase was a man of strong and clear convictions and left no one in doubt as to his belief on any given public question."

In speaking of his avowed antagonism to the use of alcoholics it says:

"It can never be said of him that he contributed to the downfall of any man by arousing in him a thirst for alcoholic drinks through the agency of his prescriptions. In other ways he helped the cause of morality here. He lived a long and useful life and his influence was ever for the best. He was a man of kindly instincts, a man of social nature and of large information.

"His career has reflected honor on the profession, and on the community and merits eulogy and appreciation."

BISHOP PHILANDER CHASE.

Philander Chase, the youngest son of Deacon Dudley and Alice (Corbett) Chase, was born December 14, 1775. All of his brothers leaving the paternal homestead for professional life, he indulged the fond dream of being the chosen son to remain on the farm with his parents and care for them in their declining years. On the other hand, these self-sacrificing parents had a deep anxiety that the last of their sons should become a minister of the gospel, and such was their constant prayer. Unfavorable providences discouraged the plans of the young man, while at the same time they seemed to open the way for the fulfillment of the parents' desire. Upon his recovery from a serious accident, it was decided that he should begin his studies preparatory to entering college. This accomplished, he entered Dartmouth College in the fall of 1791. While there, his religious views underwent a change, the results of which are, in part, related in the history of Trinity Church in Cornish.

He graduated from Dartmouth in 1795, the summer before he became of age. His aim now was the study of the ministry and he soon became a candidate for holy orders in the Protestant Episcopal Church, with a temporary residence at Albany, N. Y. Efficient instructors, together with free access to well-chosen theological libraries, were favorable circumstances in forming his character and fitting him for the great work before him. A portion of his time not thus spent was devoted to teaching.

During this period, in 1796, he married Mary Fay of Hardwick,

BISHOP PHILANDER CHASE.

Mass., daughter of Daniel and Mary (Page) Fay. He was ordained, May 10, 1798, to the diaconate in St. George's Church, New York. After this he devoted himself to missionary work and the organization of parishes in various sections of the country.

The Protestant Episcopal Church in America was then in her infancy and her constituency at that time were few and much scattered. To be a missionary at that time involved many hardships.

Mr. Chase was ordained to the priesthood in St. Paul's Church,

New York, November 10, 1799. From this time until October, 1805, he was engaged in the organization of parishes and in having charge of the Seminary at Poughkeepsie, N. Y. On the latter date, having received an appointment, he sailed from New York to New Orleans, La., where he organized Christ Church and became its rector and teacher. He remained there six years, devoting all his energies to the establishment of the church in this section. He then returned north to Randolph, Vt., where his two children had been left during his southern labors.

In the autumn of 1811, he became established as frector of Christ Church in Hartford, Conn., where he remained until March 2, 1817.

Being still prompted by the spirit of missions, he left this happy rectorate for the wilderness of Ohio, where he took charge of three churches, and also of the Worthington Academy. While there, on May 5, 1818, Mrs. Chase died, and a memorial tablet was erected there to her memory. On June 3, 1818, he was elected to the bishopric of the diocese of Ohio, and on February 11, 1819, was duly consecrated as such in the city of Philadelphia as the first bishop of Ohio. In 1819 he married Sophia May Ingraham of Philadelaphia.

Mr. Chase began to realize sensibly the need of help. His labors were great. His remuneration small and the prospects of the church in Ohio were anything but flattering, and he conceived the idea of visiting England to solicit aid from the mother church, and so he left Worthington, August 4, 1823, and returned East where he spent a few weeks among his kindred. He embarked for England, October 1, following.

Opposition to his plans arose on both sides of the Atlantic, but feeling his cause was of God his faith was equal to the hour. It was then he adopted the inspiring motto: "Jehovah Jireh," which was ever after his watchword of success.

The opposition to his well-intended plans began to assume a serious form. The English press published articles well calculated to prejudice the public mind against contributing funds to the furtherance of church and educational interests in America. It was under these disheartening circumstances that he landed in England.

Mr. Chase had previously formed the acquaintance of Henry Clay, then in Congress, who was a warm personal friend of Lord

Gambier in England. Mr. Clay sent letters of introduction by
Mr. Chase to his friend, explaining the object of his contemplated
visit to England. These were finally favorably received and
Mr. Chase received an invitation to visit Lord Gambier at Platt
Hall, his home. Lord Gambier also told him of the opposition
to his scheme, admitting that he, himself, shared in a measure
the same sentiments. Mr. Chase expressed desire that opportunity be granted of disabusing his mind by full explanation.
This favor was granted the day following and resulted in the
assurance of Lord Gambier's support for the cause in Ohio. In
this he was soon joined by Reverend Mr. Pratt and others. A
meeting of the clergy was called, the subject fully discussed and
a series of resolutions were adopted, all commendatory of Bishop
Chase and the object of his mission, promising him full sympathy
and support. Many fortunate circumstances tended to promote the success of the Bishop's mission. Many who at first
were prejudiced, being touched by his manly and earnest life became kind and generous friends. His unfeigned desire to spread
"the faith once delivered to the saints," was so sincere that many
generous souls responded, and it was said "England had not seen
such a bishop in a thousand years." During the remainder of his
stay in England (until July 17, 1824), he received little less
than a bounteous ovation at the hands of the clergy and faithful
laity. On the latter date he sailed for America in the *Orbit*,
the same ship that brought him to England. He was forty-three
days on this voyage. Some time after his return a convention
was called which met November 2, 1824. The bishop recited
the kindness shown him by English friends and told of their generous gifts for the purpose of founding an institution of religion
and learning in Ohio. The next question was, *where* shall such a
college be built? The academy at Worthington, Ohio, was still
in successful operation and under the immediate care of the
bishop, but it was deemed best to locate the new college elsewhere. Eight thousand acres of land were purchased in Knox
County, Ohio. This tract was chiefly in its primitive state,
requiring vast outlays for its development. Students from
Worthington, and others, all under the lead of the bishop, cut
their way through the tangled forest to an elevated plain
whereon the college was to be located. Willing hands were not
wanting; buildings were hastily erected. The right to confer

degrees was granted by the state and the college received its
name "Kenyon College" from Lord Kenyon of England who was
its largest donor.   The tract of land was called "Gambier Hill,"
in honor of Lord Gambier whose gifts were large.   The chapel
was "Rosse Chapel" in honor of Lady Rosse of England, who
contributed largely to this object.   The school at Worthington
was removed to the new college and thus Kenyon College began
its life in 1828.

This college owes its inception, its founding, its growth, its
career of usefulness, its honorable record, its rank among sister
colleges to the far-sighted sagacity and untiring zeal and energy
of Bishop Chase.   Never was a greater undertaking so swiftly
accomplished by the sole power of one man.   There is scarcely
a parallel to it in all the history of American educational
institutions.

He was a man of heroic mold in every way, physically of gigan-
tic proportions, with a strength and endurance seemingly almost
fabulous, and with a mind of the same commanding proportions
as his body.

He was, in fact, a man of national reputation, both as a scholar
and a teacher, and with a personality that commanded the instant
attention and respect of everyone.

The original design of Bishop Chase in founding this college
was to make it solely a religious institution for the education of
the clergy and lay members of the Protestant Episcopal Church,
"a school of the prophets."   The trustees, on the other hand,
were willing, and even desirous that it also serve the purposes of
an institution for general education.   This gave occasion for a
breach between Bishop Chase and his faculty which could not be
healed.   The latter prevailed, much to the sorrow and disappointment of the bishop, who without any contention and for the
sake of peace, made the great sacrifice and resigned the presidency
of the college and took solemn leave of the same in the early
summer of 1832.

For three years he resumed missionary labors as aforetime, but
in the summer of 1835 he was notified of an appointment to the
Episcopacy of Illinois.   At this time there was but one finished
church in all Illinois.

Although well advanced in years, Bishop Chase now stood
upon the threshold of another vast state beholding her needs.

The motto on his shield, "Jehovah Jireh" was still untarnished, and he again summoned those wondrous powers to action. He resolved to again visit England for aid. He accordingly sailed October 1, 1835, landing at Portsmouth. He returned the following May.

While in England he received many tokens of love and respect, beside much substantial aid for the furtherance of his mission in Illinois.

Like the "Star of Empire," he moved westward and pitched his tent on the fertile prairie lands of Peoria County. Here he purchased 3,200 acres of land whereon he located and erected the new college. He named it "Jubilee College," for, as he says, "that name of all others suits my feelings and circumstances. I left those dear places by me named Gambier Hill and Kenyon College and now in 1838 I can again blow the trumpet in Zion for joy that another school of the prophets, 500 miles still farther towards the setting sun, is founded to the glory of the Great Redeemer."

In a marvelously short time all the preliminary stages were passed, and the second college founded by Bishop Chase came into successful operation.

Thus two prominent educational institutions of the West, whose influence has been great and world wide, owe their existence to the devoted and sanctified energy of a Cornish boy—Philander Chase.

It is not out of place to add the following from the gifted pen of Marie M. Hopkins, president of the Chicago Branch of the Woman's Auxiliary of the Board of Missions: "Our prairie wind tells us of heroes of Church as well as of State. If you will pardon a personal allusion, my grandmother was Alice Chase, who claimed as her youngest and best beloved brother, Philander Chase, first Bishop of Ohio and later of Illinois. To this pure and sensitive boy, a son of New England's soil, the mystical voice of the unknown beckoned as alluringly as it had beckoned to his great progenitor La Salle, so many years before, La Salle and Chase—Chase and La Salle—they were men cast in the same mold. The voice sounded from the great Middle West, whose broad acres teemed with harvests that could support the world, whose vast plains afforded ample room for a population of millions then unborn. Philander Chase listened to this voice, and came to the Middle West. It is like reading a romance to read the life of this great man. He founded Kenyon College and then Jubilee; he worked for years without a salary, supporting his family by the produce of his farm. His Episcopal palace was a log hut which he called 'Robin's Nest,' 'because it was made of sticks and mud and was filled with young ones.' He endured perils by land and perils by water, the deadly pestilence, the violence of the persecutor, doubt and impatience, discouragement and discord and all the devices of the powers of darkness. Obstacles existed before him to be annihilated; hindrance rose in his path to be trampled under foot. Philander Chase did not coo like a dove; he roared like a lion. Even as Richard, that lion-hearted king of old England spent the best years of his life in ridding the Holy Land from the polluting touch of the infidel, so did Philander Chase spend his great strength in wresting the Middle West from the iron grip of heathenism and religious indifference. As long as time shall endure, so long will this portion of the country bear the indelible impress of this lion-hearted Bishop."

But the end came as it comes to all.

On Monday, September 20, 1852, Bishop Chase entered into rest. He calmly approached his end with undimmed eye, and with natural, mental and spiritual forces unabated. His mortal part rests in the cemetery at Jubilee.

SALMON CHASE.

This son of Dea. Dudley and Alice (Corbett) Chase was born July 14, 1761. He was the second of eight brothers, all of whom after obtaining a liberal education became distinguished in the medical, or legal profession, while a portion of these became eminent in the political arena.

The subject of this brief sketch was a graduate of Dartmouth College in the class of 1785, choosing the legal profession for his life work. On leaving college, he went to Portsmouth, N. H., and there studied law in the office of Judge Henry Sherburne.

On completing his studies, he was admitted to the bar and established himself in Portland, Me., then a thriving young town of great promise. Here he continued in the practice of his profession until his death, August 14, 1806, at the early age of forty-five. The degree of eminence to which he might have attained had his life been prolonged is simply one of conjecture, but the brilliant talents manifested during his brief career gave assurance of great ultimate success in life.

Mr. Chase was a sound, well-read lawyer and had such a reputation throughout the state that he came to be called the "law-book." His opinions were implicitly relied upon in cases of doubt and difficulty.

James D. Hopkins, Esq., a contemporary, said of him: "He was not only an able lawyer, but he was well versed in all the branches of solid learning; in legal science and in mathematical and metaphysical learning he had few superiors." And further said: "Mr. Chase was held by all his contemporaries in very high respect as a lawyer." His practice was very extensive, more so than any lawyer of the time in the state, and confidence in him was unlimited.

Another contemporary said of him: "Salmon Chase was a sound lawyer, but not an eloquent advocate." He could not plead as well as he knew. By many it was said of him that "he was a kind and amiable man, easy and accessible in his manners and of fine personal appearance. From his sincerity and frank manners he always had great influence with a jury." The late Judge Dawes of Boston said of him that he never saw him enter the court but with feelings of profound respect.

Salmon Portland Chase, his nephew and namesake, was so named to perpetuate his uncle's name, as also the place of residence.

Mr. Chase was twice married. First, to Miss Mary Stinson of Portsmouth, by whom he had one son, George, born September 29, 1800, who graduated at Harvard College in 1818 and commenced the study of law in Portland with great promise, but died November 11, 1819. The mother had died in 1801. Second, in 1804, he married Mrs. Sarah L. Waldo of Portland, by whom he had one daughter, Elizabeth, who married Doctor Howard of Boston. The mother and daughter and also the son survived him several years.

Mr. Chase's death was very sudden. He was at his office on Monday and on the following Sunday he died of bilious fever.

He was tall, erect and handsome and an excellent model of a lawyer and gentleman of his day. (Extracted from the "Annals of Portland, Me.")

SALMON PORTLAND CHASE.

CHIEF JUSTICE U. S. SUPREME COURT.

Salmon Portland Chase[7] was born January 13, 1808, in Cornish. When eight years of age, he, with his father's family, removed to Keene, N. H. He was but nine years of age when his father died, leaving him to the sole care of his mother. To the praise of this excellent woman it is said "that a Christian's faith and a mother's love, as high and pure as ever ennobled the most famous matrons of history, stamped the character and furnished him the equipment for the labors and triumphs of his life."

His uncle, Bishop Philander Chase of Ohio, assumed for a time the care and expense of his education. This drew him West, where he spent two years pursuing academic studies. He then returned to his mother's charge and entered the Junior class of Dartmouth College, from which he graduated in 1826 at the age of eighteen. At this time he wrote in his diary: "Knowledge may yet be gained and a golden reputation. I may yet enjoy the consciousness of having lived not in vain. Future scenes of triumph may be mine."

After spending four years in Washington in the study of law and teaching a law student in the office of William Wirt, he was admitted to the bar December 14, 1829, and at twenty-two he established himself at Cincinnati, O., thus transferring once and forever his home from New England to the ruder and more expansive society of the West.

During boyhood's tender years, under the pious instruction of his mother and the inculcations of the bishop, he accepted the Episcopal Church as the body of Christian believers, in whose communions he ever found the best satisfaction. His adherence to the Christian faith was simple, constant and sincere; he accepted it as the rule of his life and no modern speculation ever shook the foundations of his belief. His reliance upon God was evident when laying out all the important plans of his busy and strenuous life. His education had been of a kind to discipline and invigorate his natural powers. His oratory was vigorous, forcible and earnest, his rhetoric ample, his delivery weighty and imposing. "With him the sum of practical wisdom seemed to be, in regard to all earthly purposes, to discern the path of duty and then pursue it. His force of will to accomplish was prodigious, his courage

SALMON PORTLAND CHASE,
Chief Justice United States Supreme Court.

Birthplace Salmon Portland Chase.

to brave, and fortitude to endure, were absolute. Equality of right, community of interest, the reciprocity of duty were to his mind the adequate principles by which the virtue, strength and permanence of society were maintained, and he did not hesitate to oppose vigorously everything that endangered them."

A man possessed of such endowments necessarily confers authority among men, while they are prepared to successfully antagonize the endangerments of great and valued principles.

In the ten years of professional life following his admission to the bar, he established a reputation for ability that in due time brought him high rewards. During this time, in his leisure hours, he compiled the Ohio statutes, then a mighty work.

This period was the quieter part of his life, but was soon broken. The high offices awaiting him were not to be reached by the path of jurisprudence, but by statesmanship. His first political move was, after the death of Harrison in 1841, to make *slavery* the touchstone of politics and the basis of political action. Neither of the political parties could be pressed into the services of the principles and course of action he believed to be right. Each tolerated slavery, though under different restrictions.

The history, growth and development of the anti-slavery principle affords a chapter of great interest to the student of our national history. Its adherents bore the names of: "Liberty party," "Abolition party," "Free Soil party" and "Independent Democrats."

The sentiment continued to expand until it culminated in the election of Mr. Lincoln in 1860.

Through all these years Mr. Chase was ever championing the cause of the slave. To him must be awarded the full credit of having resolved upon, planned, organized and executed this political movement, himself either leading or coöperating.

From 1840 to 1849, Mr. Chase was simply a citizen and could expect no political station or honor until it should come from the prosperous fortunes of the party he was striving to create. All at once, by a surprising conjunction of circumstances, he was elevated at a bound to the highest and widest sphere of influence which our political establishment presents, to the Senate of the United States. He entered that body March 4, 1849. A handful of Liberty party men held the balance of power to prevent or determine a majority.

He was the anti-slavery champion of the Senate, whose
speeches summed up the calm argument of unflinching anti-
slavery men, and spread it through the country in the crises of
1850–54. More than any other man he is credited as being the
founder of the Republican party. His term in the Senate ended
March, 1855. The highest authority then said of him: "We
always counted on his opposition to all corruption or extravagant
expenditure and depended on his coöperation to restrain action
of the federal government within its proper sphere. He ever
showed a consciousness of moral responsibility in all his political
services."

His term in the Senate was followed by two successive elections
to the governorship of Ohio. In this high station, all the official
functions as governor were discharged with benefit to the legislation of the nation and to the administration of the state. At the
close of his gubernatorial terms, he was reëlected to the Senate.

The presidential election of 1860 approached. The Republican party, the party he had assisted in creating, now took the
field for the first time with an assurance of ultimate success.

As a candidate for the presidency, Mr. Seward seemed to lead
in public favor, while Mr. Chase, with a following scarcely less,
stood second. In the Republican convention in Chicago, May 16,
1860, the chances of these two men were so nearly equal that their
friends resorted to a *third* candidate, and Mr. Lincoln received the
nomination and was elected.

Recognizing the mental and moral worth, as also the invalu-
able services rendered by these two men, Mr. Lincoln invited both
of them into his cabinet, giving Mr. Seward the office of secretary of state and Mr. Chase that of secretary of the treasury,
which he held three years.

The Civil War was precipitated. The financial problems of
these times assumed a magnitude never before known, and
seemed to require almost superhuman wisdom to solve them.

Mr. Chase seemed to rise equal to all the requirements of the
hour, and his management of the finances of the Civil War was
the marvel of Europe and the admiration of our own people.

He resigned the portfolio of the treasury in June, 1864, and on
the December following he was appointed chief justice of the
United States, which office he held for the remainder of his life.

The distracted and disrupted condition of the country,

the best policy to pursue in the construction of the same, were problems now confronting all the heads of government, including the judiciary. In all matters brought before the chief justice, even the trial of President Johnson, he displayed the dignity, tact, sagacity and sound judgment befitting his exalted station. "As a constructive statesman, Mr. Chase must ever stand among the greatest Americans." Mr. Lincoln said of him: "Chase is about one and a half times bigger than any man I ever knew."

It is not claimed that Mr. Chase was free from faults, or that his judgment was infallible. This can be claimed by none; but taking his entire record before the world's impartial tribunal, their verdict would be as expressed in the language of his distinguished friend and associate, Hon. Wm. M. Evarts: "A lawyer, orator, senator, governor, minister, magistrate, whom living a whole nation admired; whom dead a whole nation laments. Upon an eminent stage of action, the tenor of his life was displayed on all the high places of the world. . . . The places he filled were all of the highest, the services he rendered were the most difficult, as well as the most eminent."

Mr. Chase was thrice married. His wives were all ladies of the State of Ohio. His first wife was Catharine J. Garniss, whom he married March 4, 1834. She died December 1, 1835, leaving a little girl, who lived only four years longer. September 26, 1839, he married his second wife, Eliza Ann Smith. They had three children: Kate (later Mrs. Governor Sprague) was the only one who lived. Mrs. Chase died September 29, 1845. A third marriage took place November 6, 1846, with Sarah Bella Dunlop Ludlow. Two children were born to them, of whom the only one that lived was Jeanette Ralston (later Mrs. Hoyt). On June 13, 1852, Mr. Chase was again bereft of his wife. Thenceforward he lived a widower to the end.

His last visit to his native town was in July, 1866. A reception in honor of him was held July 24 at Chester Pike's, where, as chief justice, he met his townsmen and friends in pleasant social reunion. The occasion was one of great interest and enjoyment, as the writer, who was there, can testify.

The activities and responsibilities of his strenuous life were proving too much for his physical constitution, and after a second paralytic shock, on May 6, 1873, he died May 7, 1873, at the age of sixty-five.

WINSTON CHURCHILL.

Winston Churchill, the author of " The Celebrity," " Richard
Carvel," "The Crisis," "The Crossing," "Coniston," etc., was born
in St. Louis, Missouri, November 10, 1871, only child of Edward
Spalding and Emma Bell (Blaine) Churchill. He is of old New
England ancestry, being ninth in descent from John Churchill,
the ancestor of the Plymouth branch of the Churchill family in
America, and on the maternal side is descended from Jonathan
Edwards, "the most eminent graduate of Yale College," and
amongst whose descendants are numbered the presidents of ten
colleges and universities, a remarkable and unequalled record.

Mr. Churchill was educated at Smith Academy, a well-known
private school in St. Louis, connected with the Washington
University, and later was appointed to the United States Naval
Academy at the age of eighteen and graduated in the class of
1894. The year after he entered the Naval Academy, he organized and was captain of the first eight-oared crew which represented the navy and revived at Annapolis the sport of shell
racing which had been dead since the seventies.

The chief qualities which are inculcated into a youth at the
United States Naval Academy are self-reliance and determination, and those graduates of it who have not chosen the navy for
their career have usually made eminent successes of what they
have elected to do. This is signally true of Mr. Churchill. He
had not been a year at the Naval Academy before he became
interested in American history and American problems, and
before he had finished his course he made up his mind to devote
his life and energies to these,—not only with the pen, but as an
active participant. Much of the atmosphere and some of the
material for "Richard Carvel" was gathered by him while he was
still a midshipman, and in the brief intervals between the scientific studies and drills he began to read at the Naval Academy
library some of the history which he used in that and subsequent
books.

Upon graduating, Mr. Churchill became the sub-editor of the
Army and Naval Journal, and within a year was managing editor
of the *Cosmopolitan Magazine* at Irvington. In order to devote
his time exclusively to the book "Richard Carvel," at which
he was then at work, he resigned from the *Cosmopolitan.* Just

WINSTON CHURCHILL.

about this time he wrote the first of his well-known novels, a
humorous sketch called "The Celebrity," and this he submitted
to the Macmillan Company. The immediate result of this book
was a contract with the Macmillan Company for "Richard
Carvel," then unfinished. This book, published in 1899, the
first of a series dealing with vital epochs in American history,
was so far above the class of the so-called historical novel, the
craze for which was then at its height, that it at once raised the
author to the front rank of novelists, a place which has been
well sustained by his subsequent books, as Mr. Churchill is a
painstaking writer. The publication of "Richard Carvel" was
followed, after an interval of two years by "The Crisis." Two
years later came "The Crossing," that wonderful tale of George
Rogers Clarke's conquest of the Northwest, and in 1906 he
published "Coniston." We of Cornish feel more than a passing
interest in the story of Coniston, this true picture of New England life and politics. From our hills we can look on Coniston
Mountain, can follow the myriad windings of Coniston Water;
can even see on a clear day what was once the home of
"Jethro Bass," that wonderful, rugged figure around which
the story of Coniston is woven. Those of us, and there are
many, who hold in loving memory "Jethro Bass" and his wife,
"Aunt Listy," are grateful to Mr. Churchill for immortalizing
them. "Jethro Bass" had his detractors, but Mr. Churchill
is not one of them.

In 1898 Mr. Churchill bought from Leonard Spalding, his farm
house, barns, etc., and about one hundred acres of land, this
property being formerly known as the Ayer homestead. A
part of this land overlooked the Connecticut, and Mr. Churchill
cleared the woods at this spot and erected "Harlakenden House,"
considered to be one of the finest residences in New Hampshire.
In 1903 Mr. Churchill purchased the adjoining property, known
as the Freeman homestead, and he has now something over five
hundred acres, mostly of excellent timber land. Mr. Churchill
is gradually foresting this timber land on scientific principles.
The Freeman house has been practically rebuilt and is now one
of the most attractive and commodious houses in the neighborhood. Since making his home in Cornish in 1898, Mr. Churchill
has been actively interested in the town's welfare. He has done
much for it in the matter of good roads, and any appeal to

21

him for the betterment of the town's interests is always met with
a hearty response.

Mr. Churchill represented the town of Cornish for two successive terms in the Legislature from 1903 to 1907. At the conclusion of his second term, he had planned a temporary rest and
retirement from politics, but he was appealed to by prominent
men in Claremont and surrounding towns to be the candidate
for the state Senate from this district. Looking upon this appeal
as a duty not to be lightly disregarded, he acceded, making it a
condition, however, that if he were elected he would do his utmost
to aid in any movement tending to "put the power of government into the hands of the people where it belongs." The direct
result of this announcement, strengthened by the effect of "Coniston," which had just been published, was an invitation signed by
such eminent and conservative citizens of the state as the Rev.
W. W. Niles, bishop of New Hampshire, Prof. James F. Colby, head of the law department of Dartmouth University, and
others, asking Mr. Churchill to be a candidate for governor on a
reform platform. Mr. Churchill was a young and courageous man,
and an indefatigable worker during his terms in the Legislature,
and it was believed that his name would give the reform movement an impetus which could be gained in no other way. And
so it proved. Mr. Churchill, as the candidate of the Lincoln
Republican Club, inaugurated campaign methods which were an
innovation to New Hampshire, delivering on an average of ten
speeches a week, besides writing weekly articles for the newspapers. It was a short campaign—of only six weeks duration,—
but the results of that vigorous six weeks were far-reaching. Mr.
Churchill and his associates in the campaign had no idea that he
would be elected—that was not the end for which they were working, but the people were aroused, as the people will be at times,
and here was the opportunity to lay facts before them, which
they did. The sole issue, as it is almost needless to say here,
was the control of the state government by the Boston and Maine
Railroad, a control which had existed for so long, that by most
people it was accepted as a state of things which must be endured
because it could not be cured. Never was such a convention
known in New Hampshire as followed that memorable campaign
of six weeks. Unlike previous conventions, the results were not
known the night before. The principles of the Lincoln Republi-

MRS. WINSTON CHURCHILL.

can Club were embodied in the Republican state platform. Five candidates were in the field, and on the first ballot Mr. Churchill had 157 delegates. He led the candidates on the eighth ballot, but did not have the required number of votes for election, and he was defeated by a margin of fifty-two votes on the ninth. The nominee of the convention failed of election at the polls in November and his election was made by the Legislature when it met in January.

One of the victories of the reform element in the Legislature ("Churchill Republicans," as they were pleased to call themselves) was the passage of the present anti-pass law, this being one of the important planks in the platform.

Early in the spring of 1907 Mr. Churchill was again requested to be a candidate, but this honor he declined, believing that he could do more good for the cause he had at heart by being in a disinterested position.

Mr. Churchill was married in St. Louis, Mo., October 22, 1895, to Miss Mabel Harlakenden Hall, of illustrious English descent, and they have two children, Mabel Harlakenden, born July 9, 1897, and John Dwight Winston, born December 21, 1903.

LEVI HENRY COBB, D. D.

A truthful sketch of Doctor Cobb is but little short of an eulogy. His useful life chiefly transpired within the radius of the remembrance and knowledge of the writer, who is therefore prepared to heartily endorse the many tributes offered to his memory. Chief among these memorials is that of Charles H. Richards, D.D. of New York, from whose gifted pen the writer has quoted extensively and for which he would return all grateful acknowledgment.

Levi Henry Cobb was born in Cornish, June 30, 1827. He was the son of Levi and Calista (Bugbee) Cobb, who lived the simple and quiet farmer life in the northern part of the town. Here the son had the practical training of the farmer boy, which was of great value to him in his after life. The influence, too, of that Christian home was mighty in molding his character for fitness for the service he afterwards rendered. He became a member of the Congregational Church in Cornish on March 3, 1839. After this he resolved to obtain a liberal education with the hope that God would open the way for him into the Christian ministry.

He seemed inspired with an ambition to make the most of his powers that he might be of the greatest possible service to his fellowmen.

With this end in view he entered Kimball Union Academy in 1847. This famous school gave him the intellectual drill and spiritual development which he needed. He was a diligent student and a leader in the religious life of the academy.

Graduating from the academy in 1850, he entered Dartmouth

REV. LEVI H. COBB.

College and graduated from it in the class of 1854. He had many distinguished classmates, among whom he made his mark as a young man of vigorous intellect, inflexible principle, genial and devotedly Christian. Rev. Charles Caverno, a classmate of his, thus writes of him: "I know of no other one of my classmates who has seemed to walk so continually and directly to the end he had in view as Levi H. Cobb. There seems to me a straight line from the time I first knew him to the time of his departure to the life of Heaven,—just a straight line and the duties done that belonged to that line. That he was *good*, we all knew; but he was a *great* man. He not only did *good* work, but a great amount of it. He did not write in the sand, but in human souls and that will live in influence in this world, and in the world to come forever and ever."

He completed his preparation for his life work at Andover Theological Seminary in 1857. A parish was already awaiting him in North Andover, Mass., whose call he had accepted and he was ordained there the following autumn.

Of his feelings concerning the great work he had undertaken he has written: "From an early day, far back in my home life on the paternal farm, my soul has gone out warmly and with constancy towards the work of the ministry. And when, after years of waiting, on the 28th day of October, 1857, ordaining hands were laid upon my head, setting me apart to the work of the ministry, it was the happiest day of my life up to that point. The work has grown in endearment. The seven years of my first pastorate were an upward inclined plane of increasing enjoyment in it, and love toward my co-workers there. There was not an office in the gift of my nation, nor a throne on which any nation in the old world could have placed me, which I would have exchanged for the place God gave me in the hearts of that people."

During this pastorate, on January 12, 1858, he married Miss Harriet J. Herrick of Essex, Vt., whose acquaintance he had formed at the academy in Meriden. She has been a true helpmeet in all his fields of service. Four children have gladdened their home. (See Cobb Gen.)

The condition of his health required him to give up his pastorate at North Andover, and he went south to Memphis, Tenn., where, for nearly two years he was superintendent of schools for white refugees and colored people. After this he returned to New England and took an important position as teacher in Kimball Union Academy, where he had prepared for college. Here he was exceedingly popular and successful in his work. But greatly as he enjoyed teaching, his heart was in the ministry.

After two years at Meriden, he was unanimously and enthusiastically called to the pastorate of the church in Springfield, Vt. Entering upon this work May 2, 1867, he enjoyed another pastorate of seven years. Those years were very fruitful. More than ninety new members were received into the church the second year. The church grew so they were led to the building of a new and attractive sanctuary, all paid for by the grateful people. During these seven years he had the joy of welcoming into his church two hundred and sixty-four members. Other records of the church and pastor during those years gave evidence of a remarkably successful pastorate.

Again, by reason of his health, he was induced to sever his loving connection with this people and try the climate of the Northwest. He was appointed Home Missionary superintendent for Minnesota, with home at Minneapolis. Here, again, he put in seven years of heroic service. The statistics of these services and their results are truly wonderful. The limits of this sketch will not allow their mention.

During the year 1881, by request he became General Home Missionary secretary for the Rocky Mountain district with headquarters at Denver, Colo. This extensive and important field he was obliged to relinquish owing to his election in February, 1882, as secretary of the American Congregational Union, which at that time, was the name of the Congregational Church Building Society.

He entered at once upon that office which he held for twenty-one years. It proved to be the greatest work of his life and the one by which he will be longest remembered. The recital of his activities and of the vast results accomplished during these twenty-one years would fill volumes. More than two thousand churches and nearly half that number of parsonages, scattered throughout our country, all owe their existence to the prayerful and untiring efforts of Doctor Cobb. What monuments to his memory as viewed from the earth side, while from the heavenward side no human being can estimate their importance! *Eternity alone can reveal.*

With lavish expenditure of vital power, he gave himself to this work which he loved. He traveled from the Atlantic to the Pacific, from the Lakes to the Gulf, visiting the churches and estimating their opportunities. He was in every national council to tell how the work was faring. He was delegate to the two international councils—in London in 1891 and in Boston in 1899. He was trustee of Carlton College in Minnesota, and of Rollins College in Florida. He was for thirty-three years a corporate member of the "American Board." He was a member of the

Anthropological Society and of the American Institute of Christian Philosophy. He also edited twenty-one volumes of the *Church-Building Quarterly.*

At length, when seventy-five years of age, his health suddenly failed. Up to that time his form had been as erect and his step as strong and steady as that of one twenty years younger. He was compelled to retire from active service, but as an expression of respect and honor for his long and distinguished services, he was made secretary emeritus of the society.

In his enfeebled condition, his indomitable spirit, though sweetly submissive to the Divine decree, was restless on behalf of the cause he loved so well. He still continued to send out articles and letters which were effective helpers in the good cause. His parting message, published in the *Quarterly* almost on the day of his death, shows the same clear intellect, the same ardent devotion to the Kingdom of God as aforetime. 'Twas like the dying soldier's bugle call for a charge as he falls upon the field.

Thus he passed within the vale. God called him with all his trained powers to a still larger service in that unseen country. For him, death was a promotion.

On the 8th of February, 1906, three days after his decease, his weary form was laid to rest beside his dear ones in his former parish in Springfield, Vt.

> "Servant of God, well done;
> Rest from thy loved employ."

DR. DAVID L. M. COMINGS.

Dr. David L. M. Comings was the son of Uriel and Sarah (Robinson) Comings and was born in Cornish, October 14, 1825. After leaving the district school he pursued a three years' course of study at Norwich University, then under the charge of the lamented General Ransom.

In 1847 he commenced the study of medicine and graduated from the Medical School at Castleton, Vt., in the spring of 1850. Soon after this he began the practice of his profession at Plainfield, where he remained two years. While there he made the acquaintance of Eliza W. Wardner of Plainfield, whom he married November 24, 1851; they never had any children. In the

spring of 1852 he located at the village of West Swanzey, N. H.,
where he continued in the practice of his profession with increasing
success until he entered the military service of his country at the
opening of the Civil War. Those who knew him best during this
active practice in Swanzey, remember him not merely for his
devotion to his profession. They remember him also as the
upright and conscientious citizen who did not turn from the path
of duty through fear or favor, but interested himself in whatever
pertained to the peace and good order of society. He was ever
found faithful to the cause of education, temperance and social
improvement. His kindly and Christian bearing in the domestic
circle can be appreciated only by those who had the opportunity
to observe him at his own fireside, surrounded by those whom he
most loved and trusted. The perfect control which he ever
maintained over his feelings, the self-discipline which never
allowed an angry or unkind word to escape his lips gave him a
serenity of temper which hardly belonged to one of his ardent
temperament.

At the breaking out of the Rebellion, although not in political
sympathy with the administration, he cheerfully put forth his
efforts to put down armed treason and to uphold the government
of his country. He did not stop to inquire what course others
intended to pursue, but chose his position promptly and maintained it to the end.

When further surgical assistance was required in the Department of the South, in the spring of 1862, he cheerfully offered his
services and was commissioned as assistant surgeon of the
Fourth Regiment, New Hampshire Volunteers. He remained in
sole charge of that regiment for some time, much to the satisfaction of the soldiers and officers. After some months of faithful and devoted service to the sick and wounded, his health
failed, and he was reluctantly compelled to leave the scene of
his active and useful labors. After a protracted and painful
journey he reached his home in Swanzey accompanied by his
faithful companion in life, who was at his side from the first of
his illness. After a lapse of some weeks of suffering and weak-
ness, which medical skill could not overcome, he closed his
earthly career without a murmur, and with full consciousness
to the last.

Doctor Comings died on the first day of August, 1863, leaving to the world the example of a man who had performed his duties with integrity and fidelity. In the language of one who knew him best, and was with him to the last, "he died as he had lived, a *Christian*."

AUSTIN CORBIN.

This man was not a native of Cornish, nor did he ever reside within its limits. The writer, however, feels justified in presenting his name and merits by reason of the fact that he purchased and owned more of the territory of Cornish than any other individual, unless we except the primitive owners of the town. For account of this, the reader is referred to "Blue Mountain Park Association" (which see).

Austin Corbin was born July 11, 1827, in Newport, N. H. After a good public school education, he went, in 1846, to Boston and was employed as a clerk one year. He then studied law; graduated from Harvard Law School in 1849, and he began practice in New Hampshire in partnership with Ralph Metcalf, who afterwards became governor of the state. Like many other young men he longed for the West. In 1851, he went to Davenport, Ia., in the practice of law. This he soon abandoned and gave his attention to schemes of finance that opened propitiously and developed successfully. He was a man of large conceptions and sought to use his capital for the development of plans along large enterprises. He first gave his attention to the improvement of Manhattan Beach, and the building thereon of two hotels, etc. He then gave his attention to the "Long Island Railway," then insolvent, and established it upon a sound and profitable basis. He did the same with the Reading Railroad—then in bankruptcy. This was the most stupendous undertaking he had ever assumed and he became its president. He also became deeply interested in making the extreme eastern end of Long Island a terminus for a trans-Atlantic steamship line, which would considerably lessen the time in going to Europe. Had he lived, this latter enterprise would doubtless have been carried out.

When Mr. Corbin left Davenport, Ia., he came to New York City, where he organized the "Corbin Banking Company" on Broadway. This institution continued in a thriving condition during, and in connection with, all his other vast business enterprises.

Mr. Corbin never lost his love for nature or for his native town. He established his summer home in Newport, N. H., on the homestead where he was born. This home and its surroundings was admirably fitted up with everything needful and attractive. He purchased fourteen hundred acres more of land adjoining it on which he contemplated making great improvements. After this he bought large tracts of land and established the extensive game preserve, called the "Blue Mountain Park Association" (which see).

His purposes regarding this park and the many landholders adjoining it were on a large and munificent scale, and had he lived a few years longer, he would have verified the wisdom of his plans.

But a sad and tragic death awaited him. When seemingly in the midst of, and near the fulfillment of many of his designs, he was violently thrown from his carriage on June 4, 1896, receiving injuries that terminated fatally within a few hours. His sudden death was a great shock to all his friends and wide circle of acquaintances.

Mr. Corbin was a man of great energy and activity. When asked why he did not retire from active business and *enjoy* his fortune, he replied: "I already get my enjoyment in attending to my business."

"His robust and active mind, his keen intelligence, his indomitable will, his rugged independence and self-reliance made him a natural leader among men.

"Whatever he did, was done with his whole strength. He devoted his talents to the accomplishment of worthy objects. His mission was to build up, and not destroy. Aggressive, masterful and fearless as he was, he also possessed the gentler traits of a genial manner, a hearty honesty, and kindly and generous disposition which endeared him to all his associates."

JACOB FOSS.

Jacob Foss, the son of Walter and Lucy (Cook) Foss, was born October 17, 1796, in Cornish. He married Martha Abbie Howland of Boston; they had no children. When he became of age he went to Boston. He took great pleasure, after he became a successful man with large means, in telling the story of leaving

JACOB FOSS.

his country home, with all of his earthly possessions tied up in a bandanna handkerchief.

He had decided that after reaching Boston he would accept the first offer made him for steady work, and very soon he engaged with Guy Carlton for employment in his morocco factory in Roxbury. Here he remained six months. He then went to Charlestown to the distillery of Putnam and Pratt. Here he worked for small wages at first, but being an industrious and observant man, in whom his employers soon learned to confide, they kept promoting him in the business until he reached the position of foreman or superintendent. He gave himself up to his business, making economy and improvement his chief study, leaving himself no time for anything outside of it. Every day and evening he could be found at his post watching the process of fermentation, evaporation and condensation, the changing of molasses into spirits, or overseeing the preparation of packages for shipment for market. So closely did he confine himself that his health became impaired, and with a constant asthmatic tendency, he was an invalid for years; but he kept on his course until his pecuniary growth was an assured fact, and he was looked upon as a rich man.

While attending to his regular duties, he discovered that carbonic acid gas, as it escaped from the fermentation of molasses, would convert pearl-ash into saleratus and he obtained permission to place boxes of pearl-ash over the vats in the distillery for this purpose. The foundation of his fortune was now made. Out of this business his gains were sufficient to purchase the distillery, and he entered into partnership with Mr. Addison Gilmore, and carried on the distillery in conjunction with making saleratus. The business continued for a long period and they took their places among business men of high rating and large means.

Mr. Foss purchased a fine residence on Chelsea Street, Charlestown, which is still standing. He also erected a brick building with a hall named by him, "Constitutional Liberty Hall." Mr. Foss was a Democrat, but never a zealous partisan. He believed in the American form of government and the ability of the people to carry it on.

He was an intense admirer of Andrew Jackson as a soldier and a statesman. Constitutional liberty was another of his settled convictions, which accounts for the name given his hall. He was a great admirer, too, of Daniel Webster; and the *character* of Washington was to him the very foundation on which our republic was built.

He was a large contributor to the fund for the purchase of the paintings of Webster and Washington; and that of Jackson was almost wholly at his own expense. The pictures hang in the old city hall in Charlestown.

Mr. Foss was a lover of his country and a true patriot. When the war with Mexico broke out a regiment of 770 men was raised in Massachusetts, having one company from Charlestown. A meeting was called for the purpose of raising $1,500 in aid of the families of the enlisted men; but the meeting was called in an illegal way and the town treasurer refused to pay the amount. Meanwhile the money was needed, as the company was nearly ready to be mustered into the service. In this emergency Mr. Foss came forward and advanced the amount; so the necessary funds were provided.

On the opening of the Civil War in 1861, when the city guards and artillery were ordered to the national capital, a public meeting was held in the city hall, April 17, 1861, and a committee chosen to see that the company from Charlestown was provided with all necessary supplies, and to make provision for the care and comfort of their families. Mr. Foss was chosen a member of this committee, but his health was such that he could not actively engage in the work, but he acknowledged the honor of the position and his appreciation of its meaning in a letter as follows:

"CHARLESTOWN, April 22, 1861.

"*Gentlemen*:—Having been chosen by the citizens of Charlestown at the mass meeting held in the City Hall on the 17th inst. one of the committee to aid the Charlestown military, it is impossible for me, on account of my feeble health to attend personally to the details of the service required in this crisis, which is the noblest work for all loyal citizens. I have this day deposited in the Bunker Hill Bank in this city $3,000 (a certificate of which I enclose) to be at the disposal of the committee, for them to draw and disburse without recourse to me."

In his will were the following bequests:

$2,000, the income to be expended towards celebrating the anniversary of the battle of Bunker Hill, either by ringing the bells, firing salutes, music, or decorating the streets.

$2,000, the income to be expended in the purchase of United States flags for the use of the city of Charlestown on all occasions.

$2,000 to the poor fund, the income to be expended for the worthy poor of Charlestown.

$2,000 to Tufts College.

$1,000 to Cornish, his native town, the income to be expended for the purchase of United States flags; and

$2,000, the income to be expended for the benefit of the worthy poor in said town.

These legacies to Cornish were received September 14, 1866. Their sum of $3,000, less the revenue tax of $180, leaving $2,820. Mr. Foss' whole estate was appraised at about $350,000.

He died in Charlestown, Mass., June 2, 1866. His remains were carried to the cemetery with the old flag, which he loved so well, wrapped about his casket.

ANDREW JACKSON HOOK.

Andrew Jackson Hook, only son of Moody and Eliza (Carroll) Hook, was born December 7, 1864, on the old farm which his father occupied for over sixty years, now included in "Corbin's Park" in the eastern part of Cornish, N. H., where the first nineteen years of his life were spent in caring for his aged parents, and obtaining what education he could get in the old No. 8 schoolhouse. On leaving the farm he attended business college in Manchester, N. H., from which he was graduated in the spring of 1885. He at once entered the employ of A. C. Carroll & Son, general merchants of Warner, N. H. This position he held six years; resigning this, he leased and managed the Kearsarge Hotel in Warner for one year, after which he conducted a retail grain business for about seven years when his health failed and he was compelled to retire from active labor for a time. In 1898, he was appointed postmaster of Warner, which position he has held by numerous reappointments until the present time.

In 1898 he was also appointed railway mail clerk, but was obliged to decline the same on account of his post-office duties. He has filled many positions of trust, having been elected selectman, high school committee, town clerk and for the past fourteen

years has been treasurer of the town of Warner, also has been
clerk and treasurer of the Warner Village Fire District and of the
Kearsarge Creamery Association ever since their organization,
and is a trustee of the Sugar River Savings Bank at Newport,
N. H. Notwithstanding his numerous duties he has found time
to settle many estates in probate court, and has done considerable

ANDREW J. HOOK.

business in lumber and real estate, now owning about 1,300 acres
of timber lands. He has also built up an insurance business in
and around Warner, until he now has one of the best country
agencies in the state. Being musically inclined he has been at
the head of one of the church choirs in Warner for the past
twenty-one years. He is a Granger, and has received all the
degrees in Free Masonry from the first to the thirty-second,
inclusive, having held office in most of the bodies including

that of Master of Harris Lodge, No. 91, and is a member of the
Order of the Mystic Shrine, one who appreciates the true principles of Free Masonry. He married November 17, 1888, Florence
B. Colby of Warner who was a cousin of ex-Governor Harriman
of New Hampshire. They have no children.

ERI HUGGINS, JR.

Eri Huggins was the youngest son of Eri[4] Huggins and was
born February 14, 1848. When the Civil War broke out, his
father and two older brothers at once gave themselves to the service of their country. This, doubtless, inspired the youngest of
the family to do in like manner. So he, then but fourteen years
of age, went to Alexandria, Va., where on April 1, 1862, he
enlisted with his father and brothers and other relatives, in the
famous "Iron Brigade" from Wisconsin, which is said to have
lost the largest per cent. of any brigade in the Northern Army.
He enlisted as a private and carried a musket until he was
appointed assistant commissary of his regiment. This position
he held nine months. He was in all the battles, some twenty in
number, in which the brigade was engaged, including the battles
before Petersburg and Richmond, and at Appomattox when
General Lee surrendered. In all this service he escaped serious
injury and received his discharge April 24, 1865.

It may not be out of place to here notice a fact in the history
of his father's family. The cases are few where the love of country
is so strong that it could not only induce a father to enlist, but
that he should be followed by every one of his sons. Such was the
case here. In the great struggle for national life, these four noble
men, a father and three sons, pledged their *all* to the success of
the Union cause. The father alone yielded his life, but the sons
were all permitted to live and enjoy, at least for a time, the
fruition of peace. Well may Cornish be proud of such a record of
her sons.

The war being over, Mr. Huggins traveled for wholesale
houses for several years, and finally in 1886 located at Fort
Bragg, Cal., which has since been his residence. Here he has been
superintendent of the supply and mercantile department of the
"Redwood Company," the largest milling company on the
Pacific Coast. During these years he has also held the following
offices: Agent for Wells Fargo Express Company; president of
Board of Education; city treasurer; president of Board of City

Trustees and also of the People's Building and Loan Association; postmaster, auctioneer, etc. He was married January 27, 1888, to Miss Harriet R. Wilson of Ticonderoga, N. Y. They have no children.

Mr. Huggins is still in the prime of life with a commanding personality and hosts of admiring friends, who are proud of his record.

JOHN C. HUGGINS.

John C. Huggins was the oldest son of Eri Huggins.[4] He was born in Cornish, March 3, 1840. He early sought to try his fortune in life by himself, so at fourteen years of age he left the parental roof and went to West Acton, Mass., where relatives were residing and afterwards to Petersburg, Ill., where an uncle of his had resided since 1849. Here he completed his education and went to Racine, Wis., and engaged in teaching. This he followed until the opening of the Civil War when, at twenty-one years of age, he enlisted in the Second Wisconsin Regiment, which formed a part of the famous "Iron Brigade," which rendered such distinguished services during the war. Here he was promoted, first as private commissary and afterwards as colonel on General Fairchild's staff. While here he was joined by his youngest brother, Eri, his "pet," then but fourteen years of age. They passed through the war together and both came out unharmed, although they passed through many hard-fought and bloody battles.

After the war was over, he engaged in mercantile business in St. Louis and Chicago for a few years.

After this he returned to Racine, where he united with the "Fish Brothers" in establishing a large carriage manufactory, in which business he continued several years. Here he was an active citizen, holding many offices of trust and honor. But for a time he was induced to change his business for a more lucrative one. He engaged with other capitalists in the lumber business on the Pacific Coast with headquarters at San Francisco and Fort Bragg, Cal., with his family residing at Oakland, Cal. In this enterprise, too, he was successful.

After he left Racine, Wis., it appears that the carriage manufactory there suffered a financial depression, and he was induced to return for a time (leaving his family still in Oakland) that he might rehabilitate the manufactory and put it again in a prosperous condition. He had nearly accomplished his purpose, when he was attacked by la grippe, and after a relapse, superinduced by overwork and exposure, he returned to his family in Oakland, shattered in body and mind, and died December 19, 1892.

Mr. Huggins' life was a busy and active one. Possessed of superior ability and character, he was the most genial of associates and truest of friends. He inherited from a long line of uncorrupted ancestry all those virtues, inborn courage, unfailing hope, and manly aspirations that have individualized the genuine New Englander in every part of the world.

In 1870 he married Eva J. Bowers.

PHILANDER CHASE HUGGINS.

Philander Chase Huggins was born in Cornish, February 28, 1814. At the tender age of fourteen, his father died, thus leaving him to work out his own fortune. He had received only a common school education, but the school of hard experiences to which he was called afforded him an equipment such as no university can confer, and he became an accomplished man of affairs.

Soon after the death of his father in 1828, he entered the store of Newton Whittlesey on Cornish Flat, where as a faithful and efficient clerk, he served several years.

In 1837 he resolved to try his fortune in the then "far West," so he left Cornish and was one of the early pioneers of the State of Illinois. He first settled in Woodburn, where he opened a store. Here he remained until 1840, when he removed to Bunker Hill, Ill. Just previous to this he made a visit to his native town, and on his return he took with him a bride, Mary L. Whittlesey, daughter of his former employer. They were married November 18, 1839. She was born June 7, 1801, and died November 11, 1845. They had no children. His second marriage, which occurred November 6, 1846, was to Mrs. Elizabeth F. Knowlton of Bunker Hill, who was born in Ashford, Conn., March 13, 1817, and who survived him, dying May 17, 1903. They had seven children, the first five dying in infancy; the next, a daughter, Mary E., born December 24, 1857, who married Henry B. Davis, attorney-at-law in St. Louis, Mo.; the other, a son, Frank E., born July 11, 1860, now (1905) a wholesale shoe dealer in Columbus, Ohio.

On removing to Bunker Hill, Mr. Huggins opened a general store which was a great accommodation to the people as well as

22

profit to himself, it being the only store in the place. He became postmaster, and also engaged in various manufacturing interests; built and operated the first flouring mill there, also a castor oil mill.

In 1852 the Alton and Terra Haute Railroad was projected, and Mr. Huggins, through great effort, was successful in securing Bunker Hill as one of the stations on the road in spite of great opposition by rival neighborhoods. This accomplished, it opened a prosperous career for the place. In like manner, Mr. Huggins was ever a prime mover in every public enterprise that contributed to the welfare and prosperity of his adopted township. The academy, the Congregational Church, the church of his choice and devotion, with all its fine improvements, Bunker Hill Bank, the cemetery with its beautiful soldiers' monument, and the public library, *all* owe their establishment to him in no small degree. He was also an honored Mason and Odd Fellow and member of the local lodges. In politics, he was originally a Whig, while his township was largely Democratic. His personal popularity so reduced the Democratic majority of 900, that he lacked but a few votes of an election twice to the state Legislature. When the great Free Soil agitation arose, he became a Republican to which party he adhered until his death. Whenever he was a candidate for office, he received a large part of the opposition vote.

In 1869 he was nominated for, and elected as county judge. Here, as in other responsible positions he displayed that tact and fidelity to true principle so characteristic of the man.

In 1879 he was elected supervisor of his township, and at the time of his death, January 16, 1892, he was police magistrate of the city, having accepted the position through the earnest solicitations of his many friends, in spite of his own personal objection. A few years before his death, he received a severe hip injury which obliged him to relinquish active labor, much to his distaste, and accept a more quiet indoor occupation.

The life of Judge Huggins was a beautiful one. Truly it was an object lesson which many a young man might study and imitate with profit. His biographer says of him, that, "in every relation of life he was as nearly the perfect man as we ever see in the human. As a husband and father he was the personification of affection and devotion. As a citizen, neighbor and friend

HON. SAMUEL L. POWERS.

he was self-sacrificing and sympathetic, ever giving his best efforts
in behalf of the community and those appealing to him for aid.
As a companion he was cheery and helpful. His well-trained
mind, his wide knowledge of men and events, made him a most
entertaining and instructive conversationalist and wise adviser.
To his foresight and judgment are due, not only the private fortunes of many who sought his counsel, but the present existence
of interests upon which depend in great measure the prosperity
of his own, and other towns of the county. Indeed his influence
did not cease here, but it may be said he stood side by side with
the foremost men of the state in zealous and intelligent effort
in aiding its development.''

SAMUEL LELAND POWERS.

Samuel Leland Powers was born at Cornish, October 26, 1848;
prepared for college at Kimball Union and Phillips Exeter Academies; graduated from Dartmouth College in the class of 1874;
studied law at Nashua, N. H., at the Law School of the University
of the City of New York, at Worcester, Mass., and was admitted
to the Massachusetts Bar in November, 1875; has since been
admitted to practice in the federal courts, courts of the District
of Columbia, and the Supreme Court of the United States. He
became a resident of the City of Newton, Mass., in 1882, where
he has since resided; has been a member of both branches of the
municipal government, and of the school board of that city,
being president of the city council in 1883 and 1884; was elected
to Congress from the Eleventh Massachusetts District in 1900,
and reëlected in 1902, declining the nomination in 1904. While
in Congress he was a member of the committees on judiciary,
District of Columbia, and elections, and was also a member of
the special committee of five appointed by the speaker in 1903
to draw the Anti-Trust Bill, which passed the Fifty-eighth Congress. In 1903 he was elected by the House of Representatives
as one of its managers to prosecute the Swayne impeachment
trial before the United States Senate. He had charge of President Taft's canvass in Massachusetts for his nomination to the
presidency in 1908. In 1910 President Taft appointed him a
justice of the Customs Court of Appeal of the United States,
which he declined.

Mr. Powers is a member of many of the leading clubs in Massa-

chusetts. He is president of the Middlesex Club, vice-president
of the University Club and the Newton Club. While living in
Washington he was president of the famous Tantalus Club of
that city.

He is senior member of the law firm of Powers & Hall, one of
the large and active legal firms of Boston, which is prominently
identified with corporations engaged in electrical development.
The firm is counsel for the telephone interests in New England,
and formerly represented large street railway interests in Massachusetts, Mr. Powers at one time being president of no less than
eight street railway companies. In 1905 he was elected a life
trustee of Dartmouth College, and has always taken a deep interest in educational matters. He was married in 1878 to Eva
Crowell, and they have one son, Leland, who was born in 1890,
and graduated with honors from Dartmouth in the class of 1910.
He is at present pursuing a post-graduate course for Master of
Arts degree, and is going to Harvard Law School the coming year.

DAVID SIDNEY RICHARDSON.

David Sidney Richardson was born in Cornish, September 1,
1821. He early manifested a strong love for literary pursuits.
Nature seemed to have paved the way and implanted in him a
strong desire to obtain an education, not exclusively for himself
but that he might thereby become a blessing to others by becoming an instructor of youth. This ambition became his ruling
passion—the high calling towards which all his youthful energies
were directed. He early sought the means of preparation for
his life work by attending the academies of Kimball Union, New
Hampton, and finally, Dartmouth College from which he afterwards received honorary degrees. He left the college in the
midst of his course that he might engage in teaching. From this
time forth to the end of a protracted life he followed it as his life
work.

It is said that he founded six academies in New Hampshire
and North Carolina. At Franklinton, N. C., he founded a
flourishing institute of which he was the principal for several years.
Here he established the *North Carolina Journal of Education*
and edited it several years.

While here, he married on January 1, 1851, Mary Cleora Stone,
a gifted teacher of similar aims and experience, who was also a native of Cornish. The union proved a happy one in every respect.

His former prosperity and influence thus augmented, brought increased prosperity to the institute which continued until the opening of the Civil War. This had a disastrous effect upon the school. The young men of the school were all conscripted into the Confederate Army and himself among the rest. The school buildings were converted into a hospital. The academy never recovered from this misfortune.

PROF. D. S. RICHARDSON.   MRS. MARY C. RICHARDSON.

He soon after left Franklinton for Mobile, Alabama, where he opened a military academy, and continued in charge of it fifteen years.

In 1884, he removed to California and became professor of ancient classics in McClare's Military Academy at Oakland. He remained thus connected with this institution several years, until age and failing health induced him to relinquish all further public effort as an instructor.

Still retaining his love for teaching, he, in his own private home in Oakland, continued to instruct a choice few who earnestly sought his tutelage.

In 1903, being eighty-two years of age, he bade a final farewell to his life-long profession, and retired to San José, the "Garden City," where, in the home of his only son, he died April 7, 1905.

In many respects Mr. Richardson was a remarkable man. The sprightliness and vivacity of childhood and youth never seemed to leave him. He was mirthful, optimistic, versatile, and withal was possessed of a very tender and affectionate nature. He was also resourceful, having at hand an almost limitless fund of information and anecdote. Therefore, as a conversationalist he greatly excelled. These beautiful characteristics rendered him a magnet that won many friends in every community. It was the writer's privilege to know, and in some degree to associate with the subject of this sketch, and he can cheerfully inscribe this brief tribute to his memory.

MARY CLEORA (STONE) RICHARDSON.

The excellent models of female character which Cornish has produced have been many. It is not possible to tell the whole story of the scores and hundreds of the worthy, faithful and self-sacrificing women who have become the "mothers of men." The pen of the recording angel alone can render them the justice and honor they deserve. Hidden away from the rude observation of the world, have these performed their high and holy mission and the world has received the benefit of their toil.

A beautiful exemplification of this is found in the life record of Mrs. Richardson. Hers was a life ennobled by useful work, sanctified by suffering and self-sacrifice, and crowned by the love and veneration of all who knew her.

She was born in Cornish, December 23, 1827, the daughter of Capt. Josiah and Experience (Stevens) Stone. This household was one of mutual love and good-will. Piety was its ruling note, while its other distinguishing characteristics were intelligence, refinement and activity. Under such influences as these a family of seven children were reared to go out into the world to fill places of trust and usefulness.

She early professed the religion of her fathers and became a consistent member of the Congregational Church. At fourteen years of age she taught her first public school, wherein she manifested such aptitude for the work as gave abundant promise of brilliant success as a teacher in after years.

She obtained her education from New Hampton and Kimball Union Academies, and the Washington Female Seminary near Pittsburg, Pa. Near the close of her course in the last-named institution, while valedictory honors were surely awaiting her, she accepted a position as teacher in Ray's Academy at Louisburg, N. C. At this time, 1845, the schools of the South were few and inefficient, presenting an inviting field for teachers from the New England States, many of whom there found their life work. As yet, the bitter sectional animosities had not made their appearance, and teachers from the North were welcomed and treated with every respect and consideration. Her acceptance of the position in Louisburg marked the opening of a career which covered her best years. All unconsciously to herself the gates were opening upon the theater of her life work. Here came love, joy, and suffering. Upon this chosen field of duty she was destined to experience all of Life's bitter sweet, its shade and sunshine, and finally to emerge, chastened and ennobled, the perfect fulfillment of the promise of her youth.

At Louisburg her reputation was soon established among pupils and parents; but near the close of the second year, owing to impaired health, she was compelled to resign her charge and return North. Soon after, she returned to North Carolina and opened a select family school in Bedford, about twelve miles from Louisburg. From the start it was a pronounced success. Such devotion as existed between teacher and pupils is seldom seen. Her whole heart went into the work, and the result could not be other than one of love and progress.

It was while engaged in this school that she made the acquaintance of David Sidney Richardson, her future husband. Although both came from Cornish, they had no previous acquaintance. He, too, had sought the South as a fitting field for the exercise of his chosen profession of teacher and educator. The acquaintance grew to friendship and from friendship to love. They were married January 1, 1851. The union thus formed was destined to endure for over half a century. Henceforth their lives became one in every purpose, sympathy and aim, and hand in hand they went down the years together, mutually comforted and sustained by the faith and trust of perfect union. The life of this

gifted, devoted woman, and that of her husband sounds like a
romance of more than ordinary interest. The founding and establishing of academies at Cedar Rock, Franklinton and Wilson,
N. C., and the marvelous success attending each, proved the beautiful realization of their youthful dreams.

But this good fortune could not always remain unalloyed.
Trials must come. The loss of three little children brought
sorrow to the mother heart. A sister and co-worker in their
academy also sickened and died. Then came the dark and
stormy days of the Civil War when they saw the institution
which they had so laboriously built up, engulfed and over-
whelmed in the turmoils and passions of that fearful strife.
From beginning to end, they saw it all. Their institution was
converted into a soldiers' hospital, and Mrs. Richardson became
the ministering angel to relieve suffering and to tender comfort
and sympathy to all about her.

While the deep convictions of her early Northern training still
existed, yet it did not impair the love and confidence of those to
whom she ministered. No bitterness of sectional hatred could
exist in her soulful presence, and when distress and ruin was every-
where, it was impossible for a soul like hers to fail in sympathy.
The war at last came to an end. It was not possible to maintain
their loved institution amid the wreck and chaos of war and
reconstruction. Their fortune was gone; patrons were dead;
accounts could not be collected. The furnishings of the academy with libraries and musical instruments went for nothing.
The people were bankrupt, they could not pay, and their labors
as educators at Wilson were abandoned. But there yet remained
with them the love for the school room.

At Mobile, Ala., in 1868, Mrs. Richardson opened her
"School of Fine Arts," while her husband established his "Mobile Military Academy." Both of these enterprises were successful from the start and during a period of fifteen years. Here Mrs.
Richardson turned her attention exclusively to art, although her
talent as a painter had long been recognized. The best talent of
the time became interested in her work and her studio was
crowded with pupils. Among these were Amelie Rives, since
Princess Troubetskoy and Robert McKenzie and many others.
The masterpieces, the results of her genius, were many. Thus,

in the center of a constantly growing circle of devoted pupils and friends, the years went by.

In 1883, needing rest and change, they decided to go to California which ever after became their home. They located in the city of Oakland. For a time she reopened her studio and continued her art work with marked success, but advancing age and failing health compelled her to stop. Her art receptions were discontinued, and the number of pupils limited.

A son, Frank Harper Richardson, born August 11, 1867, their only living child, had married in 1890 and a few years later became a widower with three helpless children, little girls, from two to five years of age. Mrs. Richardson, the grandmother, now nearly seventy years of age, with true heroism assumed the care of these helpless orphans and took the mother's place. Only a mother can know what that means. The burden thus self-imposed she was destined to carry to the end. How bravely and tenderly she did it needs no laudation here.

One further change of home before the end. In 1903 their son Frank, who had now become the stay and support of his aged parents, and whose business was in San José, desired to make that city the parental home. To Mrs. Richardson the mere wish of her idolized son was sufficient for any sacrifice. So the home in Oakland was disposed of, and their goods transferred to a beautiful residence in the "Garden City." Her stay here, however, was brief and transient, from November, 1903, to the afternoon of July 3, 1904, when the light faded out of those tired eyes, and her beautiful spirit found its release. Her remains rest in Cypress Lawn Cemetery, a beautiful spot overlooking the sunset sea, but her noblest monument is in the hearts of the many who knew and loved her.

Mr. Richardson, too, was a beautiful character, a fitting companion for the subject of this sketch. He was ever optimistic and mirthful under all the severe trials of his life, unless we except the last one—the loss of his beloved companion. For her he truly and sadly mourned, but not for long. On the seventh of April, 1905, he passed away. His last words were of Cleora, and he passionately kissed her portrait until he breathed his last. He was buried by her side in Cypress Lawn Cemetery.

REV. JOSEPH ROWELL.

Rev. Joseph Rowell was the fifth son of the senior Rev. Joseph
Rowell and was born in Cornish, April 22, 1820. He fitted for
college at Kimball Union Academy, class 1844. He graduated
at Yale College in 1848 and Union Theological Seminary in 1851.
He chose the profession of his father, and like him became a bold

REV. JOSEPH ROWELL.

and fearless preacher. Choosing the world at large as his field of
labor, his tendencies were to mission fields abroad rather than to
domestic pastoral labor. He was employed several years at Pan-
ama and New Grenada, S. A., as missionary. In 1858 he organized
the "Mariners' Church" in San Francisco. This has seemed to
be the chosen field for his life work, a noble work instituted and

maintained in the interests of mariners, a class whose spiritual needs are much too often neglected. He has continued his connection as chaplain of this church in the "Golden Gate" ever since. The fruit of his labors there has been rich and abundant.

Record has been kept of the converts made through his efforts in the Mariners' Church since his connection with it, and they reach the total of 5,700 souls. With good reason it is said that Chaplain Rowell has been remembered in prayer in every part of the globe, for his converts have entered every port in both hemispheres. Like "Father Taylor" of Boston, he has been called the "Sailors' Friend."

He is still a man of remarkable physical and mental vigor, being at this writing (1909) in his ninetieth year. Seldom has man been so well preserved in all his faculties as has Mr. Rowell. His has been a robust, strenuous, active, as well as a useful life. In order to give the reader a better idea of Rev. Joseph Rowell, we append a characteristic letter written by him to the writer a year since, in reply to an invitation for him to attend the annual meeting of the aged people of Cornish in 1908. We give the letter entire:

San Francisco, 7-23-08.

Dear Bro. Child:

Your invitation to attend the "Old People's Association" annual meeting is before me. I had thought it quite possible that I might be at the meeting this year, as I have been very near you this last spring. I have returned from a trip to the Mediterranean Sea, and particularly the Holy Land, where I traveled the paths which Jesus used, visited his birth-place and the scenes of his miracles, his death, and burial place, his resurrection and ascension—the joy and privilege of my life. I suppose that I am the oldest person that ever made this trip; but I bore the fatigue and trial better than many who were younger than myself; indeed, it was commonly said of me: "He keeps at the head of all exploring parties," and not seldom: "He is the youngest man aboard the ship!"

I traveled 15,000 miles or more and did not miss a meal on the whole trip. I was a pretty good specimen of Cornish vigor, and in this way, did you all credit. I should be glad to be with you, though there are so few eyes there now that ever saw me,

and nearly all my old friends have gone over the river. The
Book speaks of "the things that remain,"—Yes, the *things* remain—the hills and valleys, and even the old houses, but the
people, where are they?

Possibly I may visit the dear old town again—God knows.
But I shall certainly see the old faces again, "over Jordan."

Kindest regards to all.
                                               JOSEPH ROWELL.

AUGUSTUS SAINT-GAUDENS.

Augustus Saint-Gaudens, the celebrated sculptor, was born
in Dublin, Ireland, his father being a southern Frenchman and
his mother an Irishwoman, but was brought to America when
six months old, and his childhood and youth were passed in New
York City. He attended the public schools until his thirteenth
year when he was apprenticed to a cameo cutter. The trade was
a fortunate choice for one destined to future mastery of work in
low relief, and he exercised it for his support during his student
years in Europe. He went to Paris to study sculpture in 1867,
and entered the studio of Jouffroy in 1868. In 1870 he went to
Rome and remained there about three years. He returned to
New York in 1872 and opened his studio there. He married
Augusta F. Homer in 1877, and returned to Paris in 1878 to
execute there the statue of Farragut, the earliest of his important
works, which was exhibited in plaster at the Salon of 1880. Its
success was immediate and conclusive. A great career was begun,
and from that time he moved forward from triumph to triumph
until he was universally recognized as not only the greatest
sculptor of America, but the foremost of American artists and one
of the first artists of his time in any country. The esteem in
which he was held by his fellow artists was perhaps most clearly
shown when, at the Pan-American Exposition held in Buffalo in
1901, he was, on the unanimous recommendation of the jury of
fine arts, composed of architects, sculptors and painters, awarded
a special medal of honor "apart from and above all other awards."

His connection with the town of Cornish came about through
his friendship with the late C. C. Beaman, from whom he purchased in 1885 the old brick house then known as "Huggin's
Folly," and the land about it, and gradually transformed it into
his beautiful home of "Aspet." At first it was a summer residence
only, but when he went abroad again in 1897 to execute the great

AUGUSTUS ST. GAUDENS

equestrian statue of General Sherman, which is perhaps his masterpiece, Saint-Gaudens gave up his New York abode, and on returning to America in 1900 he made "Aspet" his permanent residence the year around. The final work on the Sherman statue was done here, and all his subsequent work was carried on from sketch to completed model in the two studios which he erected. The larger studio was destroyed by fire in 1904, when much of his work then under way was lost, as well as some souvenirs of other artists, including two portraits of himself, one by Bastien-Lepage and the other by Kenyon Cox,—the only portraits painted of him in his prime. The studio was rebuilt in more permanent form and the lost work re-begun, and in that studio his assistants are still busy (1907) reverently completing the work left unfinished at the time of his death.

Other artists were brought to Cornish by the attraction of Saint-Gaudens's presence, as well as by that of its beautiful scenery and fine air, and by degrees the artistic and literary colony was formed which has gradually spread over a part of the neighboring town of Plainfield. Its members looked upon Saint-Gaudens not only as a great artist and a beloved friend, but as the founder of the colony, and on June 23, 1905, celebrated the twentieth anniversary of his coming to Cornish by that fête and open air play, given upon the grounds of "Aspet," which has already become almost legendary and which the sculptor himself has immortalized by the creation of a charming plaquette which he presented to all who took part on the occasion. The altar, under its columned canopy, which was the background of the play, still stands in a recess of the pine groves of "Aspet," though much dilapidated by weather. To many friends of Saint-Gaudens it has seemed that no more fitting memorial could be erected to his memory than a reproduction of it in permanent material and suitably inscribed.

The artist had returned from Paris in 1900 an ill man, and from that illness he never recovered. At times he seemed again fairly vigorous, and he was able, with the assistance of a corps of devoted assistants, to do much valuable work. Upon their aid he became, however, more and more dependent as time went on. In the summer of 1906 his illness took so grave a form that work was altogether suspended and he ceased to see even his intimate friends. From that attack he rallied somewhat, but he was greatly altered. The end came on August 3, 1907. According to his wish his body was cremated, and his ashes are deposited in the cemetery at Windsor, Vt. An informal service was held at his studio on August 7 in the presence of friends and neighbors, but of only a few of his many friends in other parts of the world.

As a man Augustus Saint-Gaudens combined great energy and power of will with a singular patience and a natural gentleness and sweetness that made him greatly loved by those who knew him, and most loved by those who knew him best. As an artist his leading characteristics were mastery of design and great decorative feeling combined with exquisiteness of workmanship, as shown in the many works he executed in low relief—works unsurpassed in this kind since the Florentine Renaissance; a profound insight into human character as shown in many of these reliefs and in his great portrait statues such as the Farragut, the Lincoln and the Sherman and that ideal portrait, as real as any of them, the Deacon Chapin; a creative imagination as shown in such typical figures as the "Angel of Death" in the Shaw Memorial, the "Victory" of the Sherman group, above all, the brooding figure of the Adams Memorial—an imagination which gives these figures a strange individuality and raises them out of the rank of conventional allegories into that of original inventions. He was less interested in the problem of the expressive modelling of the human figure and cared little for the study of the nude, but his work steadily advanced in mastery of the purely sculpturesque qualities of mass and movement until his greatest works are nearly as fine in these respects as in decorative beauty of composition and imaginative beauty of conception. His great Sherman group is indubitably one of the half dozen finest equestrian statues in the world.

The fame of Saint-Gaudens belongs to America—his art to the world at large. To the town of Cornish it will be an abiding glory that it contains his chosen home.

"In his life in Cornish, Saint-Gaudens drew around him many friends of artistic and literary repute, and his beautiful home, 'Aspet,' with his numerous little studios has for many years been the Mecca of the world of sculpture in America, and that it should be *there* that the hand which touched the clay and marble into life became still, was the wish of Augustus Saint-Gaudens."

LOUIS SAINT GAUDENS.

Born on Lispenard Street, New York, January 7, 1854. Ran away from the public school at the age of thirteen. Served occasionally as apprentice until the age of eighteen, when he went to Italy, where he made a living setting cameos, a trade taught him by his brother. He lived in Rome three years, in this time he was seriously ill with pneumonia and later with Roman fever. He sometimes worked in the art classes of the French Academy at Rome. After this he went to France and studied art in Paris, then wandered through England or worked with his brother until he returned to America in 1880. He rented a studio in New York and did work for architects, including the "Piping Fun" ordered by Stanford White for the house of P. T. Barney, and the medallion portrait of Commodore De Kay. For ten years, from about 1883, he worked most of the time in his brother's studios, although part of the time upon his own orders. The "Angels of the Church of the Ascension" were modelled there. In a studio in Harlem he modelled a relief for the Union League Club and the lions for the Boston Library.

In 1901 Mr. Saint-Gaudens came to Cornish where he worked in collaboration with his brother for two years. He then built a house and studio and modelled two of the statues for the new custom house in New York, "Prince Henry" and "Van Trump," and the portrait of Mr. Breierly.

In 1905 he began the sculpture of the new union station in Washington, D. C., D. H. Bernham, architect. President Eliot of Harvard chose the subjects for the statues for the exterior decoration, "Fire," "Electricity," "Freedom," "Inventive Imagination," "Ceres," "Archimedes." These statues are being cut on single stones of white Bethel granite at Northfield, by the Daniel Ellis Company.

Mr. Saint-Gaudens is now modelling studies of three Roman soldiers, seven feet in height, which are to be reproduced for the forty-six statues which will decorate the waiting room of the station. College athletes have posed for most of the statues, which is a departure made because the college men more nearly approach the perfection of the antique statues. This work will be in place on the station about 1912.

Mr. Saint-Gaudens has modelled these statues almost without

assistance even with the manual labor and has dispensed with many of the ordinary mechanical helps and methods—and has made numberless sketches and changes to gain the classical ideal.

ANNETTA JOHNSON SAINT-GAUDENS.

Born in Flint, Ohio, September 11, 1869. Her ancestors were early pioneers to Ohio, from New England, Virginia and New Jersey.

She was educated at home until the age of thirteen when she and her sisters attended private school.

At thirteen she began modelling by herself in native clay and at the age of sixteen was sent to the Columbus Art School, where she studied for three years with Dora M. Norton, graduating from the school in 1888. After two years spent at home she went to the Art Students' League in New York, where she studied drawing with Troachtanam and modelling with Augustus Saint-Gaudens. She worked with Saint-Gaudens as student and assistant most of the time for five years, with the kindness of friends earning her own way much of that time, working on the statue of General Logan for one year and a half. She returned to Ohio, being worn out with the work in New York. In Ohio she modelled the bust of Professor Orton and President Canfield of the Ohio State University. In the summer of 1898 she returned to New York to model the portrait of Emerson MacMillin.

In 1901 the family moved to Cornish, where they have lived, excepting two winters spent with her parents in Claremont, Cal.

Mrs. Saint-Gaudens assisted her husband for several years, and for two years has been experimenting in cutting marble and modelling small statues, vases and portraits for terra cotta.

DR. DAVID S. C. H. SMITH.

David S. C. H. Smith was born in Cornish, June 27, 1797. He was educated at Dartmouth and Yale Colleges. His father, the renowned Dr. Nathan Smith, was connected with both of these institutions. Having chosen the medical profession for his life work, he went to Sutton, Mass., and commenced its practice in 1819. There were already three other doctors there, all quite distinguished men in their profession. This circumstance made his place a hard one at the first for the young man. But his thorough training and the prestige of his father's fame, soon made him the most popular physician in that part of the country. He was called in consultation by many of the doctors for miles around. He drove to Rhode Island almost every week for years and was frequently at Providence.

He was a large man of fine personal appearance, had large piercing gray eyes and some of his patients thought he could look straight through them and tell exactly what ailed them; and, indeed, *diagnosis* was his forte.

To understand the complicated and intricate mechanism of the human system requires great research, as well as intuitive genius, judgment and skill. All these Doctor Smith possessed in a remarkable degree. So when other physicians had a human machine on their hands that they could not keep going, they sent for him to find out what cog was broken, what pin loose, or what pulley disbanded. Some seemed to think that he could put in a new mainspring, wind up the system like a clock, give motion to the pendulum of life and restore a defunct body to animation, strength and vigor. He used to say that other doctors would send for him when they thought their patient was dying, and once in many cases, such a person would recover; then he got the credit of the case, giving him an increased reputation. He said he had no proof that he ever cured any one, though circumstances sometimes seemed to indicate it, and that the recuperative power was more frequently due to the constitution and courage of the patient, than to the skill of the doctor.

He was a great naturalist and seemed to know all about animated nature. He was almost as intimately acquainted with the American birds as Audubon himself. He also gave much attention to entomology. His hat was frequently lined with insects which he had pinned there to be placed in his cabinet. He furnished Professor Harris several thousand specimens for his valuable work. He also gave a description of the reptiles of New England for President Hitchcock's great work. He traveled one year through the Western country that he might master the study of botany. So he became a great botanist and could classify and give the medical properties of nearly all the known plants that grow in this country.

Like his father he was a great man, but never became rich; indeed, at one time he was quite poor and deeply in debt, and his creditors attached his horse, so that he had no way to visit his

23

patients, and he became discouraged. One day a man came for him to go to Thompson, Conn., but the doctor told him that he could not go as he had no horse. The man told him that he would take him there in his own carriage and bring him back. "Well," said the doctor, "if you will do that I will go." So he went. When he reached home the man asked him what was to pay. "Oh, nothing," said the doctor, "you have had trouble enough already." "But I am going to pay you for all that," and the man gave him a ten-dollar bill and left. The next day a man came for him to visit a poor family in the south part of the town. He said: "If they are poor I'll go, for I am poor myself." When he reached the home he found they were poor indeed, and he said that starvation was all that ailed them; so he took out his ten-dollar bill and gave it to the poor woman to buy wholesome food for her sick children. It was all the money he had. He thought their rich neighbors could doctor that family as well as he could.

During this season of financial embarrassment, Doctor Shattuck of Boston sent his son with a good horse as a present to Doctor Smith. Doctor Shattuck formerly was one of his father's students, and had a great regard for the family. Soon after this Mr. James Phelps volunteered to build him a house, telling him he could pay for it from his earnings in small installments as was most convenient.

At one time he was quite skeptical, although his mother was a pious woman and read her Bible through in course as often as she could. When she died, her book-mark was at one of the Psalms. He had her Bible and sacredly kept the mark where she left it. So thinking of his good mother and her Bible, he learned to love it for her sake. This led to his conversion and he was made happy in his new-found hope.

He was thrice married. His first wife, Lucy Hall of Sutton, Mass., whom he married July 26, 1820, was the mother of his five children. She died September 23, 1850. He left Sutton in 1848 and removed to Providence, R. I., where he died April 6, 1859.

JOSIAH FRANKLIN STONE.

Josiah Franklin Stone, the fourth son of Capt. Josiah and Experience (Stevens) Stone, was born in Cornish, October 16,

1822. He was educated at Kimball Union Academy and New Hampton Institute. At nineteen years of age he engaged in mercantile pursuits, first with his brother Samuel, and afterwards by himself. He married Malvina Clark of Sanbornton. His friends were numerous, his credit good, and his business flourishing, until his generous impulses overruled his better judgment and he signed papers for his friends, and all his earnings were swept away. After this misfortune he resorted to other occupations. He settled in Winchester, Mass., in 1850. His fellow townsmen, recognizing his sterling qualities and business abilities, thrust upon him every office of honor and trust within their gift—seven years as selectman, eight years assessor, trustee of savings bank, representative to state Legislature in 1879, where he was on the committee on banks and banking. He was justice of the peace for more than twenty-five years. He had a general charge of the public schools and settled many estates. In 1880 he was again chosen to the state Legislature where he was on the committee on railroads. During this session he was stricken with pneumonia and suddenly passed away, February 2, 1881. His biographer says of him:

"There was silence in the street and overwhelming sorrow in every heart. It was like a loving father's death. It was therefore fitting that at his funeral services, the governor of the state, committee from each branch of the Legislature, trustees of the bank, fellow-officials of every position should attend, and the flags to be at half-mast, and business places all closed. All classes felt they had lost a personal friend, a helper, whose sympathy and counsel had lifted them over many hard places, and on whom they had leaned with confidence. Rarely do we meet a man whose personality combines so much nobility and inspires so much confidence, and makes such strong impressions on a community. All felt intuitively that behind the public man was *character* so sound that no temptations of designing, grasping, dishonest men could ever degrade it.

It was in the family circle that his inner life of purity and beauty shone like Ben Adhem's "great awakening light," and happy was that favored guest, who by chance was sometimes present and participated in those private "feasts of reason and flow of soul": to grasp the strong warm hand and feel the glow of the Heaven-lit face and hear the jubilant greeting when the loving

father of the devoted family circle was the "Presence in the room."
The writer was that favored guest and still lives (1903) and offers
this feeble tribute to one of the truest friends he ever had on earth.
The love between them was like the love of Damon and Pythias.
And should Cornish ever erect a memorial shaft for those whom
Cornish hath loved, or who loved Cornish, let the names of these
two friends be graven side by side: Josiah Franklin Stone, David
Sydney Richardson."

GEORGE H. STOWELL.

Among natives of Cornish, N. H., to achieve honor and success in after years, is George H. Stowell, son of Amasa Stowell.
He was born October 28, 1835, and his boyhood days were passed
on the home farm.   He lived the rugged life of the times, with
more work than play, assisting in the cultivation of the farm, and
attending the public schools whenever opportunity afforded.   Of
hardy, persistent New England stock, the heritage of ancestry
and the early training of a New Hampshire mountain farm had
their influence in forming habits of thrift and industry that
eventually placed Mr. Stowell's name prominent among the list
of New Hampshire's public men.

In March, 1860, ambitious promptings led him to give up farming and he removed to Claremont, the town adjoining Cornish
on the south, a prosperous and growing community offering
inducements and possibilities that appealed to Mr. Stowell's
instincts and temperament.

His first venture was in the gravestone and marble manufacturing business, which he carried on successfully until 1864, when he
purchased the hardware stock of Levi B. Brown.   Mr. Stowell
made no change in the location of the business, in the northwest
corner store of Oscar J. Brown's brick block, and for thirty-seven
years, or as long as he remained in business, he occupied this
site.   "Stowell's Corner" became a landmark; a synonym of business prosperity and a place of far-reaching influence in affairs of
both town and state.

The business grew until it became one of the best known hardware firms in New Hampshire.   The stock was increased to cover
a wide range of commodities, and when coal revolutionized the
fuel business, the first car-load of anthracite coal for house use,

GEO. H. STOWELL.

was brought to Claremont by Mr. Stowell. Eventually, coal became an extensive branch of his trade.

Meantime, he was actively engaged in other occupations that called for executive power and careful financial management. To meet the demands of Claremont's growing population, tenement houses were needed, and Mr. Stowell was one of the pioneers in erecting a number of first-class structures for this purpose. And when, in 1887, the old wooden "Brown Block" on the corner opposite Mr. Stowell's store was destroyed by fire, he was the leader in organizing the syndicate that procured the site of the burned property, and built thereon Union Block, one of the finest and best appointed business blocks in the state. His last building venture of public consequence was in 1895, when he built "Stowell Block," a handsome, modern business structure on Pleasant Street.

With multitudinous and increasing business cares, Mr. Stowell has never been too busy to neglect public affairs, in which he is prominently identified. His advice, influence, and sound conservative judgment has contributed much to promote Claremont's importance as a town. His own business success, by his own efforts, made him a power in any enterprise where careful financial discrimination was needed. In return for these qualifications his town has honored him in various ways as an able representative citizen. He was a member from Claremont in the New Hampshire Legislature in 1871 and 1874; a state senator in 1875 and 1876; member of the governor's council from 1881 to 1883; aide, with rank of colonel, on Governor Prescott's staff from 1887 to 1889; member of the state constitutional conventions of 1876 and 1889 and a delegate to the Republican National Convention at Chicago in 1884.

In 1888 he was in Europe several months on a pleasure trip, and to restore his health, which had partially failed.

In town business his name is always found on important boards and committees, and with the exception of the year 1878, he served continuously from 1873 to 1894, as chief engineer of the local fire department. In this important public service he kept pace with larger towns in maintaining fire fighting facilities, and saw the department reorganized from hand tubs to modern steam equipment.

Mr. Stowell sold out his hardware business in 1901, but is still a busy man of affairs, and occupied in the management of the People's National Bank, a sound financial institution which he helped organize and of which he is vice-president and a director. Not yet willing to retire from active business, he, in May, 1906, with three other well-known business men, bought the Monadnock Mills of Claremont, the largest cotton manufactory in the northern part of the state. This seemingly stupendous venture again evidenced the sagacity and sound judgment of Mr. Stowell, for the mills have ever since been running successfully.

It was also characteristic of Mr. Stowell that he should cherish a tender regard for the town of his nativity. As an expression of this, he conceived the idea of erecting and furnishing a beautiful library building on Cornish Flat at an expense of six thousand dollars, and presenting the same to the town of Cornish under the name of "Stowell Free Library." After the site was determined the town purchased the lot, and in May, 1910, active labor was begun on the building. This was continued throughout the season, and although not entirely completed at this writing, a beautiful brick building greets the eye of every beholder, and is a perpetual reminder of the benevolence of him who conceived and erected it.

December 24, 1857, Mr. Stowell married Miss Sarah E. Field, the union proving a happy one. Their only child, Cora E. Stowell (Putnam) born June 24, 1860, died March 8, 1903. In her memory, Mr. Stowell has erected a granite and bronze mausoleum in Mountain View Cemetery at Claremont. Mrs. Stowell died September 14, 1908.

The Stowell residence at the corner of Pleasant and Summer streets is attractively located, and conspicuous in its handsome architectural design. Here, amidst the comforts of his own acquiring, enjoying the confidence and good will of his fellow citizens, he approaches his declining years, ripe with the fullness of a well-ordered life, and keenly in touch with the men and the movement of the times.

JAMES ALBERT WELLMAN.

James Albert Wellman, son of Albert E. and Emily (Dodge) (Hall) Wellman, was born in Cornish, May 4, 1867. After attending the schools of his native town he prepared for college at Kimball Union Academy. He entered Dartmouth College in

REV. J. W. WELLMAN. D. D.

1885, and graduated therefrom in 1889 with the degree of Bachelor of Science. Immediately after this he entered upon the business of life insurance as special agent of the Connecticut Mutual Life Insurance Company. Later he became the general agent of this company for Vermont, with headquarters at Burlington, Vt. After five years he resigned this position to accept the New Hampshire state agency of the National Life Insurance Company of Vermont, with headquarters at Manchester, N. H. He has a large number of men under his direction, and the annual business of his agency is about $800,000. Insurance in force, over $6,000,-000. In the amount of premiums collected it has now become the second largest in the state. The new business written by this agency exceeds by a large per cent. that written by any other state agency in New Hampshire. Mr. Wellman is president of the Agents' Association of the National Life Insurance Company of Vermont. He is an ex-president of the New Hampshire Underwriters' Club, and he has represented New Hampshire on the executive committee of the National Association of Life Underwriters. He is accredited to be one of the ablest and best-informed life insurance men in New England. Mr. Wellman is a director of the Manchester National Bank, one of New Hampshire's greatest financial institutions; a director of the Manchester Safe, Deposit and Trust Company; and a director of the Franklin Street Congregational Church. He is a thirty-second degree Mason, and a member of Trinity Commandery, Knights Templar. He is a member of the Derryfield Club, the Intervale Country Club, the Society of Colonial Governors, the Society of Colonial Wars, and the Society of the American Revolution. He has demonstrated the fact in many ways that he is a thoroughly successful business man. In 1898 he married Florence Vincent of Burlington, Vt., daughter of Dr. Walter S. Vincent and Harriet (Laurence) Vincent. They have two children: (1) Harriet Vincent, born February 22, 1900; (2) Dorothy Hall, born October 30, 1901.

REV. JOSHUA WYMAN WELLMAN, D. D.

Rev. Joshua W. Wellman, D. D., was born in Cornish, November 28, 1821. He was the eldest son of Dea. James Ripley and Phebe (Wyman) Wellman. Deacon Wellman, the father, was a son of James and Alethea (Ripley) Wellman, and a grandson of Rev. James Wellman, who was installed the first pastor of "the first Church in Cornish," September 29, 1768, three years after the settlement of the town. (See Church History, also Wellman.) Alethea (Ripley) Wellman, the grandmother, was a descendant in the sixth generation from Gov. William Bradford of the Plymouth Colony.

At the age of fifteen the subject of this sketch entered Kimball Union Academy where he fitted for college. He graduated from the academy in 1842, and from Dartmouth College in 1846.

In the winter of 1838–39, he taught his first school in Hartford, Vt., and later, during his college course in Upton and East Randolph, Mass. (now Holbrook). From 1846 to 1849 he taught in Kimball Union Academy a part of each year, and in 1847 was principal of the academy in Rochester, Mass., for two terms. Entering the Andover Theological Seminary in 1847, he graduated therefrom in 1850, and was then a resident licentiate in the seminary for one year. He was ordained to the Christian ministry and installed as pastor of the historic "First Church in Derry," N. H., June 18, 1851, where he remained five years. He was installed pastor of the "Eliot Church" in Newton, Mass., June 11, 1856, and was dismissed therefrom October 23, 1873. His pastorate in Newton included the exciting period of the Civil War. During the early part of the conflict he visited the South and saw something of the horrors of war. He was strongly opposed to slavery and supported the war as necessary to save the Union. The plain statement of his views in his sermons produced considerable excitement at a time when many believed that the pulpit should be silent on such subjects. He continued, however, in every way that seemed to him to be proper, to help forward the cause of the right. The church became eminently patriotic and twenty-seven men from the congregation enlisted in the war.

During this pastorate the church grew from a small membership to be one of the largest and most prominent churches in the state.

March 25, 1874, Mr. Wellman was installed pastor of the "Ancient First Church" in Malden, Mass., and which under his care also grew into a large and influential church. He remained its pastor until May 6, 1883, when he was dismissed from its pastorate. Since that time he has had no pastoral charge but has done considerable pulpit work in his own and among neighboring churches. During this period he has devoted much of his time to literary work, still retaining his residence and church relationship in Malden.

October 24, 1854, he married Ellen M., daughter of Caleb Strong and Prudence (Durfee) Holbrook of East Randolph, Mass. (now Holbrook), who died June 24, 1901. Their children were: (1) Arthur Holbrook, a lawyer, who practices in Boston, who married October 11, 1887, Jennie Louise Faulkner; (2) Edward Wyman, who married October 1, 1884, Emma R. Patch and died April 17, 1891; (3) Ellen Holbrook, who married October 24, 1883, Robert Cushman King; (4) Annie Durfee, who died April 7, 1903.

Mr. Wellman was elected a corporate member of The American Board of Commissioners for Foreign Missions in 1867; was one of the managers of the Congregational Sunday School and Publishing Society, and a trustee of Pinkerton Academy and of Phillips Academy in Andover, serving on each of these boards for several years. He is a member of the New England Historic Genealogical Society, a corporate member of the General Theological Library of Boston, and for many years a director of the American College and Educational Society. He was a leading advocate in the formation of the Congregational Club of Boston, of which he was an original member. Olivet College in 1868 and Dartmouth College in 1870 bestowed upon him the degree of D. D.

He has published: (1) Church Polity of the Pilgrims, 1857. (2) The Organic Development of Christianity in the Direction of Education and Learning: Address before the Society for the Promotion of Collegiate and Theological Education in the West, Boston, Mass., May 30, 1860. (3) Sermon: Our Nation Under the Government of God, Newton, Mass., August 3, 1862. (4) The Good and Faithful Servant: Memorial Sermon of John C. Potter, Newton, Mass., 1870. (5) Tract: Christianity and Our Civil Institutions, 1870. (6) Sketch of Rev. James Munroe Bacon, 1875. (7) Free Public Libraries: Address at the Opening of the Free Public Library, Newton, Mass., June 17, 1870. (8) In Memory of Mrs. Maria Brigham Furber, 1883. (9) Transcendent Value of the Christian Sanctuary: Rededication Sermon, First Church, Derry, 1885. (10) The Andover Case, with introductory, historical statement, careful summary of arguments of respondent, full text of arguments of complainants, and decision of board of visitors, pp. 194, 1887. (11) The Questions at Issue in the Andover Case, 1892. (12) Historical Discourse: 250th Anniversary of the Organization of the First Church of Christ, Malden, Mass., 1899. (13) Origin and Early History of the Eliot Church, Newton, Mass., 1904.

BIRTHS, MARRIAGES AND DEATHS IN CORNISH NOT RECORDED IN GENEALOGIES.

A PARTIAL LIST OF BIRTHS IN TOWN NOT FOUND IN ITS GENEALOGIES.

IN ALPHABETICAL ORDER UNTIL 1863.

Abbott, Samuel and Betsey, son, Samuel S., July 6, 1811.
Abbott, Samuel and Betsey, son, John, Aug. 4, 1813.
Ashley, Seymore and Martha, dau., ————, Feb. 7, 1864.
Ballard, Israel and E., son, Daniel, Nov. 12, 1778.
Bancroft, Timothy and Matilda, dau., Louisa, Jan. 13, 1817.
Belden, Samuel and Abigail, dau., Abigail, Sept. 21, 1810.
Blodgett, Buzzell and Rhoda, son, Joshua Nathaniel, Nov. 16, 1863.
Brown, H. N. and Hannah, dau., Eugenia M., June 24, 1861.
Coats, Charles W. and Calista, dau., Annie C., May 10, 1862.
Coil, Peter and Anna, son, Peter, Feb. 8, 1862.
Cole, Samuel and Rebecca, dau., Mary, March 31, 1794.
Conlin, John and Mary, dau., Sarah J., Aug. 4, 1860.
Conlin, John and Mary, son, Patrick, April 5, 1864.
Comings, George B. and Olive, a child, Jan. 11, 1862.
Crossman, John and Elizabeth, son, Charles H., Oct. 21, 1858.
Dearborn, John and Elizabeth, son, George L., July 17, 1854.
Dorman, Lewis and Sarah, son, Henry, Feb. 28, 1861.
Eddy, Zechariah and Phebe, dau., Eunice, Feb. 26, 1796.
Eddy, Zechariah and Phebe, son, Elias Newbury, Jan. 12, 1798.
Farwell, John H. and Eliza, son, Fred, June —, 1861.
Farwell, John H. and Eliza, son, Frank D., Oct. 30, 1862.
Flanders, Stephen and Susanna (Lucy), son, Alba, March 26, 1803.
Flint, J. J. and Silvia, son, John, May 28, 1863.
Flint, J. J. and Silvia, son, ————, March 26, 1865.
Follett, Jesse and Judith, dau., Louisa Adelaide, May —, 1813.
Follett, Jesse and Judith, dau., Sarah Ray, April 30, 1815.
Graves, Eldad and Sarah, son, Eldad, Jr., March 15, 1773.
Greely, Thomas and Ann, dau., Sarah C., Jan. 20, 1860.
Hawley, Richard and Keziah, dau., Lucy, Jan. 21, 1778.
Hibbard, Daniel and Hannah, son, Daniel, July 6, 1776.
Horton, Zenas and Nancy, son, Valentine Baxter, June 29, 1802.
Johnson, George F. and Frances, a child, ————, March 21, 1863.
Kennedy, Bartholmew and wife, twin sons, ————, Feb. —, 1859.
Knight, Lorenzo M. and Calista, dau., Kate, July 1, 1860.
Knight, Lorenzo M. and Calista, dau., Elma, Aug. —, 1862.
Lewis, T. B. and wife, dau., Hattie L., Dec. 13, 1861.

Lewis, ———— and wife, dau., Dec. 31, 1850.
Marston, Ezra and wife, son, ————, March 17, 1859.
McCarty, Michael and Catherine, son, Martin, May 1, 1860.
Morey, Willard and Lydia, son, Williard, Aug. 28, 1788.
Packard, Judson and Abigail, dau., Eunice, March 23, 1861.
Powers, Phinehas and Elizabeth, dau., Tirzah, Nov. 22, 1768.
Powers, Abraham and Rachel, dau., Rachel, June 25, 1770.
Remington, David and Sybil, dau., Susanna, Oct. 31, 1777.
Robinson, George H. and wife, son, ————, Aug. 12, 1851.
Royce, Henry and Emeline, dau., Lucy, May 26, 1863.
Sargent, Stephen and Lucy, son, Moses, June 26, 1804.
Shedd, Reed and Electa, son, Marcellus R., May 15, 1860.
Simonds, Isaac and Mehitable, son, Samuel Curtis, May 29, 1797.
Smith, Abraham and Abigail, dau., Harriet, May 18, 1798.
Snow, Amos and Lydia, dau., Esther, Sept. 16, 1774.
Spaulding, Elisha F. and Lucy, son, Ed. E., Nov. 21, 1859.
Stearns, Edward and Mary, dau., Jennie M., July 15, 1860.
Tuket, Israel and wife, son, Charles Henry, April 9, 1850.
Warner, Jerry and wife, son, Jerry Bradley, March 1, 1810.
Warner, Jerry and wife, son, Charles Henry, Feb. 4, 1812.
Watkins, Oren and Marcia, dau., Georgianna, March 7, 1862.
Wilder, James and Mary, dau., ————, Sept. 26, 1859.
Wilder, Sylvanus and Mary, dau., Mary J., May 26, 1859.
Wilder, James and Mary, twin sons, ————, Feb. 6, 1862.
Wilder, James and Mary, dau., Bertha, Dec. 26, 1863.
Wilson, Levi and Sarah, dau., Sally, April 29, 1799.
Witherill, Theodore and wife, dau., ————, Feb. 27, 1859.

PARTIAL LIST OF BIRTHS IN TOWN NOT IN GENEALOGIES, 1863–1887.

IN CHRONOLOGICAL ORDER.

Lucy C. Royce, May 26, 1863.
John W. Flint, May 28, 1863.
Joshua N. Blodgett, Nov. 16, 1863.
Bertha G. Wilder, Dec. 26, 1863.
Patrick Conlin, April 5, 1864.
Ida M. Wilder, July 7, 1865.
Arvilla Baskwell, Dec. 19, 1866.
John W. Wilcox, Dec. 30, 1866.
Everard C. Wilder, June 26, 1867.
Etta M. Parkhurst, June 6, 1868.
Albert Shedd, Nov. 16, 1869.
Flora Ada Smith, Jan. 21, 1870.
Herbert A. Whiting, April 20, 1870.
Fred A. Shallies, July 26, 1870.
Edwin H. Shedd, Aug. 12, 1870.
John A. Wakefield, Sept. 12, 1870.
Franklin S. Ashley, Oct. 13, 1870.

Grace M. Parkhurst, Jan. 27, 1871.
Jane Sargent, Feb. 1, 1871.
Eddie S. Loverin, April 4, 1871.
Henry Dana, Aug. 30, 1871.
Abby Fiske Howard, Sept. 25, 1871.
Edna Stearns, Feb. 8, 1872.
Nellie Royce, March 3, 1872.
Mary W. Curtis, April 12, 1872.
Son of Carlos Messer, Aug. 27, 1872.
Effie Jordan, Feb. 9, 1873.
Dau. of Carlos S. Gee, March 4, 1873.
Velzora H. Comings, March 28, 1873.
Fanny V. Thayer, Sept. 16, 1873.
Florence Harris, Dec. 10, 1873.
Child of Enoch Quimby, ———, 1873.
Henry H. Royce, Feb. —, 1874.
Fred Vadney, April 27, 1874.
Almeda Whitmore, July 21, 1874.
Charles Joseph St. Johns, Dec. 11, 1874.
Shirley Walter Humphrey, April 8, 1875.
Fred W. Knight, April 17, 1875.
Lizzie A. Pope, May 3, 1875.
Lucius R. Jordan May 14, 1875.
Susan M. Skinner, June 25, 1875.
Walter E. Bailey, Sept. 8, 1875.
Charles W. Vadney, Oct. 1, 1875.
Maria Stearns, Nov. 27, 1875.
Fred P. Messer, Dec. 31, 1875.
Alexander Wilder, April 4, 1876.
Charles Austin, June 5, 1876.
Carl E. Farwell, ———, 1876.
Son of Alfred Lucas, Nov. 20, 1876.
Ann L. Hutchinson, Dec. 28, 1876.
Dau. of Daniel Whitmore, Dec. 28, 1876.
Willie Spencer, twin, Jan. 15, 1877.
Willis Spencer, twin, Jan. 15, 1877.
Dau. of John P. Small, March 21, 1877.
Dau. of David Marcott, March 31, 1877.
Winslow Jacobs, April 18, 1877.
Wallace Harris, April 27, 1877.
Dau. of Warren S. Whipple, July 10, 1877.
Bertha Skinner, July 10, 1877.
Son of Warren H. Fletcher, July 20, 1877.
Morris Jordan, May 14, 1878.
Franklin Curtis, June 21, 1878.
Grace E. Morgan, Nov. 13, 1878.
Eliza A. Messer, Nov. 21, 1878.
Son of Keron Ryan, Dec. 9, 1878.

Son of Daniel Whitmore, Dec. 30, 1878.
Son of George F. Davis, Feb. —, 1879.
Lena A. Pope, March 8, 1879.
Ernest Whitmore, March 21, 1879.
William McCarty, July 26, 1879.
Molly B. Mason, Nov. 4, 1879.
Chester A. Spaulding, Nov. 14, 1879.
G. J. A. Benjamin, Dec. 25, 1879
Jessie Noyes, July 1, 1880.
Patrick Reynolds, Oct. 7, 1880.
Roy M. Harris, Oct. 24, 1880.
Son of Ozro V. Eastman, Dec. —, 1880.
Son of Daniel Whitmore, March —, 1881.
Lena E. Kempton, May 16, 1881.
Louis L. Comstock, Oct. 15, 1881.
Lulu Boyd, Jan. 19, 1882.
Nellie L. Eastman, Jan. 31, 1882.
T. R. Francis, April 15, 1882.
Mary E. Wiley, April 17, 1882.
Guy H. Eaton, May 18, 1882.
Amy B. Anthony, Aug. 10, 1882.
Lena M. Spaulding, Jan. 22, 1884.
Cleveland H. Curtis, Oct. 17, 1884.
Dau. of Wm. A. Sweet, Jan. 4, 1885.
Dau. of Frank H. Cass, May 16, 1885.
Dau. of Edmund Curtis, Jan. 10, 1886.
Dau. of Sumner U. Dunsmoor, Feb. 9, 1886.
Herman C. Terry, May 6, 1886.
Son of Leonard Hadley, June 4, 1886.
Max W. Cole, Aug. 28, 1886.
Son of Fred A. Spaulding, Nov. 17, 1886.
Dau. of Rufus G. Smith, Dec. 7, 1886.

In all 317 births in town *not* included in genealogies.

BIRTHS IN CORNISH NOT RECORDED IN GENEALOGIES, 1887–1910.

IN CHRONOLOGICAL ORDER.

To William F. and Allie (Chambers) Terry, a son, Sept. 4, 1887.
　　Napoleon and Mrs. Ruth (Spaulding) Miller, a son, Frank Orin, Nov. 12, 1887.
　　Leander and Susan (Browe) Bordeau, a dau., ———, Jan. 19, 1888.
　　Edmund and Jennie L. (Bythrow) Curtis, a son, ———, Feb. 5, 1888.
　　Darwin and Etta (Sweet) Jordan, a dau., ———, March 10, 1888.
　　James L. W. and Ella M. (Carroll) Thayer, a son, ———, May 24, 1888.
　　Winfield S. and Mary (———) Newman, a dau., ———, June 8, 1888.
　　Frank F. and Julia F. (Lewis) Royce, a son, Chester Pike, July 17, 1888.
　　Fred and Kate S. (Marshall) Billings, a son, ———, Sept. 22, 1888.

To Fred A. and Emma (Olson) Spaulding, a dau., Oct. 19, 1888.

Harry A. and Jessie (Robinson) Harris, a dau., Susan, Dec. 13, 1888.

Joseph and Martha (Beers) Jondro, a son, Clayton Elmer, May 18, 1889.

Philander C. and Mary J. (Newman) Sargent, a son, Nov. 5, 1889.

Charles F. and Gertie C. (Elmer) Wright, a dau., Alice May, Nov. 7, 1889.

Charles M. and Lucy (Nash) Bythrow, a dau., Maude, Nov. 30, 1889.

Napoleon and Mrs. Ruth (Spaulding) Miller, a dau., Myrtie May, Dec. 11, 1889.

Martin M. and Alice L. Williams, a son, ———, Jan. 29, 1890.

Thomas and Kate (Lee) Burke, a son, Thomas Francis, Feb. 28, 1890.

James L. W. and Julia M. (Olney) Thayer, a son, James L. W., Jr., July 16, 1890.

Dwight and Rosa J. (Spaulding) Hammond, a dau., ———, Aug. 18, 1890.

Aleck and Louise (Burg) Duclos, a son, ———, Dec. 13, 1890.

John W. and Mary J. (Kenyon) Flint, a dau., Ida May, Feb. 2, 1891.

Clarence M. and Bertha L. (Hewes) Kenney, a son, Ralph Hewes, March 6, 1891.

Henry and Grace (———) Nash, a dau., ———, April 20, 1891.

Dana and Jane (Sargent) Martin, a dau., May 2, 1891.

Fred and Kate S. (Marshall) Billings, a son, Edward Percy, May 8, 1891.

John H. and Laura S. (Morse) Bellair, a dau., ———, June 2, 1891.

C. A. and Ida (Fletcher) Wardner, a son, ———, June 14, 1891.

Thomas and Nellie (Conlin) Cary, a son, Thomas C., July 15, 1891.

Napoleon and Mrs. Ruth (Spaulding) Miller, a son, Willie N., Dec. 13, 1891.

Erwin and Jennie M. (Dana) Williams, a dau., Hardie L., Dec. 27, 1891.

Elmer E. and Minnie Bell (Hayes) De Goosh, a son, ———, April 25, 1892.

Charles and Alice (Chapman) Alexander, a dau., ———, May 2, 1892.

Ernest E. and Nellie (Donahue) Hill, a dau., ———, June 22, 1893.

Edmund and Kate (Quigly) Marcott, a dau., ———, Sept. 4, 1893.

Winfield S. and Mary F. (White) Newman, a dau., ———, Sept. 6, 1893.

Charles M. and Lucy M. (Nash) Bythrow, a son, ———, April 15, 1894.

Frank and Hattie (Davidson) Williams, a dau., ———, May 1, 1894.

Daniel and E. Areanna (Spaulding) Headle, a dau., ———, July 6, 1894.

Elwin and Mary (Small) Sherwin, a dau., ———, Sept. 19, 1894.

Lendel B. and Lena O. (Nelson) Chase, a son, Lewis, Nov. 14, 1894.

Oliver and Zoe (Cardia) Feeteau, a dau., ———, Jan. 30, 1895.

Edmund and Kate (Quigly) Marcott, a son, ———, June 2, 1895.

Fred L. and Hattie M. (Chase) Lasure, a dau., ———, June 5, 1895.

Charles and Minnie (Brown) Haven, a son, ———, July 18, 1896.

Charles M. and Lucy M. (Nash) Bythrow, a dau., ———, Aug. 24, 1896.

William E. and Vinnie E. (Jordan) Curtis, a son, ———, Sept. 2, 1896.

Webster and Agnes (Donald) Pratt, a dau., ———, Sept. 4, 1896.

Herbert and Ellen M. (Nelson) Leslie, a son, ———, Sept. 6, 1896.

Oliver and Zoe (Cardia) Feeteau, a son, Ubel, Oct. 13, 1896.

Frank and Bertha (Jones) Sherwin, a son, ———, Oct. 15, 1896.

To Joseph and Louisa (Chamberlain) Dolan, a son, Raymond, Nov. 1, 1896.
Edmund and Kate (Quigley) Marcott, a son, ———, Nov. 23, 1896.
Lewellen and Alice (Biglow) Gibson, a son, Elwin, May 30, 1897.
James W. and Ella (Moore) Smith, a son, Leonard E., June 20, 1897.
Duane W. and L. Minnie (Lobdell) Small, a dau., ———, Aug. 22, 1897.
F. E. and Alice (Frost) Demary, a dau., ———, Sept. 14, 1897.
Chester and Catherine (Hammond) Smith, a dau., ———, Oct. 21, 1897.
Frank H. and Hattie (Davidson) Williams, a son, ———, Oct. 23, 1897.
Eugene E and Nellie (Kimton) Webster, a dau., Lillian R., July 8, 1898.
George R. and Abbie S. (Blood) Gassett, a son, ———, Aug. 8, 1898.
Justin and Martha E. (Whitlock) Judd, a dau., ———, Aug. 11, 1898.
Joseph and Louisa (Chamberlain) Dolan, a son, ———, Aug. 21, 1898.
Will and Jennie J. (Sargent) Brace, a dau., ———, Sept. 21, 1898.
Lendel B. and Lena O. (Nelson) Chase, twins, Lynne D. and Lettie L.,
    Oct. 3, 1898.
Herbert I. and Ellen M. (Nelson) Leslie, a dau., Gertie E., Nov. 5, 1898.
Ernest E. and Nellie (Donahue) Hill, a dau., Eva M., Dec. 15, 1898.
Walter and Cora B. (Packard) Jordan, a dau., Hazel D., Feb. 1, 1899.
Alfred and Ellen (McGuire) Cody, a son, Frank, May 9, 1899.
Justin and Martha E. (Whitlock) Judd, a dau., June 16, 1899.
A. C. and Lena M. (Dodge) Bowness, a son, Arthur L., June 18, 1899.
Edward F. and Bella (Devoe) Van Epps, a son, ———, July 3, 1899.
George C. and Minnie (Mobbs) Redman, a dau., ———, July 29, 1899.
James W. and Ella (Moore) Smith, a son, ———, Aug. 2, 1899.
Fred C. and Blanche (Perkins) Smith, a son, ———, Sept. 14, 1899.
Joseph and Louisa (Chamberlain) Dolan, a dau., ———, Nov. 22, 1899.
Frank C. and Carmen P. (Gordon) Harris, a son, Francis C., March 18,
    1900.
Dr. Henry B. and Alice (Shedd) Ketchum, a dau., Grace, March 23, 1900.
Duane W. and Minnie (Lobdell) Small, a son, ———, April 5, 1900.
David J. and Emma (Blaize) Chamberlain, a son, ———, April 5, 1900.
Louis and Lena (Pope) Herschell, a son, Deane, April 15, 1900.
Ernest E. and Nellie (Donahue) Hill, a dau., ———, Aug. 21, 1900.
Zeb. and Mary (Goodrow) Fountain, a son, James, Nov. 2, 1900.
A. A. and Nellie (Royce) Lawton, a son, ———, Nov. 29, 1900.
Rev. Charles V. and Abbie E. (Hall) French, a dau., Dorothy, Dec. 8, 1900.
Guy and Hattie (Spaulding) Hammond, a dau., ———, Feb. 12, 1901.
Herbert I. and Ellen M. (Nelson) Leslie, a dau., Nettie E., Feb. 25, 1901.
Fred and Rosa (Pressy) Leach, a dau., Gladys, Feb. 26, 1901.
Joseph and Elizabeth (McCreedy) Marcott, a dau., ———, July 2, 1901.
Antoine and Maie (Fouquet) Tonachella, a son, ———, Sept. 15, 1901.
Edward and Delia (Gerrow) Chamberlain, a son, ———, Sept. 21, 1901.
Henry W. and Margaret (Sullivan) Dana, a son, ———, Oct. 5, 1901.
Frank C. and Carmen P. (Gordon) Harris, a dau., ———, Nov. 25, 1901.
Joseph and Louisa (Chamberlain) Dolan, a dau., ———, March 15, 1902.
Stephen M. and Aurilla (Hurd) Thornton, a dau., Stella A., April 1, 1902.
James R. and Martha A. (Davis) Marshall, a dau., ———, April 7, 1902.
Justin and Martha E. (Whitlock) Judd, a dau., ———, April 18, 1902.

To Maurice W. and Mary F. (Jenny) Colby, a dau., ———, May 27, 1902.
Joseph and Elizabeth (McCreedy) Marcott, a son, ———, Sept. 15, 1902.
Duane W. and Minnie (Lobdell) Small, a dau., ———, Oct. 19, 1902.
Ara M. and Mabel W. (Hastings) Hastings, a son, ———, Dec. 13, 1902.
Clifford C. and Lizzie (Begnon) Phillips, a dau., ———, June 17, 1903.
Henry W. and Margarett (Sullivan) Dana, a dau., ———, July 27, 1903.
Peter T. and Nellie V. (Spaulding) Saunders, a son, ———, Aug. 2, 1903.
F. P. and Margarett (Abbott) Dunne, a son, ———, Sept. 2, 1903.
Fred and Evangeline (Child) Wilkins, a son, ———, Sept. 12, 1903.
Stephen M. and Aurilla A. (Hurd) Thornton, a son, Adelbert C., Oct. 6, 1903.
Frank C. and Carmen P. (Gordon) Harris, a dau., ———, Oct. 26, 1903.
Henry B. and Clara M. (Dorwin) Howe, a dau., Bernice A., Jan. 19, 1904.
Joseph and Louisa (Chamberlain) Dolan, a dau., ———, April 2, 1904.
Frederic and Phebe (Frye) Redman, a son, George F., April 15, 1904.
Justin and Martha E. (Whitlock) Judd, a son, ———, April 29, 1904.
Charles E. and Nellie S. (Pequin) King, a son, Henry E., July 4, 1904.
Edward and Delia (Gerrow) Chamberlain, a son, John, Aug. 30, 1904.
Joseph and Elizabeth (McCreedy) Marcott, a dau., ———, Sept. 13, 1904.
Maurice W. and Mary (Jenny) Colby, a son, Carlos D., Oct. 7, 1904.
Ivan L. and Kate M. (Stickney) Davis, a son, ———, Feb. 23, 1905.
Herbert H. and Emma (Leems) Royce, a dau., Aretha P., March 7, 1905.
Alexander and Ida (Campbell) Harper, a dau., ———, March 20, 1905.
Henry B. and Clara (Dorwin) Howe, a son, ———, March 26, 1905.
Fred and Evangeline (Child) Wilkins, a son, ———, July 21, 1905.
Charles A. and Eleanor (Hardy) Platt, a son, ———, Aug. 6, 1905.
Solomon and Soprina (Arnold) Bilow, a son, ———, Aug. 16, 1905.
Earl W. and Elnora C. (Benway) Brown, a son, ———, Sept. 2, 1905.
Fred E. and Lena M. (Woodward) Emery, a dau., Charlotte L., Dec. 10, 1905.
Duane W. and Minnie (Lobdell) Small, a dau., ———, Dec. 22, 1905.
James W. and Mary (Peyson) Pratt, a dau., Ida M., Jan. 3, 1906.
Israel and Mary M. (Spaulding) Chamberlain, a dau., Louisa, Jan. 28, 1906.
Henry B. and Clara M. (Dorwin) Howe, a dau., Elizabeth I., Jan. 28, 1907.
Octavius J. and Elizabeth (Pardy) Bishop, a son, ———, April 7, 1907.
Lewis and Maggie (Gerrow) Chamberlain, a dau., ———, July 9, 1907.
Harry and ——— (Jarvis) Weeden. a dau., ———, July 23, 1907.
Duane W. and Minnie (Lobdell) Small, a son, ———, Aug. 25, 1907.
James W. and Mary (Peyson) Pratt, a dau., ———, Sept. 4, 1907.
Solomon and Soprina (Arnold) Bilow, a son, ———, Sept. 18, 1907.
Arthur A. and Margarett A. (Nichols) Shurtleff, a dau., ———, Oct. 1, 1907.
Joseph and Louisa (Chamberlain) Dolan, a dau., ———, Oct. 20, 1907.
Fred and Evangeline (Child) Wilkins, a son, ———, Oct. 28, 1907.
Willie L. and Velona F. (Picknell) Nelson, a son, Alfred J., Jan. 16, 1908.
Edward F. and Sarah (Mahoney) O'Brien, a son, ———, Feb. 5, 1908.
Clark A. and Ida (Fletcher) Wardner, a dau., ———, March 1, 1908.
John M. and Elsie (Lull) Tewksbury, a son, ———, March 8, 1908.
23

To Earle W. and Elnora (Benway) Brown, a dau.. ———, March 31, 1908.
   Samuel F. and Cora G. (Judd) Smith, twin daughters, ———, ———,
      April 9, 1908.
   William J. and Isabella (McKavey) Hanley, a son, ———, June 6, 1908.
   Julian and Mabel S. (Robinson) Burke, a dau., Persis E.. Aug. 25, 1908.
   William and Esther (Kellogg) Bugbee, a son, ———, Sept. 17, 1908.
   Stephen and Ellen M. (Griffiths) Duling, a son, ———, Sept. 21, 1908.
   Henry B. and Clara M. (Dorwin) Howe, a dau., Ruby M., Nov. 23, 1908.
   Percy and Marion (Morse) MacKaye, a dau., Christiania L., Jan. 10, 1909.
   Louis and Lena R. (Pope) Herschell, a son, ———, Jan. 28, 1909.
   Leon and Mildred (Robertson) Munroe, a son, ———, Feb. 4, 1909.
   Stephen M. and Aurilla A. (Hurd) Thornton, a dau., Elsie, Feb. 24, 1909.
   Edward F. and Sarah (Mahoney) O'Brien, a son, ———, March 30, 1909.
   Homer and Carlotta (Dollery) Saint Gaudens, a son, Augustus, July 8,
      1909.
   Maurice and Mary F. (Jenny) Colby, a dau., Charlotte, Nov. 14, 1909.
   Orrel F. and Huldah E. (Scribner) Atwood, a dau., Bulah, Nov. 24, 1909.

EARLY MARRIAGES, 1770–1834.

A List of All Marriages in Town Recorded Prior to 1834, Except Those
Appearing in Family Genealogies.

In Chronological Order (Nearly).

Joseph Vinson and Eunice ———, Sept. 4, 1770.
Joseph Kee and Mary Nichols (both of Plainfield), Aug. 30, 1773.
Joseph Marsh and Betty Marsh, Sept. 29, 1773.
Thomas Wilson and Esther Spaulding, Nov. 24, 1774.
Robert Dunlap and Mary Vinson, Sept. 26, 1775.
Richard Vinson and Abigail Messenger (second wife), Jan. 30, 1776.
Ethan Clark and Lucy Eager (both of Claremont), Dec. 29, 1788.
Stephen Dexter (Claremont) and Prudence Hubbard (Newport), Oct. 4, 1789.
David York and Eunice Bugbee (both of Claremont), Oct. 21, 1789.
Joseph Edmonds and Wid. Esther Hilliard, Nov. 25, 1790.
Samuel McColly and Abigail Wilson, July 15, 1790.
Charles Waterman and Sarah Aplin, April 22, 1790.
Elisha White and ——— Sampson (both of Claremont), Dec. 30, 1790.
Nathan Rand and Mollie Parker, Oct. 18, 1792.
Amasa Grover (Bethel, Vt.) and Mary Jones, Dec. 9, 1792.
Benjamin Shaw (Woodstock, Vt.) and Hannah McColly, March 27, 1793.
Sanford Tracy (Washington) and Elizabeth Hildreth, June 11, 1794.
Nathaniel Wheeler and Anna Read, Feb. 13, 1794.
Dr. Thomas Fields (Plainfield) and Thankful Townes (Claremont), Feb. 5,
   1795.
Lemuel Richardson and Polly Chase, March 12, 1795.
Jacob Whipple (Croydon) and Rhoda Whiting, June 25, 1795.
Elisha Herrick and Sarah Bridge, July 4, 1795.
Ebenezer Clark and Eunice Chase (both of Keene), Sept. 5, 1795.

Ansel Burrows and Hannah Eliot, Dec. 30, 1795.
Francis Dean and Lucy Eaton (both of Plainfield), Jan. 5, 1796.
Eldad Hart and Polly Farrington, Nov. 6, 1796.
Nathaniel Pierce and Submit Curtis, June 23, 1796.
Isaac Simonds and Mehitable Pierce, Aug. 30, 1796.
Bryant Brown and Betsey Day, Nov. 14, 1796.
John Hildreth and Sukey Crague, Dec. 14, 1796.
Stephen Parker and Ame Ayers, April 2, 1797.
William Temple (Plainfield) and Wid. Lucy Lucus, Feb. 14, 1798.
Bartholomew Harris and Hannah Read, March 1, 1798.
John Rich (Dummerston, Vt.) and Elute Burbank (Hartland, Vt.), July 15, 1798.
Samuel Chase and Polly Barstow, Feb. 18, 1801.
Joseph Barstow (Windsor, Vt.), and Nabby Kenerson, March 15, 1801.
William Lyon Tucker and Elizabeth Perkins Smith, March 25, 1802.
Daniel Dudley (Newport) and Zurviah Fitch, March 30, 1802.
Barna Tisdale and Martha Wright, Dec. 30, 1802.
Asaph Belmont and Sally Simpson, Nov. 4, 1803.
Jonathan Hilliard and Susanna Lucy, Dec. 13, 1803.
William Johonnett (Windsor, Vt.) and Abigail Brown, Feb. 29, 1804.
Warren Smith and Peggy Williams, April 26, 1804
Caleb Thompson and Eunice King, May 14, 1804.
Pearce Luther and Sally Sweet, May 22, 1804.
Thomas Straight and Sarah Stone (both of Plainfield), May 31, 1804.
Dr. Jonathan Badger (Concord) and Eliza Hall, Nov. 5, 1804.
Israel Hall (Windsor, Vt.) and Marion Wood, Nov. 17, 1804.
Abel Gates (Plainfield) and Ida Chase, Jan. 26, 1805.
Francis McCarty (Hanover) and Martha Dustin, March 14, 1805.
Simeon A. Freeman (Fairlee, Vt.) and Polly March, April 2, 1805.
Thomas Penniman and Zurviah Dudley, Oct. 4, 1805.
Peter Abbott and Olive Read, March 6, 1806.
Winthrop Merry (Windsor, Vt.) and Olive Ayers, March 15, 1806.
William Butman (Barnard, Vt.) and Olive Hildreth, June 24, 1806.
——— Nichols (Crownpoint, N. Y.) and Alice Young, Jan. 13, 1809.
Samuel Williams and Abigail Belden, Dec. 28, 1809.
John Davis (Epsom) and Rachel Davis, Jan. 5, 1810.
John Hale and Aehsa Smith, Aug. 30, 1810.
Wyman Stevens (Plainfield) and Deborah Thompson, March 7, 1811.
Samuel Clark and Bathsheba Porter, Nov. 21, 1811.
Joseph Little (Boscawen) and Sarah Burns Lucy, March 12, 1812.
Aaron Post, Jr., and Eliza Gibson Lucy, April 19, 1812.
Samuel Huggins and Mary Russell, July 9, 1812.
Barna Palmer and Dorothy Bissell Shapleigh, Jan. 28, 1813.
Daniel Kingsbury (Plainfield) and Sybil Aldrich, Nov. 23, 1814.
David Dana (Pomfret, Vt.) and Rebecca H. Chase, Feb. 23, 1814.
Samuel Read and Mary Stevens, Dec. 22, 1814.
Levi Nichols (Enosburg, Vt.) and Rachel Smith, Jan. 10, 1815.
Philip Walker (Croydon) and Betsey King (Grantham), Jan. 12, 1815.

Josiah B. True (Salisbury) and Abigail Roberts (Plainfield), Jan. 15, 1815.
John Gove, Jr., and ———— Scott (both of Grantham), Aug. 19, 1815.
Oliver Sawyer and Betsey Russell, Sept. 24, 1815.
David Elliott (Coventry, Vt.) and Laura Chase, Feb. 18, 1816.
Josiah Bemis and Esther Riggs, April 13, 1817.
Theodore Clark and Betsey Davis, Sept. 30, 1817.
Abner Wilder and Ruhama Paine, Dec. 21, 1817.
John Gage (Grantham) and Hannah Norton, Feb. 15, 1818.
Josiah Putney (Hopkinton) and Eliza True (Plainfield), Feb. 15, 1818.
James Emerson (Haverhill, Mass.) and Betsey Bradley, Feb. 19, 1818.
Otis Copeland (Braintree, Vt.) and Rebecca Wilder, March 19, 1818.
Josiah Gove and Mary Brown, April 21, 1818.
Amos Rice (Weathersfield, Vt.) and Anna Whiting (Claremont), May 3, 1818.
Moses Abbott and Abigail Burrill, Aug. 10, 1819.
Relief Spaulding and Dorothy Lamberton, Aug. 9, 1819.
Eliab Ripley and Fanny Clark (Plainfield), Dec. 3, 1819.
Perley Fifield and Miriam Morgan (both of Plainfield), Jan. 23, 1820.
Joshua York and Hannah Bishop (Windsor, Vt.), March 13, 1820.
William E. Smith (Grantham) and Lucy M. Johnson (Plainfield), April 12, 1820.
Stephen Pingrey (Lebanon) and Judith True (Plainfield), Dec. 18, 1820.
Asa Collins and Sally Brown (both of Plainfield), Feb. 7, 1821.
Lovell Spaulding (Northumberland) and Laura Clark (Plainfield), Oct. 22, 1821.
Wilbur Andrews and Orinda Ross (both of Plainfield), Oct. 22, 1821.
Nathaniel Goodale (Morristown, Vt.) and Mary Thompson, Jan. 26, 1823.
John Allen, Jr., and Dorothy Gove, March 20, 1823.
Paschal E. Burnham (Windsor, Vt.) and Asenath Williams, Nov. 20, 1823.
Moses Wright (Enosburg, Vt.) and Ruth Smith, Jan. 12, 1824.
Charles Stanley (Dublin) and Lucy Winch, Nov. 30, 1824.
Stephen M. Bush (Orwell, Vt.) and Salome M. Morse, Sept. 9, 1827.
Rufus Wheeler (Plainfield) and Sarah Bingham, April 8, 1830.
James Stone and Mary Whitby (both then of Cornish), Dec. 29, 1824.
Edward Aiken and Lucinda Stone, Feb. 27, 1823.
Mr. Tucker (New York City) and Louisa Wigginson Brown (Boston), Jan. 17, 1826.
George A. Simmons (Boston) and Belinda R. Wells, Sept. 5, 1832.
Lemuel Thompson (Boston) and Eliza Hall, Nov. 11, 1833.
Danford Belden (Orwell, Vt.) and Betsey Tasker, June 1, 1834.
Alvah Smith and Eliza Thomas, June 5, 1834.

The marriages of this list, that should follow, have not been fully secured, excepting since 1861. After this date the record shows the entire list up to the present time. Beginning with 1887 the law compels an elaborate tabulated record of all vital statistics. This has been a great aid to the compiler.

MARRIAGES FROM 1861–1910.

Martin V. Chapman and Matilda Jordan (both of Plainfield), Dec. 31, 1861.
J. J. Ferson and Rhoda A. Doyle, May 13, 1861.

Abial Lane and Marian Butman, Jan. 1, 1863.
C. H. Hopkins and Susan C. Logan, March 17, 1863.
Ezekiel Place and Sophronia Albe, Oct. 24, 1863.
George H. Corliss and Susan A. Austin, Nov. 12, 1863.
Edward A. Worthen and Marietta Simonds, Dec. 12, 1863.
William Goodwin and Amanda Willey, Dec. 12, 1863.
William A. Wells and Celia A. Hill, Dec. 15, 1863.
Charles Watriss and Mary Mead, Oct. 18, 1863.
Rufus Cobb and Julia Brown, Feb. 6, 1864.
James D. Squires and Mary E. Hall, July 25, 1864.
Denison Pratt and Cynthia Smith, Sept. 9, 1864.
Cyrus R. Bagley and Jennie E. Sleeper, Aug. 17, 1864.
David Morrison and Sarah D. Bartlett, Oct. 18, 1864.
Leander Sanderson and Eliza M. Paine, Feb. 26, 1865.
John Conlin and Ellen Gilbert, Oct. 28, 1865.
Joshua B. Wilcox and Hannah M. Redmond, Dec. 27, 1865.
Samuel E. Barnard and Janette Burr, Oct. 13, 1865.
George F. Johnson and Adeline Willey, Dec. 31, 1865.
Henry F. Sears and Sarah J. Walker, Aug. 21, 1866.
Edgar A. Chapman and ———— Laughton, Dec. 31, 1868.
Henry J. Pollard and H. W. Barrows, Nov. 2, 1869.
Benjamin F. Foster and Nettie B. Spaulding, Dec. 7, 1869.
Eugene Parker Robinson and Hattie Abbie Fitch, May 12, 1869.
Leonard W. Newell and Abbie A. Jones, Dec. 24, 1870.
John P. Foster and Mary J. Kenyon, Dec. 9, 1870.
James Moran and Lucia A. Chapman, Aug. 18, 1870.
George W. Hunt and Minerva Kendrick, Aug. 18, 1871.
William W. Cook and Clara Ferguson, Dec. 16, 1871.
D. F. Cutting and Luella Stearns, May 29, 1872.
Justus O. Cole and Lizzie Ann Hilliard, Oct. 26, 1872.
Charles F. Blaisdell and Katharine A. Wadrobe, April 20, 1872.
Charles H. Hobart and Lizzie L. Spaulding, Feb. 18, 1873.
Calvin T. Dunklee and Amoret S. Felt, July 12, 1873.
Edwin J. Fletcher and Mary Sears, Sept. 28, 1873.
Albert O. Davis and Mary Livingston, Oct. 23, 1873.
Joseph S. Stickney and Emily F. Jordan, March 25, 1874.
Atwood W. Reed and Sarah Moores, June 22, 1874.
Ransom G. Hastings and Ella M. Davis, Nov. 27, 1874.
Jabez P. Reed and Mrs. Lydia B. Rice, April 13, 1875.
John E. Bradley and Alice Martin, June 1, 1876.
Thomas T. Burnham and Ida Carlisle, Sept. 25, 1876.
Homer L. Morgan and Susan A. Hathorn, Sept. 30, 1876.
Henry P. Crandall and Ella F. Willis, July 4, 1876.
Orlando C. Boynton and Louise A. Chase, Feb. 8, 1877.
Adam Sawyer and Ada Dodge, July 3, 1877.
Isaac Godfrey and Abbie White, Aug. 9, 1877.
George E. Wilson and Jennie P. Jackson, Jan. 1, 1878.
Darwin L. Dow and Sarah E. Cheney, Sept. 17, 1878.

Arthur W. Britton and Tilla C. Chadwick, March 22, 1879.
Albert Monroe and Fannie J. Martin, Jan. 14, 1880.
Giles Pratt and Lucy A. Chapman, Feb. 24, 1880.
Henry Hoisington and Linda Thompson, April 10, 1880.
Edgar A. Royce and Ada E. Cutts, Nov. 24, 1880.
Martin M. Williams and Alice S. Williams, Feb. 16, 1881.
James W. Dana and Eva Boyd, Feb. 27, 1881.
William A. Sweet and Alvira Strong, Jan. 28, 1882.
Fred B. Newman and Minnie White, Nov. 27, 1882.
George A. Burke and Rosa B. Gardem, June 6, 1883.
Rufus A. Kidder and Delia A. Fairbanks, March 22, 1884.
Lemuel A. Price and Celia A. Buck, April 26, 1884.
Edmund Pendleton and Lizzie Shattuck, June 2, 1884.
Lucian I. Pingree and Lurette E. Sargent, July 2, 1884.
J. A. Graves and Carrie Nichols, Aug. 18, 1884.
Carlos D. Royce and Kate Adams, Nov. 16, 1884.
George W. Whittle and Bertha Wilder, Nov. 25, 1884.
Willard A. Northrop and Ada C. Webster, Sept. 6, 1885.
Napoleon Miller and Mrs. Ruth Spaulding. Feb. 2, 1886.
Albert C. Stafford and Mrs. Mary C. Barrows, May 4, 1886.
Dana Martin and Jennie J. Sargent, July 19, 1886.
James H. Purrey and Clarissa L. Spaulding, Sept. 4, 1886.
Charles B. Weeden and A. Joslyn, Feb. 9, 1887.
Frederic Billings and Kate Marshall, Aug. 17, 1887.
Winfield S. Newman and Mary F. White, Nov. 23, 1887.
John Nelson and Jennie E. Home, Jan. 10, 1888.
Clarence G. Osmore and Nillar F. Thayer, March 9, 1889.
Charles F. Wright and Gertie E. Elmer, April 29, 1889.
James L. W. Thayer and Julia M. Olney, Oct. 13, 1889.
Dana Boyd and Mary E. Plant, Feb. 9, 1890.
Michael J. Regan and Ella B. Rowe, Sept. 7, 1890.
Erwin E. Williams and Jennie M. Dana, Sept. 20, 1890.
Clark McCane and Rosa Stone, ———, 1890(?).
Charles E. Curtis and Emma G. Andrews, Jan. 21, 1892.
Albert A. Lawton and Nellie A. Royce, Aug. 17, 1892.
Freeman T. Watton and Estella E. Davis, Jan. 17, 1893.
Hosea L. Hadley and Ann M. Mattoon, Jan. 23, 1893.
Fred S. Shepard and Gertrude Sturtevant, April 17, 1893.
Edmund Marcott and Kate Quigly, June 16, 1893.
Webster W. Pratt and Agnes Donald, April 15, 1894.
Daniel W. Ackley and Catherine McCreedy, April 17, 1894.
Oliver W. Bythrow and Lavina Sterling, July 4, 1894.
Willis Willey and Ella J. Hugaboom, Sept. 25, 1895.
A. Willett and Caroline Norton, May 26, 1896.
Fred H. Elliott and Lena E. Kempton, Nov. 25, 1896.
George A. Sargent and Mary Monet, April 30, 1897.
John W. Stewart and Mary B. Brown, Sept. 6, 1897.
George R. Gassett and Abbie S. Hunt, Oct. 6, 1897.

Edward E. Webster and Nellie Kimpton, Dec. 27, 1897.
John C. Fairchild and Charlotte E. Houston, Sept. 27, 1898.
Louis Herschell and Lena O. Pope, March 30, 1899.
Fred C. Smith and Blanche A. Perkins, April 25, 1899.
Chester A. Spaulding and Myrtie W. Packard, Sept. 2, 1899.
Scott E. Jordan and Addie E. Packard, Sept. 2, 1899.
Loren C. Horton and Effie J. Rollins, Sept. 19, 1899.
Stephen M. Thornton and Aurilla A. Hurd, March 11, 1901.
George M. Hodgman and Martha A. Harrington, March 22, 1901.
Daniel W. Ackley and Bertha A. Rice, April 2, 1901.
Alfred E. Kirk and Gertie G. Magoon, Dec. 25, 1901.
Leonard F. Johnson and Mrs. Clara D. Kempton, Dec. 26, 1901.
Israel Chamberlain and May M. Spaulding, Sept. 4, 1904.
Fred E. Emery and Lena M. Woodard, Feb. 28, 1905.
Samuel F. Smith and Cora G. Judd, Aug. 12, 1905.
Robert A. Walker and Mary Ellen Leslie, Dec. 24, 1905.
Harry L. Kellogg and Ethel H. Pardy, Oct. 24, 1906.
George J. Compton and A. Maude Kitchen, Nov. 20, 1906.
Nelson A. Potwin and Myra A. Smith, Aug. 16, 1907.
Frank V. Walker and Ina A. Pardy, Sept. 18, 1907.
Cleveland H. Curtis and Mrs. Helen B. Peabody, Nov. 7, 1907.
John B. Wright and Mrs. Frances L. Whitney, March 1, 1908.
Herbert L. Robinson and Julia A. Howard, Aug. 12, 1909.
Noel J. Huggins and Louise D. Rodgers, Oct. 18, 1909.
Jesse O. Dwyer and Amelia H. Colton, Nov. 16, 1909.
Leonard Smith and Viola C. Chapman, Feb. 14, 1910.
Clarence H. Stygles and Mary E. Gordon, Feb. 22, 1910.
John Bean and Mary A. Kewak, March 22, 1910.
George McDonald and Viola Picknell, April 24, 1910.
Henry M. Bean and Josephine L. Bean, May 26, 1910.
Darwin B. Johnson and Flora B. Jordan, June 8, 1910.
Justin White and Nora E. Despe, June 8, 1910.
Webster O. Sanders and Idella Quimby, Oct. 17, 1910.
William H. Curtis and Carrie E. Clark, Dec. 4, 1910.
Chester A. Wright and Ola W. Gay (of Boston), Dec. 10, 1910.

Two hundred forty-four marriages not in genealogies.

LIST OF DEATHS NOT FOUND IN GENEALOGIES.

Abbott, Moses, Nov. 17, 1848, 77 yrs.
Allds, Sarah, widow of James, June 14, 1814, 72 yrs.
Allen, Hosea, Nov. 26, 1843, 45 yrs.
Allen, Lydia, Feb. 12, 1875, 84 yrs.
Allen, dau. of William, April 22, 1833, 16 yrs.
Allen, child of John, Jr., ———, 1826.
Allen, child of John, Jr., April 27, 1827.
Arguin, Louise, June 20, 1902, 82 yrs.

Austin, Wilbur M., March 26, 1860, 4 yrs.

Austin, George S., Sept. 18, 1871.

Bachelor, Peter C., son of Caleb and Prudentia, Aug. 12, 1803, 5 yrs.

Bachelor, Betsey, dau. of Caleb and Prudentia, Aug. 10, 1803, 3 yrs.

Bachelor, child of S., March 24, 1827, 6 yrs.

Bachelor, ———, child of James, March 23, 1842, 6 yrs.

Bachelor, child of "Mrs. Bachelor," June 27, 1846.

Bachelor, Sam., Sept. 7., 1892 (infant).

Bailey, Walter E., son of Emma, Jan. 12, 1876.

Baker, Hattie A., wife of Elder L. F., Aug. 4, 1880, 24 yrs.

Barney, Mrs. Harvey, June 9, 1878, 79 yrs.

Barton, Russell, Aug. 17, 1899, 12 yrs., 9 mos., 7 d.

Bartlett, Mrs. Alonzo J., July 27, 1883, 43 yrs.

Bartlett, infant of Gamaliel, July —, 1826.

Bartlett, child of Gamaliel, April 12, 1832, 2 yrs.

Bartlett, Chester, son of Nathaniel and Amy, April 28, 1799, 1 yr.

Bartlett, Erastus, son of Gamaliel, Sept. 18, 1825, 2 yrs.

Bean, Henry E., May 19, 1885.

Beers, Charles M., Sept. 1, 1888, 39 yrs.

Benton, Olive, wife of Jonathan, March 18, 1846, 88 yrs.

Benway, Charles E., April 29, 1867.

Billings, Edward P., Dec. 30, 1894, 3 yrs., 7 mos., 22 d.

Billings, Fred M., Jan. 4, 1895, 6 yrs., 3 mos., 12 d.

Bixby, Amasa, Aug. 5, 1850, 85 yrs.

Bixby, wife of Amasa, Jan. 8, 1845, 81 yrs.

Bixby, Amos, April 15, 1904, 84 yrs., 10 mos.

Bernard, Samuel, April 9, 1846, 60 yrs.

Bernard, Huldah Gilbert, his wife, Aug. 28, 1882, 78 yrs.

Bernard, Hollis G., their son, Oct. 1, 1841, 1 yr.

Blanchard, child of Henry, Dec. 8, 1835, 4 yrs.

Blanchard, Amarilla, dau. of Nathaniel and Sarah, Aug. 5, 1824, 24 yrs.

Bomar, Katie, July 24, 1908, 33 yrs.

Boyd, David, Sept. 10, 1871.

Boyd, Lulu, March 24, 1882.

Brewer, "Mrs." (No further inscription.)

Brewer, Experience, dau. of Betsey, Oct. 30, 1795.

Brigham, Lucy, wife of Enoch, Aug. 18, 1828, 36 yrs.

Brocklebank, James, Sept. 25, 1903, 74 yrs.

Bryant, Calvin, Feb. 18, 1810, 27 yrs.

Burbank, Franklin, June 28, 1896, 80 yrs., 7 mos., 9 d.

Burbank, Mary, his wife, Nov. 8, 1890, 84 yrs.

Burham, Abigail, Feb. 19, 1899, 74 yrs., 9 mos., 10 d.

Burr, Versel, Aug. 14, 1837, 11 yrs.

Burke, Lucy, wife of Benjamin Franklin, March 25, 1841, 27 yrs.

Burke, Susan M., her dau., July 11, 1840, 1 yr.

Burnham, M. M., July 24, 1882.

Butman, Mrs. Olive, Feb. 5, 1836, 87 yrs.

Butman, Sybil, Feb. 27, 1883.

Bythrow, Horace A., Jan. 14, 1901, 72 yrs., 10 mos., 10 d.
Bythrow, Charles N., his son, Aug. 9, 1898, 36 yrs.
Bythrow, infant of Charles N. and Lucy, Aug. 24, 1896.
Bythrow, Mabel M., dau. of C. N. and Lucy, Sept. 16, 1890.
Campbell, Josiah, infant of David and Lydia, March 25, 1807, 2 yrs.
Carroll, James, Oct. 7, 1873, 83 yrs.
Carroll, wife of James, July —, 1835.
Carroll, infant child of James, June 2, 1835.
Cass, dau. of Frank, May 16, 1885.
Chase, Elizabeth, dau. of Cotton, May —, 1843.
Chase, Elizabeth, infant dau. of A. and M., Jan. 4, 1845.
Chase, Sarah, Aug. 1, 1872.
Chaffin, Palmer, Nov. 7, 1862.
Chamberlain, Harry P., June 27, 1874.
Chambers, infant of "Mrs. Chambers," Feb. 25, 1831.
Chapman, Mary Jane, Nov. 10, 1903, 62 yrs., 3 mos., 15 d.
Chapman, Alvin, infant son of Stephen and Lydia, Jan. 8, 1813.
Chapman, Caroline Matilda, infant dau. of Rev. Benjamin, March 17, 1800.
Clapp, "Mr. Clapp," Jan. 1, 1841, 18 yrs.
Clark, Harry, Oct. 16, 1841, 57 yrs.
Clark, Samuel, Jan. 23, 1873, 90 yrs.
Clark, Bathsheba, his wife, Nov. 25, 1855, 68 yrs.
Clark, Samuel W., their son, Oct. 13, 1855, 2 yrs.
Clark, Elizabeth Bean, his wife, Jan. 1, 1892, 67 yrs.
Clark, Polly, July 3, 1817, 41 yrs.
Clement, Roxana, wife of William, March 4, 1832, 43 yrs.
Clement, child of William, April 8, 1829, 4 yrs.
Coats, "Mrs. Coats," Aug. 6, 1829, 29 yrs.
Colby, Rebecca, July 19, 1889.
Corser, Mary M., June 2, 1887, 74 yrs.
Cotton, Ebenezer, July 20, 1865, 78 yrs.
Cotton, Mary, Oct. 21, 1876, 81 yrs.
Cotton, Ellen, Feb. 15, 1861, 20 yrs.
Coburn, Smith, July 17, 1864.
Cole, Francis A., June —, 1871.
Coburn, child of Ellen, Feb. 21, 1875.
Coult, Peter, March 23, 1875, 26 yrs. (See Fatalities.)
Conlin, Mary, Aug. 3, 1891, 63 yrs.
Corliss, Ella H., Aug. 24, 1906, 62 yrs., 20 d.
Cranford, Jane L., Jan. 10, 1892, 72 yrs.
Cummings, infant dau. of Edward W. and Carrie, March 22, 1892.
Currier, Polly. (Date effaced by time.)
Curtis, Widow Dorcas, Sept. 3, 1827, 78 yrs.
Curtis, Franklin H., son of Hartley, June 23, 1888. (See Fatalities.)
Curtis, William E., brother of last, April 10, 1897, 29 yrs.
Curtis, infant son of last, Sept. 5, 1896.
Curtis, Horace, Aug. 21, 1886.
Daniels, William H., July 28, 1881, 37 yrs., 10 mos.

Dannatt, Robert, Aug. 26, 1890, 79 yrs.
Dannatt, Robert, son of above, May 21, 1906, 35 yrs., 3 mos., 3 d.
Dannatt, Emma C., June 6, 1902, 35 yrs., 4 mos., 24 d.
Davidson, Ira, March 26, 1875, 76 yrs.
Davis, Bailey, Oct. 8, 1875, 54 yrs.
Davis, Albert O., March 13, 1892, 39 yrs.
Davis, Nellie M., Jan. 10, 1904, 33 yrs.　(A teacher.)
Deming, Mary A., Oct. 10, 1893, 28 yrs., 2 mos., 24 d.
Deming, Lizzie M., Dec. 16, 1869.
DeGoosh, Ann, Sept. 8, 1893, 81 yrs.
DeGoosh, infant of Elmer, Jan. 7, 1896.
Dodge, Amos, Aug. 29, 1881, 73 yrs.
Douglas, son of Ansel, Sept. 21, 1883, 19 mos.
Duncklee, Calvin T., May 30, 1898.
Duncklee, Mary J., Feb. 15, 1896, 69 yrs., 2 mos., 15 d.
Dunbar, Charles, Feb. 10, 1875, 89 yrs.
Dunlop, Robert, Jan. 16, 1801, 47 yrs.
Dudley, Mary, Oct. 24, 1862.
Dustin, Widow Jemina, Sept. 23, 1836.
Dutton, Amasa, Aug. 5, 1832.
Eager, Abraham, Jan. 11, 1834, 6 yrs.
Eaton, Charles, July 28, 1876, 20 yrs.
Edgerton, Calvin, son of Eliphalet, Sept. 28, 1828, 18 yrs.　(At K. U. A.)
Elms, infant of E., March 12, 1829.
Emery, Peter, April 12, 1897, 68 yrs., 9 mos., 20 d.
Emery, Eliza, his wife, March 8, 1908, 78 yrs., 11 mos., 7 d.
Emerson, Moses, July 16, 1847, 70 yrs.
Emerson, Sarah, his wife, Nov. 10, 1854, 75 yrs.
Emerson, Moses B., only son of last, Aug. 20, 1841, 24 yrs.
Esterbrook, Eliza, April 11, 1865.
Esterbrook, Chauncy, Jan. 29, 1908, 78 yrs., 5 mos.
Farnum, Moses, Sept. 19, 1828, 54 yrs.
Farnum, wife of Moses, Sept. 27, 1828, 55 yrs.
Fisher, Horace, Aug. 22, 1831, 19 yrs.
Fitch, James, Oct. 25, 1803, 23 yrs.
Flint, Dea. Josiah, Jan. 6, 1842, 79 yrs.
Flint, Rebecca, his wife, April 24, 1840, 78 yrs.
Flint, J. J., June 10, 1884.
Flint, John W., May 21, 1894, 30 yrs.
Follett, Levi, Feb. 1, 1837, 76 yrs.
Follett, Sarah, his wife, Oct. 12, 1823.
Forehand, Christopher C., April 12, 1882, 61 yrs.
Forehand, Eliza C., his wife, May 15, 1883, 56 yrs.
Forehand, Willie L., their son, Sept. 17, 1876, 10 yrs.
Forehand, Charles E., son of Sullivan, Nov. 25, 1901, 29 yrs., 3 mos.
Forehand, Maude E., his wife, Jan. 27, 1905, 28 yrs., 1 mo., 4 d.
Freeman, Edward J., April 4, 1888, 64 yrs., 10 mos., 1 d.
Frost, Eleanor B., March 30, 1896, 45 yrs., 10 mos., 4 d.

Fifield, Charles P., July 30, 1871.

Fitch, Julia A., Oct. 30, 1871.

Foster, Anna, dau. of Jacob and Sarah, Sept. 4, 1803, 19 yrs.

Gates, child of Trobridge, Oct. —, 1838.

Gates, "Mr. Gates at the river," Dec. —. 1842.

Gates, John, June 26, 1879, 80 yrs.

Garland, Harold A., infant son of E. H., Feb. 25, 1907.

Gee, Carlos, March 26, 1876, 3 yrs.

Gentle, Louis, infant of Louis and Sarah, Feb. 21, 1897.

Gilkey, Laura A., Feb. 9, 1897, 77 yrs.

Gilkey, Charles, son of James, Feb. 11, 1901, 74 yrs., 4 mos., 12 d.

Goodrich, Dr. Josiah, son of Hezekiah, May 18, 1802, 34 yrs.

> "His duty finished to mankind.
> To God his spirit he resigned."
>
> (Epitaph.)

Gould, Daniel, April 11, 1814, 18 yrs.

Gleason, Elizabeth P., April 10, 1877.

Griggs, Charles, Oct. 23, 1798, 17 yrs.

Grow, Adeline, March 18, 1869.

Grover, Patience, wife of William, April 9, 1871, 74 yrs.

Grover, Eldad, infant of Eldad and Sarah, March 30, 1773.

Graves, Sarah, wife of Eldad, June 15, 1774.

Hadley, Florence, dau. of James and Jane, Jan. 20, 1900, 17 yrs.

Hadley, Avis, Feb. 23, 1909, 76 yrs.

Hall, Widow Olive, Aug. 14, 1829, 73 yrs.

Hardy, Timothy, Sept. 26, 1873, 80 yrs.

Hardy, Ann Nichols, his wife, April 24, 1870, 72 yrs.

Harris, Nathan, Feb. 22, 1900, 61 yrs., 9 mos.

Harris, Leroy, his son, June 14, 1899, 19 yrs., 7 mos., 25 d.

Hart, Benjamin, Feb. 19, 1881, 84 yrs.

Hawley, Franklin Z., son of Zebina and C. M., Nov. 3, 1842, 3 yrs.

Haynes, John, son of Nathan and Hannah, Aug. 24, 1799, 2 yrs.

Haynes, Joshua, son of Nathan and Hannah, Aug. 17, 1803, 3 yrs.

Haynes, Mrs. Joseph, March 14, 1828, 71 yrs.

Heady, child of "Mrs. Heady," Jan. —, 1837, 7 yrs.

Heath, Truman L., July 13, 1892, 62 yrs. (See Military.)

Heath, Sarah I. Russell, his wife, Aug. 22, 1861, 32 yrs.

Heath, Maurice, their infant son, July 20, 1859, 2 yrs.

Herrick, Elizabeth, wife of Elisha, Oct. 19, 1794, 24 yrs.

Herrick, Amos, their infant son, Nov. 20, 1794.

Herrick, Sarah, wife of Elisha, Aug. 17, 1803, 39 yrs.

Herrick, infant of Sarah and Elisha, April 15, 1796.

Herrick, Betsey, dau. of Elisha and Sarah, Aug. 30, 1803.

Hibbard, Daniel, Oct. 21, 1776, at Ticonderoga, N. Y.

Hicks, Levi, Dec. 28, 1875, 78 yrs.

Hicks, Tamson, his wife (?), May 11, 1866, 77 yrs.

Hickson, George H., Sept. 15, 1897, 47 yrs., 1 mo., 11 d.

Hitchcock, Edward, Sept. 10, 1864.

Horton, Zenas, Jr., Feb. 25, 1829, 28 yrs.

Hodgman, Lucy Ann, Jan. 8, 1890, 54 yrs.

Hodgson, Flossie, May 21, 1901, 19 yrs., 6 mos.

Humphrey, Samuel, March 19, 1886, 80 yrs.

Humphrey, H. Maria, his wife, Feb. 13, 1888, 75 yrs.

Humphrey, Shirley Walter, son of Willard, March 9, 1876, 1 yr.

Hunt, Clementine M., June 20, 1903, 19 yrs., 10 mos., 25 d.

Hyde, Mary Ann, dau. of Asaph and Dorothy, June 25, 1829, 18 yrs.

Jones, Fred L., son of Silas L. and M. K., Aug. 17, 1878, 23 yrs.

Jondro, Clayton A., son of J. and M., Aug. 16, 1893, 4 yrs.

Johnson, Nancy, Feb. 11, 1865.

Jordan, Ellen, Nov. —, 1878.

Jordan, Morris, Feb. —, 1879.

Jordan, Margaret, June 10, 1879.

Judd, Wilbur H., infant of Charles and Lucy E., Sept. 3, 1865.

Judd, infant son of Justin and Mattie E., Aug. 21, 1897.

Judkins, Marcellus, Dec. 23, 1861. (See Soldiers' Monument.)

Kelley, Charles, June 30, 1871.

Kenney, Mehitable S., Nov. 13, 1870, 80 yrs.

Kenney, Clarabell, June 18, 1866, 20 yrs.

Ketchum, Grace, infant of Dr. Henry B., Nov. 6, 1900.

Keating, son of Thomas, June 30, 1878, 11 yrs.

Kimball, Clarissa, wife of James, Oct. 18, 1806, 19 yrs.

Kimball, her infant child, Oct. 18, 1806.

Kimball, Ella, March 6, 1901, 44 yrs., 1 mo., 5 d.

Knight, Henry C., Aug. 10, 1880.

Lamson, Jonathan J., July 10, 1896, 72 yrs., 11 mos., 13 d.

Lane, Hannah, Aug. 19, 1829, 64 yrs.

Locke, Lavinia A. (Russell), Jan. 26, 1899, 81 yrs., 3d.

Locke, Charles E., April 22, 1892, 49 yrs.

Lougee, Joseph. (Grave unmarked.)

Lougee, Lucy Dodge, his wife, Jan. 28, 1871, 44 yrs.

Lyscom, Sarah Payne, wife of Darius, Oct. 31, 1864, 78 yrs.

Marble, infant son of Enoch and Anna, March 16, 1801.

Marcott, Nelson, Oct. 13, 1901, 49 yrs.

Marcott, Mary E., Jan. 12, 1905, 72 yrs.

Marcott, Thomas, July 18, 1905.

Marcy, Stephen, son of George S., July 18, 1900, 23 yrs., 1 mo., 22 d.

Marcy, John S., Sept. 28, 1838, 38 yrs.

Marston, Jonathan, April 24, 1834, 19 yrs.

Marston, wife of William, Sept. —, 1842, 26 yrs.

Marshall, James, June 7, 1900, 70 yrs.

Marshall, Emily, Feb. 8, 1899, 45 yrs.

Martin, Mr., of Northboro, Mass., Nov. 25, 1838.

Mathews, Lucy, Feb. 15, 1889, 98 yrs., 5 mos., 7d.

McGovern, Mary, May 9, 1892, 44 yrs.

McAllister, Lydia, March 15, 1891, 87 yrs.

Merrow, Mary, dau of. John and Clara, Aug. 12, 1863, 4 yrs.
Mellen, Eleanor C., May 6, 1906, 86 yrs.
Miller, Ruth R., wife of Napoleon, Feb. 2, 1898.
Moore, Fred, July 10, 1879, 17 yrs.
Morrill, infant of Levi, Nov. 11, 1829.
Morrill, child of William F. C., Sept. 3, 1849.
Morse, Betsey, June 23, 1834, 34 yrs.
Muzzy, Jonathan, Jan. 9, 1846.
Muzzy, wife of Jonathan, Aug. —, 1844.
Nelson, Eunice D., Jan. 15, 1890, 74 yrs.
Nelson, Alfred J., April 3, 1908.
Nelson, Benjamin F., Feb. 5, 1909, 29 yrs., 1 mo., 1 d.
Newman, Mrs. Franklin, Oct. 22, 1880, 58 yrs.
Newman, Frank P., son of Fred, Oct. 15, 1889, 2 yrs.
Newton, Harriet M., Sept. 27, 1857, 17 yrs.   (Suicide.)
Newton, Laura W., Feb. 9, 1896.
Newton, Francis, April 7, 1830, 77 yrs.
Norton, Harriet, Aug. 3, 1864.
Norris, Mary, dau. of Senator Moses Norris, May 2, 1897, 51 yrs., 6 mos.
Nutting, Cyrus, son of Timothy, July —, 1841.
Paine, Sarah, wife of Darius Lyscom, Oct. 31, 1864, 78 yrs.
Parker, Mary, first wife of Capt. Stephen, July 27, 1793, 54 yrs.
Parker, Sarah P., wife of Joseph, April 24, 1821, 25 yrs.
Parker, Mrs. Rev. John, Oct. 27, 1876, 55 yrs., 6 mos.
Parkhurst, Abbie J., Aug. 18, 1867.
Peach, Julia A. Bailey, dau. of P. A. Hardy, Nov. 30, 1871, 36 yrs.
Penniman, Zurviah, wife of Thomas, July 30, 1832, 84 yrs.
Perry, Wid. of Capt. David, (Anna Bliss), Oct. —, 1835, 90 yrs.
Phelps, Calista, Feb. 15, 1898.
Phillips, Zephaniah, Aug. 23, 1808, 43 yrs.
Pierce, Elizabeth, wife of Nathaniel, April 5, 1863, 65 yrs.
Phillips, George F., son of Hiram, Feb. 14, 1887, 32 yrs., 6 mos., 10 d.
Pike, Miss Ruth, June 6, 1828, 50 yrs.
Picknell, Clifford A., Aug. 13, 1905, 9 mos.
Platt, Captain, Dec. 27, 1828.
Platt, Mrs., March 16, 1828. "Old Age."
Poland, Lucinda, dau. of A. and M. P., Jan. 16, 1847, 14 yrs.
Porter, Sarah, wife of Isaac, Oct. 8, 1828, 24 yrs.
Porter, Mrs., Jan. —, 1837.
Porter, Wid. Lucy, Sept. 19, 1830, 76 yrs.
Porter, Ruth, wife of Lyman, June 15, 1871.
Porter, Arlettie, her dau., June 8, 1871.
Prout, Henrietta, dau. of Thomas E., Oct. 3, 1878, 9 yrs.
Prout, Willie, brother of last, May 3, 1879, 19 yrs.
Putney, Sarah D., wife of Charles E., July 15, 1881, 28 yrs.
Quimby, Enoch, July 18, 1878, 70 yrs.
Quimby, wife of Enoch, Aug. 26, 1881, 50 yrs.
Rawson, George H., son of Enos and Elvira, April 18, 1849, 6 yrs.

Rawson, James K. P., son of Enos and Elvira, March 2, 1849, 4 yrs.
Reynolds, Mrs. Patrick, Dec. 30, 1876, 50 yrs.
Read, Elisha, April —, 1839, 85 yrs.
Read, Mary, his dau., Nov. 12, 1843.
Read, Ernest P., Sept. 18, 1884.
Redman, George, March —, 1902, 35 yrs.
Rice, Alonzo V. P., Aug. 6, 1894, 81 yrs., 3 mos., 18 d.
Rice, Rosarah (Spaulding), Nov. 28, 1893, 63 yrs., 28 d.
Rickard, Levi, March 16, 1865.
Rickard, first wife of Levi, May 9, 1846.
Rickard, Lucy Allen, second wife of Levi, Jan. 6, 1885, 72 yrs., 11 mos.
Robinson, George, May 24, 1865.
Root, Elias, Jan. 17, 1868.
Royce, Joel, March 27, 1875, 83 yrs.
Royce, Seba, his wife, Nov. 20, 1846, 51 yrs.
Royce, Calvin, their son, Nov. 30, 1834, 4 mos.
Royce, Harvey, their son, May 9, 1837, 7 yrs.
Russell, Hannah W., Jan. 10, 1894, 85 yrs., 2 mos., 2 d.
Russell, Sarah, June 18, 1874, 76 yrs.
Russell, Allen D., May 7, 1906, 67 yrs., 9 mos.
Ryan, William P., Aug. 10, 1880.
Ryan, James W., his son, Sept. 25, 1901, 75 yrs.
Ryan, Forest C., Jan. 19, 1879, 6 yrs.
Sanborn, Mary A., Oct. 19, 1900, 87 yrs., 3 mos.
Sargent, Lovinia, wife of John E., Sept. 29, 1870.
Sargent, Flora, dau. of P. C. and M. J., Feb. 5, 1895, 1 yr.
Sargent, Electa, wife of J. R., May 15, 1878, 33 yrs.
Sargent, infant of Mary, Sept. 5, 1896, 1 mo.
Sargent, Mrs. Mary, Aug. 3, 1877, 83 yrs.
Sawins, Sarah Richard, wife of Samuel, Jan. 20, 1842, 69 yrs.
Sawyer, Sarah, Dec. 24, 1869.
Seaver, Henry, Jan. 31, 1872.
Seton, Christopher, June 15, 1830, 75 yrs.
Shapley, Jabez, Sept. —, 1836, 90 yrs.
Shaw, Mrs. Susan R. Stevens, June 14, 1892, 79 yrs.
Shedd, John S., March 18, 1865.
Smith, Hannah, Oct. 2, 1869.
Smith, Lydia, March 7, 1873.
Spaulding, Theodosia, Feb. 2, 1865.
Spaulding, S. L., March 22, 1883.
Stearns, Ida E., April 5, 1862.
Shaw, John S., Nov. 20, 1893, 81 yrs., 11 mos., 5 d.
Shepard, Rebecca M., Jan. 9, 1906, 87 yrs., 11 mos., 18 d.
Sherwin, infant of Frank and Bertha Jones, Oct. 18, 1896.
Shelly, Calvin, March —, 1847.
Shedd, Bertie E., son of Reed and Electa, Sept. 4, 1875, 5 yrs.
Silloway, Warren, son of William and Abigail, Sept. 15, 1889, 56 yrs., 5 mos., 20 d.

Skinner, Miss Betsey, Dec. 6, 1827, 22 yrs.

Smart, Sarah S., dau. of Joseph and Polly. Nov. 28, 1897, 80 yrs., 11 mos.

Small, J. M., son of Duane and L. N., Sept. 9, 1897, 17 d.

Smith, Calista B., April 17, 1897.

Smith, Sarah, wife of Capt. Samuel, March 1, 1815, 38 yrs.

Smith, Albert, her son, Feb. 26, 1815, 9 yrs.

Smith, Pethuel, son of Warren and Peggy, June 29, 1815, 7 yrs.

Smith, Joseph, son of Walter and Anna, May 7, 1787, 17 mos.

Solgee, John Jacob, Jan. 20, 1835, 84 yrs.

Spofford, "Widow Spofford," Oct. 18, 1830, 95 yrs.

Spaulding, Mary J., wife of Nathan, Feb. 21, 1887, 54 yrs., 6 mos., 2 d.

Spaulding, Clarissa, dau. of Leonard and Sally, Aug. 5, 1803, 2 yrs.

Spaulding, Lena May, dau. of Leonard, Jan. 5, 1887, 3 yrs.

Spaulding, Mrs. Rhoda, Dec. 7, 1884.

Spaulding, Anna, wife of Capt. Abel, Feb. 8, 1826, 37 yrs.

Spaulding, Leonard D., Dec. 7, 1909, 71 yrs., 9 mos., 12 d.

Spencer, Junius A., Feb. 12, 1889, 60 yrs., 7 mos., 12 d.

Stearns, Harriet, Oct. 29, 1843, 47 yrs.

Stone, Mary Jane (at Faith Home, Portsmouth), Feb. 24, 1881, 65 yrs.

Stone, Wid. Elizabeth, March 31, 1850, 89 yrs.

Stearns, Mary J., dau. of Charles, Oct. 1, 1894, 36 yrs., 4 mos., 25 d. (Suicide.)

Stearns, Benjamin, March 20, 1875, 88 yrs.

Story, Sarah W., May 14, 1902, 77 yrs., 3 mos., 25 d.

Straw, Mrs. George H., Jan. 6, 1885, 41 yrs.

Strong, Carter O., July, 1856, 19 yrs. (See Casualties.)

Strong, G. B., brother of last, Oct. 3, 1907, 73 yrs., 11 mos., 23 d.

Sturtevant, Elsie E., June 10, 1902, 18 yrs., 5 mos., 10 d.

Tappan, Wid. Judith Solgee, March 21, 1836, 63 yrs.

Tasker, Mrs. Rebecca H., April 4, 1838, 66 yrs.

Thomas, Miss Sarah, Oct. 1, 1813, 44 yrs. "She by her own labor acquired the sum of 500 dollars, which she gave wholly by her will to the support of the gospel among the heathen." (Inscription.)

Terry, Mary E., Feb. 1, 1908, 74 yrs., 6 mos., 7 d.

Thatcher, "Mrs. Thatcher," May —, 1835.

Thomas, Ann, Sept. 24, 1904, 70 yrs.

Tinkham, child of Peter, Feb. 26, 1831, 9 yrs.

Tinkham, infant of Peter, Oct. —, 1826.

Tift, Joseph L. W., April 29, 1891, 62 yrs., 9 mos., 18 d.

Town, Moses, May 28, 1841, 31 yrs.

Town, Eliza Jane, dau. of Aaron and Mary, March 30, 1840, 5 yrs.

Town, Wid. Betsey, Oct. 14, 1846, 68 yrs., at alms house.

Tracy, Etta, July 3, 1874, 32 yrs.

Trobridge, Mrs. James, July 27, 1883, 47 yrs.

Tucker, Lucy, wife of Abijah, Jan. 12, 1796, 58 yrs.

Turner, Laura Ann, Jan. 27, 1820, 2 mos.

Thompson, J. M., April 28, 1874.

Truman, N. T., June 28, 1885.

Trodden, James W., Sept. 30, 1863.

Vinton, "Grandchild of Daniel," April 20, 1829.

Voorhees, Henry, May 31, 1876, 40 yrs.

Walker, Helen R., May 16, 1903, 58 yrs., 3 mos., 2 d.

Walker, Katie, Sept. 16, 1900.

Wardner, Frederic, Jan. 16, 1904, 76 yrs., 29 d.

Waterman, Mrs. Albert, Dec. 26, 1877, 31 yrs.

Welden, Alexander, Jan. 12, 1876, 26 yrs.

Wetmore, Mary, dau. of David Marcott, Oct. 12, 1898, 30 yrs.

Whitmore, Mrs. William, July 31, 1874, 23 yrs.

Whitmore, Mrs. William (second wife), Dec. 22, 1879, 27 yrs.

White, a child of "Mrs. White," Sept. —, 1834.

Whipple, Benjamin, son of Jacob and Rhoda, July 9, 1799, 4 yrs.

Whittaker, child of "Mrs. W.," Jan. 1, 1841.

Wheeler, Diana, April 13, 1875, 76 yrs.

Wellman, Merton, son of William P. and Ella L., July 11, 1868.

Whitmore, Lillie, Nov. 28, 1870.

Whitmore, Lydia, Sept. 8, 1872.

Whitmore, Frances E., Feb. 13, 1876.

Wiley, Susan, wife of Andrew, June 21, 1862, 63 yrs.

Wilton, Guy, Jan. 9, 1892, 4 mos.

Wilder, Gerrard S., Dec. 16, 1866, 17 yrs.

Wilder, James, Dec. 31, 1873, 58 yrs.

Winch, Luther, Feb. —, 1827.

Williams, Mrs. A., Jan. 11, 1865.

Williams, Edna M., April 11, 1871.

Williams, Maria, March —, 1870.

Williams, Amy Gates, Feb. 2, 1875.

Williams, Electa, wife of Elisha, April 19, 1834, 33 yrs.

Williams, Jonathan W., their son, April 27, 1833, 5 yrs.

Williams, Eliza Ann, their dau., Jan. 21, 1837, 15 mos.

Williams, "Widow Williams" in 1826.

Williams, Gertie May, dau. of M. M. and A. L., Dec. 3, 1891, 9 yrs.

Williams, Orlando E., Jan. 23, 1890, 55 yrs.

Williams, Lucius F., son of Frank H., Feb. 8, 1899, 1 yr., 3 mos., 21 d.

Williams, child of Frank H. and Norma K., Sept. 6, 1903.

Williamson, Caleb B., Sept. 10, 1885, 67 yrs.   (Accident; see Casualties.)

Wood, Thomas, May 20, 1838, 36 yrs.

Woodard, Rosa, March 17, 1898, 26 yrs.

Wright, Thomas, Oct. 8, 1878, 50 yrs.

Wright, Moses, Feb. 4, 1856, 91 yrs.

Wright, Mary, his wife, June 1, 1833, 65 yrs.

Wright, Loami, infant son of Eb. and Martha, July 20, 1785.

Wyman, Leonard, infant son of Benjamin, Feb. 24, 1809.

In all 429 names, mainly in alphabetical order.

GENERAL INDEX

24

INDEX OF NAMES

Lightning Source UK Ltd.
Milton Keynes UK
UKHW011129260420
362298UK00002B/265